Introduction and Overview

This Report investigates an important yet largely unexplored topic: the relationship between women's rights and welfare and the democratization and market-oriented transformation of Central and Eastern Europe and the former Soviet Union.

The 150 million women and 50 million girls who live in the 27 transition countries are not a special interest group. Women represent half of the population, and their particular concerns affect fundamental social questions. Typically, when women are at the lower steps on the gradient of advantage, this is because of the demands of their role in providing and caring for the new generation. This socially established linkage, rooted in childbearing, reinforces the bonds between the well-being of women and that of children. Women's experiences, however, also exert a tremendous influence on all of society, and women's progress is a sensitive indicator of human development in general.

Through its Regional Monitoring Reports, UNICEF has been examining the ways in which the collapse of the communist governments has affected the lives of children. This Report asks: Did gender equality exist behind the egalitarian rhetoric of communism? How have women fared under the emerging market democracies? Is the actual and potential contribution of women to healthy change fully recognized and realized?

The answers to these questions provide particular insights into people's lives in the transition countries, as well as into the links between development and gender equality. Indeed, women's rights and human development have been two of the most prominent social issues of the 20th century. In this light, the premise of this Report is that the transition offers an historical opportunity for the countries in the region to exercise genuine leadership in addressing gender questions and that women's broader participation is crucial if the social, economic and political targets of the transition are to be achieved.

Was there gender equality?

Discrimination against women blocks the development of nations just as it blocks progress for girls, women and their families. The 1979 UN Convention on the Elimination of All Forms of Discrimination against Women defines discrimination against women as "any distinction, exclusion or restriction made on the basis of sex which has the effect or purpose of impairing or nullifying the recognition, enjoyment or exercise by women . . . of human rights and fundamental freedoms in the political, economic, social, cultural, civil, or any other field." All the transition countries are signatories of the Convention, as well as of the 1989 Convention on the Rights of the Child: this is a noteworthy declaration of intent.

So, how are these countries measuring up? Analysis of human development indices shows that the transition countries have a relative advantage in terms of gender equity and child and maternal health compared to countries at a similar level of development outside the region. This comparative edge is widely attributed to the historical achievement of the former governments in securing universal access to basic health care and education services and offering paid employment to most women.

Indeed, the Central European countries spent relatively large amounts on health and education services, and the Soviet Union had a ratio of physicians to population comparable to that of the richest nations in the world. In contrast to the situation in many other countries, there is no evidence that unequal treatment of girls caused gender differences in child and adolescent mortality or in basic educational attainment. Moreover, in the Baltic States, Russia and Ukraine, for example, the gender gap in labour force participation rates was comparable to that in Sweden, the leader in this regard among Western nations. The workforce participation rates of women in Poland, Romania and Azerbaijan were comparable to or higher than those in the United States or France, with the notable difference that, in the planned economies, women generally held full-time jobs throughout their working lives.

The Report finds that women's wages relative to those of men and women's representation among professionals and economic decision makers compare favourably to the levels in advanced market economies. This is linked to the generally significant attainments in the education of women – an asset which remains important in the new market environment. Women in the workplace had access to an extensive state-run system of family and childcare supports, including lengthy paid maternity leave, family allowances attached to wages, and nursery, kindergarten and after-school services for children.

From Czechoslovakia to Albania, from the Baltic to Central Asia, there was considerable diversity in terms of cultural traditions, lifestyles and degree of urbanization. This certainly influenced the average number of children born to families and the strength of kinship systems. Yet, at the same time, in many ways women's roles in the family, including their contribution to and command over the household economy, were strikingly similar across the region. For example, the right of women to marry or initiate divorce was guaranteed in constitutions everywhere, despite traditions to the contrary in some places.

With a huge appetite for able labour, the state encouraged women to study, marry and have jobs and babies, and, where kinship support was weak, the state provided the means to help women manage the competing demands. These state-directed initiatives often favoured concrete advancements among women. However, many other apparent achievements were superficial rather than genuine, and women's well-being and their opportunities were often compromised under communism. Significantly, the underlying process was authoritarian rather than rights-based; a semblance of equity which often came closer to uniformity than genuine equality was imposed from the top down. Human rights and fundamental freedoms were denied; civil society was suppressed, and the family was neglected or viewed with suspicion.

When communist rule collapsed at the end of the 1980s and the beginning of the 90s, it left behind many basic economic and national issues unresolved, including the issue of gender equity. People did not immediately realize that the paternalistic communist state, despite all the proclamations, had actually failed to deal with fundamental questions of gender equality. These "missing achievements" were closely linked to the lack of market forces and the shortcomings in civil society – the same areas which the transition is supposed to address.

The missing links

The thinness of the veneer of equality under communism is revealed most graphically in the representation of women in parliaments, where women often accounted for as many as one-third of the seats – a share matched elsewhere in the world only in Nordic countries. This remarkable female presence disappeared during the first democratic elections in the region. This attests to the profound failure of the communist governments to cultivate gender equality which is legitimized and sustained by citizens.

The Report confirms the existence of additional weaknesses which must be dealt with.

● Women did not have equal career opportunities. They were poorly represented among party leaders and planners and among the directors of large state enterprises – the few top positions which really counted in these hierarchical societies. Occupational segregation – whereby women dominate in certain occupations and men in others – was considerable. The findings of this Report counter the frequent claim that the gender gap in wages in the transition countries does not reflect gender discrimination in the workplace. The in-depth investigation carried out for this Report could attribute only a rel-

atively small part of the 10-30 percent gap to differing job characteristics, skills, or experience.

● Health care was delivered by the state health care system. However, the returns were disappointing given the level of investment. For example, despite an emphasis on maternal and infant health care, there was large variance in maternal and infant mortality rates across the region, and the rates were often far above the targets of the World Health Organization. Health awareness and the need for healthy lifestyles were neglected, as evidenced by the widespread abuse of alcohol and the poor nutrition.

● Outside the context of work, there was little official social support for family life, and families functioned in isolation. Fertility rates among teenagers were high, often several times higher than the corresponding rates in Western countries. Services to help strengthen families and support women's capacity to prevent or cope with situations of risk were glaringly absent. The state applied too many last-minute, half-way measures: medical abortions rather than access to family planning services, or the separation of children from parents for placement in institutions instead of, for example, securing parental counselling.

● Despite laws ostensibly guaranteeing equality between women and men within marriage, the gender distribution of power in families remained one-sided. By taking over the responsibility for certain areas of family life, the state did not help women and men share these responsibilities more equally. Instead, it contributed to the weight of the "double burden" borne by women – long hours on the job followed by unpaid work at home. Data show that the total workload of women in Central and Eastern Europe averaged close to 70 hours per week, about 15 hours more than the workload of women in Western Europe.

● Another serious barrier to women's equality is the blanket of silence over violence against women that still covers the region. The evidence reviewed in this Report shows that violence against women is widespread, but that professionals in criminal justice, health care, social work, and education are largely untrained in recognizing and addressing violence against women, particularly domestic violence. This also represents an inheritance from the communist period.

These shortcomings confirm that the legacy of gender equality in the region is less robust than often assumed and raise concerns about whether and how these problems are going to be put on the agenda. By shattering the state monopoly over economic, social and political issues, the transition has exposed women to an environment in which the conditions for equality have yet to be explored.

New economic opportunities and risks

During the first half of the 1990s, GDP dropped by 15-25 percent in Central Europe, 35-45 percent in Southeastern

Europe and about 50 percent or more (with a few exceptions) in former Yugoslavia, the Baltic States, the western Commonwealth of Independent States, and the countries of the Caucasus and Central Asia. Economies have begun to rebound since then, but only Poland and Slovenia seem to have been able to surpass the level of output in 1989. Despite impressive growth in the private sector, many structural problems are still hindering economic recovery.

Market reforms and declines in output have led to large drops in real wages and pressure on employers to reduce the number of jobs. Losses in real wages – not infrequently larger than the falls in GDP – have been accompanied by considerable increases in wage differentials. The Gini coefficient, a common measure of the extent of wage inequality, has risen by one-third on average in Central and Southeastern Europe and by one-half in countries of the former Soviet Union. At the same time, governments have endured a huge drop in revenues, while their ability to raise taxes has not been adequately expanded.

Since 1989, an estimated 26 million jobs have been lost in the region – 13 percent of the pre-transition total. Available data suggest that almost 14 million of these jobs were held by women. Nonetheless, in the formal economy, women have managed to maintain their share of employment in the 40-50 percent range. Although the incidence of part-time work (a choice desired by many women) has increased in several countries, more than 90 percent of employed women still have full-time jobs. Yet, in parts of the region many jobs exist only on paper, and even the meagre wages many jobs provide are paid out after considerable delays.

Registered unemployment has soared in the former centrally planned economies, from almost zero to more than 10 million. Women represent a higher share of these jobless; six million women were on unemployment registers in 1997. In addition, more and more women and men who are without work are being excluded from these registers and are ineligible for unemployment compensation.

Economic change has affected women within the workforce, but also in the household. The need for two incomes in a household is still being felt, often even more strongly than was the case under communism, but it is more difficult to satisfy. The fact that both women and men have lost jobs in great numbers has undoubtedly influenced the gender balance of power within families, shifting sometimes towards the woman, sometimes towards the man.

Jobless women are more likely to become economically inactive, while men find work in the "grey" economy. Nonetheless, as the Report reveals, women often have a crucial role in ensuring household survival. As state commitments to childcare have shrunk, women's responsibilities within the family have curtailed their ability to seek and find work. Enrolment rates in nurseries (for children up to age 2) have fallen across the region, most noticeably in the Baltic and western CIS countries, and nurseries have practically ceased to exist in the Czech Republic and Slovakia. The number of kindergarten places is also declining in many countries.

The analysis finds that older jobless women and local communities have taken on a greater role in childcare. Meanwhile, falling fertility rates have reduced populations of young children by 10-50 percent in the region – a striking outcome. This can offer some immediate relief in economic and health terms to families and communities, but might generate several long-term economic and social problems.

There is evidence that in some countries employers are less willing to hire women and less willing to accommodate maternity and parental leaves. Analysis has found that, in Poland, because of their marriage status, unemployed married women, but not unemployed married men, are hindered from securing work.

Adequate, accessible and affordable childcare is crucial in the effort of families with young children to balance employment and household responsibilities. Government policy measures such as extended maternity and parental leave show some success in encouraging parents to stay at home to raise their children, but produce mixed results in terms of gender equity. Because of the reduction in childcare services and income support, the gender gap in wages has become more acutely felt.

However, a striking finding of the Report is that this gap has remained stable despite significant increases in overall wage inequality during the 1990s. The gender pay gap has widened the most in Bulgaria (which has been slow to reform) and then only by 5 percentage points. It has stayed the same in many countries and even declined in some, such as the Czech Republic, Hungary and Russia. Detailed analysis reveals that the strong educational attainment of women is a key factor. There is also some evidence that occupational segregation by gender has lessened during the transition.

At the same time, there is now a risk that gender segregation in employment is becoming linked to the type of ownership exercised by the employer. Thus, while women continue to fill public-sector jobs, men are making greater inroads in the private sector. As many as three-quarters of the employees in education and health care are women, and these fields account for a significant share of all female employment. Analysis shows that gender is a determinant in access to private-sector jobs, even independently of other factors. Women are also less likely than men to be self-employed or employers themselves. Still, available evidence suggests that women have established or own about one-quarter of new businesses – a promising start, given the recent emergence of entrepreneurial freedom in the region.

Women's health and safety

A shocking and unanticipated deterioration in life expectancy accompanied the early years of the transition. Of 23 countries for which time series are available, male life expectancy worsened in 22, and female life expectancy in 16. In many countries, the decline was small and only temporary; in others, the drop was large and more difficult to reverse. In Russia and Kazakhstan, the cumulative drop in life expectancy for men was 6.3 and 5.5 years, respectively, and among women 3.2 and 3.3 years. In 1997, life expectancy worsened or did not improve in Southeastern Europe, Estonia, Belarus, Moldova, Ukraine, and Turkmenistan – about one-third of the countries for which data are available.

It is increasingly recognized that women respond to health threats and medical treatments differently than men. This gender difference is apparent in the changes in life expectancy noted above, changes largely wrought by the strains of transition expressed through the poorer nutrition, unhealthier lifestyles, alcohol abuse, emotional distress, and violence which, according to some evidence, are more common among people with weak social networks.

The changes which have been triggered by the transition and which shape health have affected women both positively and negatively. In economic terms, women's health is influenced by lower incomes, greater income disparity and reduced funding for health care systems. Values and social environments are changing, and this is sometimes accompanied by healthier lifestyles, but not infrequently also by greater risk-taking behaviour.

Some indicators of maternal health have improved, demonstrating that the transition can harvest the previous investments in the health and education of women. Data show that infant mortality rates have remained largely stable or have declined, while maternal mortality rates have decreased across most of Central and Eastern Europe.

However, maternal mortality rates in Albania, Romania and most western CIS countries are still above the WHO target for Europe (15 maternal deaths per 100,000 live births), and the progress achieved in Russia during the 1980s has not continued during the 90s.

More frequent birth complications and worsening health status among infants are evidence of the poorer health of women as well. For example, in Belarus, the rate of hæmorrhage and eclampsia has almost doubled; in Russia, the incidence of birth complications has almost tripled, and in many countries the proportion of low birthweight babies has risen. These outcomes may in part be linked to demographic shifts, such as the higher share of births outside marriage, particularly to teenage mothers. However, women's poor nutrition and the erosion in access to services are also factors. In this regard, it should be noted that, in Central Asia, maternal mortality is still relatively high, often higher than it was in 1989.

Abortion remains common throughout the region, though the absolute number of legal abortions has declined in every country. Rates are especially high in Southeastern Europe (except Albania), western CIS and the Baltics (except Lithuania). The only countries where the number of legal abortions per 100 live births is around or below the European Union average are Poland (where abortion laws became much more strict in 1993), Croatia, Azerbaijan, and Tajikistan. In Russia, there are two abortions for every live birth, that is, about 2.5 million abortions in 1997.

Though legal and usually performed by qualified health professionals, abortions still involve serious emotional and physical complications for women. Surveys show that around 70 percent of women feel depressed or traumatized by the experience. Abortion is a leading cause of maternal death, accounting for up to 20-25 percent of maternal deaths in some countries. The main reasons for persistently high abortion rates are inadequate access to family planning and little knowledge of reproductive health issues, especially among young women.

Young women are also particularly vulnerable to the increased incidence of "social diseases" in the region. There are indications that adolescent girls are catching up to both their male counterparts and Western European girls in alcohol and tobacco use. For example, evidence shows that the percentage of adolescent Latvian girls who smoke has doubled, as has the share of 15-year-old Polish girls who report having been drunk at least twice.

Some health threats are relatively new to the region, including drug abuse, HIV infection and trafficking in women for the purpose of sexual exploitation. The number of recorded HIV cases jumped from around 30,000 in 1994 to about 270,000 at the end of 1998, with an estimated 80,000 new infections in 1998 alone. This frightening surge is associated with intravenous drug use, which has been growing rapidly in parts of the region. About 70 percent of all HIV infections in Ukraine occur among drug users, and there is an important overlap between drug use and prostitution.

The booming sex industry across Central and Eastern Europe puts many women at very high risk. The negative impact of prostitution on the status of women in the transition countries cannot be understated. Prostitution affects perceptions about the role of women in society, places women in positions of economic and physical vulnerability and raises the risk to women of health problems and violence. There is evidence that the number of women from Central and Eastern Europe involved in street prostitution in many of the major cities of Western Europe is rising rapidly. Frequently, these women are forced migrants who have been coerced into prostitution through deception, kidnapping and intimidation.

There are also indications that violence against women, including domestic violence, is becoming more common. The culture of lawlessness seems to be spreading, and the rise in violent crime is alarming. Rape seems to be inadequately addressed through the criminal justice system, and cases of domestic violence do not even attract the attention of the courts. Indeed, domestic violence is not specifically recognized as a crime in some countries. In the weakened economy, women are more vulnerable to spousal violence, but also to sexual exploitation in the workplace. These risks call for urgent improvement in the capacity of health professionals, social workers, police officers, and judicial authorities to provide adequate remedies and promote prevention.

Particularly disturbing is the use of violence against women, including rape and forced pregnancy, as weapons of war in ethnic conflicts. Estimates of the number of women raped as part of a deliberate pattern of abuse during the 1992-95 conflict in Bosnia-Herzegovina, in the former Yugoslavia, vary from 20,000 to 50,000. Women refugees and displaced persons – of which there are hundreds of thousands from Croatia to Tajikistan – are also vulnerable to sexual exploitation and abuse. New waves of physical, sexual and mental violence against women have been generated by the struggle in Kosovo in the Balkans, a region which has already experienced the tragic outcomes of ethnic strife.

Making the transition work for women

This Report makes clear that gender equality needs to be placed higher on the political agenda of the transition countries if they are to turn their impressive assets in human capabilities to full advantage. These countries face the enormous challenge of revitalizing civil society from the grassroots up.

It is critical that women act as agents of change in this process of linking political, social and economic reforms together into a foundation for development. The Report finds that, so far, female voices have been only faintly heard in the new democratic institutions of the region and that women politicians, ministers, ambassadors, and senior government decision makers are largely lacking. In most countries less than 10 percent of the parliamentarians are women, and the ratio of senior government posts occupied by women – 11 percent in Central Europe and 4 percent in CIS countries – is also very low.

Empowering women to act as agents of change requires both immediate action and long-term commitment in order to build women's participation in society at all levels. As the authority expropriated by the communist state from communities, families and individuals is regained by citizens, parents and entrepreneurs, there is an historic opportunity – and endless numbers of individual opportunities – for the gender balance of power also to be reset. Certainly, a broad-based women's movement which acts in concert with other equality-seeking organizations, civil institutions, economic actors, and governments is a primary conduit for such a process.

Reducing the role of the state is a basic goal of the transition, but government has a vital part to play in promoting the gender balance in society. Ways need to be found to reform, rebuild and sustain public services, such as health care, social care and education. Tax systems need to be reformed so that governments can raise revenues to pay for these services. National machinery for the advancement of women must be established, as has been done in several countries in the region. Using gender-based analysis in the development of public policies – holding a gender lens to statistics and planning – is a recognized "best practice" which promotes equal outcomes for women and men. This involves paying special attention to issues particular to women and mainstreaming a gendered viewpoint.

The aim of this Report is to stimulate the development of national agendas and public policy frameworks for gender equality. The regional perspective offered by the analyses of the Report suggests that the following issues merit special focus.

- Mobilizing women and men within political parties to encourage women's participation in the democratic political process.
- Developing workplace policies and practices which expand the opportunities for women.
- Supporting women micro-entrepreneurs through business training and access to financing.
- Encouraging public discussion on gender issues and women's equality through grassroots organizations, the media and education and awareness campaigns.
- Developing a multi-faceted strategy to deal with violence against women.
- Promoting a fairer sharing between women and men of responsibility for child-rearing.
- Targeting public support for single parents, most of whom are women.
- Maintaining and strengthening women's educational attainment.
- Reaching WHO and UNICEF targets for maternal and child health.
- Favouring a broader life-cycle and social determinants approach to women's health.
- Focusing on and involving children and adolescents in the effort to achieve gender equality within families and communities.

Importantly, the principles which underpin the transition – the expression of diversity and genuine political representation, economic development and the expansion of choice – are the same values driving the movement for women's equality. They are simply somewhat different perspectives on the same process. In this light, the bid for women's equality should not be set apart from the transition, but should be a part of the transition. Equality cannot be imposed as it was under communism, but equality also cannot thrive in the wild as those who champion an unfettered marketplace would claim. Equality is a civilized and civilizing influence which needs to be carefully and constantly cultivated in order to advance human development. It is not a static state to be achieved; it is a living process to be continuously attended to.

Gáspár Fajth
MONEE Project Officer

1 The Transition, Children and Women

This Report is the sixth in the series of Regional Monitoring Reports from the MONEE project of the UNICEF International Child Development Centre. It focuses on the rights of women and changes in their well-being since the collapse of communism in the 27 countries of Central and Eastern Europe and the former Soviet Union. A better understanding of the status of women in the context of the transition is crucial for advancing human development in the region.

Women are important as economic and social actors and as agents of change. Women are vital participants in the economy through paid and unpaid work and vital contributors to political life and individual endeavour. They play a pivotal role in child welfare and a central role in family, social and community life – areas in which development is essential to the future of the countries in transition.

Under communism, the state became the main social institution in these countries, marginalizing the function of the market, the family and other civic institutions. In so doing, it became the dominant arbiter and official enforcer of social norms and values, including those around gender equality. The communist state espoused an egalitarian ideology and enshrined equality rights in legislation, but its promise was unfulfilled in the daily lives of women. With civil society weak and the family shut in against the state, there was little space for women's equality to develop and grow from the grassroots.

There are some important areas where the status of women was relatively enhanced under communism. These command economies promoted equal education and high employment for women, as well as generous and comprehensive childcare and maternal health services. This investment in women was probably motivated more by economic necessity than by social justice, but the outcome was a concrete advancement for women.

The economic, social and political transition in the region has shattered the state monopoly on gender equality and exposed women to a wide-open environment where the conditions for equality are quite different, a territory rich with possibilities but not without risks. In some ways, the transition process has cut into the employment and social welfare gains of women – a regression often linked to the sudden and significant shrinkage in the role of the state. In the gap between the retreat of former regimes and the development of democratic society, there is room for concern that the commitment to women's full participation in society that is required from a broad coalition of actors may fail to materialize.

Nevertheless, this Report is presented in the spirit that women have much to gain by the transition to market economies and democratic governments – as individuals, as workers and mothers, as family and community members, as women in association, and as a political force. It is important to raise the alert about new risks to women that have emerged in the transition, but it is equally important to focus on the rewards of conquering these challenges.

This chapter provides an overview of the transition and updates some of the trends described in previous Regional Monitoring Reports to highlight the larger economic, social and political context behind the changes in women's lives. It is followed by five thematic chapters that explore women in the transition. These are related to the labour market, family, health, violence against women, and participation in decision making.

In this chapter, Section 1.1 looks at the region from a human development perspective which weighs both economic and social welfare. Section 1.2 maps out the economic changes taking place in the region. Section 1.3 explores social trends. Section 1.4 reviews commitments to women's rights, the overarching theme of the Report. As with earlier Regional Monitoring Reports, attention focuses on changes that have taken place since 1989, the pre-transition benchmark used by these Reports.

■

1.1 The Region in a Human Development Perspective

In 1989, 154 million women, 135 million men and 122 million children were living in the part of the world now constituted by Central and Eastern Europe, the Baltic countries and the Commonwealth of Independent States (CIS). The transition to market economies and democratic governments in this region covers a huge geographical area and a population base that is characterized by diversity and disparity both within and among countries. Sometimes the differences are so great and the circumstances so divergent that questions must be raised about the extent to which these countries form a region and about what links them together. The answers lie in the common heritage embedded in the institutions and structures during the shared history of the past several decades and in the goals set for the transition. This introductory section maps the overall development level of the region using aggregate statistical measures that embrace the main aspects of development.

Human development rankings

The Human Development Index (HDI) of the UNDP was created to measure human progress in more than narrow economic terms. As Box 1.1 describes, the HDI provides a broader measure of development by combining an income indicator (per capita GDP expressed in purchasing-power parities) with two "human capability" measures (a health and an education index).

The 27 countries of the transition region, grouped in the seven sub-regions conventionally used by the MONEE project, are introduced below. Figure 1.1 shows the 1995 development rankings for 25 of the countries in an international field of 174 nations, as published in the 1998 *Human Development Report*. The black HDI column represents the distance each country falls behind the top-ranked country, that is, the longer the column, the lower the standing. The transition countries run from Slovenia at 37th to Tajikistan at 118th, with development standings generally decreasing from west to east. This picture confirms the considerable disparity among the seven sub-regions and, at times, also within these sub-regions.

The Central European countries of the Czech Republic, Slovakia, Hungary, and Poland ranked highest among the transition countries, belonging to the UNDP's "high human development" group of nations. However, their nearest neighbours there were the more well off countries of Latin America rather than the countries of the European Union. The Czech Republic and Slovakia

Figure 1.1

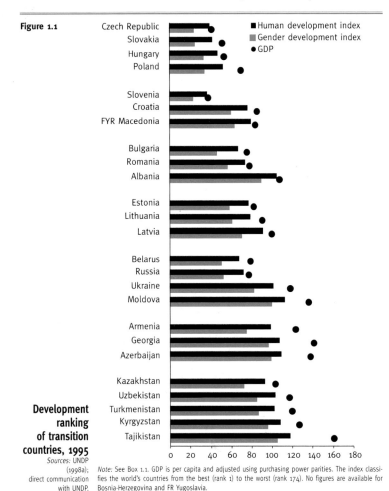

Development ranking of transition countries, 1995
Sources: UNDP (1998a); direct communication with UNDP.

Note: See Box 1.1. GDP is per capita and adjusted using purchasing power parities. The index classifies the world's countries from the best (rank 1) to the worst (rank 174). No figures are available for Bosnia-Herzegovina and FR Yugoslavia.

Box 1.1

Measuring development

The Human Development Index was first introduced in the 1990 *Human Development Report*. Its purpose was to give a broader measure of the well-being of a nation than simply GDP. The HDI is designed to reflect three fundamental aspects of human welfare: standard of living, health and education. Currently, the index uses the following indicators to capture these elements of human development: purchasing power adjusted to per capita income, life expectancy at birth, and a combination of literacy figures and education enrolment. A country's scores for each variable are standardized on a scale from 0 to 1. The composite index, which is intended to reflect the country's overall development level, is calculated as a simple arithmetic average of the three scores.

The HDI is both admired and criticized. It has had a great impact on the way people think about development, breaking the exclusive hold of income-based indicators of welfare. However, critics maintain that the index measures are so basic they may miss what they strive to measure. For example, long life expectancy

does not necessarily mean people are healthy; school enrolment shows the opportunity to learn, not necessarily the level or quality of knowledge attained, and personal income is not the only factor in the standard of living. Critics question whether the simple averaging of the components is adequate and have raised the issue of the correlation among the factors and whether the transformation of indicators into scores is correct. Finally, the picture drawn by the HDI refers only to national averages and does not reflect inequality between groups in society, such as women and men.

In response, the HDI has been refined, and companion indicators developed, such as the income-distribution-adjusted index, the human poverty index, the gender empowerment measure, and the gender-related development index (GDI). Introduced in the 1995 *Human Development Report*, the GDI has the same three elements as the HDI, each adjusted for gender inequality. The greater the inequality between women and men, the lower the GDI compared to the HDI. (See the Glossary for details on the GDI.)

ranked 39th and 42nd, close to Argentina, Uruguay and Panama; Hungary was 47th, between Venezuela and Mexico, while Poland was 52nd, just before Colombia.

The HDI rankings underline the staggering disparities among the countries that have emerged from the violent breakup of the former Yugoslavia. (Only three of these countries were covered by the UNDP report.) Slovenia, at 37th, ranked best among all the transition countries, but the Former Yugoslav Republic of Macedonia fell into 80th place. Croatia's ranking also reflects the impact of the 1992-95 civil war. There is no HDI score for Bosnia-Herzegovina, as the civil war there was just ending. Similarly, 1995 data were unavailable for the Federal Republic of Yugoslavia (Serbia and Montenegro), which was under the constraints of an international embargo. Available social and economic indicators suggest that the ex-Yugoslav countries – with the exception of Slovenia – would have fallen into the medium human-development group in 1995.

In Southeastern Europe, Albania was extremely isolated before the transition. In 1995 it had the poorest development ranking in Eastern Europe at 105th, a score similar to that of China or Egypt. Neighbouring Bulgaria, at 67th, and Romania, at 74th, fell into the medium human-development cluster of nations.

The countries of Estonia, Latvia and Lithuania ranked poorly, which was surprising given that the Baltic sub-region was a highly developed area within the Soviet Union before the transition.

In the western CIS, Russia and Belarus fared relatively well (ranking close to Bulgaria and Romania, or, outside the region, Brazil, Ecuador and Turkey). Ukraine and Moldova, the other two western CIS countries, ranked closer to countries of the Caucasus and Central Asia. Uzbekistan, the most populous country in the Central Asia sub-region, was close to the area average at 104th. Kazakhstan, which is regarded in this Report as a Central Asian country, had a better ranking than the other four. Tajikistan, with the lowest standing in the region at 118th, ranked lower than Mongolia or China, but still considerably higher than Pakistan or India.

As mentioned, the HDI ranking contains measures for both economic and social development. It is enlightening to analyse the international rankings of the transition countries further with these components in mind.

Comparing economic and social development

In Figure 1.1, the black dots show the rankings the countries would have if only the economic component of the HDI indicator were considered. Ranking the 25 transition countries by GDP per capita in comparative prices would push all countries lower in the rankings. Hungary, for example, would drop six places, Bulgaria eight, Ukraine 16, Azerbaijan about 30, and Tajikistan 43. This suggests the transition countries enjoy a comparative advantage in the development of

human capabilities, such as health and education – a pattern with important implications for child development. The downward shift might also suggest the transition countries suffer a systematic disadvantage in their economic development compared to countries outside the region.

Figure 1.1 also presents the country rankings using a gender-related development index (GDI), a refined human development indicator that considers gender disparities in earned income, life expectancy and schooling (Box 1.1). Based on the GDI, as the blue columns illustrate, all the transition countries move up 10-15 places over their HDI ranking. By this measure, Slovenia and the Czech Republic overtake Portugal and approach Italy and Ireland; Hungary and Poland overtake Argentina and come close to Uruguay. This indicates that the countries in the region enjoy a systematic gender equality advantage relative to other countries. It also demonstrates that the first five years of the transition – whatever hard times there may have been – did not eliminate this comparative edge.

Two important qualifications must be added. On the one hand, a wider set of statistics suggests the HDI rankings underestimate the development levels of the transition countries in certain regards. For example, UNICEF's *State of the World's Children* ranked the countries of the region relatively higher – Slovenia 16th (1995 HDI, 37th), Croatia 32nd, Poland 36th, Russia 57th, and Uzbekistan 89th (HDI, 104th). The basis of the UNICEF ranking is the under-5 mortality rate. This effective indicator of child welfare also reflects the health and education of the mother and is a good proxy for access to basic social services.

Other evidence confirms the systematic social-development advantage indicated by the GDI and UNICEF rankings. The share of the urban population in Central and Eastern Europe is similar to that in Latin America, but access to water, sanitation and health services is considerably better in the post-communist region. Central European countries spend relatively the same on health care or education as the OECD countries; CIS countries tend to spend less, but have no fewer teachers, physicians, or hospital beds per capita. In the Central Asian countries of Tajikistan and Turkmenistan, the physicians-to-population ratios were comparable to those of Switzerland and the United States in the early 1990s.

On the other hand, more in-depth investigations and refined measurements reveal that the crude indicators of access to services often seriously overestimate the value of the services provided. Evidence for this comes in various forms. For example, the 1994 Adult Literacy Survey of 12 industrialized countries, including Poland, from the transition region revealed weak performance in functional literacy. Of Poles surveyed, 75 percent scored in the lowest two levels for the ability to locate and use information in documents, compared to 35-45 percent of persons in the Netherlands and Germany.

In other countries, reassessments of immunization records of children have revealed discrepancies in public health services. In Kyrgyzstan, Turkmenistan and Uzbekistan, the share of valid immunizations – those carried out within the proper time intervals – is considerably lower than official immunization data imply. These findings suggest that the actual value of the capabilities-based welfare indicators for the countries may be generally lower than believed. Nonetheless, they do not necessarily impugn the HDI rankings of the countries. The HDI scores placed the region in a developing country environment in the mid-1990s. While there are few available in-depth comparisons between this region and Latin America or Asia, it is likely that countries in those regions also have problems with the effectiveness of services.

In any case, there does appear to be a greater gap in the transition region between the efforts and resources put into social development and the results achieved. Policies and delivery systems inherited from the past are proving ineffective in the new circumstances associated with transition. This points to the need for serious reforms in the social sectors, or the transition countries risk losing their current comparative advantages in gender development and child welfare. Unfortunately, the situation since 1989 has not been very encouraging.

The large deterioration in many welfare indicators noted by earlier Regional Monitoring Reports is reflected in the changes in the HDI rankings of the transition countries between 1990 and 1995. In 1990, Czechoslovakia ranked 26th, Hungary 28th, Armenia 47th, Poland 48th,

---

Box 1.2

The United Nations and a rights-based approach to development

The 1995 *Human Development Report*, devoted to the issue of gender equality, stated that the objective of development is to enlarge people's choices. This involves equality of opportunity for all people in society, sustainability of such opportunities from one generation to the next, and the empowerment of people so they can participate in and benefit from development. The promotion and protection of human rights, including equal rights for women, are primary instruments for realizing these goals.

The historical roots of a rights-based approach to development are found in the aftermath of the Second World War. The 1948 Universal Declaration of Human Rights was a political response to the horrors of that war. It recognizes that all people, regardless of gender, race, language, or religion, are entitled to participate in society with rights and dignity, and it embraces a vision of global human values endorsed by the entire international community. At the same time, institutions like the International Monetary Fund and the World Bank were established to plan against the kind of economic disaster that had precipitated the war and to focus on alleviating poverty through economic growth. From these beginnings, a sophisticated appreciation of the complex inter-relationships among political, economic and social rights and conditions has evolved around the consensus that addressing the root causes of development problems is essential.

One of the most important advances has been the recognition that de jure equality – equality in the law – does not automatically deliver de facto equality. Despite legal guarantees, structural barriers and systemic discrimination continue to exclude women and other traditionally disadvantaged groups from equal opportunities. A rights-based approach to development calls for substantive equality. This approach recognizes that special measures which promote positive discrimination may be necessary to overcome long-standing barriers. It also holds that like-treatment may perpetuate inequalities, so the goal is equal outcomes rather than identical treatment of women and men. This approach strives to ensure that equality and inclusion are built into the design and implementation of services, supports, funding allocations, programmes, policies, and laws.

As instruments of international commitment, the 1979 Convention on the Elimination of All Forms of Discrimination against Women (CEDAW) and the 1989 Convention on the Rights of the Child have moved forward from simply declaring rights to identifying issues that need to be addressed and the measures that need to be taken to realize these rights. The Platform for Action of the 1995 Fourth World Conference on Women identifies a set of steps to fulfil the provisions of CEDAW and dedicates a chapter to the rights of the girl child. Discrimination against women and girls in the allocation of economic and social resources is recognized as a direct violation of economic, social, political, and cultural rights.

Established in 1976, the UN Development Fund for Women (UNIFEM) has integrated a rights-based framework into its efforts to promote women's empowerment and gender equality. UNIFEM is dedicated to building stronger women's organizations and networks and, in recent years, has focused on how women can use CEDAW and the 1995 Platform for Action to advance their positions.

CEDAW, the Platform of Action and the Convention on the Rights of the Child have shaped UNICEF's 1996 Mission Statement "to work on the rights of children in general, the rights of girls in particular, as well as the rights of women and the promotion of gender equality at all stages of the life cycle". UNICEF has arrived at a rights-based approach to development through decades of practical work on the ground. In the 1960s-70s, UNICEF learned the effectiveness of targeting support to women in order to reach children. This women-and-development approach focused on women as agents of child welfare. In the 1980s, UNICEF recognized that tactical actions were often ineffective and inefficient without broader political and economic support. In the early 1990s, framed by the World Summit for Children, UNICEF explicitly shifted to a rights-based "gender-in-development" philosophy. This approach holds that meeting the human rights of women and children is essential for development to occur and that gender discrimination often impairs the ability of women and children to exercise their rights.

Bulgaria 40th, Kazakhstan 54th, and Tajikistan 88th. The comparison over time is not straightforward: it is affected by the higher number of countries included, changes in calculating methods, and weaknesses in GDP estimates for the initial transition period. Nonetheless, the change in HDI rankings from 1990 to 1995 is often staggering, for example Russia falling from 37th to 66th place.

The main reason for the downshift in development in the region in 1990-95 was the fall in economic output. The inefficient, non-market production system inherited from the communist past simply could not meet the needs of the emerging marketplace. The result was a pronounced devaluation of national outputs on the world market. The relative HDI rankings of the transition countries also fell because indicators measuring human capability have been tending to drop in the region during the 1990s, while countries in other parts of the world are making progress. As later sections highlight, there has been an absolute deterioration not only in economic, but also in health and education indicators in the region, mainly but not exclusively in the former Soviet Union.

The transition countries face the challenge of advancing a balanced and integrated agenda of economic and social development that will bring the desired prosperity and well-being to the region. There are many differences and disparities across the region, but this important political challenge is common to all countries. The comparative advantage the countries enjoy with the gender and children's indices provides a good foundation for a human rights-based approach to development – an approach increasingly undertaken by international organizations (Box 1.2) and among the advanced countries in different parts of the world. Rights-based development aims to promote the growing equality of opportunity among people and nations.

■

1.2 Changes in the Economy

Changes in the economy have been high on the reform agenda of the region – macro-economic stabilization, development of the market and integration into the main economic institutions of the world. This thrust is welcome from the perspective of the rights and well-being of women and their families. Economic output and entrepreneurial freedom are essential for meeting development needs and enlarging people's choices.

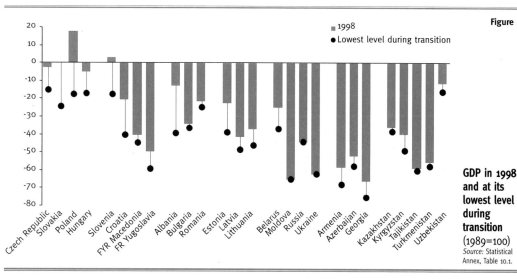

Figure 1.2

GDP in 1998 and at its lowest level during transition (1989=100)
Source: Statistical Annex, Table 10.1.

The international comparison in the previous section illustrates that the transition countries are relatively weak in the economic dimension of human development. However, it is important to note that, since 1995, the returns of economic reforms have become more apparent.

Uneven recovery in outputs

The cumulative changes in real GDP during the transition period are shown in Figure 1.2 using official data on measured output for 26 of the 27 countries. The figure illustrates both the large falls that took place after 1989 and the current status of economic recovery in the region.

The large black dots below the horizontal axis in the diagram show the maximum extent of the contraction of these economies since 1989. It is clear that all the countries portrayed underwent a considerable regression in economic output. The biggest drops occurred in former Yugoslavia (with the exception of Slovenia) and in the Baltic and CIS countries (with the exception of Uzbekistan). In Central Europe, Slovenia and Romania, economies contracted by 15-25 percent. Output fell by 35-45 percent in the rest of the Balkans and by almost 60 percent in FR Yugoslavia. There were no data available for war-torn Bosnia-Herzegovina.

The blue columns in Figure 1.2 indicate the current status of economic recovery, that is, how much the 1998 GDP falls short of or exceeds the 1989 level. (The European Bank for Reconstruction and Development, EBRD, estimated the 1998 figures.) It is clear that most countries have rebounded, but still fall short of 1989 levels.

Only Poland and Slovenia have increased the size of their economies; Slovakia has only just recovered, while both the Czech Republic and Hungary are slightly below the 1989 levels. The economies of Central Europe bottomed out around 1992-93, and of the Baltics and most

CIS countries around 1994-95. In contrast, the economies of Ukraine and Moldova are still on a downward slide, and Russia was hit with a new economic crisis in 1998. It is unclear how the violent events in the Balkans that erupted in spring 1999 and that have taken a heavy human toll are going to set back the economic situation in FR Yugoslavia and neighbouring countries.

The GDP figures presented in Figure 1.2 may well underestimate the real size of the economies in the region, given the substantial growth of the informal economy, as Box 1.3 discusses. Still, it is clear GDP fell substantially across the region during transition. Moreover, the growth of the informal sector does not necessarily have positive effects on human development and welfare. For example, lawful employment provides access to social security entitlements, limits on working hours, and safety and other protective regulations. Moreover, the growth of the informal sector is often associated with illegal activities, including organized crime.

Structural changes and reforms

Changes in economic output levels across the region have been accompanied by major structural shifts. In Central Europe, Slovenia, Croatia, and the Baltic States small-scale private enterprises in the service sector have played an important role in the recovery. Large-scale privatization of state enterprises has also moved the transition forward. In some cases, most prominently in Hungary, this progress has been driven by substantial direct foreign investment. (See Statistical Annex, Table 10.4.)

In Albania, Armenia, Georgia, and Kyrgyzstan, agriculture, mostly family farms, has helped spur economic renewal. Indeed, agriculture is once again more important to the economy than industry as many large state-owned factories are paralysed or shut down. In Georgia, for example, agriculture accounted for 28 percent of GDP in 1997, compared to 15 percent for industry and construction and 22 percent for trade. In Albania, Armenia and Kyrgyzstan, agriculture now makes up one-third or more of the economy (Statistical Annex, Table 10.3).

In the other half of the region, the direction of the change is less clear. In some countries, such as Russia, Azerbaijan, Kazakhstan, and Turkmenistan, the huge energy and mining industries built up to serve a bigger economy now target export markets. However, inadequate infrastructure and transportation are a problem, especially in the last three countries, but anticipated foreign investment could ease that difficulty. Some CIS countries, like Belarus, continue to draw on Russian energy and raw materials. Others, like Uzbekistan, have pursued a gradualist reform strategy, building upon the industrial and agricultural capacity inherited from Soviet times. These strategies have helped offset the fall in economic output in the short term, but their potential for long-term economic growth remains uncertain.

In Russia, the export of energy and mineral resources may have softened the economic shocks of transition, but it has also contributed to delays in tax reform and enterprise restructuring. Corporate taxes, cross subsidies through low energy prices, the delayed payment of energy bills, and credit operations have all helped sustain production and consumption levels. This consolidation strategy collapsed in 1998, following the sharp fall in oil prices on the world market and a more cautious environment in international lending sparked by wildfire recession in East Asia. Earlier projections on economic growth for Russia have been adjusted downward, raising fears of a prolonged economic recession that may destabilize the region.

Figure 1.4 illustrates the level of reform achieved in the region. The figure shows the estimated share of the private sector in GDP, as well as a score which is a composite average of indicators that have been developed by the EBRD to measure economic transition. (A score greater than 4 indicates full marketization.) The chart confirms the link between private-sector development and market-oriented reforms. It also shows that many countries still lag considerably. Nevertheless, there are some areas – like trade and the privatization of smaller enterprises and ventures – where most countries had made important progress by 1998.

Box 1.3

Estimates of the size of the informal economy in the transition region

One prominent feature of the transition economies has been the growth of the informal sector and its associated labour markets. Figure 1.3 reports the estimated size of the informal sector in a selection of transition economies based on energy usage, which has not decreased in line with reported economic output. (Reduced energy efficiency may also play a role in energy-use figures in countries with abundant nuclear power, like Ukraine and Russia, or in oil-rich Azerbaijan.) The growth of the informal sector appears to be most pronounced in Russia, Ukraine and some other countries of the former Soviet Union. It is a worldwide experience that this "grey" activity grows in response to punitive tax systems and costly and sometimes corrupt bureaucratic procedures.

Figure 1.3

Estimated size of the informal sector, 1990 and 1995 (percent of GDP) Source: Johnson, Kaufman and Schleifer (1997).

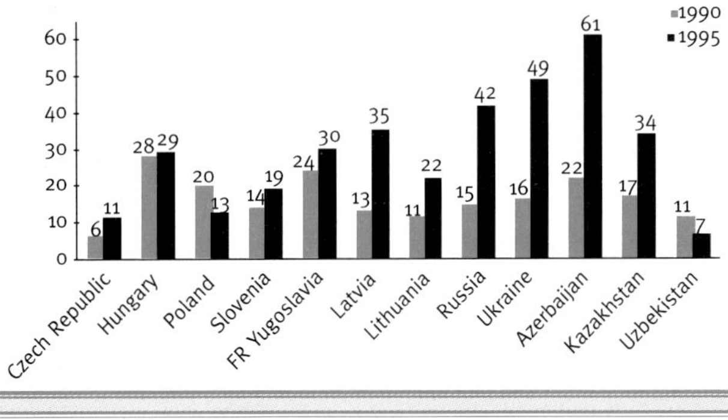

Estimated size of the informal sector, 1990 and 1995 (percent of GDP) — bar chart. Values (1990, 1995): Czech Republic 6, 11; Hungary 28, 29; Poland 20, 13; Slovenia 14, 19; FR Yugoslavia 24, 30; Latvia 13, 35; Lithuania 11, 22; Russia 15, 42; Ukraine 16, 49; Azerbaijan 22, 61; Kazakhstan 17, 34; Uzbekistan 11, 7.

Large gaps in employment and wages

People mainly experience the impact of economic reform as a change in paid employment and in what wages can buy. Falls in economic output across the region have also entailed large drops in real wages and pressure on employers to reduce their workforces. These effects have been amplified by the need to improve labour productivity and to reduce the over-staffing and labour hoarding common in the former planned economies. This suggests that, even when GDP recovers, employment levels and real wages may not, as illustrated in Box 1.4.

Big losses in real wages were, moreover, accompanied by considerable increases in measured wage differentials in all countries for which data were available. (See Statistical Annex, Tables 10.8 and 10.12.) The Gini coefficient, a common measure of the extent of inequality, rose on average by one-third in Central and Southeastern Europe and by one-half in the former Soviet Union (where some countries, such as Russia, had a high degree of earnings disparity by OECD standards before transition).

Overall, the number of jobs lost in the region since 1989 has been estimated at 26 million – 13 percent of the initial level. As Figure 1.6 shows, employment has declined in 23 countries of the region during the 1990s,

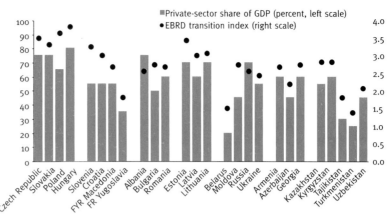

Figure 1.4

Private-sector share of GDP (percent, left scale)
EBRD transition index (right scale)

Note: The values of the transition index are MONEE project calculations and are unweighted averages of the EBRD scores on eight different dimensions of the transition (for example, privatization, enterprise restructuring, price liberalization, and banking reform).

Progress in economic transition, 1998
Source: EBRD (1998), Table 2.1.

remained stable in Azerbaijan, and increased in Turkmenistan and Uzbekistan. Some countries, notably in the western CIS, the Caucasus and Central Asia, have endeavoured to protect employment levels in the face of plunging GDP. Workers accept even low-paying jobs or periodic employment because these offer them access to social security, employee benefits and social ties.

The emergence of significant unemployment is a relatively new phenomenon in the region after decades of central planning and policies of full employment. The number of registered unemployed grew from about one million in 1989 (found mostly in the southern states of communist Yugoslavia) to eight or nine million by 1993-94 following the first waves of economic reforms. Three-

---

Box 1.4

Two patterns of change in GDP, employment and wages

There are two distinctive patterns of change in the region related to GDP, employment and real wages. Hungary represents the trend in Central Europe and some other countries where the drop in economic output has been relatively moderate and a steady recovery has been under way for some time. In Hungary, GDP has almost recovered, but less so real wages, and not so jobs. The number of jobs in 1997 was 71 percent of that in 1989, and these jobs paid a per-earner wage worth 23 percent less in real terms. Higher labour productivity – reflected in the widening gap between Hungarian GDP and employment in Figure 1.5 – has improved the prospects for economic growth, but the price has been two-digit unemployment rates since 1992. The data suggest that economic recovery has been more effective in raising wages than in creating new jobs. Hungary, like some other countries leading in economic reform, faces problems associated with high unemployment, such as growing social exclusion.

In Azerbaijan, the pattern is characteristic of countries, mostly the CIS, where

declines in GDP were so abrupt and large that a similar, or bigger, cut in employment was politically untenable (and often demographic factors also put pressure on employment). So, Azerbaijan shows a huge fall in GDP and in real wages that bottomed out in 1995 and has recovered only slightly since. Meanwhile, employment has remained constant, which means labour productivity per employee has crashed. The result is much less overt unemployment, but much lower real wages (see the dotted line in the graph) and a big rise in the number of working poor.

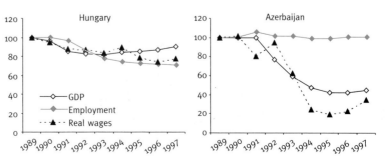

Figure 1.5

Hungary

Azerbaijan

◇ GDP
◆ Employment
▲ Real wages

Note: Employment refers to the total number of persons employed. Wages refers to real wages.

Change in GDP, employment and wages in Hungary and Azerbaijan, 1989-97
(1989=100)
Source: Statistical Annex, Tables 10.1, 10.8, 10.9.

quarters of these people were registered in Central Europe and in the Balkans. Currently, the number of registered unemployed is estimated at more than 10 million across the 27 countries of the region, about six million of whom are women. The ratio of women among the registered unemployed is around 50 percent in Central and Eastern Europe and exceeds 60 percent in Ukraine, Belarus, Russia, Armenia, and Kazakhstan.

steadily in Russia, with no signs of stabilizing or recovering. The number of jobs shrank by 14 percent between 1989 and 1997. The registered unemployment rate is still low, around 3 percent. Official estimates, using international standards, put the actual rate at more than 9 percent in 1997. Unregistered unemployment is common across the CIS, where labour market institutions are weak or lacking.

The evidence suggests, therefore, that most countries are still having difficulties improving labour productivity without aggravating macro-economic and social problems. In 1997, registered unemployment increased in 13 of the 24 countries for which recent data were available, and in six countries this followed temporary improvements. (See Statistical Annex, Table 10.10.)

The example of the countries leading in economic reform in the region shows that stimulating the growth of small- and

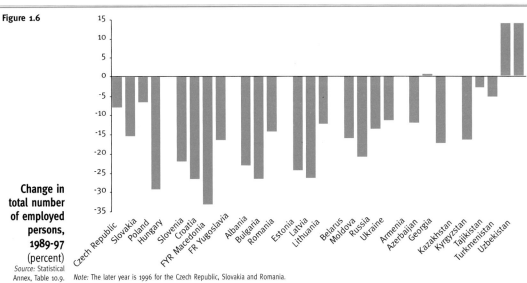

Figure 1.6

Change in total number of employed persons, 1989-97 (percent)
Source: Statistical Annex, Table 10.9.

Note: The later year is 1996 for the Czech Republic, Slovakia and Romania.

Although unemployment has stabilized or increased at a slower pace in recent years, employment prospects have generally remained dim. Further macro-economic adjustments, enterprise restructuring and other changes meant that more people were driven out of jobs in the Czech Republic and Slovakia in 1997. That same year, GDP fell by 7 percent in Albania following financial frauds and civic strife, and Romania saw a similar drop in output associated with efforts to speed up reforms. In Bulgaria in 1996-97, real wages fell by one-third, and registered unemployment rose from 11 to 14 percent. In FR Yugoslavia, one-quarter of the workforce was registered as unemployed in 1997, and about two-fifths in Bosnia-Herzegovina and FYR Macedonia.

Employment has declined relatively slowly but

medium-sized enterprises is strategically important to improving productivity and reducing unemployment. By providing an alternative to big companies, it also helps tackle the political and economic gridlock occurring at the level of large institutional employers. Studies have shown that self-employment and small ventures have played an important role in cushioning the welfare impact of enterprise restructuring in Poland. In Hungary, the growth of micro-enterprises employing less than 10 persons, often family businesses, is seen as key to a sharp increase in labour productivity. In 1995, the small-enterprise sector provided 44 percent of GDP and employed about one-third of the workforce. In contrast, the small-enterprise sector accounts for about 10 percent of employment in Russia, and in several CIS countries even less.

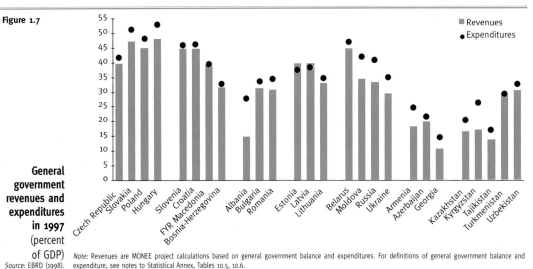

Figure 1.7

General government revenues and expenditures in 1997 (percent of GDP)
Source: EBRD (1998).

■ Revenues
● Expenditures

Note: Revenues are MONEE project calculations based on general government balance and expenditures. For definitions of general government balance and expenditure, see notes to Statistical Annex, Tables 10.5, 10.6.

Declines in government revenues

One of the biggest and most important challenges facing the countries in transition is to be able to collect enough taxes to meet essential public spending requirements and so avoid growing fiscal deficits. The social upheaval associated with the transition process in many countries has put governments under enormous pressure to keep expenditures at a level that will prevent widespread poverty and preserve social order and cohesion. However, at the same time, the combination of severe recession and deeply flawed tax systems has led to a large decline in government revenues. The result has been persistent fiscal imbalances in most countries of the region. Estimates for 1997 (see Statistical Annex, Table 10.5) showed that, with few exceptions, governments in transition countries were running budget deficits and that, in many cases, the deficits were large relative to the size of the economy.

Since one of the purposes of the transition is to reduce the pervasive role of the state, a decline in government revenues and spending (as a percentage of GDP) is not necessarily a bad thing. However, in a number of countries, the decline in government revenues has been so large, it has impaired the functioning of vital state institutions and made the reform of institutional arrangements extremely difficult. Figure 1.7 shows government revenues and expenditures expressed as a percentage of GDP for each country.

The unweighted average of the ratio of revenues to GDP in 1997 was less than 30 percent in the CIS countries. It was close to 40 percent in Central and Eastern European countries. While the general pattern of a close association between low revenues and high fiscal deficits is apparent, there are exceptions. Russia and Moldova, for example, collect a relatively high share of revenues, but their deficits are among the highest in the region because their expenditure levels are closer to those of Central Europe rather than other CIS countries. Here, as in a number of countries, the decline in expenditures has been brought about by artificial means, including arrears in public-sector payments, wages and pensions. Persistent fiscal imbalances associated with insufficient revenue collection jeopardize macro-economic stability and output recovery, as the recent crisis in Russia illustrates. Box 1.5 focuses on some of the underlying causes of weak government-revenue performance, particularly in many CIS countries.

Box 1.5

Tax collection and reforms

The structure of government revenues shows characteristic differences between countries in Central and Eastern Europe and those of the CIS. These differences help explain lower revenue collection in the CIS. Overall, as Figure 1.8 illustrates, taxation has shifted away from the corporate sector, but this shift has been far less pronounced in the CIS. In Central and Eastern Europe, the combined share of enterprise-profit taxes and domestic taxes on goods and services fell from 62 percent of tax revenue in 1989 to 41 percent in 1997. Moreover, with the exception of Albania, personal income taxes have not declined as a share of GDP, and the decline in indirect domestic taxes, like the value-added tax, has been marginal. Hence, almost the entire drop in tax revenues represents a fall in tax revenues on corporate profits.

For a variety of reasons, the CIS continues to exhibit a much greater reliance on the corporate sector. Countries slow to reform, such as Belarus, Turkmenistan and Ukraine, still raised over 6 percent of GDP in 1997 from corporate income taxes, compared to an average of less than 3 percent in advanced transition countries. In the context of the low income-generating capacity of state-owned enterprises, the failure to shift the tax base away from the corporate sector has contributed to the decline in revenues.

There is no easy solution to the problem of tax collection in transition economies, but there are two significant areas where changes can bring substantive progress. First, the tax systems of the transition economies, particularly in the CIS, can reduce their reliance on corporate taxation and put more emphasis on personal

income and expenditure-based taxes. These taxes need to be carefully designed to mitigate against any negative impact on consumer demand and low-income households. A simple broad-based tax structure with reasonable rates is particularly important for the success of small businesses and entrepreneurs who do not have the resources to manipulate complex tax structures to their advantage.

Second, changes in the structure of the tax system must go hand in hand with more transparent tax administration. In many countries, the definition of the tax base is problematic. Taxes are prone to being changed arbitrarily on short notice and are sometimes applied retroactively. This capricious environment encourages the owners and managers of firms to find ways to avoid paying taxes. Research has shown the strong correlation between distortional tax systems with excessive regulations and the size of the unofficial economy. Simply put, companies and individuals are more willing to pay taxes, and hence revenue will be higher, if the tax system is seen as simple, transparent and fair.

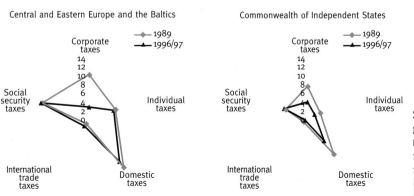

Figure 1.8

Note: Central and Eastern Europe excludes Albania and Bosnia-Herzegovina. CIS excludes Belarus and Uzbekistan. The initial year is 1990 for Hungary and 1991 for Armenia, Azerbaijan, Estonia, Georgia, FYR Macedonia, Moldova, Latvia, Slovenia, and Ukraine. Data for Russia for 1989 refer to the USSR and in the case of the Czech Republic and Slovakia to former Czechoslovakia.

Structure of government revenues in 1989 and 1996/97 (percent of GDP)

Source: EBRD (1998), page 59.

A number of countries have made significant reforms to their tax systems, and in some cases these changes are already bearing fruit in terms of higher government revenues. Additionally, there is room for more efficient spending, particularly on social transfers, as tight expenditure management will continue to be crucial. Social reform, therefore, is an integral part of economic change.

■

1.3 Social Trends and Reforms

Social issues have generally received less attention than economic problems during the transition. The timetable for reform and the associated social costs have generally been underestimated. Social systems that delivered positive benefits in the past have turned out to be inefficient or difficult to sustain under the new conditions. Reduced revenues have paralysed rather than inspired governments to carry out social reforms. Considering the inheritance of the past, there is a tremendous amount of work to be done to strengthen the responsibility and the capacity of individuals, families and civic society to act as partners in health, education and social protection services. The need for action is urgent, as the human costs of the transition have been high.

Poverty and social dislocation have hit hard

Before transition, poverty was limited in the region. Access to employment and basic health and education services was easy and widespread; income security was high, and disparity moderate; social supports included universal pensions, generous family benefits and childcare subsidies and services.

The falls in GDP, employment and real wages that have characterized the transition mean that rising poverty must have affected a large part of the region's population. Measuring the increase in poverty is, however, not clearcut. The results depend on the definition of poverty used and on the availability of adequate statistical surveys. A study relying on a poverty threshold of US$4 per day concluded that, in 1993-94, about 120 million people – almost 30 percent of the 414 million in the region – lived in poverty, compared to 13.6 million in 1988-89. According to this estimate, 30-40 percent of the population were living in poverty in Bulgaria, Estonia, Russia, Ukraine, and Uzbekistan, about half the population was poor in Kazakhstan, Lithuania and Turkmenistan, and about three-quarters in Kyrgyzstan. According to the same poverty threshold, only a small percent of Czechs, Slovaks, Hungarians, and Slovenians would appear to be poor. However, other studies, using different poverty lines, suggest poverty has increased to sizeable measures in Central Europe.

Increased unemployment or wage disparity implies that income inequality among households is also growing, unless mitigated by public transfers. Experts agree that the gap between rich and poor has widened in the region, but in Central Europe has remained within the range of OECD economies. At the same time, inequality in household income has risen to very high levels in several countries of the former Soviet Union, including Russia, and is comparable to that found in some South American countries. There are signs the growth in income disparity is abating in some countries, such as Estonia, Lithuania and Russia, but still remains high. Income inequality continues to expand slowly in countries, like the Czech Republic and Hungary, where increasing disparity was contained in the early transition period. (See Statistical Annex, Table 10.13.)

The appearance of widening income disparity calls into question how equitably the fruits of economic growth will be shared. In Poland, which shows the strongest economic recovery in the region, the poorest 20 percent of the population claimed 9 percent of total income in 1989; by 1997 this share had declined to 7 percent. So those who had little before now have less.

Available evidence suggests families with children have suffered greater income losses than households without children. In Russia, for example, an estimate using data from the Goskomstat showed that 37 percent of families with two children, 50 percent of families with three children, and 72 percent of families with four or more children were below the official poverty line in 1997. By comparison, 17 percent of pensioner households were living in poverty. Another study, using data from the Russia Longitudinal Monitoring Survey, found that the real income of pensioner households improved by more than 6 percent, while that of families with two or more children deteriorated by 34 percent between mid-1992 and late 1996. Similar trends have been reported in Central Europe.

A 1996 survey in Armenia found that the presence of a child increases the risk of extreme household poverty by 7 percent, independent of any other factors. Households twice the average household size have twice the risk of being extremely poor. Box 1.6 uses the case of Bulgaria to illustrate how falling income and greater income disparity affect food consumption among various population groups.

Box 1.6

Inequalities in the consumption of protein-rich food, by income, in Bulgaria

The consumption of protein-rich products like milk and meat has declined steadily during the transition in Bulgaria. A decrease in per capita consumption was first noted in 1991 following price liberalization. The consumption of milk and yogurt has continued to decline, while a slight increase in meat consumption in 1992 has reversed.

Data from the 1992-97 Household Budget Survey show that not only has the average consumption of milk, yogurt and meat decreased, but the disparity in consumption has widened. In other words, most people are eating less protein, but the poor are eating far less. For example, the annual per capita consumption of meat dropped from 19 kilograms to 7 kilograms among the poorest 10 percent of the population, and from 56 kilograms to 37 kilograms among the richest 10 percent. So, the consumption gap has grown, as Table 1.1 illustrates: the richest went from eating three times as much meat as the poorest in 1989 to eating five times as much meat in 1997.

The overall decline in milk and yogurt consumption and the increase in disparity have been especially pronounced in recent years. The per capita consumption of milk and yogurt was 78 kilograms in 1992, already one-third less than it had been at the beginning of the 1990s. Among the richest 10 percent of the population, consumption was 96 kilograms, 1.6 times more than it was among the poorest 10 percent. By 1997, yearly consumption by the highest income group (87 kilograms) was almost four times that of the lowest income group (22 kilograms). Since there are three times more children on average in the lowest income group than in the highest, as Figure 1.9 shows, children are disproportionately affected.

Before transition, milk and yogurt were affordable across the Bulgarian population and were commonly used to make up for inadequate access to other foods.

The sharp drop in consumption among lower income persons that became even worse by 1997 raises real concerns about the health and nutrition of a significant share of the Bulgarian population, particularly children.

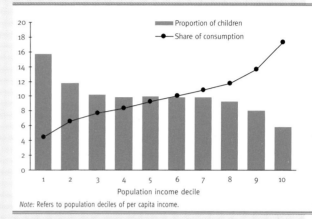

Figure 1.9

Note: Refers to population deciles of per capita income.

Share in total consumption of milk and yogurt and proportion of the total number of children, by income decile, Bulgaria, 1997
Source: NSI (various).

Table 1.1

Per capita consumption of meat, milk and yogurt in low- and high-income groups, Bulgaria, 1992-97

(kilograms)

	1992	1993	1994	1995	1996	1997
Meat						
first decile	19.0	16.9	14.0	12.6	12.0	7.4
tenth decile	55.5	54.7	44.4	45.4	45.6	36.8
ratio	2.9	3.2	3.2	3.6	3.8	5.0
Milk and yogurt						
first decile	61.7	43.0	40.1	30.5	32.1	22.4
tenth decile	96.0	94.0	101.0	98.4	93.5	87.1
ratio	1.6	2.2	2.5	3.2	2.9	3.9

Source: NSI (various).

Note: Refers to average annual per capita consumption and population deciles of per capita income.

Finally, it should be noted that hostilities and ethnic clashes have created a particular type of poverty related to the presence of refugees or internally displaced persons. In most countries experiencing this problem, hundreds of thousands of people have been living in abject conditions for several years now. For example, although hostilities had come to an end in Georgia by the mid-1990s, nearly 300,000 people were still registered as displaced in 1997. Children under age 16 accounted for one-third of these people. Women, mostly of working age, made up 53 percent. A survey in the capital, Tbilisi, found that one-third of the displaced families had no regular income. Many displaced persons have been compelled to migrate, mostly to Russia or other CIS countries, where their citizenship status is unclear and their prospects dim. In Russia alone, the number of refugee or displaced children has reached 300,000, according to estimates from the Federal Migration Service. International aid, which has been considerable, can only lessen the problem of refugees and displaced persons to a degree. Recent tragic events in the Balkans demonstrate that the region is still vulnerable to ethnic conflict and violence.

Changes in life expectancy and adult mortality

At the end of the 1980s, male life expectancy was relatively low in the region, varying from 62 years (Turkmenistan) to 70 years (FYR Macedonia, Bosnia-Herzegovina and Albania), with heavily industrialized countries in the middle of the range. Female life expectancy showed less variance, with Turkmenistan the only country below 70 years (68.4 in 1989). In nine countries – Albania, Bulgaria, the Czech Republic, Georgia, Latvia, Lithuania, Slovakia, Slovenia, and Ukraine –

Figure 1.10

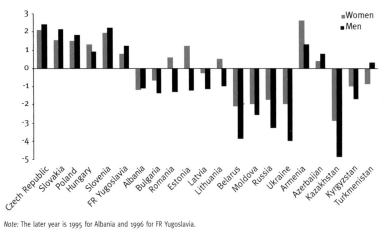

Change in male and female life expectancy, 1989-97 (years)

Source: Statistical Annex, Tables 4.2, 4.3.

Note: The later year is 1995 for Albania and 1996 for FR Yugoslavia.

female life expectancy was above 75 years; Slovenian women averaged almost 77 years.

Deterioration in life expectancy, especially among men, was an unanticipated and shocking outcome of the transition. In 22 of 23 countries on which time series are available, life expectancy has worsened during the 1990s. In many cases, the decline has been small and only temporary; in others, like Russia, the drop has been large and more difficult to reverse. In 1997, life expectancy worsened or did not improve in Southeastern Europe, Estonia, Belarus, Moldova, Ukraine, and Turkmenistan – about one-third of the countries for which data were available.

Figure 1.10 shows the difference in life expectancy in 1997, compared to 1989, for women and men across the region. The data suggest an improvement in Central Europe, but considerable worsening elsewhere, especially among the male population of the western CIS and Central Asian countries. Kazakhstan, Belarus, Ukraine, and Moldova currently seem to be most affected by a mortality crisis, with men dying three to five years earlier than the average before the transition. In these countries and in Albania, Bulgaria, Latvia, Kyrgyzstan, and Turkmenistan, women's life expectancy is down by one to three years. Over the full transition period, life expectancy declined

most in Russia, dropping 6.6 years for males and 3.2 years for females by 1994. More than 1.5 million people died over and above the numbers anticipated on the basis of pre-transition age-specific mortality rates. Since 1995, life expectancy in Russia has been rising again, although it is far from recovering to 1989 levels.

Notably, increases in mortality have hit young and middle-aged men harder than the usual vulnerable populations – children, pregnant mothers and the elderly. Most of the "excess" deaths are due to cardiovascular and circulatory diseases and accidents and violence, causes that were already responsible for a significant part of adult mortality. Women and children are likely also to be adversely affected by this trend of men dying in their prime – losing husbands, fathers and breadwinners and enduring the ill health of a family member and, perhaps, increased alcohol use or violence and the stresses associated with all these circumstances. An examination of mortality in the region underscores the influence of both economic and social environments on health.

Figure 1.11 uses GDP as a proxy indicator to illustrate the importance of economic factors in adult male mortality in the region. The graph presents the way changes in GDP and in mortality among men aged 40-49 have correlated over the transition period. The diagram shows that, in many countries where GDP declined 20 percent or more from 1989 levels, mortality has also increased, sometimes enormously. There are other countries – Georgia, Tajikistan, Armenia, FR Yugoslavia – where GDP has declined greatly, but male mortality has not greatly increased or has even decreased. This suggests that non-economic factors, such as social cohesion created by strong family ties and ethnic pride, may have had a mitigating effect.

Figure 1.12 uses the divorce rate as a proxy indicator to illustrate the importance of social factors in adult male mortality during the transition. It shows the correlation between the mortality rates among men aged 40-49 and the general divorce rate across the region. (This figure compares the average level of the rates themselves – the incidence of death and the number of divorces per marriages – over the period.) The graph demonstrates that high mortality rates have occurred in countries with high divorce rates, while low mortality rates have coincided with low divorce rates. It is a worldwide experience that divorced, widowed and unmarried adults – males more than females – are at higher risk of premature death than are those

Figure 1.11

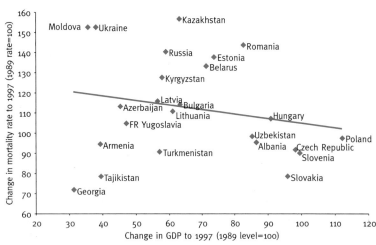

Changes in mortality rates for men aged 40-49 and in real GDP, 1989-97

Sources: MONEE project database; Statistical Annex, Table 10.1.

Note: The later year is 1996 for Albania, Tajikistan, Turkmenistan, Uzbekistan, and FR Yugoslavia.

sharing a roof with others. This confirms that strong personal and social bonds influence health and may counteract the deleterious effects of reduced income, deteriorating material conditions, insufficient housing, and inadequate social services. Box 1.7 looks at the social determinants of health and a new vision of "healthy societies".

parity in infant and young-child mortality rates remains in the region. Given that most child deaths are preventable, this needs to be addressed. Moreover, a wider range of indicators, such as child neglect and youth suicide, reveals that child welfare has been seriously compromised during the transition years.

The health and social risks of children

It has already been noted that the under-5 mortality rates of the transition countries offer a more favourable picture of human development in the region in the 1990s than do international rankings based on other economic or social indicators. In part, this reflects the health achievements inherited from the past and the success during the transition in preventing a major deterioration. Nevertheless, a significant dis-

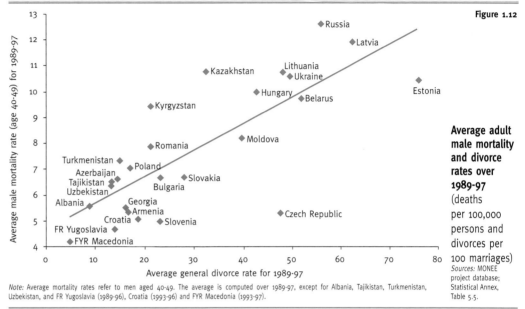

Figure 1.12

Average adult male mortality and divorce rates over 1989-97 (deaths per 100,000 persons and divorces per 100 marriages)
Sources: MONEE project database; Statistical Annex, Table 5.5.

Note: Average mortality rates refer to men aged 40-49. The average is computed over 1989-97, except for Albania, Tajikistan, Turkmenistan, Uzbekistan, and FR Yugoslavia (1989-96), Croatia (1993-96) and FYR Macedonia (1993-97).

Box 1.7

Social determinants of health

The view that health is the product of health care systems was especially common in Central and Eastern Europe and the USSR under state planning. It is ironic that mortality trends in the region are now widely quoted to underpin Western research arguing that health is determined by socio-economic factors to a much larger degree than has been generally supposed.

Epidemiological investigations have concluded that infection-related pandemics have receded in the industrialized world over the last two centuries more because of social, economic and environmental changes than because of medical breakthroughs. The latter often came too late to be responsible for the changes in health and disease patterns. The link between poverty and certain diseases (tuberculosis, respiratory diseases, malnutrition) has been clear for a long time. Education and life skills have also been increasingly recognized as "health assets". More recently, research in industrial countries is broadening the range of social factors considered important.

Studies have found correlations between the degree of income disparity in a society and health status. It has been claimed that life skills have a positive health impact not only by helping an individual avoid material deprivation (such as of food and shelter) and biochemical risks (such as from germs and poisons), but also through psychosocial factors. For example, coping skills are strongly associated with a lower risk of cardiovascular diseases and contribute substantially to the explanation of socio-economic gradients in health status.

Psychosocial factors, rather than only material rec-

iprocity or the sharing of knowledge, may explain why the strength of family ties and social networks based on trust – referred to as "social capital" – is an important determinant of individual health. Surveys in the United States, for example, have found that markers of social cohesion, collective efficacy and residential stability, measured at the neighbourhood level, are strong predictors of homicide, crime and violence.

This broadening in the approach to health issues in the West has been motivated by both the high expectations of citizens for lifelong good health and the rising costs of meeting these expectations through a cure-driven health care system. (Research in the United Kingdom and the United States has shown that only about one-fifth of health care interventions actually improved health.) Most important, however, is the growing recognition that health promotion and disease prevention are more efficient and effective than medical treatment in raising the overall health of a population. (Reports have found that 70 percent of medical and health care interventions in the United Kingdom addressed preventable conditions.)

These findings suggest that maintaining good access to health services and improving the quality of health care may be important investments for the transition countries. However, to be truly successful, these investments must be built upon a broad health foundation that includes better access to good nutrition, sufficient information, proficient life skills, and the cultivation of cohesive social networks and a supportive social environment.

Figure 1.13 provides an update on changes in the infant mortality rate (IMR) since 1989 for selected countries. The disparity in the region is apparent. For example, in 1989, Czech babies faced three or four times less risk of death than did Kyrgyz infants. Changes in the Czech rate are typical for Central European countries in transition – some initial increase followed by a steady decline. However, in other parts of the region, the IMR has been more resistant to improvement. In Russia, infant mortality peaked in 1993-94 and has subsided to slightly below 1989 levels. (It should be noted that Russia moved from the Soviet definition of "live birth" to the WHO concept in 1993.)

Figure 1.13

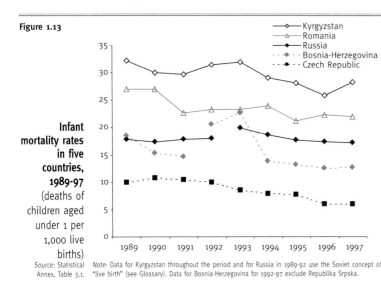

Infant mortality rates in five countries, 1989-97
(deaths of children aged under 1 per 1,000 live births)

Source: Statistical Annex, Table 3.1.

Note: Data for Kyrgyzstan throughout the period and for Russia in 1989-92 use the Soviet concept of "live birth" (see Glossary). Data for Bosnia-Herzegovina for 1992-97 exclude Republika Srpska.

The IMR shot up in Bosnia-Herzegovina in 1992-93. The large fall in 1994 – a year before the end of the war – presumably reflects worsening registration among high-risk groups rather than actual improvement. International efforts to save children and women by transporting them to other countries may have played a role as well. Although rates declined in Kyrgyzstan over 1994-96, there is reason to think that an increasing share of infant mortality is not being registered there and in some other parts of the region. In neighbouring Kazakhstan, a 1995

Figure 1.14

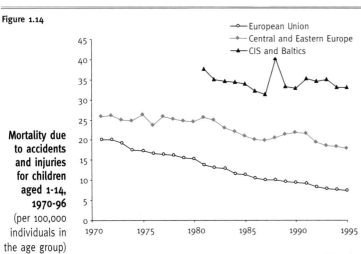

Mortality due to accidents and injuries for children aged 1-14, 1970-96
(per 100,000 individuals in the age group)

Source: Ecohost (1998).

Note: The age-standardized mortality rates represent what the crude mortality rates would have been if the populations had the same age distribution as the standard European population.

study carried out through the National Institute of Nutrition found that the infant mortality rate was substantially higher and showed somewhat less decline than indicated by official data from the Ministry of Health.

In conclusion, although measurement problems blur the picture, increases in the IMR appear generally to have been contained over the transition, and, in a number of countries, improvements have taken place. In part, this may be associated with a large decline in the total number of newborns. In 1989-97 the number of infants born annually decreased from 6.9 million to 4.7 million – a more than 30 percent decline on average – relieving some of the pressures on parents and existing health services.

For different reasons, child mortality rates have also shown relative stability during the transition period. In 1997, in 17 of 22 countries for which data on 5-19 mortality were available, rates showed stability or fell compared to 1989. (See Statistical Annex, Table 3.4.) However, the rates exhibit considerable variance across the region, and there is still much room for improvement. Many of the deaths are preventable since they are caused by accidents and injuries, a serious and under-recognized problem in the transition countries.

As a recent study has explored, mortality rates from external causes (rather than illness) among children and adolescents are 2-2.5 times higher in Central and Eastern Europe than they are in the European Union, and 4-5 times higher in the Commonwealth of Independent States. This gap has existed for a long time and shows no evidence of diminishing, as Figure 1.14 shows.

Table 1.2 presents mortality rates due to external causes by gender for four age groups in Central and Eastern Europe, the CIS and the Baltics, using European Union data as a benchmark. While patterns by age and gender are similar across these sub-regions, the difference in mortality levels between the European Union and the transition region is striking, especially in the case of children under age 10 in the CIS and the Baltics.

Adolescents, especially boys, have a high risk of dying from injuries and accidents; in fact, in this age group, external causes are the leading factors in death. In the case of boys aged 10-19, reducing mortality rates from accidents and injuries to the EU level would close the survival gap with the EU entirely in Central Europe, by more than 90 percent in the Baltics, and by more than 80 percent in the western CIS (Russia, Belarus and Ukraine). In the southern parts of the region, smaller reductions of 20-65 percent would be achieved (largely due to the greater incidence of communicable diseases), but, in absolute terms, the number of children saved would be high. Overall, if mortality rates from accidents and injuries in the transition countries had been reduced to the EU average during the 1990s, there would have been 30,000 fewer deaths of children and youths every year. This represents about 31 percent of all deaths among those aged 1-19 in the transition countries.

Addressing health and social risks for children in the region requires the development of a new relationship among families, the public and non-governmental institutions caring for and educating children. The child protection systems inherited from the communist era addressed risk largely by having the state "rescue" children from what was seen as poor parenting and placing them in big centrally directed institutions. It has been clear from the beginning of the transition that social reforms must promote the responsibility and capacity of families to care for their children.

The fourth Regional Monitoring Report revealed that institutional care of high-risk children was still prevalent across the region after transition began. In a context of no new types of support or alternatives, the percentage of children left without parental care and placed in institutions has increased. At the same time, the sharp decline in state funding has caused the quality of institutional care, already scandalous in some countries, to deteriorate. In a few countries, such as Moldova or Georgia, the public child-protection system has virtually collapsed.

Figure 1.15 shows changes in the proportion of children aged 0-3 placed in infant homes. This indicator is sensitive to short-term changes in the social environment and is a telling measure of the state of child protection reform because alternatives to institutionalization at this young age are both highly preferable and relatively easy to secure. The graph shows the trend in 1989-95 presented in the fourth Regional Monitoring Report and updates the picture with 1997 data which reveal that the proportion of young children in institutional care has risen even higher in almost all countries for which information was available.

In the worst case, Estonia, the rate of institutionalization had risen 80 percent by 1995 and more than doubled by 1997. With the exception of Hungary, which has initiated comprehensive reforms, institutionalization rates have worsened, often alarmingly, since 1995. Table 8.1 in the Statistical Annex shows that, despite the larger increases in many other countries, Bulgaria still has the highest proportion of children in infant homes, followed by Romania and Latvia.

Other data confirm the disheartening evidence of growing family vulnerability and the difficulties in "deinstitutionalizing" children. In Romania, after some initial decline, the number of children in homes and orphanages in each of the last four years has remained above 50,000, and the number placed with foster parents grew from 7,549 to 10,999 in 1996. In Russia, the steady rise in the numbers of children "left without parental care" (Figure 1.16) drove up the total number of children in institutions. 1997 data suggest that there

were further increases in the number of children separated from their families. Although the total number of children in institutions stopped growing that year, the number of children placed with guardians (usually a grandparent) grew by 15,500, and the number of international adoptions shot up from 3,251 to 5,730. The data suggest that current efforts to reform child protection systems have had little impact on the high rates of children who live without their parents. At best, some progress has been made in placing children in alternative environments rather than in institutions.

Earlier Regional Monitoring Reports called attention to increases in youth suicide in the region. For example, suicide rates among young males grew by 62 percent

Table 1.2

Externally caused mortality rate compared to the European Union, 1992-93

(by age group, European Union=1.0)

| | 1-4 years | | 5-9 years | | 10-14 years | | 15-19 years | |
	Male	Female	Male	Female	Male	Female	Male	Female
Central and Eastern Europe	2.5	2.5	2.5	2.4	2.1	1.6	1.2	1.1
CIS and Baltic States	5.0	5.2	5.1	4.5	4.0	3.0	2.5	2.5

Source: Ecohost (1998).

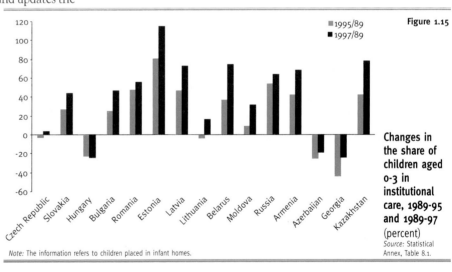

Figure 1.15

Changes in the share of children aged 0-3 in institutional care, 1989-95 and 1989-97 (percent)
Source: Statistical Annex, Table 8.1.

Note: The information refers to children placed in infant homes.

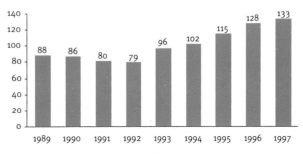

Figure 1.16

Children without parental care placed in institutions in Russia, 1989-97 (1,000s)
Sources: MONEE project database; MLSD (1995), (1997).

Note: The data refer to the total number of children without parental care living in institutions each year.

in the Czech Republic, 56 percent in Lithuania and 77 percent in Russia in 1989-95. Recent data suggest there has been little improvement in the last few years.

The total number of youth suicides in Russia fell in 1996, after peaking at 2,930 cases in 1995, but rose again in 1997. A similar pattern has been documented in FYR Macedonia, Bulgaria, Estonia, Lithuania, Moldova, and Kazakhstan. (See Statistical Annex, Tables 3.7 and 3.8.) These findings underline the need for young people to receive more support from families, social networks and services. Social cohesion is an important determinant of health, and youth suicide is a sensitive indicator of the state of social bonds.

The evidence above highlights risks that should be addressed with urgency in the transition countries. In many cases, prevention programmes are non-existent, weak, or poorly coordinated. International donors and institutions could help out through research and advocacy, by supporting the development of local capacity and by facilitating linkages and partnerships with countries, inside and outside the region, where effective prevention strategies have been implemented.

Changes in education

Universal access to basic education for both girls and boys was a noteworthy achievement of the communist period. Good international marks in literacy and education enrolment – primary, secondary and tertiary – improved the human development standing of the region. The strong legacy of these education systems is sometimes striking. A 1995 international survey of learning achievement among 13-year-olds in 41 countries ranked the Czech Republic 2nd in science and 6th in maths, compared to ranks of 18th and 23rd for Germany and 17th and 28th for the United States. Russia and several other former communist countries also scored well, although others, such as Romania, did not.

Earlier in this chapter, it is noted that the command economies of the communist era promoted the significant participation of women in the workforce and that there was considerable progress in achieving gender equality in education. A strong commitment to educational opportunities for girls and boy exists in all countries of the region. Enrolment rates in basic education remained relatively

high in Central Europe and many other countries after 1989 with little evidence of a gender gap appearing. Recent studies in the Baltics, however, reveal that a significant share of children either do not start school at the compulsory age, or do not finish school.

There is some evidence of larger declines in enrolment, especially in the countries of the former Yugoslavia, the Caucasus and Central Asia, but less-stringent population registers and under-reporting (often due to ethnic hostilities), as well as methodological changes, make it difficult to review the situation. The available data, however, still do not suggest any systematic gender gap. For example, in 1997, 251,000 girls and 256,000 boys were enrolled in basic education in Armenia, and 467,000 girls and 480,000 boys in Turkmenistan. Some anecdotal evidence points to cases in Central Asia where the education enrolment of girls is lower than that of boys, especially in rural areas.

There is a more marked gender difference in secondary school enrolment, but this favours girls. Enrolment in general secondary education – where girls have been over-represented in the past – increased in all countries, except in Moldova and the countries of the Caucasus and Central Asia. On the other hand, many fewer students are enrolled in technical and vocational schools (a traditional male preserve).

Figure 1.17 shows that in countries where females had a high share of enrolment in tertiary education this share has increased. However, where this share was lower, as in some countries of the Caucasus and Central Asia, it has tended to decline since 1989. Some sources suggest that, in these countries, women from rural areas, in particular, now have a relatively poor chance of receiving tertiary education.

While recognizing past progress and current efforts in education, the fifth Regional Monitoring Report stressed the need for educational reforms across the region. To maintain their comparative "knowledge" advantage under the new market conditions, the transition countries have much to do to strengthen the equity and efficiency of their education systems. In many countries the system that produced the relatively positive education picture of the 1990s is now "running on air".

In Russia, real government expenditures on education in 1997 were less than one-third of those in 1990. About half the unpaid wage bill from federal and regional budgets and almost all strikes occurred in the educational sector. In Bulgaria and Kyrgyzstan, only one-quarter of former funding levels for education were secured in 1997, and, in Georgia, slightly over one-tenth. Staff numbers remained stable or even increased in most countries, but these levels may be hard to maintain with shrinking state resources and teachers who are often demoralized by low pay and wage arrears.

Under these conditions, parent and community involvement in and funding of pre-school, extra-curricu-

Figure 1.17

Share of women among tertiary education students, 1989 and 1997 (percent)

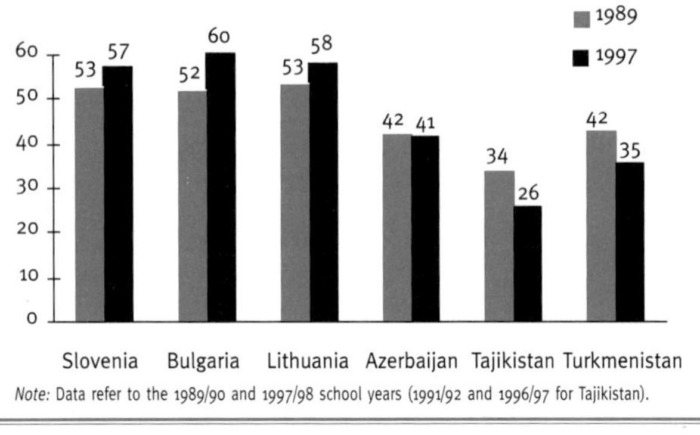

Source: Statistical Annex, Table 7.5.

Note: Data refer to the 1989/90 and 1997/98 school years (1991/92 and 1996/97 for Tajikistan).

■ 1989
■ 1997

Slovenia: 53, 57
Bulgaria: 52, 60
Lithuania: 53, 58
Azerbaijan: 42, 41
Tajikistan: 34, 26
Turkmenistan: 42, 35

lar, remedial, and leisure programmes have proved crucial in many cases to sustaining vigorous schools – even though there is often no commensurate participation in school decisions and affairs. Parental and community involvement in early childhood education is especially important because, as later chapters discuss, state-run and workplace nurseries and kindergartens have been cut back massively in many countries.

Promoting and supporting the capacity of parents to provide for and raise their families require a commitment to gender equality. When women endure inequality, so do children, especially girls. In this light, the last section of this introductory chapter reviews the political commitments of countries to women's equality – an important area of transition-related reforms in the region.

■

1.4 Commitments to Women's Equality

As the preceding sections make clear, the process of transition in this region of the world is the profound process of reforming the relationships among individuals, society, the economy, and the state. The transition countries have the opportunity to adopt the "best practices" of the 20th century's most successful nations, which, in short, means embracing democratic government, a liberalized marketplace and concern for human rights. Linking political, social and economic reforms together is a challenge, but it is the fundamental architecture of rights-based human development. This section examines the status of women's rights as human rights in the transition countries on the basis of the implementation of the 1979 UN Convention on the Elimination of All Forms of Discrimination against Women (CEDAW). Advancing equality for women involves expanding the choices available to women, and, it is understood, advancing equality for women entails broader benefits for children, men and society.

Implementing CEDAW

Under communism, women were guaranteed equal rights in the law, and the governments of the region signed and ratified CEDAW. (See Box 1.8 for a summary of CEDAW.) However, the participation of the communist countries in the international process to review compliance and enforcement of CEDAW within their borders was largely ceremonial. Under communism – where ideology, politics, government, law, the economy, and society were fused – there was only one place for rights to reside: in the state. In practice, human rights were not recognized as inherent and inalienable individual rights, but treated as collective rights best expressed through the instrument of the state. In this monolithic environment, many of the most fundamental human rights, including the right to form civic associations, were denied.

The desire to enjoy individual human rights was one of the primary engines behind the collapse of communism, and integrating human rights into the foundation and every aspect of these new societies is an overarching goal. The fact that, by August 1998, all 27 post-communist countries of the region had signed and ratified both CEDAW and the Convention on the Rights of the Child is important. These countries can now fully participate in the international processes that monitor compliance with these rights covenants. These processes can be invaluable in measuring progress, pointing out shortcomings and recommending remedies. This is the work of the monitoring committees, elected bodies of independent experts who review national reports prepared by participating countries.

Since 1989, the CEDAW Committee has reviewed 16 national reports on the elimination of discrimination against women from countries in the region. (See Table 1.3.) The committee commended countries for their efforts to date, especially given the tremendous difficulties of the transition, including economic hardship and war. At the same time, it drew attention to some of the major challenges that remain for the full implementation of the Convention throughout the region. The committee's main findings – based on 12 reports reviewed between 1994 and 1998 – are examined below. These relate to adequacy of legal equality and government machineries, to cultural images and patterns around the role of women, and to violations of fundamental rights.

Laws and government machinery promoting equality

The CEDAW Committee concluded that, despite constitutional affirmations that women and men are equal in the eyes of the law, women do not actually have de jure equality in most of the countries reporting. This is because there is no clear definition of discrimination in constitutions or laws, and there are few mechanisms to strengthen the prosecution of discriminatory actions against women. Moreover, the revised laws do not reflect an understanding of indirect and structural discrimination – which is behind de facto inequality – and of the concept of temporary special remedies. For example, labour laws in many countries still prohibit women from performing certain types of heavy work and dangerous occupations, and this restricts women's economic opportunities and does little to improve the working conditions of men.

The committee also found elements of structural discrimination in family laws among the countries reporting. The rules of joint property in the Czech Republic and Azerbaijan do not adequately support women in divorce

Box 1.8

The UN Convention on the Elimination of All Forms of Discrimination against Women

The preamble of the Convention notes that:

- women and men have the equal right to enjoy all economic, social, cultural, civil, and political rights;
- discrimination against women hampers not only women's participation in and contribution to the political, social, economic, and cultural life of their countries, but the growth in the prosperity of society and the family;
- welfare of the world and the cause of peace require the maximum participation of women on equal terms with men in all fields;
- a change in the traditional role of men, as well as the role of women, in society and in the family is needed to achieve full equality between women and men.

Basic rights
Article 1 defines discrimination against women as "any distinction, exclusion or restriction made on the basis of sex which has the effect or purpose of impairing or nullifying the recognition, enjoyment or exercise by women irrespective of their marital status, on a basis of equality of men and women, of human rights and fundamental freedoms in the political, economic, social, cultural, civil or any other field."

Article 2 makes it clear that signatory states agree to pursue, without delay, a policy of eliminating discrimination against women in all its forms. The government must make equality a legal reality by embodying it in the constitution, establishing legal protection of the rights of women, including tribunals and other mechanisms, and adopting appropriate legislation and other measures, including sanctions, to prohibit discrimination.

Article 3 says governments shall take "all appropriate measures, including legislation" in all fields to ensure the full development and advancement of women towards equality. Specifically noted are measures to modify conduct based on the idea of the inferiority or superiority of either of the sexes or on stereotyped roles for women and men, to ensure that family education recognizes the social contribution of mater-

nity and the common responsibility of men and women in the upbringing and development of their children, and to suppress "all forms of traffic in women and exploitation of prostitution of women".

Public life
Part II focuses on the elimination of discrimination against women in the political and public life of the country. This includes the right to vote and to hold public office and perform all public functions at all levels of government. It ensures the right of women to participate equally in the formulation and implementation of government policy and to participate in non-governmental organizations and associations concerned with the public and political life of the country. Governments must also ensure that women have equal opportunity to represent their governments internationally and to work in international organizations.

Education, employment, health
The articles of Part III pertain to the economic and social equality of women. Article 10 considers equal rights for women in education. Article 11 states all people have the right to work and women should enjoy equal opportunities, free choice, equal pay, social security, and employment protection in case of pregnancy. Importantly, it requires measures which encourage social service supports that enable parents to combine family obligations with work responsibilities and participation in public life, particularly the development of childcare facilities. Article 12 agrees that equal access to health care includes family planning services.

Civil liberties
Article 15 states women shall be accorded "equality with men before the law", including all civil matters such as concluding contracts, administering property and the freedom to choose residence. Article 16 states that women have equal rights in all matters relating to marriage and family relations, including the right to choose a spouse, to enter and to leave a marriage, and to make decisions about children.

situations or in non-marital unions. Laws in Bulgaria, Ukraine and Armenia actively discriminate against women and fail to protect the rights of the girl child by explicitly permitting a lower legal age of marriage for girls than for boys. Relatively early ages for marriage and childbearing are common across the region and, as Chapter 3 of this Report explores, have implications for young women's autonomy.

Violence against women is a major problem in the region, as it is around the world, and violence, in general, has increased during the transition. Chapter 5 of this Report provides detailed analysis of this subject and con-

firms the CEDAW Committee's finding that, in the countries reporting, legal and judicial responses to violence against women tend to be inadequate.

In reforming the role of the state in the transition countries, the government has a crucial part to play in promoting equality among citizens, including advancing equality between women and men. Given the oppressive role of the state in these former communist countries, there is now great sensitivity, even an allergy, to state intervention in social norms and values. However, as the Platform for Action of the 1995 Fourth World Conference on Women, held in Beijing, clearly states, government machinery and institutional mechanisms are essential for the advancement of women's equality.

At the time of the CEDAW review, a government capacity dedicated to implementing, coordinating and monitoring commitments on equality for women was non-existent in the Czech Republic, Hungary, Croatia, Bosnia-Herzegovina, FR Yugoslavia, and Armenia and present but limited in effectiveness in the other countries. In some instances, such as in the Czech Republic, Slovakia and Hungary, the state places responsibility for equality on individual women, an abdication of state responsibility. The CEDAW Committee criticized Hungary for stating women's issues are not a priority during the transition and reminded its government that meeting women's human rights is central to solving transition-related economic and social crises. (As Chapter 6 notes, some countries, including Hungary and the Czech Republic, have since set up agencies on gender equality.)

The committee found that many of the governments reporting lacked a clear understanding of their responsibility under CEDAW to take affirmative action measures in the short term that enable women and men to overcome systemic barriers to equality. Although there is resistance to fixed quotas for women's representation – a largely decorative and derided feature of the communist political system, there are many other, less controversial ways governments can engage in positive discrimination that promotes equality. Chapter 6 takes a closer look at the whole issue of the importance of women in decision making – in government, business and civil society.

One of the main purposes of this Report is to analyse gender-disaggregated data from the region, because these data are the hard evidence that underpins the story of women and the transition. The Beijing Platform for Action recognized that the collection of such data is essential to the development of government programmes and policies that meet the real needs of women. The CEDAW Committee concluded that such data are frequently missing in the region, especially those that would allow an analysis of gender inequality within families and in the workplace and those related to the health and safety of women. Certainly, a lack of data on the causes and extent of violence against women obstructs progress on this pressing issue.

Lack of legislative and government support for women's equality has also inhibited the development of the community of non-governmental organizations, an essential pillar of and primary player in women's equality. Internationally, the NGO sector has expanded its role as advocate and activist for women's rights to become a powerful civic partner of governments – advisor, as well as critic. The CEDAW Committee reminded governments that they have a responsibility to facilitate the establishment of a network of NGOs, which are often short of technical and financial resources. It noted the decline of

Table 1.3

Status of CEDAW in the transition countries

(as of 1 March 1999)

Country	Date of ratification, accession, or succession to CEDAW		Date last report considered by the CEDAW Committee
	Date	Note	
Central Europe			
Czech Republic	February 1993	a, b	January 1998
Slovakia	May 1993	b	June 1998
Poland	July 1980	c	1991
Hungary	December 1980	a	January 1996
Former Yugoslavia			
Slovenia	July 1992	b	January 1997
Croatia	September 1992	b	January 1998
FYR Macedonia	January 1994	b	n/a
Bosnia-Herzegovina	September 1993	b	January 1994 d
FR Yugoslavia	February 1982	e	January 1994 d
Southeastern Europe			
Albania	May 1994	f	n/a
Bulgaria	February 1982	a	January 1998
Romania	January 1982	c	1993
Baltic States			
Estonia	October 1991	f	n/a
Latvia	April 1992	f	n/a
Lithuania	January 1994	f	n/a
Western CIS			
Belarus	February 1981	a	1989 g
Moldova	July 1994	f	n/a
Russia	January 1981	a	January 1995
Ukraine	March 1981	a	January 1996
Caucasus			
Armenia	September 1993	f	July 1997
Azerbaijan	July 1995	f	January 1998
Georgia	October 1994	f	n/a
Central Asia			
Kazakhstan	August 1998	f	n/a
Kyrgyzstan	February 1997	f	January 1999
Tajikistan	October 1993	f	n/a
Turkmenistan	May 1997	f	n/a
Uzbekistan	July 1995	f	n/a

Source: CEDAW website (http://www.un.org/womenwatch/daw/cedaw).

Note: CEDAW = Convention on the Elimination of All Forms of Violence against Women. a. Reservation subsequently withdrawn. b. Succession. c. Declarations or reservations. d. Oral reports submitted on an exceptional basis. e. Former Yugoslavia. f. Accession. g. New report submitted in 1993. n/a. No report yet considered.

NGOs since 1989 in the Czech Republic and called on governments in Hungary, Croatia and Bulgaria to increase the involvement of NGOs in their national machineries.

The participation of women in decision making is essential for advancing women's equality, as Chapter 6 shows, but women are largely excluded from politics and government decisions in these countries – a situation that has worsened during the transition. The CEDAW Committee has highlighted this as a serious obstacle to women's equality for all 12 transition countries of which the CEDAW reports form the basis of the review. It did commend Hungary for including instruction on human and women's rights in all primary and secondary schools and universities.

Persistent gender stereotypes

The CEDAW Committee pointed out that pervasive gender stereotypes and systematic cultural patterns in the region impede the implementation of the Convention in the region. It cited all 12 countries for a failure to address gender inequality in the home and found that governments tended to perceive women as mothers within the context of families, rather than as individuals and independent actors in the public sphere. This stereotypical view of women lies at the root of many of the discrepancies between de jure and de facto equality in the countries reviewed, the committee concluded. It called on all the countries to deal with ingrained patriarchal attitudes and to take active measures to eliminate the tendency to view women primarily as mothers and wives.

The committee found that sex-segregated schools, curricula and textbooks, and the media still encouraged gender stereotyping, notably in the Czech Republic, Slovakia, Slovenia, Bulgaria, and Russia. It called for creative measures, especially in the media, to portray women in a more representative and expansive manner, showing women as direct actors in all aspects of society at all ages and stages of their lives.

Violation of rights

The CEDAW Committee drew attention to the continuing and, in some cases, worsening violations of women's rights throughout the region. It stated emphatically that women's rights were being threatened by what it described as the alarming incidence of poverty. It found that many countries have failed to take measures to assist unemployed and rural women or to support entrepreneurship among women. Women's rights have also been violated by the deterioration in their health and in health care systems since the onset of the transition, according to the committee, especially in Hungary, FR Yugoslavia, Russia, Armenia, and Azerbaijan. It cited levels of infant or maternal mortality as a concern in Croatia, FR Yugoslavia, Bulgaria, Ukraine, Armenia, and Azerbaijan and commented on the lack of adequate access to reproductive health care, including family planning.

The committee cited violence against women, the subject of Chapter 5 in this Report, as one of the most overt violations of women's rights in the region. In almost every case, it called for greater efforts to combat violence against women, to enact laws that adequately address the issue and to support victims. It stated that current laws are inadequate to deal with the growing volume of prostitution and trafficking of women. Also of particular note is the targeting of civilian women for ethnic cleansing, forced pregnancies and systematic rapes in wars and ethnic conflicts in the region, including in Croatia, Bosnia-Herzegovina, FR Yugoslavia, Armenia, and Azerbaijan.

Some groups of women are especially vulnerable to rights violations. Refugee and displaced women in Hungary, Croatia, Bosnia-Herzegovina, FR Yugoslavia, Armenia, and Azerbaijan were not being adequately supported, the committee found. It also called attention to the exclusion of minority women and children and of women and children with disabilities in Hungary, Croatia, Bosnia-Herzegovina, FR Yugoslavia, Bulgaria, Ukraine, and Armenia.

1.5 Conclusions

This chapter illustrates that – given their economic output – the transition countries have impressive assets in human capabilities, gender equity and child development. However, development remains uneven in the region in many ways – geographically, economically and socially. This is due, in part, to weak or rigid social and economic institutions inherited from the past – infrastructure that is bloated in some areas and sparse in others, notably at the grassroots of society. Still, it is clear that during the transition the economic and social achievements of the countries of Central and Eastern Europe and the former Soviet Union have fallen short of expectations, and, in many cases, serious deterioration has taken place.

While documenting the growing disparity in the economic and social indicators of countries, the analysis does find some encouraging signs. Economic growth is on the upswing in most countries, and in some countries the economies are not only more flexible and efficient than in 1989, but bigger. The sudden and shocking drop in life expectancy in the region has proved to be temporary or moderate not only in Central Europe, which leads in economic recovery, but often also in the region's southern countries which are still in economic difficulty. Education indicators have, for the most part, shown remarkable resistance, and despite problems in numerous areas tertiary enrolment has increased in many countries.

These much-anticipated and long-awaited signs of success are not only the result of years of political and government endeavour, but the fruit of extraordinary and often unheralded effort by individuals and communities.

The broader economic trends and structural changes reviewed have significant, though mixed, implications for the economic independence, security and status of women across the region. The substantial drop in real wages creates pressure for two-income households and, thus, high female participation in the labour market. Yet, there is less job security and fewer jobs, for which women must compete with each other, as well as with men. At the same time, increases in wage inequality and higher costs for childcare may promote the one-earner household model, and, given the gender gap in wages, women are likely to be the ones who stay home. The success of some countries in modernizing industry and developing the service sector may actually lead to a more open and competitive marketplace in which women can rise. In other countries, the growing significance of sectors traditionally dominated by men, such as agriculture, may close rather than open doors for women. Chapter 2 explores how the emergence of a labour market has affected the employment and earning position of women during the transition, revealing often surprising results.

The social changes reviewed in this chapter suggest that the transition has had an enormous impact on the private and public dimensions of women's lives. Growing poverty, especially child poverty, indicates the tremendous pressures that are straining the capacity and resources of women. This stressful and unsettled environment is also influencing women's decisions about whether and when to get married and have children, with important demographic implications, which Chapter 3 explores. On the bright side, enrolment in education remains equitable for girls and young women.

The rise in adult mortality that has accompanied the stress of transition has killed more men than women. However, women's health has also been adversely affected, as Chapter 4 discusses in detail, and often, as Chapter 5 explores, the health toll is violence at the hands of women's own spouses and partners. The higher number of children abandoned by parents or placed in the care of the state and the increase in youth suicides are also powerful indicators of the stress on families.

The review of the findings of the monitoring committee of the Convention on the Elimination of All Forms of Discrimination against Women raises questions about whether the prospects for rights-based development in the region are as bright as suggested by the international development rankings. While the broad legal framework for equality seems to be in place in the transition countries, there is still much to do in terms of making the spirit of the law a daily reality in the workplace, the family and the community. Progress on gender equality can accelerate the success of the transition and ensure that women, men and children get a fair share of the opportunities. It is therefore of great importance that these issues be thoroughly explored and that the voice of women be heard in all the countries in transition.

■

2 Women and the Labour Market

If the purpose of the transition is to raise the living standards of people and to promote their rights, then examining the economic status and prospects of women in the transition region is essential. The participation of women in the labour market is important for many reasons. It is the source of women's economic autonomy, a passport to social security, pension and health benefits, and an opportunity for social and personal development. In a household context, women's paid employment influences the relative role and power of women within the family and provides not only income, but a role model for family members, especially children.

The process of economic transition is reshaping the working lives of women. Since 1989, as Chapter 1 outlines, there has been a very serious fall in GDP, employment and real wages – and considerable institutional change – in many of the 27 countries of the region. These circumstances affect the immediate economic status of women and their households, but they also affect decisions related to fertility, family and higher education. In turn, these conditions and decisions influence the structure of the transitional labour markets.

Under communism, constitutions guaranteed the right to employment for the entire working-age population and the right to equal pay for equal work among men and women. There was no formal unemployment, and women generally worked full time throughout their adult lives. The public sector, which dominated the economy through state-owned enterprises, supplied jobs seemingly without limit.

Did these circumstances remove the gender gap on the job? Statistics show that women's participation in the workforce was, in fact, outstanding by international standards. Still, as in most countries, women were clustered in lower paying, lower status occupations and were not equally represented in senior and decision-making positions. However, they did enjoy generous formal and informal benefits related to family and childcare responsibilities. In Central and Southeastern Europe, for instance, women could count on both maternity leaves and parental leaves, including the option of caring for children at home for several years with employment guarantees on their return to the labour force. In the Soviet Union, nurseries, kindergartens and health care facilities were common in larger state-run enterprises. Informally, women were often allowed time off work to manage household shopping because goods were scarce and queues long.

The transition to a market economy presents women with a changing work environment, one with obstacles and opportunities. Women must now compete for jobs at a time when secure state jobs are being eliminated. It is also expected that alternative forms of employment, such as part-time work and fixed-term contracts, will increasingly appear, as they have in Western economies. "Non-standard" employment may not always improve women's economic autonomy, but it does offer flexibility.

The shift to less secure employment for both women and men reduces the likelihood of a family model based on a dominant male breadwinner. It is probable that women and men will share more versatile roles, taking on responsibility for income-earning and childcare as changing circumstances dictate. The transition to a market economy also offers both women and men the opportunity to take up self-employment and entrepreneurship.

Women in the transition region do have a positive legacy of high levels of education, a capital of great importance in the transforming economies. There is an expectation, embedded in social norms and life strategies, that women will perform work for pay for much of their lives. However, women's burden of family responsibilities will make it harder for them to pursue careers, especially with weakened state support for families. The prevailing attitude in society is that the tension between work and family must be borne by women and eased by the state. The challenge now for local and central governments, businesses, communities, families, and men is to cultivate an adaptable and supportive public environment that enables women to contribute to and benefit from the marketplace in a way that suits their circumstances and permits them to realize their potential.

Economic power is the foundation of women's equality and the muscle that helps women to exercise their human rights. UN conventions and other international commitments are clear about the imperative of advancing economic equality between women and men. They acknowledge women's right to the same working conditions as men, including equal pay for equal work or work of equal value, the right to maternity leave with pay and sufficient social security benefits and without loss of employment, seniority, or social allowances, the right to an adequate standard of living for oneself and one's family, the right to social services, including access to childcare for the children of working parents, and the right to recognition of the value of unpaid work.

This chapter focuses on paid employment, a major axis of change in the institutional transformation of the region and the main channel through which macro-economic stabilization and structural adjustment affect household welfare. The discussion and analysis presented are constrained by the data limitations, including a lack of gender-disaggregated statistics, and by the use of conventional economic terms which presume a male model of work. For example, most unpaid work in the household economy is technically considered "inactivity" though it is crucial for the economic survival of many families, especially in current circumstances. Still, it is clear that participation in and earnings from the emerging labour markets in the transition region are keys to the future.

Section 2.1 explores trends in women's employment and unemployment in the transition economies. Section 2.2 reviews and analyses evidence on the gender pay gap, the structure of employment and the occupational segregation of women. Section 2.3 looks at the contribution and importance of female employment and earnings in terms of household income. The Conclusions offer a summary of the main findings and outline some policy implications.

2.1 Women's Employment is under Pressure

Employment for women is important not only because of the direct contribution it makes to household welfare, but because of the personal power it provides for women in shaping and making family decisions and in establishing social ties and networks beyond the family. It is therefore essential to monitor how women are participating in the emerging labour markets of the transition region and call attention to any sign that they are being "squeezed out" of the new employment picture.

Changing participation in the labour force

Historically, the participation of women in the labour force in the region has been outstanding by international standards. However, it is worth asking whether high female participation rates characterized all parts of Central and Eastern Europe and the former Soviet Union. Figure 2.1 presents the share of economically active women and men in the working-age populations of the region. For international comparison, the figure includes data for six market economies – Turkey, Greece, Brazil, France, the US, and Sweden.

The graph reveals a somewhat surprising pattern across the region at the beginning of the transition. The highest activity rates were found in the Baltic States and in the countries which now form the western part of the Commonwealth of Independent States – Belarus, Moldova, Russia, and Ukraine. In these countries, the gender gap in labour force participation was very small – less than 2 percentage points in Belarus and Ukraine. This compares to Sweden, which leads the Western nations in this regard. Even taking into consideration that Soviet methodology counted women on maternity leave as active in the labour force and used a lower retirement age, female activity rates in these countries were impressive.

Not surprisingly, female participation rates were appreciably lower in the less industrialized, less urbanized countries of the Caucasus and Central Asia. In Uzbekistan, the gender gap in labour force participation was 9 percentage points. However, even these participation rates were high by international standards. Thus, female activity rates in the Asian countries of the former Soviet Union were higher than those in the more urbanized countries of Central and Eastern Europe with relatively fewer children, such as Poland, Hungary and Romania (though not Czechoslovakia). In Hungary, the gender gap was 11 percentage points, and in Poland, 13 percentage points. Figure 2.1 shows that these rates were comparable to or even better than those in the US or France at the end of the 1980s. However, there was one notable difference in that, unlike women in France or the US, women in Poland, Hungary and Romania, for example, were almost all employed full time.

The glorification of and

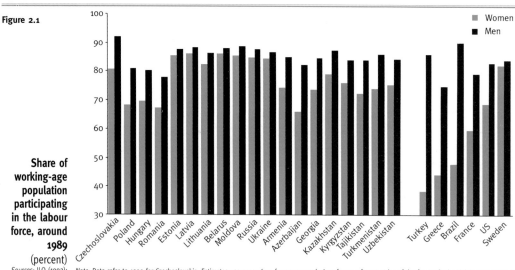

Figure 2.1

Share of working-age population participating in the labour force, around 1989
(percent)

Sources: ILO (1992); MONEE project database.

Note: Data refer to 1990 for Czechoslovakia. Estimates use ages 16-54 for women and 16-59 for men for countries of the former Soviet Union, ages 15-54 for women and 15-59 for men for Central and Eastern Europe, and ages 15-59 for both genders for the other countries. (See the Glossary for the definition of working-age population.)

■ Women
■ Men

Czechoslovakia, Poland, Hungary, Romania, Estonia, Latvia, Lithuania, Belarus, Moldova, Russia, Ukraine, Armenia, Azerbaijan, Georgia, Kazakhstan, Kyrgyzstan, Tajikistan, Turkmenistan, Uzbekistan, Turkey, Greece, Brazil, France, US, Sweden

Box 2.1

Women's paid and unpaid work: an East-West comparison

Under communism, women in Central and Eastern Europe showed high rates of employment, but they continued to fulfil substantial duties in the home, including cooking, cleaning, shopping, and childcare. Figure 2.2 shows the average hours of paid and unpaid work performed by women in selected European countries. The data refer to a wide range of years, but illustrate well the "double burden" that women in Central and Eastern Europe have carried compared to women in Western countries.

The horizontal axis indicates the average weekly hours women spend in paid employment. Countries in Central and Eastern Europe are clustered at the right-hand side of the graph, showing almost twice the weekly paid workload among women as countries in Western Europe. The vertical axis shows hours of unpaid work at home, where women in Central and Eastern Europe had a workload comparable to that of their Western counterparts. The total workload is represented by the diagonal lines, with women in Central and Eastern Europe averaging close to 70 hours per week, about 15 hours more than women in Western Europe.

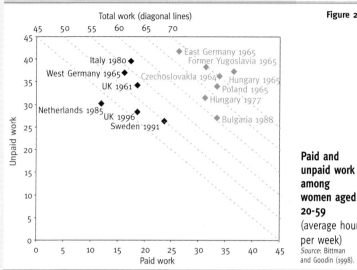

Figure 2.2

Paid and unpaid work among women aged 20-59 (average hours per week)
Source: Bittman and Goodin (1998).

entitlement to work have ideological roots in communism, but it is often argued that the high rate of female participation in the labour force was more about economic expediency and necessity than about genuine economic autonomy for women. The centrally planned economies required a large work force, and the fixed wages and prices obliged households to earn two incomes. So, women went to work en masse and were supported in this by family benefits and services such as paid leave and state-run nurseries and kindergartens. However, time-use surveys have revealed that the greater amounts of paid work did not mean fewer hours of unpaid work in the home relative to Western countries. Rather the outcome was that, because of this daily "double burden", the aggregate workload of women in the region was about two hours longer than that of women in Western countries (Box 2.1).

It is difficult to assess the effect of the transition on women's labour force activity rates across Central and Eastern Europe and the former Soviet Union. The earlier collection of labour statistics is often no longer valid, and new concepts and surveys have been slow to appear in many countries. In most cases, changes in statistical methods and surveys blur the picture. Thus, under the full-employment policies of former governments, labour force participation was equated with employment. On the other hand, in market economies the concept of participation includes both employment and unemployment. International standards for measuring unemployment require that the unemployed be ready to take up employment and be actively seeking work, for example by registering at labour offices, looking at job advertisements, or making job inquiries.

Using crude activity rates, Table 2.1 investigates changes in labour force participation in the region since 1989. These crude rates compare the total size of the

Table 2.1

Crude activity rates and the gender gap, 1989-97

	Crude female activity rate, % (a)		Rise or fall in crude female activity rate, % points	Gender gap in crude activity rates (male minus female rates), % points		Change in the gender gap, % points
	1989	1997	1989-97	1989	1997	1989-97
Slovakia (b)	40.4	40.5	0.1	11.8	11.1	-0.7
Poland (c)	43.2	39.4	-3.8	11.3	10.0	-1.3
Hungary (b)	37.4	33.2	-4.2	13.0	10.3	-2.7
Slovenia	–	44.0	–	–	9.5	–
FYR Macedonia	–	31.3	–	–	17.3	–
Bulgaria (b)	42.4	39.3	-3.1	1.9	7.3	5.4
Romania (b)	42.6	46.9	4.3	8.4	10.9	2.5
Estonia	51.3	43.4	-7.9	7.2	10.7	3.5
Latvia	51.5	42.9	-8.6	7.8	10.7	2.9
Lithuania	48.6	44.0	-4.6	8.0	10.8	2.8
Belarus	48.3	46.0	-2.3	8.9	-0.2	-9.1
Russia	47.9	40.6	-7.3	10.0	12.0	2.0
Ukraine (d)	46.4	46.8	0.4	9.6	6.9	-2.7
Azerbaijan	33.3	35.1	1.8	15.3	6.8	-8.5
Uzbekistan	36.9	–	–	6.9	–	–
Turkmenistan (e)	34.7	29.0	-5.7	14.2	15.2	1.0
Tajikistan (e)	34.8	28.2	-6.6	7.4	4.3	-3.1

Sources: ILO (1992), (1998); MONEE project database.

Note: a. Active population as a percent of total population (all ages). Data are estimates based on available and published official statistics. Persons with unpaid wage or maternity or other leave tend to be included among those who are active. b. 1990. c. 1988. d. 1995. e. 1996.

workforce (employed and unemployed) to the full population. Accordingly, they exhibit lower average values than the working-age rates used in Figure 2.1 and are more sensitive to differences in population structure such as the high ratios of older people in Central Europe or of young populations in Central Asia. Nevertheless, these crude rates capture well the gender differences in activity over the full life cycle. The gender gap, in fact, appears relatively bigger according to this measure than the working-age rates suggest because in all countries the working-age span for women was five years shorter than it was for men. In Russia, for example, 48 percent of the total female population participated in the labour force in 1989, compared to 58 percent for men. The difference in relative terms was actually about one-fifth, considerably larger than the small gap indicated by the working-age participation rates presented in Figure 2.1.

The first two columns of Table 2.1 present the crude female activity rates in 1989 and 1997 (or the nearest available year); the third column shows the rise or the fall in the rate over the period. The other three columns show the gender gap (that is, the difference between the crude activity rates of men and women) in both years, as well as the change since 1989.

In 10 of the 14 countries for which pre- and mid-transition data are available, female crude activity rates show a decline. The drop in activity rates has been greatest in the three Baltic States, Russia, Turkmenistan, and Tajikistan, where one of every five or six economically active women has been replaced by an inactive woman. The participation of men in the labour force has also decreased, but proportionally less; hence the small gender gap in labour force participation is a thing of the past in the Baltics and Russia. The same has happened in Bulgaria, where – despite the shorter work life of women – the activity rates by gender were almost equal before transition. (Data from 1997 imply that some states of the former Yugoslavia, like FYR Macedonia, may have also witnessed a big fall in female labour force participation over the 1990s.)

Declines in female activity rates have also been considerable in Hungary and Poland, but in these countries the gender gap has narrowed. Moreover, available data suggest that in some countries, for example Romania and Azerbaijan, the numbers of economically active women have actually risen. In the 14 countries for which data are available, men's participation in the labour force has climbed only in Romania and Bulgaria. In Poland, Hungary and Tajikistan, the registered economic activity of men has fallen more than that of women. Such trends, accompanied by higher middle-age mortality rates among men, have led Belarus into a unique situation in which women outnumber men in economic activity.

The gender gap in labour force participation, therefore, does not appear to show a tectonic shift with the emergence of the labour market across the region. This is not really surprising considering the fall in average real wages that has generated greater efforts to maintain two-earner households despite the shrinking number of jobs.

There have been more characteristic changes among young and older age groups. Indeed, a large part of the fall in female participation is concentrated among young and late middle-age women. There is some evidence that women over age 50, many of whom would have retired at age 55 under the former employment system, are taking on an increased role in childcare. In countries where overall female activity has fallen sharply, losses among young women have been big. In Russia, for example, labour force participation by women aged 20-24 declined by 12 percentage points from 1989 to 1996, double the decline among young men. About one-quarter of the decrease among young women has been due to higher enrolments in tertiary education, leaving three-quarters explained by other factors such as the reduced availability of childcare and jobs. The enrolment of young women in tertiary education has risen in about half of the countries in the region and may indicate poor job prospects and the understanding that future labour demand will favour the educated.

In countries where tertiary enrolment rates have increased the most – such as Hungary or Poland – the growth in economic inactivity among young women can be almost entirely attributed to higher numbers of post-secondary enrolments. In Poland, for example, household surveys found an 8 percentage point decline in labour market participation among women aged 15-24 between 1992 and 1995. During the same period, the share of young women enrolled in post-secondary education increased by 7 percentage points. Chapter 3 discusses the associated substantial changes in fertility and childcare in the region.

Falling female employment

The decline in labour force participation reviewed above does not adequately reflect the bleak economic reality faced by many women during the transition. The 1990s have witnessed a phenomenon unique in the history of the region: millions of people who have never had to deal with job loss and marketplace competition have been laid off work either in big waves, as in Central or Southeastern Europe, or gradually, as in most parts of the CIS. About half the people affected have joined the economically inactive population, but the other half have remained active by looking for work, often swelling the newly established unemployment registers. Many young people – the transition generation – who have never had an opportunity to be employed have joined these sad ranks.

Figure 2.3 shows, for a selection of countries, that female employment has decreased more markedly than female labour force participation. This is because rising unemployment has tempered the growth in economic inactivity.

It has been estimated that there were 26 million fewer jobs in the 27 countries of the region in 1997 relative to 1989. The spotty information available on gender distribution suggests that almost 14 million jobs – slightly more than every second one – were lost regionwide by women. Because of the shorter work life and the lower labour force activity rates of women before the transition, this means that since 1989 women have lost considerably more work than men. In several countries, women have also lost more in absolute terms. In Russia between 1990 and 1995, for example, women lost seven million jobs, while men lost one to two million.

The 14 million "female" jobs which have disappeared in the 1990s have involved big regional differences in other ways, too. The size of employment loss has been especially striking in countries which are more advanced in economic reform. In Hungary, a country of 10 million people, women have lost about 900,000 jobs since 1989, meaning that every third job for women is gone. Poland, home of 39 million people, has lost 1.6 million jobs for women. Cautious reform seems to have offered some protection against the erosion of jobs for women in Azerbaijan and Uzbekistan, but not in Ukraine, a country of 50 million people where almost one million jobs for women have been lost and several million more are on the verge of disappearing.

The gender disparity in the falls in employment is illustrated by the case of Lithuania. Figure 2.4 shows not only that women there have endured a disproportionate share of employment loss, but that they have continued to lose jobs since economic recovery started, while men have seized the new opportunities. However, due to high initial female employment rates, women still hold almost half the total jobs in the country, as is the case in the other Baltic States.

Figure 2.5 confirms that, despite the drops in employment, the share of women among the employed still remains in the range of 40-50 percent across the region. This is due partly to high initial female employment rates and partly to the employment losses experienced by men in many countries.

Using data from the Hungarian Labour Force Survey, Figure 2.6 sheds light on how the incidence of employment among young and middle-aged women varies according to the number of children in the family. The diagram confirms that the presence of children considerably reduces the probability of employment among women. For young women, even one child in the household entails a big drop in the employment ratio. What is striking is how much the presence of three or more children substantially reduces the incidence of employment – to a level just over 10 percent among young women and around 40 percent among middle-aged women. Although

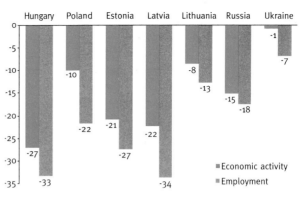

Figure 2.3

Change in female employment and economic activity, 1989-97 (percent)

Sources: OECD-CCET Labour Market Database; ILO (1992), (1998).

Note: Data refer to 1988-97 for Poland, 1990-96 for Hungary and Estonia, 1989-96 for Russia, and 1989-95 for Ukraine.

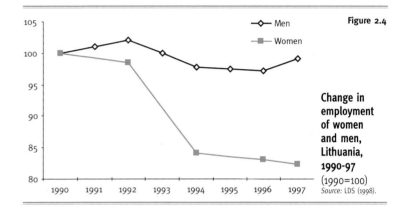

Figure 2.4

Change in employment of women and men, Lithuania, 1990-97 (1990=100)

Source: LDS (1998).

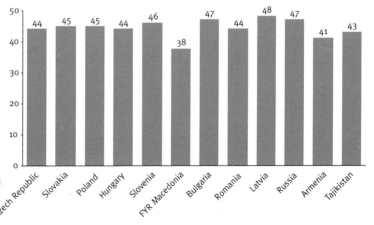

Figure 2.5

Women's share in total employment, around 1996-97 (percent)

Sources: OECD-CCET Labour Market Database; Magloutchiants (1998); ABW Khujand (1998).

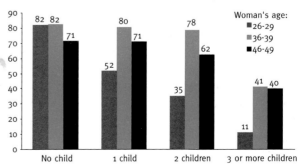

Figure 2.6

Female employment, by age and number of children, Hungary, 1996 (percent)

Source: Lakatos (1998).

Note: Percent of women employed within each category (age and number of children).

no comparable pre-transition data are available, this pattern suggests that women raising children have been among the main losers in the shift to more competitive labour markets.

Other factors may also be involved. Since larger families are more common among ethnic minorities in Hungary, women in these families may face additional discrimination in the labour market. Family policy may also play a role. In a 1995 survey in Hungary, 70 percent of women with three or more children said they planned to stay on childcare leave rather than return to work.

As Chapter 3 details, generously long parental leaves have helped offset the effect of the closing of employment-related nursery networks in many countries during the transition. However, unless these leaves take place in a gender-sensitive social climate, there is a risk that extended childcare leaves will become associated with female non-employment.

Growth in unemployment

Chapter 1 notes that the aggregate numbers of persons registered as unemployed at labour offices across the region include more women than men. It also warns that, for various reasons, registered unemployment is often a poor indicator of the actual level of unemployment. Data from administrative registers are known to be influenced by factors such as the size and entitlement conditions of unemployment compensation, the anticipated effectiveness of the employment services and the amount of coverage provided by the network of labour offices. In Central Asia, for example, it has been reported that the cost for a rural unemployed individual to travel to a labour office is often higher than the monthly benefit. On the other hand, some registered unemployed may actually be economically active. This practice may be illegal in many countries, but it is permitted in others.

Figure 2.7 presents unemployment rates for women and men from labour force surveys or similar surveys using international measurement criteria. Since unemployment is a new phenomenon in the region, the current levels tend directly to reflect the full amount of the change that has taken place since the beginning of the transition. Except for a few countries, the graph shows high female unemployment. However, since unemployment was close to zero before transition, the growth has obviously been considerable in all countries.

The data also show that, in several countries, the female unemployment rate is higher than the male unemployment rate. Still, the data from the new surveys reveal less gender disadvantage than do the data from the unemployment registers cited in Chapter 1. In many countries where unemployment registers are poorly developed, such as Russia, estimates using international concepts tend to present a more balanced gender picture or even higher male unemployment. Given relatively bigger losses in female employment, this points to a widening of the gender gap in labour market activity rates. Indeed, the countries that exhibit higher male unemployment ratios (Figure 2.7) also tend to exhibit an increase in the gender gap in labour force participation (Table 2.1) because of women's relatively more widespread withdrawal from the job market.

Labour force surveys usually do not count as unemployed those persons who do not search for work because they believe no jobs are available. Taking account of these "passive" unemployed would push female unemployment rates up by 1 or 2 percentage points in Central Europe. The inclusion of women who are inactive because they have become discouraged from job-seeking would push up the unemployment rates shown in Figure 2.7 for Latvia or Bulgaria by as many as 4 to 6 percentage points.

Much of the reduction in women's economic activity has occurred among younger and older age groups. Figure 2.8 reveals that

Figure 2.7

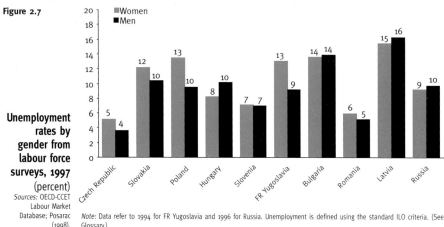

Unemployment rates by gender from labour force surveys, 1997 (percent)
Sources: OECD-CCET Labour Market Database; Posarac (1998).

Note: Data refer to 1994 for FR Yugoslavia and 1996 for Russia. Unemployment is defined using the standard ILO criteria. (See Glossary.)

Figure 2.8

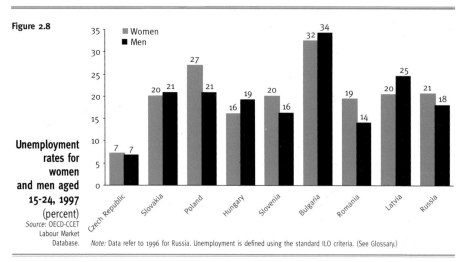

Unemployment rates for women and men aged 15-24, 1997 (percent)
Source: OECD-CCET Labour Market Database.

Note: Data refer to 1996 for Russia. Unemployment is defined using the standard ILO criteria. (See Glossary.)

Box 2.2

Gender differences in finding work in Poland

Labour force surveys performed in Poland over the 1990s make it possible to draw a portrait of gender differences in length of unemployment and success in finding work. The analysis presented here is based on a sub-sample of 2,076 people who were looking for work in November 1995 and who were re-interviewed one year later. Of the respondents, 51 percent were women.

At the time of the first interview, the women had been searching for work for just over 16 months on average. The men had been looking for work a significantly shorter time, just under 14 months. One year later, 40 percent of the men, but only 25 percent of the women had found work.

These data show that Poland's unemployed women have a relatively hard time finding work. A more detailed investigation carried out for this Report has found that, when all variables are taken into account, the main explanation for the gender difference in job-hunting success is marital status. Married men are twice as likely to find work as married women. Part of this difference may reflect women's greater responsibility for childcare, which could hamper job-hunting, limit employment options, or generate discrimination by employers.

However, the investigation has found that the same conclusion is not true for survey respondents who are employed. Holding other variables constant, the research uncovered little gender difference in terms of job security in Poland in the mid-1990s. This suggests that many women are able to balance family and job commitments and to work around, or in spite of, negative attitudes towards women who have dependent children and who are employed.

a large proportion of the young women characterized as economically active are actually unemployed. It presents the unemployment rates for women under age 25 in the same countries presented in Figure 2.7 (except for FR Yugoslavia, where data on youth unemployment are not available). These rates are much higher, showing that finding a job is particularly hard for young people. Youth unemployment rates are also often higher than the average in well-established market economies. For the transition countries, offering better prospects for well-educated young people is crucial to the effort to relieve the high current rates of poverty and social distress.

The share of the long-term unemployed – those out of work longer than one year – has become a serious problem with pressing economic and social implications for women and men across the region. Figure 2.9 shows that as many as one- to two-thirds of all unemployed women are long-term unemployed in many countries and that the rising trend continued at least from 1993 to 1997. Long-term unemployment wastes human resources and is best addressed through active measures such as retraining.

While persistent unemployment is a problem for women and men, there is evidence in the region that women are experiencing more difficulty in finding work and that the main determinant in this is women's greater

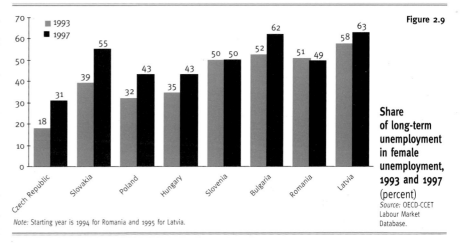

Figure 2.9

Note: Starting year is 1994 for Romania and 1995 for Latvia.

Share of long-term unemployment in female unemployment, 1993 and 1997 (percent)
Source: OECD-CCET Labour Market Database.

responsibility for childcare. A study carried out for this Report found that in Poland marriage status – a reliable proxy for the presence of children – was not a factor for unemployed men in finding work, but was a serious handicap for unemployed women (Box 2.2).

If the finding in Poland that women with children, independent of any other factors, face a harder time getting a job can be generalized for the whole region, this may explain why young women have been delaying or refusing to make a commitment to the establishment of a family. This dimension of women's life is further investigated in Chapter 3.

■

2.2 The Gender Pay Gap and the Structure of Female Employment

Wages are important indicators of economic well-being and of personal success. The relative level of women's and men's pay is revealing about women's progress in the labour market. Women's earnings can influence their status and

decision-making power within the family, as well as their choices about labour market participation and fertility. Women's wages are especially important for children. Research shows that women are more likely than men to spend their earnings directly on the needs of children.

The gender pay gap – women's disadvantage in earned income relative to men – is linked to hidden and overt discrimination in employment and wages. Wage-based discrimination occurs when workers with identical productivity characteristics receive unequal treatment in remuneration. In all countries of the transition region, laws forbid such discrimination. Although in several Baltic and CIS countries women are specifically prohibited from performing certain jobs that are considered dangerous or unhealthy or that require work at night, laws in transition countries also proscribe discrimination in employment. Nevertheless, tradition, social pressure and the commitment to the family are discouraging women from taking the more well paid jobs, and thus employment effects are very important factors in the gender pay gap.

Occupational segregation, whereby women dominate in certain occupations and men in others, is common everywhere. Occupations and skills, which are normally seen as the major determinants of the amount of earned income, are often suited to particular industries, corporate structures or types of employment.

Prior to transition, the region was no different from other parts of the world in terms of gender segregation by occupation and industry. However, at the big state enterprises which were prevalent in the economy, full-time employment was the norm for women and men, and job benefits and job security were rigidly regulated.

Since 1989, the role of the state in the economy has declined considerably in most transition countries. With economic restructuring, the private sector has grown substantially, and employment has become more diversified so that now self-employment and small-scale enterprises, often in the informal economy, are available as alternatives. These trends are expected to have major implications for female employment, the workplace environment and the gender wage gap.

Changes in the structure of employment

The emergence of private ownership has progressed considerably in the region. The private sector now accounts for 50-70 percent of measured economic activity in the majority of countries. It includes wholly new businesses, but also former state enterprises which have been transformed through privatization, a major component of institutional and economic restructuring.

Information on the participation of women in the process of private-sector growth is scarce and fragmented. However, the share of the private sector in employment clearly varies across economic branches; for example, it is often very low in health care, social services, education, and public administration. It is therefore useful to examine the share of women in different economic branches as a first step in the analysis. Figure 2.10 illustrates the overall position of women in selected branches of the economy in Latvia, a highly industrialized Baltic country where women still account for half of total employment.

The graph shows that woman held 80 percent or more of the jobs in education and health and social services, about three-quarters of the jobs in the hotel and restaurant industries and more than half the positions in wholesale and retail trade, financial services and "other" services. Women held one-third or fewer of the jobs in the construction, utilities and transport and communications sectors. Men held more than half the places in manufacturing, agriculture (with the exception of the employment on family farms), public administration, and business.

Similar patterns are observed in other parts of the region. For instance, in Hungary and Poland almost three-quarters of public employees are women. In countries where women's share of total employment is lower, their share also tends to be lower in the industries dominated by women as shown in Figure 2.10. In FYR Macedonia, for example, women make up only 38 percent of all employees and only slightly more than half those in education. They are predominant – 70 percent – only in health care and social services.

Despite restructuring, these broad profiles of gender employment have been quite stable during the transition. In Romania between 1990 and 1996, for example, women's employment dipped from 43 to 41 percent in industry (broadly defined), rose from 73 to 76 percent in health care and social services and stayed flat at 67 percent in education.

Looking at the issue from another perspective, a significant share of women's total employment is accounted for by those same sectors where women are over-represented among employees. In FYR Macedonia, about two-fifths of all female employment is in health care, education and public administration. In Latvia, one-third of total female employment is in health care, education and public administration, and a further 30 percent in hotels and restaurants, wholesale and retail trade, and financial and "other" services.

Figure 2.10

Share of women and men employed in selected economic sectors, Latvia, 1997 (percent)
Source: CSBL (1998).

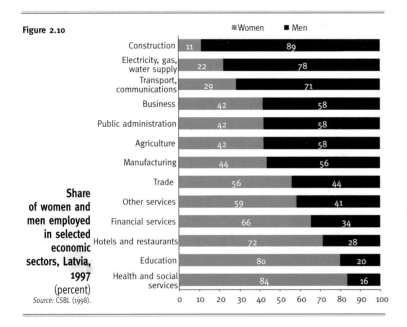

It is apparent that a substantial portion of the jobs for women is concentrated in areas that have remained and are likely to remain in the public or state sector. However, it is also clear that certain areas of the service sector where female employment is significant have been at the forefront of privatization and new business creation.

More detailed studies suggest that the rate of the movement of women from public-sector to private-sector jobs has been slower than that of men, and the high concentration of female employment in teaching and caring professions ensures women's continued attachment to the public sector at least in the medium term.

Using data drawn from the November 1992 Polish Labour Force Survey, a study has revealed that about 18 percent of employees were working in the private sector in the country, slightly more than one-third of them women. This was disproportionately lower than the 45 percent share of women in total employment. Comparable data from November 1996 showed that private-sector employees accounted for 34 percent of all workers, but that only 37 percent of the private-sector employees were women. These findings are in accord with studies in Russia which have found that men made up 55-60 percent of private-sector employees in 1996. These studies concluded that, with other variables constant, males had an appreciably greater probability of private-sector employment.

The data available on private-sector wages for women are limited to a few transition countries. Estimates for Hungary suggest that the earnings of women are 10 percent higher on average in the private sector relative to the public sector, while the Polish survey referred to above found the relative private-sector earnings of women 6 percent lower. It should be noted that private-sector workers in Poland are generally younger, with women in the private sector some six years younger on average than their counterparts in the rest of the economy. This issue needs further research, but the available evidence points to few wage incentives for women to join the private sector. However, it may be that private-sector wages are systematically under-reported (for example to avoid taxes), so caution is warranted in interpreting the numbers.

The emergence of the private sector may have accentuated gender discrimination in the workplace, and this may partly explain why relatively fewer women are switching to private-sector jobs. Evidence of gender bias has been reported in the recruitment practices of some employers in Hungary, Poland, the Czech Republic, and Slovakia, despite employment laws guaranteeing women equal treatment. Private-sector employers who face a newly competitive business environment may, for example, associate higher non-wage costs with women because of their family responsibilities.

A further factor may be "vertical job segregation". As Chapter 6 discusses, women have been under-represented at the level of management. This circumstance may have implications for the development of self-employment and small-scale entrepreneurship that has been strategic during the transition. The extent of women's participation in these areas is a largely under-researched aspect of the role of women in the economic and social changes accompanying transition.

Figure 2.11 reports the share of self-employment in total female and male employment for a selection of transition economies. (The data are not readily comparable among the countries; they tend to include employers, the self-employed, and unpaid family workers, but self-employment in certain types of ventures may be excluded.) On average, men appear to have a higher share in self-employment. The graph shows that the ratio of self-employment is high among women in countries where family farms are important, a sector that is strong in Poland and has re-emerged in Romania (where 90 percent of self-employment is in agriculture). The case of Romania suggests that in the countries – mostly in the southern part of the region, as Chapter 1 indicates – where private, often small family plots have been crucial in private-sector development, women's labour may have played a major part.

A prominent feature of employment for women in market economies is part-time work. Women account for 80 percent of all part-time employment in the European Union, where 32 percent of all female employees are in part-time jobs. Part-time work is a significant avenue for women seeking to earn income and manage family responsibilities. However, in the region, part-time work was uncommon before transition and has shown relatively few signs of growth since. In Hungary, for example, the share of women working part-time had climbed from 1-2 percent before the transition to 9 percent by 1997. The available data presented in Figure 2.12 confirm that part-time work is still uncommon in many transition economies, despite the demand among women for part-time employment, as Chapter 3 notes.

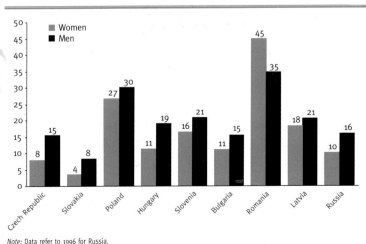

Figure 2.11

Share of self-employment in total male and female employment, 1997
(percent)
Source: OECD-CCET Labour Market Database.

Note: Data refer to 1996 for Russia.

Figure 2.12

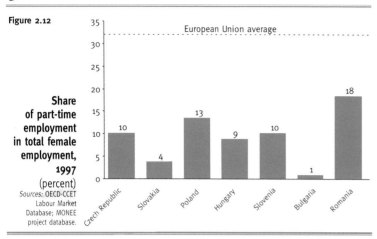

Share of part-time employment in total female employment, 1997
(percent)
Sources: OECD-CCET Labour Market Database; MONEE project database.

The small number of part-time jobs appears to be the result of supply factors. Managers trained within the state-enterprise system may not see part-time employees as cost-effective, or the tax system may not provide adequate incentives for the recruitment of such employees. However, it has also been argued that women and men simply cannot afford to work part time when two full-time incomes are required in most households to reach an acceptable standard of living.

The informal sector and its associated labour markets are growing in many transition economies. The flexible nature of the informal sector and the absence of entry barriers may promote the participation of women in this sector. Evidence on the hidden labour market is difficult to obtain. According to an estimate for Poland in 1994, women made up 36 percent of all informal workers who, in turn, represented 10 percent of all labour market participants. Most informal workers had lower levels of education. A survey undertaken at the beginning of 1998 by the Institute for Economics in Belgrade showed that 30 percent of employees were engaged in unregistered labour market activities in the form of second jobs. Most of these

employees said they were motivated by economic necessity. About 40 percent of the employees working a second job were women, with the highest participation among women aged 30-40. Women were working slightly more than 50 hours extra per month, compared to 63 hours for men. Some 37 percent of women engaged in the extra work while on the job at their main place of employment, compared to 29 percent of men. A more detailed analysis found that, when variables such as age, education and earnings on the main job are taken into account, women are less likely than men, by an estimated 17 percentage points, to engage in unregistered labour activity. On the other hand, reports from Central Asia suggest that women dominate in the booming and highly visible "shuttle tours" and informal "suitcase" trade in consumer goods brought in from neighbouring countries.

There are clear data collection problems, and survey respondents may be less than truthful about their participation in the informal sector. Informal sector activity often involves second jobs to earn crucial extra income. Informal activities may also take the form of unpaid work in the household economy, including the production of goods and services for sale or barter in the community – a coping strategy to deal with the rising risk of poverty. In any case, the growth of the informal labour market means that greater numbers of women and men are relatively unprotected and vulnerable to exploitation in their jobs. As Box 2.3 highlights, the booming sex industry, in particular, puts women at a very high risk of violence and exploitation.

The gender pay gap: is it shrinking?

The first step in exploring the gender gap in earnings is simply to compare the average monthly pay for women relative to men. Figure 2.13 provides recent data for 15 countries across the region. It shows that women earn less

---

Box 2.3

The growing sex industry

It is difficult to measure the scale of the sex industry, given its unregulated and often criminal nature, but it is widely observed that the upheaval of transition has led to a rapid rise in the number of women from the region who are working as prostitutes. Several cities in Central Europe and the Baltics have become destinations for sex tourism.

Evidence from Latvia shows that more than 3,000 sex workers, mainly women, have been employed in sex clubs in Riga, the capital, during the 1990s. Police there estimate that, during the decade, 10,000-15,000 prostitutes have been active in the city. According to a survey carried out in Riga in 1995 by the Centre for Criminological Research, more than 60

percent of the prostitutes said unemployment caused them to enter the sex trade. Police estimates, combined with data from the Latvian Labour Force Survey, suggest that almost 2 percent of the employed women in Latvia were working in the sex industry in the mid-1990s.

Women from Eastern and Central Europe now dominate street prostitution in a number of major cities in Western Europe. As Chapter 5 presents, many have been deceived or forced into migrating. There is cause for alarm at the impact of this growing, illicit business on women and society. The serious implications for personal and public health and for the status and rights of women need to be examined and addressed.

than men in every country, with women's wages averaging between 70 and 90 percent of men's wages. Most of the ratios reveal a gender pay gap comparable to or smaller than those prevailing in Western countries. For example, in Great Britain, the wages among women averaged about 70 percent of the wages among men in 1990.

By including available pre- and mid-transition data, Table 2.2 provides insight on how female-male wage ratios have changed over the last decade. Only Bulgaria reports a big rise – 5 percentage points – in the gender

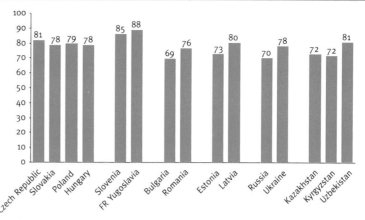

Figure 2.13

Average monthly earnings for women as a share of male earnings, around 1997 (percent)
Source: Table 2.2.

Table 2.2

Gender pay ratios, selected countries and years

(female monthly wages as a percent of male monthly wages)

	Ratio	Year	Note
Czech Republic	66.1	1987	a
	73.0	1992	b
	81.3	1996	b
Slovakia	66.1	1987	a
	73.3	1992	b
	78.2	1996	b
Poland	73.7	1985	a
	79.0	1992	c
	79.0	1996	c
Hungary	74.3	1986	a
	80.8	1992	d
	78.1	1997	d
Slovenia	87.0	1987	e
	88.6	1991	f
	85.4	1996	f
FR Yugoslavia	89.9	1995	g
	88.8	1996	g
	88.4	1997	g
Bulgaria	74.0	1990	h
	69.1	1997	h
Romania	78.6	1994	i
	76.2	1997	i
Estonia	79.8	1992	j
	72.6	1996	j
Latvia	79.9	1998	k
Lithuania	65.0	1997	l, m
	71.0	1997	l, n
Russia	70.9	1989	a, o
	68.5	1992	p
	69.5	1996	p
Ukraine	77.7	1996	q
Azerbaijan	52.6	1995	r
Kazakhstan	72.3	1996	s
Kyrgyzstan	73.3	1995	t
	71.5	1997	t
Uzbekistan	80.5	1995	u

Note: a. Atkinson and Micklewright (1992), Table 4.2. b. Social Stratification Surveys. c. Polish Labour Force Surveys. d. Lakatos (1998). e. Orazem and Vodopivec (1995). f. Shircel (1998). g. FR Yugoslavia Labour Force Survey. h. Tzvetkova-Anguelova (1998); refers to the public sector. i. NCS (1998). j. Papp (1998); refers to hourly wages. k. CSBL (1998). l. LDS (1998). m. Refers to manual workers. n. Refers to non-manual workers. o. Data for 1989 refer to the former Soviet Union. p. Russia Longitudinal Monitoring Survey. q. Ukraine Household Income and Expenditures Study. r. Azerbaijan Survey of Living Conditions; dataset may not be nationally representative, and results should be interpreted with care. s. Kazakhstan Living Standards Survey. t. NSCKR (1998). u. EUI/Essex Survey in Uzbekistan.

pay gap between 1990 and 1997. The data suggest that there has been a considerable narrowing in the gender pay gap since the introduction of reforms in the Czech Republic, Slovakia, Poland, and Hungary. The ratios for Slovenia, FR Yugoslavia, Romania, Russia, and Kyrgyzstan appear relatively stable. This stability is a striking outcome in the context of changing labour markets and the significant growth in wage inequality, as Chapter 1 indicates.

In the investigation of the structural factors in the gender pay gap, the methodologies developed for established market economies assign great importance to what is referred to as the "selectivity bias problem". Whenever a considerable portion of the female working-age population does not participate in the labour market, it is reasonable to assume that the skills, talents and employment capacities of the women who do participate (the "select pool") are different from those of women who do not participate. In this respect, the productivity characteristics and wages of women may not be readily comparable to those of men, who tend to exhibit full participation rates.

In the transition region, this "selectivity bias" is generally a new issue. Under communism, the labour force participation of women was high and close to that of men, thereby dampening the potential of positive or negative selection bias. It seems logical to assume that the observed stability or improvement in the gender gap during transition may reflect structural impacts. Studies in the new Federal Länder in Germany, for example, have found that the average wages of women rose by 10 percentage points relative to men's wages during the first four years after German unification. About 8 percentage points represented simply a reaction to the withdrawal of many poorly qualified – and, therefore, less competitive – women from the labour market. Certainly, other post-communist states face economic conditions which are starkly different from those in the former German Democratic Republic. In many parts of the region, the selectivity bias may be limited, since rising poverty has pressured women, no matter their abilities, to continue to work.

The gender pay ratios in Table 2.2 do not take into

account the number of working hours, which, even among full-time employees, may differ considerably. (Thus, for example, teachers typically have shorter working days.) Moreover, the ratios measure earnings from a main formal-sector job and so do not reflect the marked increase in work in second jobs and in unreported labour in the region. It is also difficult to assess the gender implications of wage arrears, notably in Russia, Ukraine and the Central Asian countries. An analysis carried out in Ukraine (Box 2.4) showed that women are heavily represented in enterprises and sectors affected by wage arrears.

Gender differences in average earnings reflect a range of structural effects. Representative household surveys, which were introduced in most countries in the region only after several years of transition, include information on a spectrum of job and personal factors relevant to employment. A regression analysis carried out for this Report has attempted to distinguish the effects of individual differences in human capital from the effects of the occupational and industrial branch on wages. Although data problems limit the accuracy of the results, the analysis closely quantifies the part of the gender gap attributable primarily to gender discrimination.

For 11 transition countries, Table 2.3 reports three measures of the gender pay gap – one unadjusted and two adjusted – that resulted from the analysis. Here is how to read the table.

- *Column 1* reports the unadjusted gender pay gap – the percentage difference between the monthly earnings of female and male employees. The percentages mirror the ratios revealed in the exploration in this chapter. (Since

Table 2.3

Three measures of the gender pay gap, selected countries and years

(difference between male and female monthly wages expressed as percent of male wages)

	Note	Year	1. Crude ratio, without controls	2. Controlling for human capital*	3. Controlling for human capital and job factors*
Czech Republic	a	1984	27.5	27.0	24.8
	a	1992	24.2	23.7	20.0
Slovakia	a	1984	24.8	24.8	24.2
	a	1992	23.7	24.2	22.5
Poland	b	1996	11.5	16.7	16.0
Hungary	a	1992	18.7	20.0	15.3
FR Yugoslavia	c	1996	10.7	12.3	11.5
Latvia	d	1996	17.4	21.3	20.0
Russia	e	1992	27.5	29.6	23.1
		1996	26.5	29.1	24.2
Ukraine	f	1996	20.0	16.0	18.7
Azerbaijan	g	1995	39.0	40.1	35.9
Kazakhstan	h	1996	24.2	28.1	29.6
Uzbekistan	i	1995	18.0	11.5	20.6

Note: Estimates computed from the following. a. Social Stratification Surveys. b. Polish Labour Force Survey (hourly wages). c. FR Yugoslavia Labour Force Survey. d. Latvian Household Budget Survey. e. Russia Longitudinal Monitoring Survey. f. Ukraine Household Income and Expenditures Study. g. Azerbaijan Survey of Living Conditions. h. Kazakhstan Living Standards Survey. i. EUI/Essex Survey in Uzbekistan. *The last two columns are based on the ordinary least square (OLS) estimation of a pooled sample (that is, male and female observations), with the estimated coefficient of the gender dummy capturing the gender pay gap.

data sources, definitions and calculations are not always identical, the pay gaps in Table 2.3 are not the precise complements of the wage ratios in Table 2.2.)

- *Column 2* reports the gender pay gap "net" of the effect of human capital factors, such as education and experience. (Age was used as a proxy for experience, an admittedly weaker proxy in terms of women.) In most cases, after removing the effect of these factors, the gender gap stays flat or widens. This indicates that women's education levels were as high or even higher than men's, a feature

Box 2.4

Wage arrears and women workers in Ukraine

Wage arrears are a serious problem in the Baltic States, Russia and other countries of the former Soviet Union, including Ukraine. Most affected tend to be the industries with the lowest relative wages, and these are often dominated by female workers.

The Ukraine-96 Project, a 1996 initiative of the World Bank and the Kiev International Institute of Sociology, collected information on wage arrears from 850 Ukrainian workers, about half of them women. Over 45 percent were owed pay, with 43 percent of women and 47 percent of men reporting wage arrears from their main jobs. Analysis confirmed that the women were negatively affected by wage arrears especially because of their higher relative participation in industries where arrears are more common, such as industry, health care, education, and finance, with one-third of women in the

sample employed in the latter three.

Other important determinants of arrears were an individual's ethnicity and years on the job. Ethnic Ukrainians were 11 percent less likely than other ethnic groups, including Russians, to be owed back pay. The longer an individual had been employed on the same job, the greater the risk of arrears. This may be explained by the fact that older workers are less employable in the changing market economy and so are less likely to leave their jobs over wage arrears. Education and occupation (except military service) had little influence, as did ownership structure (public, private, collective). Finally, gender did not appear to be a factor at the individual level, indicating that the decisions of employers and managers related to arrears were not determined by gender bias.

which gave women a comparative advantage in wages.

● *Column 3* is "net" of the effect of further factors, such as occupation, branch of employment and several other wage-determining variables. If the effect of these factors

is removed, the gender gap shrinks in most cases. This confirms that part of the gap is due to the fact that women tend to be concentrated in those occupations and economic branches which pay less.

Box 2.5

The gender pay gap in Russia

Data available through the Russia Longitudinal Monitoring Survey permit a more refined calculation of the gender pay gap in Russia that illustrates the influence of various factors and highlights changes between 1992 and 1996.

Figure 2.14 reproposes the calculation method presented in Table 2.3, but this time using both monthly wages (on the left side of the graph) and hourly wages (on the right side). The size difference between the black and light blue columns shows graphically that, if women had the same educational level as men, the gender gap would have been even wider, that is, the better education of women serves to close the pay gap in Russia. The difference between the light blue and the dark blue columns indicates that, if women also had the same type of jobs as men, then the gender gap would, in contrast, have been smaller, that is, occupational factors are responsible for part of the gap.

In comparing the gaps based on monthly wages and those based on hourly wages, the diagram confirms that the number of hours worked is an important determinant of the pay gap. For hourly wages, the "crude pay gap" is smaller, with men having a pay advantage which is about 7 percentage points narrower than the gap relative to monthly earnings. Similarly, the "net pay gap" calculated for hourly wages is 21 percent, about 3 percentage points narrower than the gap relative to monthly wages. This shows that part of the "unexplained" gender gap in monthly wages is due to the fact that women tend to work fewer hours than men.

Data from the same survey also allow an investigation of how greater wage inequality and structural changes in employment have affected the earnings position of women relative to that of men between 1992 and 1996. Based on a methodology that deconstructs the observed change – minus 0.7 percent – into four components, Table 2.4 examines factors that influence the gender pay gap over time. (A negative entry indicates an effect that reduces the gender pay gap over time.)

The first component in Table 2.4 captures the effect of changes in the gender differences in the observed job and human capital characteristics of employees. This component may provide an insight into observable "selection" effects. For example, a selective withdrawal from the labour market of less qualified women would result in a reduction in the pay gap. In fact, the value is negative, though the effect seems small. The second element of the decomposition captures the general effect of changes in the returns on characteristics like occupation, education and experi-

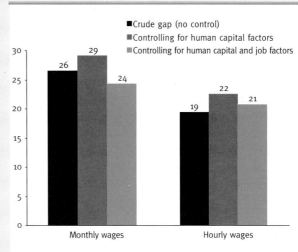

Figure 2.14

Three measures of the gender pay gap in monthly and hourly wages, Russia, 1996 (difference between male and female wages, as percent of male wages)
Source: Calculated based on the 1996 Russia Longitudinal Monitoring Survey.

Table 2.4

Gender-specific and structural effects of change in the hourly pay gap, Russia, 1992-96

(percent)

Observed change	-0.7
a. observed job and employee characteristics	-0.7
b. returns to observed characteristics	-4.3
c. "gap effect"	-1.1
d. wage dispersion	5.4
of which:	
gender-specific effects (a+c)	-1.8
wage-specific effects (b+d)	1.1

Source: Computed based on the Russia Longitudinal Monitoring Survey.

ence (for example pay raises in certain professions). The third component measures the impact of changes in the "net" gap, and the fourth reflects the net effect of changes in wage inequality.

The first and third terms measure gender-inequality effects, while the second and fourth terms capture the effects of changes in wage inequality (bigger pay differentials relative to measured job or skill characteristics and bigger wage dispersion that is unrelated to these).

The data confirm that, on balance, the small amount of movement in the observed gender pay gap in Russia results from contrasting effects. Indeed, greater wage dispersion had a widening effect on the gender pay gap. This effect, however, was offset by movements in the other three components: "selective" withdrawals, smaller "unexplained" gender pay differences and, particularly, shifts in labour market returns on education that were favourable for women.

The main finding of this analysis, however, is not that women's education level and occupation have a positive or negative effect on the gender pay gap. The main finding is that, when conventional determinants are considered, the biggest part of the gender pay gap remains, and it therefore remains technically unexplained. In the Czech Republic, for example, after all measurable structural effects have been removed, women's wages are still 20 percent lower than men's, as opposed to 24 percent with the crude measure in 1992.

These findings go against the widespread assumption that most of the gender gap is due to occupational or educational differences. Certainly, the gaps reported in Column 3 may still reflect some qualitative job differences not captured by the data, since the calculations are based on monthly wages, aggregated information on occupations and proxies for work experience. Nonetheless, these results – at the very least – do not exclude the existence of substantial hidden discrimination against women.

It is obvious that more accurate statistics and further analytical work are needed to clarify this issue further. Box 2.5 presents a more refined calculation of the "net gap effect" using hourly wages in Russia. The results show that the "unexplained" pay gap is somewhat smaller when reckoned according to hourly rather than monthly wages, though most of the gender difference is still there. However, a more positive finding is that the "unexplained" wage gap shrank somewhat between 1992 and 1996, possibly a weak but promising outcome of market reforms in this large and important country.

Measuring occupational segregation

It has already been shown that the concentration of women in lower paying economic sectors and occupations is a factor in the gender pay gap. The measurement of occupational segregation, however, is an issue in its own right.

First, the segregation of women and men into different occupations reflects prevailing gender stereotypes in society. These stereotypes define both women and men according to a limited set of expectations which are particularly confining for women in terms of economic and public achievement. As Chapter 6 discusses, gender stereotypes on the job are one of the invisible barriers that keep women from certain occupations and, in particular, senior positions. Research in Western countries suggests that women are less likely than men to be promoted and that they experience smaller pay increases when they are promoted. An ILO survey of enterprise managers in three Central European countries confirms the existence of gender bias in the workplace. Most of the managers surveyed in the Czech Republic and Slovakia believed that men have supervisory skills which are superior to those of women, and in Hungary almost 60 percent of managers preferred to recruit male supervisors.

Second, there is growing awareness, which is supported by empirical evidence in many countries throughout the world, that the pay in occupations dominated by women is lower even when the effect of variables such as the different levels of education required are taken into account. Calculations carried out for this Report have found an inverse relationship between women's presence in certain professions and the occupational wage advantage. Identifying cause and effect in this case is very difficult because numerous factors are at work. Do jobs pay less simply because they are predominantly occupied by women? Do women gravitate to lower paying and lower status jobs because they are making choices about their own career commitments, including their careers as mothers? How much does the male breadwinner model influence wage-setting in occupations? Whatever the answers, it is clear that the degree of occupational segregation tends to be a strong indicator of the disadvantage experienced by women in the workplace.

The measurement of occupational segregation is often complicated by problems in the availability, comparability and disaggregation of statistics on occupations. Moreover, results may differ depending on the segregation index used. Figure 2.15 shows the results of calculations based on the Duncan and Duncan dissimilarity index, which measures the proportions of women and men who would have to shift occupations in order to create equalized gender distribution. While its meaning is easy to understand, the index has the shortcoming of assigning equal weight to each occupation regardless of the share of the occupation in total employment.

Figure 2.15 shows the levels of occupational segregation in nine of the transition economies also featured in Table 2.3. The segregation values range mainly from 30 to 40 percent. (For Azerbaijan, which is below this range, the quality of the data is suspicious.) Segregation appears highest in Russia and Poland, where, on average, 45-47 percent of women or men would have to change jobs to

Figure 2.15

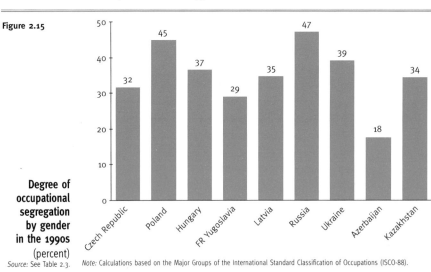

Degree of occupational segregation by gender in the 1990s
(percent)

Source: See Table 2.3. *Note:* Calculations based on the Major Groups of the International Standard Classification of Occupations (ISCO-88).

equalize gender representation in each occupation. By comparison, a 1996 study assigned to the United Kingdom a value of 44 percent, the highest in the study, while the lowest, 32 percent, was assigned to Switzerland.

There was a high degree of occupational segregation under communist rule, a legacy reflected in Figure 2.15. It is harder to tell whether and how occupational segregation has been affected by the transition. Data constraints and changing occupational definitions prevent a detailed comparison. Given the specific nature of occupational skills, the training required to change occupational groups, and ingrained attitudes and systemic barriers, it is certain that positive changes in occupational segregation will take time. This presents opportunities for policy and programme initiatives.

Table 2.5 uses data from the Russia Longitudinal Monitoring Survey to explore how occupational segregation changed between 1992 and 1996. In addition to the Duncan and Duncan dissimilarity index, it also shows the Gini concentration index to check for structural shifts in 29 "sub-major" (two-digit) occupational groupings. Both indexes reveal a high degree of occupational segregation in Russia. (By comparison, the Duncan and Duncan value for the United States was 36, which is two-thirds of the Russian value, while the Gini index for the US was even lower, about half the Russian value.) Nevertheless, the

Table 2.5

Occupational segregation, Russia, 1992-96

(percent)

	1992	1996	1996/1992
Duncan and Duncan dissimilarity index	53.8	51.3	95.4
Gini concentration index	71.3	67.6	94.8

Source: Computed based on the Russia Longitudinal Monitoring Survey.

calculations show some evidence that segregation in Russia has lessened slightly during the transition.

This positive outcome fits with earlier results showing that the impact of job-related characteristics on the gender pay gap was weaker in 1996 than it had been four years earlier. Certainly, all these findings for Russia are partial and do not appear to be very robust. They do, however, offer hope that the emerging labour market will reward the high human capital profile of women in the region and that women's rights to equal pay and participation are not necessarily in conflict with the new market orientation. On the other hand, the available data clearly signal that there is a long way to go to achieve more balanced attitudes towards issues revolving around women and work.

∎

2.3 Women's Employment and Income in the Household Context

The preceding sections discuss the position of women in the labour market largely independent of the household environment. However, women's decisions related to paid work are usually significantly shaped by this environment. The amount and type of paid work women seek are influenced by the nature of women's household responsibilities and circumstances. Conversely, the employment status and earnings level of women affect the relative status and power of women within the household and the welfare of other household members, especially children, and have implications for family policies.

Before examining the changes in the demographic behaviours and family circumstances of women during the transition (see Chapter 3), one should look at women's employment and income in a household context, as well as related issues such as women's influence on the use of incomes within the household and the impact of unemployment among men and women on households and children.

The losses in wages and in employment among women and men during the transition mean that the share of household incomes earned on primary jobs has declined in many countries. In Russia, for example, the proportion of household cash income earned from employment fell from more than 75 percent in 1989 to just under 40 percent in 1995. In many countries, households are desperate to find additional ways to earn money.

Female earnings are not only an important input in household income, but their relative contribution can influence and enhance women's status within the household. The 1996 Latvian Household Budget Survey showed that employment income comprised about 68 percent of all household income. A study carried out for this Report found that Latvian women in households with children contributed, on average, 45 percent of household income. This strikingly high average, however, can still obscure big differences across households. For example, an estimated 44 percent of Latvian children live in households where women are the main earners. One-quarter of these children live with a single female parent. The Latvian example is a useful reminder that the economic welfare of a large number of children depends directly on the employment prospects of their mothers.

While household incomes are important for the living standards of women and children, the members of a household do not automatically share the same living standard. Social and cultural factors can influence the allocation of resources within households. These factors include social norms related to gender and kinship relationships, the way in which income enters the household (for instance, as cash wages, bank deposits, or in-kind payments) and the relative economic power of individual household members.

A growing body of research in countries at all stages of development finds that the receipt of income by women boosts their economic power within the household. This has significant effects on household consumption patterns, including the relative amount of money spent to meet the needs of children. Greater economic autonomy may increase not only women's influence in household deci-

Table 2.6

Five main patterns in household financial management

Wife management	The husband has the higher income and hands the bulk of his pay to the wife, who manages most household expenditures.
Husband management	The husband has the higher income and gives the wife an allowance for parts of the family budget, for example for food.
Pooling system	All income is pooled, and both partners withdraw income from a cash "kitty" or joint bank account as necessary.
Independent management	Both partners have income, and neither has automatic access to all household funds. Each may be responsible for different areas of expenditure.
Extended family management	Members of the broader kinship system (for example the eldest in the extended family) participate in decision making.

Source: Adapted from Pahl (1989).

Figure 2.16

Opinions on who decides on family finances, Russia, 1994
Source: Bodrova (1995).

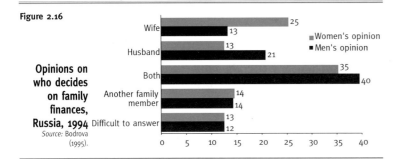

Figure 2.17

Married women with earnings: who decides how their earnings are used?
Sources: NINK and Macro International (1996); IOGU and Macro International (1997).

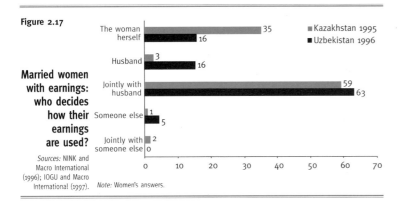

Note: Women's answers.

sion making, but their independence and ability to quit unsuccessful relationships.

However, the household resources received by women and children involve more than household income. Established gender roles and other social norms play an important part in the allocation of these resources, irrespective of who brings the money into the household. In fact, one way social norms are expressed is through different household income management strategies, as outlined in Table 2.6.

In Western countries, pooling and independent management are more common when both wife and husband have paying jobs. The high rates of female labour force participation suggest that these patterns may be prevalent in the transition countries, too, although cultural patterns may play a role in promoting the more traditional patterns of wife, husband and extended family management. Reliable and comparable data on these arrangements within households, over time and across countries would provide a telling perspective on changes in women's status within households. Unfortunately, such data are largely unavailable. Figures 2.16 and 2.17, however, offer interesting insights into women's position in household economic decision making in the region, revealing patterns that are far from predominantly patriarchal.

Figure 2.16 presents the answers of Russian women and men when they were asked who makes the decisions regarding household finances. The most common response (35-40 percent) is that wife and husband share control. However, in a sizeable proportion of households a single partner – wife or husband – makes the decisions on household budgets. Generally speaking, this sort of control is exercised by an equal share of wives and husbands, though, interestingly, both women and men attribute more control to their own gender. This implies that the actual proportion of households where both spouses make decisions on finances may be higher than indicated and that there may be conflicts over this issue.

The high female labour force participation in many other CIS countries suggests that the surprisingly balanced gender pattern shown for Russia may have been widespread elsewhere as well.

The labour force participation of women has, however, been lower in the southern part of the region. Figure 2.17 reports on surveys carried out in Kazakhstan in 1995 and Uzbekistan in 1996. In the surveys, married women with earnings were asked who decided how their earnings were used.

Interestingly, in both countries most women – around 60 percent – reported that decisions were made jointly with their husbands. In Uzbekistan, however, one in five women said decisions about how to use their earnings were made by someone other than themselves. In 16 percent of cases this was the husband, and in 5 percent of the cases this was someone else (for example older rela-

Box 2.6

Children and parental employment in Hungary

Statistics on the labour market too rarely show the importance of adult employment from the perspective of children. What proportion of children live in households where no adult works and where no income from employment is being brought into the household? How many children live in a household in which only one parent works? An examination of labour force survey data for Hungary in 1992-97 provides some striking answers.

Female unemployment and inactivity (in the sense of non-participation in the labour market) are two important reasons why a considerable number of children live in households where no working-age adult has a job or runs a business. In 1992, almost one child in 10 in Hungary was living in a "workless household". Moreover, as Figure 2.18 shows, the number continued to rise after 1993, when overall unemployment peaked in Hungary. By 1997, almost one child in seven was living in a workless household. If the analysis is restricted to parents (as opposed to any adult in the household), the number is higher still by a small margin: 15 percent of children had no employed parent living with them in 1997, up from 10 percent in 1992.

Table 2.7 shows the changes in the employment status of both mothers and fathers over the period, distinguishing between single- and two-parent families. (As with Figure 2.18, the perspective taken is that of the child, so that a parent with two children is reported twice in Table 2.7.) There was a large fall in the proportion of children living in two-parent families in which both mother and father were working, down from 48 percent to 38 percent over 1992-97. Not only were there more children in workless households as a result, but there was a marked rise in the proportion of children in households with only the father working – up by 6 percentage points.

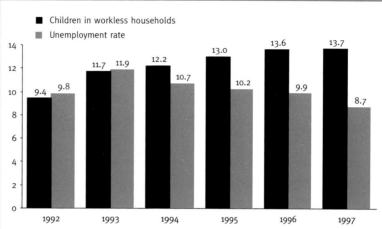

Figure 2.18

- ■ Children in workless households
- ▮ Unemployment rate

Year	Children in workless households	Unemployment rate
1992	9.4	9.8
1993	11.7	11.9
1994	12.2	10.7
1995	13.0	10.2
1996	13.6	9.9
1997	13.7	8.7

Children in workless households and the unemployment rate, Hungary, 1992-97 (percent)
Source: Labour Force Survey microdata.

Note: The graph shows the share of children living in households where no adult of working age is employed (including self-employment and casual work). Children are defined as all persons aged 0-14 and those aged 15-18 if enrolled in full-time education. The unemployment rate is the standard ILO definition. (See Glossary.)

Table 2.7

Employment status of children's parents, Hungary, 1992 and 1997

(percent)

	1992	1997
One-parent families		
mother works	7.7	7.3
mother does not work	2.9	4.3
father works	0.8	1.1
father does not work	0.3	0.5
Two-parent families		
both parents work	48.0	38.2
only mother works	6.6	5.6
only father works	26.4	32.4
neither parent works	7.3	10.6
Total	100.0	100.0
mother works	62.3	51.1
father works	75.2	71.7

Source: Labour Force Survey microdata.

Note: The data show the employment status of children's parents if these are living with the family and take the child as the unit of analysis. Also see the note to Figure 2.18.

tives). These patterns differed across ethnic groups, with "someone else" being less likely to decide how to spend the earnings of Slav women. The data confirm that cultural and ethnic factors may have an effect on gender roles, but generally they support the view that women's relatively high labour force participation in all these countries results in a relatively balanced gender pattern in household economic decisions.

In light of the losses in women's employment during the transition across the region, the gender balance of income power in the home may have shifted towards men in many cases. However, since the employment loss has also been great among men, there may have been a shift towards women in a significant number of cases, too. Using Hungary as an example, Box 2.6 looks at how this polarization in the employment and non-employment status of wives and husbands – and cases in which all adults in the household are without work – affects children.

■

2.4 Conclusions

Paid work is a key determinant of women's economic autonomy and an important foundation for women's exercise of authority in the home and participation in wider society. The former communist countries were remarkable for the high labour force participation rates among women, who, unlike in Western economies, worked overwhelmingly at full-time jobs. Before the transition, the gender gap in labour force participation in the region was very small by international standards – less than 2 percent in countries like Estonia or Belarus and in the 10 percent range in many other countries. Despite long hours on the job, women in the region continued to pull down a "second shift" of unpaid work at home. Data show that the total workload of women in Central and Eastern Europe averaged close to 70 hours per week, about 15 hours more than the workload of women in Western Europe.

The transition has generated an unprecedented phenomenon in the region: the loss of millions of jobs by people who have almost no personal experience of job loss or of a competitive labour market. Nonetheless, the gender gap in labour force participation does not appear to have widened considerably. Although female participation in the labour force has decreased in many countries, male participation has fallen as well. Yet, the financial pressure to maintain two incomes in households remains tremendous, constraining women and men to continue to work or to search for work.

The decline in labour force participation appears to have affected younger and older women of working age the most. There is evidence that, in response, more young women are now pursuing post-secondary education in many countries. Older women are taking on childcare responsibilities – presumably often for other family members.

Female employment has dropped even more markedly than female labour force participation. An estimated 14 million jobs held by women disappeared across the region between 1989 and 1997. This was well over half the total number of jobs lost. Still, due to high pre-transition employment rates, the share of women employed remains in the 40-50 percent range. Overall, there is little evidence that women are being "squeezed out" of the employment picture. However, it appears that the tensions created because of the need to care for children and the need to work for pay have grown, and flexible options for reconciling these commitments – such as part-time work arrangements – are still mostly unavailable.

Unemployment is a new phenomenon in the region, and the data show that there is substantial female unemployment in most countries. In several countries, the female unemployment rate is higher than the male unemployment rate. There is also evidence that it is harder for women to find jobs because of their greater responsibility for childcare. A study in Poland revealed that marriage status is a major factor in determining whether unemployed women find work, though this is not the case for unemployed men.

Women around the world face a gender gap in pay, and the communist countries were no different, despite their egalitarian rhetoric and the levelling hand of central planning. The available data show that in 1996-97 women earned less than men on average, with the gender gap ranging from 10 to 30 percent, amounts comparable to, or smaller than, those in Western countries. Further analysis shows that the gender gap in the region is aggravated by occupational factors and mitigated by human capital factors. This suggests that women's high levels of education often work to their advantage in closing the pay gap, while the fact that women tend to cluster in lower paying occupations acts against them. However, even when these observable determinants are taken into consideration, there remains a substantial gender gap in pay – one that remains unexplained and that demands further research and discussion.

The available data suggest that during transition the gender gap in wages has remained relatively stable or even decreased in some countries, a striking outcome considering that there has been a large rise in overall wage disparity in the same period. Analysis confirms that the economic welfare of a large number of children depends directly on the employment and wage prospects of mothers.

It is clear that there has been and continues to be significant occupational segregation by gender in the region. It appears that gender segregation is also becoming based on the ownership structure of enterprises, with women continuing to cluster in public-sector jobs, and men making far greater inroads in private-sector employment. In many countries, women make up about three-quarters of the employees in education, health care and social services, while they are under-represented in industry, agriculture (with the exception of family farms) and business. On the other hand, women are very active in the hotel and restaurant industry, in wholesale and retail trade and in financial services – growth areas which offer good prospects in the emerging private sector.

Although women appear to be less inclined or able than men to move into self-employment and entrepreneurship – a vital part of the new private sector, in many cases women already have a strong position in the private sector. Further research into women's role in entrepreneurship is needed, and support programmes and policies should be developed to boost women's participation in this area.

■

3 Women, Families and Policies

One of the main promises of the transition is to increase the ability of individuals to determine their own well-being. This new emphasis on persons having the responsibility and the capacity to make choices and realize goals extends naturally to family life.

The individual may be the basic political unit of democratic society, but families remain the basic social unit. In this regard, it is important to understand what is happening to women and families during the transition and what measures need to be taken – by individuals, partners, families, communities, and the state – to support women in their roles within and outside the home.

UN documents and international agreements accord a woman the same rights and responsibilities as they do a man during marriage, including reproductive rights related to the number and spacing of children. Women have maternity rights on and off the job and the right to own and manage adequate housing. Agreements also call for recognition of the shared responsibility of women and men in the upbringing and development of children. It is likewise clear that, although parents have the primary responsibility for ensuring their children have an adequate standard of living, the state has a duty to support the ability of parents to carry out this responsibility.

Women have many roles within the home, and the interplay among these roles is complex. Women are partners in household unions, paid and unpaid workers in the household, mothers, and often primary caregivers. The activity of women in these various functions is a major determinant of the health, education and economic welfare of family members, especially children, and also provides role models for the adults the children will become.

Under communism, women in the region exhibited notably high participation in the paid labour force, though there was greater variance across countries than is usually presumed. Overall, women's earning capacity and labour position have weakened with the emergence of more competitive and less regulated labour markets during the reform years. Still, the relative position of women to men – the gender balance – has often changed less than might have been expected, and the difference in earning capacity has at times narrowed. Given the dire economic reality in most countries, these outcomes are clearly the result of considerable individual effort with, no doubt, associated personal and social costs.

The family dimension of women's lives has also changed appreciably and often unexpectedly during the transition. This change is the focus of the present chapter, particularly women's roles in family formation.

Under communism, women were constitutionally guaranteed the same rights and responsibilities as men in marriage and child-rearing. Furthermore, the communist state provided a wide range of family support measures – including nurseries, kindergartens, after-school programmes, and parental leave benefits – as much to keep women in the workforce as to keep up fertility rates. However, the letter of the law did not necessarily translate into progress in gender equality in the private sphere of the home. The state's appropriation of many parental duties, especially childcare, meant that individual women and men were not compelled in their own homes and partnerships to address the gender balance related to household work and family responsibilities.

Family support measures, aimed largely at women, have been deeply affected by the new economic and social conditions of the transition. The functions and the resources of the state have changed tremendously. The state is no longer the single or predominant employer and provider of welfare services and benefits. In many countries, the state's resources and its ability to raise revenues are greatly diminished. Not only has there been less to go around during the transition – fewer jobs and less purchasing power, but the social and economic environment is much more diverse and, in some ways, more fragmented. The profound changes in social and economic expectations and conditions have acted upon the relative positions and inter-relationships of women and men in the region. Kinship networks and communities have increasingly taken over the social support functions formerly performed by the state.

This chapter looks at demographic trends relating to women and families during the transition and at changes in family policies. Section 3.1 examines women, family formation and related social policies in the region at the outset of the transition. This offers a useful context for understanding emerging trends. Section 3.2 presents an overview of changes in family formation. Section 3.3 looks at changes in family policies. The Conclusions outline some policy implications and areas that merit special attention.

■

3.1 Women, Families and State Policies at the Outset of the Transition

Patterns in family formation not only depend on individual circumstances and decisions, but are shaped by public policy and community supports, as well as by traditions, social values and the economic environment. In highly industrialized and urban areas, family size tends to be smaller than it is in more agricultural and rural areas, where families with many children are more frequent, where women are often engaged in unpaid household production, and where the extended family is an important source of social and economic support. These varying circumstances influence attitudes, cultural norms and the roles related to gender.

Nonetheless, although countries in Central Europe, the Baltics and the western CIS tend to be more industrialized and urban than nations in the south from the Balkans to Central Asia, demographic and family profiles often show striking consistencies among these subregions. In part, this is due to the conformity of approach by governments to family-related policies and investment in education and health services. This has been the result of a common goal of central planning: to expand industrialization by expanding the labour force through the promotion of population growth and the entry of women into the formal economy. So, governments encouraged women to have both babies and jobs, and in areas where the kinship networks were weaker the state provided the childcare bridge that allowed women to manage these competing demands.

High marriage rates and early childbearing

In Western industrialized countries, growing female education and labour market participation rates in recent decades have been accompanied by changing patterns of family formation and reproductive behaviour. Known as the "second demographic transition", the new patterns are characterized by later age at first marriage and childbirth and a diversification of family forms, including more single parents and cohabiting couples. (The "first demographic transition" refers to the decline in fertility associated with the shift from rural agrarian life to urban industrialized society.)

As explored earlier in this Report, women in the region also had good access to education and employment, and, up to 1990, their labour force participation was comparable to or even higher than that in most Western economies. So, is there evidence that trends associated with a "second demographic transition" have occurred? In many important respects, it would appear that the answer is "no". As Figure 3.1 shows, at the onset of the transition, women were entering their first marriage at a relatively young age. The average age was closer to that in Turkey or Greece – countries exhibiting much lower female labour force participation rates, as the previous chapter illustrates – rather than to that in France or Sweden – countries with comparable education and labour patterns.

Not only did women marry early, but marriage was virtually universal. At the beginning of the transition, roughly eight in ten women in the region were married by age 24, compared to two to four in most Western countries. Cohabitation was rare. Many countries had high divorce rates, as in the West, but they also had high remarriage rates, so that women in the region were more likely than Western women to remarry after divorce.

At the outset of transition, women in the region were also bearing children at a relatively young age. In most cases, however, this demographic characteristic was not associated with high fertility rates, as it is in more traditional societies. Figure 3.2 shows that, in the early 1990s, total birth rates in Central Europe, the western CIS and the Baltics were similar to those in Western Europe. At the same time, in contrast to Western Europe, fertility rates among teenagers in the region were strik-

Figure 3.1

Average age of women at first marriage, 1990 (years)

Sources: Statistical Annex, Table 5.2; CE (1998).

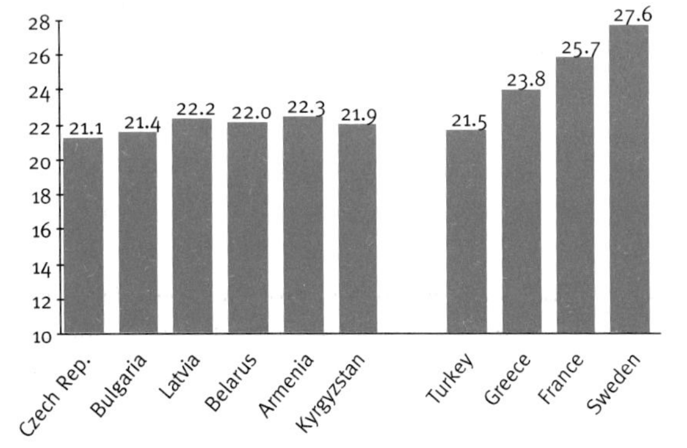

Figure 3.2

Teenage and total birth rates, early 1990s (live births per 1,000 women in relevant age group)

Sources: UN (1997a); MONEE project database.

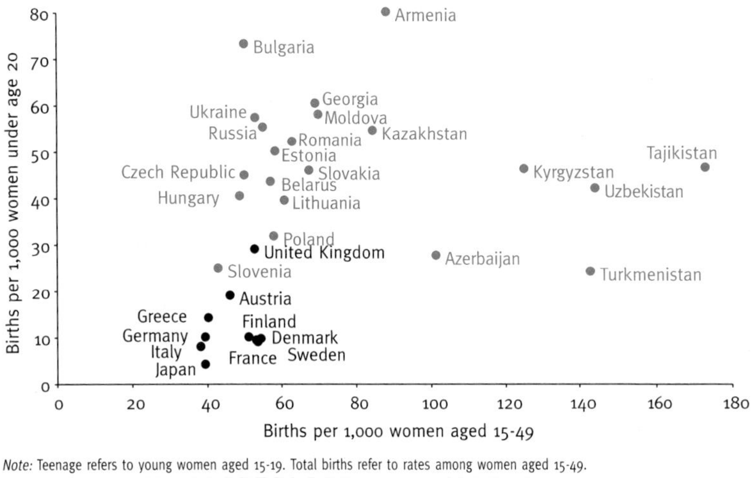

Note: Teenage refers to young women aged 15-19. Total births refer to rates among women aged 15-49.

ingly high. Only Slovenia and, less convincingly, Poland are grouped with Western European countries in the lower left part of the graph where low overall birth rates and low teenage birth rates are represented. Countries in the upper left, including those in the Baltics, the western CIS and parts of Central and Southeastern Europe, present low total birth rates relative to Western Europe, but a range of higher teenage birth rates – up to several times higher.

This difference in teenage birth rates emerged between 1970 and 1990. The rates rose across the former Soviet Union, from 35 to 57 births per 1,000 teenagers in Ukraine for example, while in Central Europe they remained stable or declined, for example in Hungary from 50 to 40 births. In Western countries, the drop was far more dramatic. Thus, in Sweden the rate fell from 34 to 14 births over the same period.

Most countries in Central Asia and the Caucasus still had high birth rates at the beginning of the 1990s, despite the relatively high labour force participation rates among women in Kyrgyzstan, Uzbekistan, Turkmenistan, or Tajikistan. Yet, this part of the region has a wide range of teenage birth rates, from relatively low rates in Turkmenistan and Azerbaijan to extremely high rates in Armenia.

As shown by census data, the countries of the former Soviet Union did experience high single-parent rates even before the pronounced growth in this phenomenon in Western countries. In the early 1970s, single-parent families were more prevalent in Russia (13 percent) and even in Georgia (10 percent) and Turkmenistan (10 percent) than in France (9 percent) or Germany (8 percent).

However, while the share of single-parent families settled around 10 percent of all households with children in the final years of communism (with the exception of the Baltic States), it grew steadily in the West and, in the late 1980s, often exceeded the rates in the transition region, as presented in Figure 3.3.

Liberal family laws and ambitious family policies

The early Soviet marriage code attempted to establish equality between husbands and wives, secularize marriage and make divorce simple. Benefits and taxation were linked to women's employment rather than to their status as spouses. Marriage remained a popular institution, partly because family laws made it easy to enter and to leave a union and partly because the state attached a range of incentives to registered marriage, including better access to housing, in-kind services and cash benefits. Not only did social norms support the tradition of marriage, but the state saw the institution of marriage as a way to produce the next generation of workers. Six of the eight countries in a UN survey conducted one year before the collapse of state socialism were still pursuing pro-natalist objectives in social policies.

The ease of marriage and of divorce and the legal

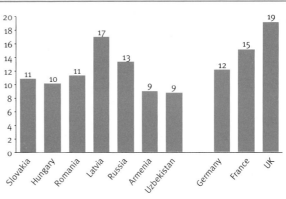

Figure 3.3

Single-parent households, late 1980s (percent of all households with children aged 0-17)
Sources: Klugman and Motivans (1999); McLanahan and Caspar (1995); SOSR (1996); Zamfir and Zamfir (1998); KSH (1995).

Note: Data refer to 1987 for the UK, 1988 for Germany and France, 1989 for Latvia, Russia, Armenia, and Uzbekistan, 1990 for Hungary, 1991 for Slovakia, and 1992 for Romania.

equality in the ownership and division of (patently limited) family assets were favourable conditions for gender equity. However, as Chapter 2 notes, the gender division of household chores and childcare added long hours of unpaid work to women's full-time jobs, a situation exacerbated by the relative lack of consumer appliances. This "double burden" (see Figure 2.2 in Chapter 2) and a relative lack of choice and flexibility in employment may partly explain the anticipation some felt that one of the benefits of the transition would be the opportunity for women to be full-time parents.

Former Soviet leader Mikhail Gorbachev made headlines in 1987 when he said perestroika offered Soviet women what they really wanted – the chance to stay at home with their children. Similarly, a 1988 survey found that the statement "what women really want is a home and children" was endorsed by 75 percent of women and 79 percent of men in Hungary, though it was strongly rejected by Dutch, British and US respondents.

At the onset of the transition, family support programmes were widely available across the region and tended to be generous and comprehensive. Most programmes were designed by central authorities, but were delivered through state enterprises, agricultural collectives and local governments. As Table 3.1 shows, relative public expenditure on cash and in-kind benefits exceeded that in many Western countries. In some ways, countries like Hungary and Czechoslovakia had systems similar to the Scandinavian or French family support model, offering universal family support benefits, generous maternity and parental leave benefits, and services such as widely accessible childcare. Non-cash programmes (such as services and subsidies for child-related goods) were more important in the Soviet Union than in Central or Southeastern Europe, where cash benefits were more popular.

Many programmes, such as childcare and children's summer camps, were attached to the workplace, a circumstance that supported women's participation in the labour force, but also made employment the main access route to childcare and related services. Women were entitled to maternity leave of four to seven months, often at

Public expenditure on family programmes in 1989

(percent of GDP)

Table 3.1

	Czechoslovakia	Hungary	Poland	Sweden	Germany	US
Total	4.4	5.5	3.0	4.4	1.9	0.6
Cash benefits	3.1	4.4	2.3	2.1	1.3	0.3
family/child allowance	2.2	3.0	2.0	0.9	0.9	0.3
maternity and parental leave	0.5	0.8	0.2	1.0	*	*
other family support	0.2	0.5	0.1	0.2	0.2	*
In-kind benefits (mostly childcare)	1.1	1.1	0.7	2.3	0.6	0.2

Sources: OECD (1996); Fajth (1996).

Note: * = low or negligible amount.

full wages. Many countries also offered paid or unpaid parental leave with a guarantee of re-employment. This leave was usually available to either parent and in some countries also to grandparents.

At the beginning of the transition, health and education services were free or available at low cost throughout the region. Kindergarten enrolment was especially high in Central Europe, with four in five children enrolled in 1989. Coverage tended to decline further east: three in five children were enrolled in Russia and Ukraine, and only one in five was enrolled in Central Asia. The quality of public childcare varied widely, too, both across the region and within countries.

While the communist state took an active interest in women and children, the perspective was not invari-

ably family-friendly. In both the education and the child protection systems, the child was seen as an individual in relationship with the state, rather than as a member of a family. Consequently, families were often blamed rather than supported, and not infrequently state institutions were considered preferable.

Numerous supportive services that exist in Western countries – from awareness initiatives and education to counselling and crisis support – were simply missing in Central and Eastern Europe, leaving family members to cope with stress and with mental health and lifestyle problems on their own – a situation that often exposed women and children to higher risks of family violence. Indeed, the nuclear family became a strongly guarded refuge against the pervasive intervention of the state. Given the weakness of kinship networks and the suppression of community life, this retreat could sometimes be a source of tension and isolation.

During the transition, women have faced both opportunities and challenges. The functions of the state are changing; the economy is being transformed, and diversity is flourishing, including the re-emergence of an awareness of national and ethno-cultural identities. These shifts are being reflected in public policies and in the private responses to the new social and economic conditions that are reshaping family life and gender roles.

■

3.2 Changes in Family Formation since 1989

Trends in the way families form, dissolve and re-form have important implications for women's equality. Responsibility for children is a major determinant of women's status in society, and the family is a key social institution through which gender roles and status are communicated and validated.

Prior to the transition, demographic behaviour had a specific profile. Marriage was universal; both marriage and childbearing usually took place at a comparatively young age, and the share of single-parent families was significant (and had been stable since the 1970s). Given this inheritance, how have demographic trends evolved during the transition? How do they match women's aspirations? Are they becoming more like those in Western countries, or have they taken a different path?

A sociological survey conducted at the outset of the transition in Poland, Hungary and Russia, as well as in Germany and Sweden, showed strong differentiation among these countries. For example, especially Polish, but also Hungarian mothers were more likely than mothers in Germany and Sweden to rank family and private life as more important to their identity than work and profes-

sional opportunities. The responses of Russian respondents fell between those in Western and Central Europe.

However, when survey respondents were asked whether women with children or women without children have better lives, only Hungarian women said overwhelmingly (89 percent) that mothers have better lives. They may have been influenced by the family support system in Hungary, the most generous in the region. Polish women were divided, and, interestingly, more than three in five Russian and German women felt that women without children have better lives.

In all countries, most women expressed the desire to maintain an attachment to the labour force. In fact, most mothers in Poland, Hungary and Russia were engaged in full-time employment. However, they showed a strong preference for part-time employment – a reality in Western countries, where the majority of mothers with small children were working part time.

While these survey results can be interpreted in many ways, they suggest that, despite women's significant commitment to labour force participation, they consider family life and children very important. It appears that women feel torn between the competing interests of work and family.

Large shifts
in demographic behaviour

The economic and social changes during the transition have been accompanied by huge demographic shifts. Birth rates have plummeted across the region, and the marriage rate is down substantially in almost every country. Divorce initially increased in countries with already high divorce rates. The share of teenage births and births outside marriage has risen in some cases, and so has the prevalence of single-parent households. The deterioration in adult life expectancy in several countries has contributed to and may also have been partly caused by the greater fragility of families.

Table 3.2 summarizes current marriage, fertility and divorce rates, as well as overall changes in these rates since 1989. At the level of sub-regional averages, the data make the following main points.

- Marriage, fertility and divorce rates were far from identical across the region in 1989. All parts of the former Soviet Union – the Baltics, western CIS, the Caucasus, and Central Asia – had very high marriage rates. However, these high marriage rates were associated with high divorce rates only in western CIS and the Baltics and with high or moderate fertility levels only in Central Asia and the Caucasus. Most countries in Central and Eastern Europe exhibited low fertility rates (with the notable exception of Albania and the southern parts of former Yugoslavia).

- Substantial change has taken place in all areas of the region, and the patterns and directions of change often show a striking consistency across all sub-regions. The number of births has decreased everywhere. In Central Europe, for example, where fertility rates were already low, the drop in relative terms has been similar to that in Central Asia. Marriage rates have declined in line with fertility rates in most countries.

- The magnitude of the change has been dramatic at times. Marriage rates have halved in the Baltics and the Caucasus – sub-regions in which countries have very different cultural traditions. Both areas have experienced large population movements and ethnic enmity, even conflict, in addition to economic hardships. Here (as well as in Romania which had aggressive pro-natalist policies before the transition), the number of births fell sharply after 1989.

- By contrast, divorce trends have taken different directions. In the Baltic countries, divorce rates soared during the mid-1990s before decreasing thereafter. In some countries, such as those in

Central Europe, divorce rates fell during the initial years of the transition before rising more recently.

Marriages rates – falling sometimes after an initial positive "euphoria" effect at the outset of transition – are now stabilizing in some countries. The decline in marriages (and remarriages) can be interpreted as a delay in family formation due to economic circumstances. However, it is more difficult to judge whether this change also entails a more profound shift in lifestyle patterns. For example, in the Caucasus and Central Asia, the delays in marriage may be due partly to the inability of families to finance the traditional marriage feast or to pay dowries. In Central Europe and the Baltics, they may reflect a decision by couples to live together prior to marriage or to pursue education or career opportunities before marriage.

Figure 3.4 presents another measure of family instability – the general divorce rate, or annual number of divorces per 100 marriages. The diagram reinforces the finding that regional differences in divorce rates have grown during the transition. In countries with the lowest initial divorce rates – Uzbekistan and FYR Macedonia in the graph – divorces fell as much as or more than marriages. The general divorce rate climbed substantially in western CIS and the Baltic States. In Estonia over 1995-97, there

	Crude marriage rate (per 1,000 population)			Total fertility rate (children per woman)			Crude divorce rate (per 1,000 population)		
	1989	1997	% change	1989	1997	% change	1989	1997	% change
Central Europe	7.0	5.2	-26	1.95	1.37	-30	2.1	2.1	2
Former Yugoslavia	6.3	5.3	-5	1.83	1.65	-10	0.8	0.8	1
Southeastern Europe	7.1	5.4	-31	2.05	1.21	-41	1.3	1.6	-12
Baltics	8.9	4.3	-52	2.08	1.25	-40	3.8	3.1	-19
Western CIS	9.4	6.9	-27	2.10	1.81	-14	3.5	3.7	5
Caucasus	8.4	4.2	-49	2.70	1.76	-35	1.4	0.6	-57
Central Asia	9.8	8.6	-31	4.01	2.89	-28	1.8	1.7	-7

Table 3.2

Summary of main trends in family formation, 1989-97

Source: MONEE project database.

Note: Rates are unweighted national averages. Marriage and divorce rates calculated using the 15-59 population show larger variations across regions due to different population structures, but the levels of change over the period are similar. Former Yugoslavia excludes Bosnia-Herzegovina. Southeastern Europe excludes Albania. End year is 1995 for Central Asia. Starting year is 1991 for former Yugoslavia. See Glossary for the definition of total fertility rate.

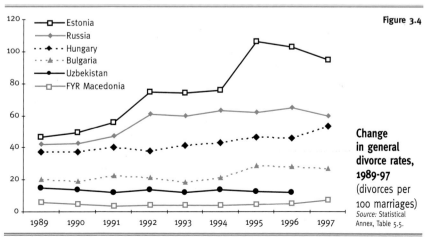

Figure 3.4

Change in general divorce rates, 1989-97 (divorces per 100 marriages)

Source: Statistical Annex, Table 5.5.

were as many divorces as marriages. This reflects a decline in marriage and an increase in divorce and signals a growing prevalence of cohabitation.

Aside from the steep drop in marriages, several factors are contributing to the higher general divorce rates. The increase in family breakups in some countries during the transition may have resulted from the economic and social stress of unemployment and poverty, changes in lifestyles and social values, liberal family laws, and newly streamlined divorce procedures.

Trends in marriage and divorce have also contributed to plunging fertility rates, which have continued to fall in most countries even in recent years. Figure 3.5 shows the pattern of the changes over time in a cross-section of countries.

The sharp drop in fertility in the region has gained international attention and, in some countries, has provoked calls for pro-natalist policies and a return to conventional family models. In some, it has undermined the political support for better access to modern family planning, an issue of concern for women's health, as Chapter 4 details.

It is worth noting that fertility rates in the region began to decline before 1989. At the start of the transition, fertility rates were already below the population-replacement rate in some countries (the dotted line in

Figure 3.5). It could be argued that, in the longer view, the trends in the region are part of the historical downward drift in fertility rates among industrialized countries, or that they are part of a response to the baby-booms occurring in certain countries in the 1980s.

Still, in many countries fertility is now at extremely low levels in absolute terms, and, if this trend continues, it will have significant social and economic repercussions. This may also reflect the heavy price women and families have paid as they try to support their children despite the economic hardships of the transition. The rise at the beginning of the transition in the number of children born in countries like Hungary, the Czech Republic and Uzbekistan suggests that there was an initial anticipation of a more child-friendly environment, though such an anticipation quickly faded.

Contrasting changes in age at first marriage

The average age at first marriage is a useful indicator of women's circumstances, with both positive and negative implications. In North America and Western Europe, the age at first marriage for women has risen during the past few decades. This is linked to the growing economic opportunities for women and the greater social acceptance of cohabitation and non-marital unions.

Marriage has been a popular institution across the transition region, with women tending to marry and to have a first child at relatively young ages. Until 1993-94, the average age of women at first marriage remained largely the same and even declined in some countries, including Russia. This stability suggests that marriage rates fell among all age groups. In the last few years, however, the average age has started to climb. Figure 3.6 shows that the average had increased in 9 of 15 countries of the region between 1989 and 1997, but women were still marrying at a younger age relative to the situation in Western countries. For example, the average age in the European Union was 26.3 years in 1994.

The average age of women at first marriage rose in the Czech Republic, Hungary, Slovenia, Croatia, FR Yugoslavia, Bulgaria, Estonia, and Latvia and stayed relatively the same in western CIS, the Caucasus and Central Asia. Slovakia, where data are available only to 1994, reported a significant drop in the age of women at first marriage – from 22.9 to 21.3 years, a decline echoed among men.

It is worthwhile investigating how the gender gap in age at first marriage has changed. It is conventional around the world that men are older on average than women at marriage – perhaps because of long-held perceptions that an older age for the man reflects economic advantage, while a younger age for the woman suggests more reproductive years ahead in which to produce many children.

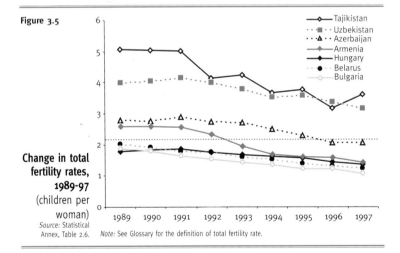

Figure 3.5

Change in total fertility rates, 1989-97 (children per woman)
Source: Statistical Annex, Table 2.6.

Note: See Glossary for the definition of total fertility rate.

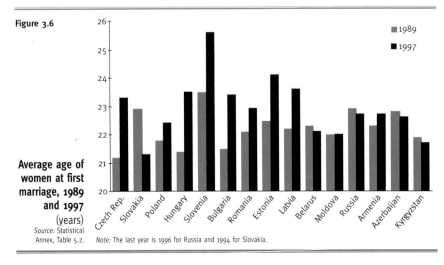

Figure 3.6

Average age of women at first marriage, 1989 and 1997 (years)
Source: Statistical Annex, Table 5.2.

Note: The last year is 1996 for Russia and 1994 for Slovakia.

In 1989, the gender difference in marriage age was around two years in western CIS, the Baltic States and Central Europe – a small gap by international standards. Little change had taken place in these countries by 1997: the age gap was about the same or less, except in Russia and Belarus, where it grew slightly. However, in countries in the southern part of the region, the gender gap was initially about four years, and recent data, where available, tend to show it widening.

Increases in non-marital births and cohabitation

Previous Regional Monitoring Reports called attention to the rising numbers of children born outside marriage. Figure 3.7 shows that the share of births to unmarried mothers ranges from less than 5 percent in Turkmenistan in Central Asia to more than 50 percent in Estonia in the Baltics, where it has doubled since 1989.

The increases indicated in Figure 3.7 imply that during the 1990s the number of births to unmarried parents – single mothers or cohabiting partners – has declined much less than the number of births to married couples. One influential element in this outcome is the larger share of first-borns among all births. Since 1989, more parents who already have one or two children have been deciding to delay or forgo the birth of an additional child. The share of first-borns in Russia, for example, rose from 46 to 59 percent between 1989 and 1997. Parents having their first child are more likely to be unmarried than are those having a second, third, or fourth child. Moreover, the incidence of single motherhood and cohabitation has gone up in many countries.

These factors make it difficult to interpret extra-marital birth rates. The implications of childbirth outside a registered marriage are certainly quite different for women and their children depending on whether a mother is alone or cohabiting. Unfortunately, demographic registers in the region still largely overlook the fact that marriage is becoming a poor indicator of parental partnerships. In some Western countries, about half the births outside marriage are registered to both parents who are living at the same address.

Figure 3.8 summarizes the results of family and fertility studies from a selection of Western, Central and Eastern European countries in the mid-1990s. It allows a comparison of the incidence of cohabitation that, as it turns out, varies greatly. More than 60 percent of women in Estonia and almost half in Slovenia reported a cohabitation experience by age 25, rates which are relatively high by Western European standards. In other

countries, such as Poland, cohabitation represented no more than a small percentage of all couples in the mid-1990s, a rate similar to that reported for Italy. However, in all transition countries, only a small share of women were bearing children during cohabitation. This suggests that, as in Western Europe, cohabitation often serves as a sort of "trial marriage".

The data on cohabitation obscure considerable differences in the behaviour of younger and older generations. The 1991 census in Slovenia reported that about 5 percent of women aged 20-34 were cohabiting and that 77 percent of these were living with a partner and a child or children, compared to less than 2 percent of women aged 35 or older. Data from a 1997 fertility study in Estonia showed that only about 15 percent of married women aged 15-19 had married without first experiencing cohabitation, compared to more than 60 percent of married women aged 45-49.

However, it appears that births to cohabiting mothers are relatively uncommon and so do not account for the rising ratios of non-marital births across the region (Figure 3.7). In Slovenia, where cohabitation rates grew rapidly, 13 percent of all births in 1996 were to unmarried couples

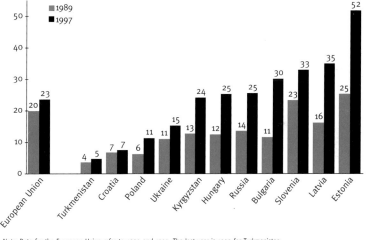

Figure 3.7

Non-marital births, 1989 and 1997 (percent of total live births)
Sources: Statistical Annex, Table 2.4; Eurostat (1997a).

Note: Data for the European Union refer to 1990 and 1995. The last year is 1995 for Turkmenistan.

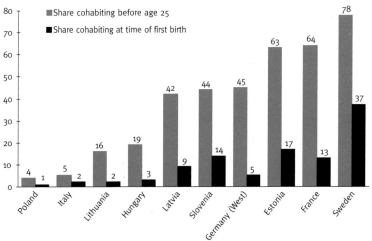

Figure 3.8

Cohabitation in Eastern and Western Europe up to the mid-1990s (percent of all women aged 25-29)
Source: Klijzing and Macura (1995).

Note: Data refer to 1991 for Poland, 1992 for Germany (West), 1992-93 for Hungary and Sweden, 1994 for Estonia and France, 1994-95 for Lithuania, 1995 for Latvia and Slovenia, and 1995-96 for Italy.

living together. This compares with the 32 percent share accounted for by all out-of-wedlock births in that year, suggesting that cohabitation explains barely more than one-third of all non-marital births. However, in most cases of extra-marital birth in Slovenia, fathers do register themselves as a parent of the child even if they do not live with the mother of the child. This is not the case in Russia, for example, where about half the births outside marriage are not registered to both parents.

High rates of teenage childbearing

As noted, women in the region marry and have a first child at a relatively young age. While the average marriage age has climbed recently, the average age at first birth has remained the same across much of the region and, in several cases, has even gone down.

Figure 3.9 charts teenage birth rates during the transition. It confirms that the rates were high in the region at the outset of transition in 1989. In four of six sub-regions – the Baltics, western CIS, the Caucasus, and Central Asia – teenage births rose immediately after transition, even against a backdrop of falling fertility rates. Since 1992, teenage birth rates have declined and in 1997 were lower – if only slightly in some sub-regions – than they had been in 1989. Still, the rates remain well above those in Western Europe.

Teenage parents and their children are at higher risk of poverty because they have typically had less opportunity to develop their "human capital" through education and work experience. Generally, fertility rates are inversely related to education or socio-economic status, that is, the lower the level of education, the higher the level of fertility. Early childbearing limits the opportunities of girls and young women to pursue education and careers. This, in turn, may promote a decision to have a greater number of children. In effect, teenage motherhood can restrict the choices available to these young women and make it more likely they will require social supports.

Figure 3.10 shows, for a selection of countries, that the share of teenage births among total births climbed early in the transition and has since receded, but, with the exception of a few countries, like the Czech Republic, is still higher than it was in 1989. In some countries, like Azerbaijan, the share of teenage births has continued to rise. Sharp drops since mid-transition have brought rates in the Czech Republic, Slovenia and Croatia close to those in Western Europe.

In Bulgaria and Romania, teenage fertility is still very high. The narrower economic opportunities and the influence of traditional values among the Roma ethnicity in these countries may play a part in this outcome. Early childbearing, large families and a pronounced gender division in household labour are frequently reported especially among Roma families in Central and Southeastern Europe.

For example, in a 1992 study in Bulgaria, more than half the Roma women who responded said they hoped to have three or more children, more than double the number desired by ethnic Turkish women, another minority in Bulgaria, or by ethnic Bulgarian women. Roma women tend to start having children in their early teens and have many children, often with a relatively short interval between births. These young women face daunting economic disadvantages, and, as a 1995 survey noted, behaviours such as early sexual activity (at younger than age 15), low educational attainment and extra-marital birth are frequently transferred from one generation to the next.

Of course, high teenage birth rates also mean high rates of teenage sexual activity and pregnancy and, in many countries of the region, high rates of adolescent abortion. In four countries, each year more than one in 10 teenagers becomes pregnant. (The issue of family planning and abortion is discussed in Chapter 4.)

Before the transition most teenage births occurred within marriage. This suggests that both the marriages and the pregnancies were planned or that the pregnancies triggered the marriages. Studies in the Czech Republic and Russia show that the majority of babies born to teenage mothers were conceived before the parents married.

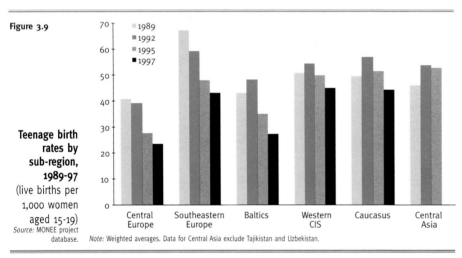

Figure 3.9

Teenage birth rates by sub-region, 1989-97 (live births per 1,000 women aged 15-19)
Source: MONEE project database.   Note: Weighted averages. Data for Central Asia exclude Tajikistan and Uzbekistan.

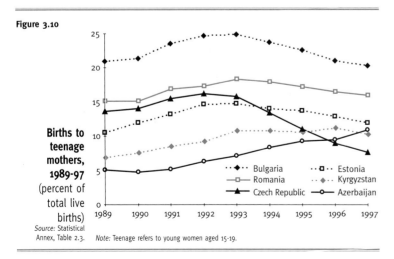

Figure 3.10

Births to teenage mothers, 1989-97 (percent of total live births)
Source: Statistical Annex, Table 2.3.   Note: Teenage refers to young women aged 15-19.

There is evidence, however, that during the transition there has been less inclination to marry because of pregnancy. Figure 3.11 shows that the share of extra-marital births among teenagers rose substantially between 1989 and 1997. Births among unmarried teenage mothers now represent more than three of four teenage births in Slovenia and Estonia. In most countries, meanwhile, the share of births to unmarried women has increased among both teenagers and older women.

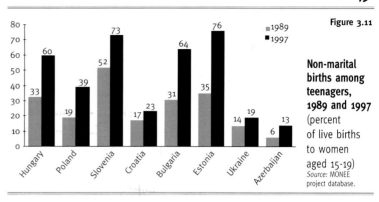

Figure 3.11

Non-marital births among teenagers, 1989 and 1997 (percent of live births to women aged 15-19)
Source: MONEE project database.

Changes in family and household structure

Demographic trends such as the rising share of births outside marriage, increasing divorce and, in several countries, premature parental mortality are having an impact on household structure. The extent to which the number and share of children living in various types of family arrangements have grown during the transition is difficult to gauge because the relevant data are usually collected in population censuses which only take place periodically. In countries where data are available, there are signs that more and more children are not living in dual-parent households, but in single-parent households or extended family households.

For example, a comparison of the data from the 1989 population census and the 1994 micro-census in Russia shows a rise in the share of single-parent households from 14 to over 16 percent. In addition, a growing number of single mothers were living with their parents. These two factors were each responsible for about half the increase of 1.7 million in the children in Russia living in households without both parents in 1994 relative to 1989.

It is difficult to judge how much single parenthood has grown in the region in general, but it appears that, even in countries where divorce rates and non-marital birth rates are lower, there has been an increase in single parenthood. In Poland, for example, the number of children living in single-parent families rose by more than 100,000 between 1988 and 1995, with almost 12 percent of children living with single mothers (while only 1 percent were living with single fathers).

Single-parent families are hardly a new phenomenon in the region. What has changed during the transition is that single parents, most of whom are women, face a tighter job market and less accessible childcare, including after-school care. For women, balancing their roles as breadwinners and primary caregivers has become especially difficult. Unemployment, poverty and income disparity have risen at the same time that the presence of the state in social protection has weakened. As state intervention shrinks, more responsibility is shifted to individuals, who, in turn, appear to rely more heavily on kinship systems and local support networks.

Social protection legislation in the region usually defines single mothers as women whose children have been born or adopted outside marriage. In reality, however, divorce is also a main route into single parenthood. During the transition, the relative number of children experiencing parental divorce has increased in many countries. (See Statistical Annex, Table 5.6.) The number is high in countries where divorce rates are high, such as the Baltics and western CIS, and low where divorce is less common, such as former Yugoslavia, the Caucasus and Central Asia. However, several Central European countries show a mixed profile of low divorce rates with high rates of children involved in divorce, suggesting that couples with more children may face greater chances of divorce.

■

3.3 The Changing Landscape of Family Policies

Before the transition, family law accorded women and men equal rights, and families received considerable public support through cash and non-cash benefits. Women's family commitments and functions were influenced by these policies, but also by public health and education services which were widely accessible and which were offered free or at low cost.

However, this seemingly strong network of family supports was particularly vulnerable to the forces of transition because it was financed and operated by the state and because many of the benefits and services were delivered through the workplace. This points to the need for reforms. Furthermore, given the emerging conditions, the family laws drafted under the former governments and still in force do not pay adequate attention to the new dimension that private property brings to the issue of family assets and to the matter of private child support to be paid by partners. Also missing is the whole environment of intermediary support and prevention services, including social care and counselling, that strengthen families and bolster the capacity of women to prevent or cope with risk situations in the household.

The weakening state role in income support

A sociological survey carried out in Poland, Hungary and Russia around 1990-91, near the outset of transition, included a question on the importance of various family policy measures. More than half of the mothers with small children in the survey ranked income support (or tax relief) first. Only a small share of women gave top priority to more childcare services, and fewer still said measures encouraging men to take on more family responsibilities were the most important.

In the early years of transition, public policy steps were taken to improve income supports. Most countries in the region introduced or enhanced universal cash benefits to families with children. The intention was to cushion the impact of the removal of the non-cash support, such as price subsidies, that came with market reforms. However, high inflation and the erosion of employment-related services reduced the mitigating effect. Nevertheless, a World Bank study on five transition countries found that the cash benefits did help families, especially poor ones, and in some countries were more effective at reaching poor families than unemployment benefits or targeted social assistance.

Using data from the Luxembourg Income Study, other research revealed that child poverty in relative terms was often more well contained in the post-communist region than in Western countries. (The research defined child poverty in terms of equivalent per-capita disposable household income which is less than 50 percent of the overall adjusted median.) In the early 1990s, Czech or Slovak children were to be found below this threshold less often than children in neighbouring Austria or Germany. Hungarian and Polish children with two parents were at lower risk of being in relative poverty (respectively, 11 percent in 1994 and 14 percent in 1992) than children with two parents in the UK (18 percent in 1995). While several factors may have been responsible for this outcome, it is clear that efforts during the first years of transition to protect the generous pre-transition

levels of family benefits had an important effect. It is worth noting, however, that child poverty rates in dual-parent households were much higher in Russia even in these relative terms: 26 percent in 1995, about twice as high as in Hungary or Poland.

Generous public transfers are usually critical to the efforts of single parents to keep their households out of poverty. The low incidence of poverty among children in single-parent families in Sweden or Denmark is generally attributed to generous welfare systems. In this regard, research has found a striking difference between the post-communist countries and Western countries outside Scandinavia. The child poverty rates among the children of single parents in Poland, Hungary and Russia during the early 1990s did not appear to be very different from those among children living with couples, but in Germany, the UK and the US the children of single parents are at much higher (40-60 percent) risk of poverty.

Families in the region received a large part of their child-related benefits – larger than in Western countries (see Table 3.1) – through regular family allowances. As the transition progressed, countries spent relatively less and less. For example, in 1997 the Czech Republic spent 0.8 percent of GDP on family allowances, half what it had spent before transition; Bulgaria spent 0.6 percent of GDP on allowances in 1997, compared to 2.2 percent in 1991.

Table 3.3 compares the per-child family allowance to the average wage for eight transition countries. The results show considerable erosion of the value of the benefit in all countries. Allowances are especially small relative to wages in those very countries – in Southeastern Europe and the former Soviet Union – where wages have also plunged in real terms. This implies an even bigger fall in the purchasing power of family benefits than the figures indicate.

Over the course of the transition, most countries have switched from universal cash benefits to family allowances targeted at low-income households, and in some countries, such as Georgia or Armenia, family allowances have been dropped altogether. In a few countries, targeted coverage has helped the benefit value of allowances to rebound. However, as the international experience shows and studies in the transition region confirm, moving from a model of universal benefits to one of social assistance entitlement raises the risk that a portion of the needy population will be excluded.

A survey of 10 countries that was carried out for this Report found that it was the mother who actually received the family allowance, usually attached to her wages. Research in Western countries documents the advantages of this arrangement for child welfare. For example, a UK study concluded that shifting the benefit from men to women

Table 3.3

The value of family allowance benefits, 1990-97

(per-child benefit for couples with two children, percent average wage)

	1990	1991	1992	1993	1994	1995	1996	1997
Slovakia	10.3	9.1	7.4	5.9	9.2	8.9	8.1	7.1
Hungary	16.1	14.3	13.9	12.0	9.6	8.2	6.8	7.7
Slovenia	9.5	9.0	8.1	9.2	8.2	7.5	6.3	5.6
Estonia	–	–	10.0	8.3	6.3	5.3	4.9	4.7
Latvia	–	–	10.8	8.8	5.8	4.6	5.1	4.0
Russia	–	–	10.2	3.5	5.5	6.6	6.3	6.1
Azerbaijan	–	–	–	5.4	3.7	2.5	7.6	6.4
Turkmenistan	–	–	–	–	1.9	2.7	1.7	1.3

Source: MONEE project database.

had a measurable positive effect on child-related family expenditures. In this light, reducing public spending on family allowances can mean less money for women.

Likewise, the shift from universal to targeted family allowances in the region may actually leave many women in a less autonomous financial position. For example, in countries where public administration is now left to local officials, women may be subjected to the discretion of patriarchal community structures and suffer when allowances are distributed in favour of more "traditional" households headed by men.

On the other hand, the effective targeting of public benefits can help fill the financial gap left when non-custodial parents, most often fathers, default on child support. The increases in divorce and single parenthood suggest that more women are finding themselves in this difficult position, as Box 3.1 discusses. Certainly, public social assistance is not an adequate replacement for the private support to which children are entitled and which parents have the right to expect and the responsibility to provide. However, establishing paternity, setting appropriate levels of support and enforcing payment are often difficult and need to be addressed through concerted effort. An intermediate solution would involve differentiating benefit values so as to favour vulnerable groups. Thus, in Russia, never-married or widowed single mothers are entitled to double benefits, and divorced parents whose partners default on child support receive 1.5 times the allowance.

However, substantial erosion in the value of family cash benefits limit the effectiveness of targeting. Since

most single-parent households are he[...] erosion raises concerns about th[...] poverty" and about the implications [...] child development.

Using absolute poverty thresh[...] found that the poverty rates among [...] gle-parent households had risen m[...] rates among children living with both parents, particularly, in recent years, among children under age 6, as shown in Figure 3.12. In 1996, more than one in three children under age 6 who were living with a single parent were living in poverty.

Although this finding cannot be generalized to other countries, it is reasonable to suppose that single-parent families everywhere face greater hardship. This may also explain why single mothers increasingly live in extended family households in many countries. There is

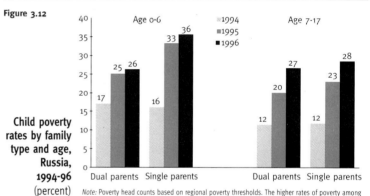

Figure 3.12

Child poverty rates by family type and age, Russia, 1994-96 (percent)

Source: Klugman and Kolev (1999).

Note: Poverty head counts based on regional poverty thresholds. The higher rates of poverty among single-parent families are also observed using the national poverty line adjusted for equivalence scales and economies of scale.

Box 3.1

Default on child support by non-custodial parents

Securing child support from a parent who does not live with the child is often difficult. Given the demographic trends in the region during transition, including increased divorce and single parenthood, it is likely that more women and children are facing the financial challenges of inadequate child support.

In many countries, the state provides a child support payment in case of default by the non-custodial parent – the father in the vast majority of cases – and uses the courts to collect arrears. In Bulgaria, this approach appears to be effective, and the number of court cases for non-payment of child support has declined since 1989.

According to survey data in Russia, in almost one in five divorces the level of child support is determined by the agreement of the parents and without court involvement. In such cases, the average support payment has been twice as much as that in court-ordered cases and is paid more regularly. In general, however, the survey reveals a bleaker picture for many custodial parents and their children after divorce:

more than half the children do not benefit from child support, and, on average, payments are one to two years in arrears.

It seems likely that the incidence of non-payment of child support has risen during the transition, and available data on court cases for non-payment seem to confirm this contention. Lithuania, Estonia, Russia, and Poland report that the number of cases grew twofold between 1989 and 1997, and Belarus registered three and a half times as many cases. However, in other countries, such as Latvia, Bulgaria and Hungary, fewer cases have reached court. This may simply reflect less will to take such cases to court, or it may mean that such cases have a lower priority in over-burdened justice systems.

Certainly, better enforcement of child support payments requires individual and political will, as well as an efficient administrative system and coordination among the institutional actors involved – the judiciary, the police, social welfare agencies, and local authorities. Still, the most important factor is changing social attitudes to recognize parental rights and responsibilities.

so a greater chance now that very young children are living with single mothers who have never married or cohabited. Older children are more likely to be living with mothers who are divorced or widowed. This distinction may be important in shaping the levels of risk and therefore also in the development of policy options.

Income tax policies affect family income and can thus influence family decisions related to women's participation in the labour force. Accordingly, they have implications for gender equity and for the distribution of net household incomes, though these are often less overt than the impact of policies on cash benefits.

Personal income tax systems in which the tax unit is the individual rather than the household tend to promote female employment, especially if the pooling of the income of spouses for tax purposes is not allowed. In contrast, tax systems based on family units, pooling, or allowances for low-income spouses create incentives for the lower income earner in the household – most often women – to take other than full-time work or withdraw from the labour market entirely.

Government revenues from income taxes are often relatively modest in the region, and the pressure for tax reform is bound to grow. As wage taxes are replaced by income taxes and as the tax base expands, the importance of ensuring that the tax structure is fair and efficient will also rise.

The brief review of existing tax arrangements in the region provided in Box 3.2 suggests that current tax systems are friendly to women's labour force participation and tend to offer concessions to families with children. However, it appears that the concessions benefit mainly middle-income rather than low-income households and that the tax systems do little to help single parents meet those costs of running a home that are similar for all households, including households with more earners.

Maternity and parental leaves: childcare choices

Balancing work and family responsibilities is a major challenge for most parents, but especially for women. A variety of measures – maternity and parental leaves and nursery and kindergarten services – exists in the region to help alleviate the conflict between work and family roles. Most options involve some kind of explicit or implicit income support, and most have a gender dimension.

Maternity and parental leaves serve different purposes and have distinctive gender implications. Maternity leave (which, as Table 3.4 shows, usually covers a period of months before and after childbirth) is based on an immediate concern for the physical survival and health of mother and child and, as such, is similar to a social insurance benefit. In keeping with this goal, maternity leave offers full-wage compensation or sick leave pay and is available only to women.

Extended maternity leaves or parental leaves, on the other hand, are generally considered more custodial in nature and therefore less significant for the well-being of the child, despite growing evidence underlining the

---

Box 3.2

Income tax systems and family support

A survey carried out for this Report on 10 countries in the region (the Czech Republic, FR Yugoslavia, Bulgaria, Romania, Estonia, Russia, Ukraine, Georgia, Uzbekistan, and Tajikistan) found that most countries levy taxes on the income of individuals. Only Estonia permits wives and husbands to pool their incomes and tax-free allowances. (Romania is reportedly considering a similar scheme.)

When the tax-rate structure is progressive (the rates increase with income level), pooling can substantially reduce the total tax paid by spouses with unequal incomes. In Estonia, the tax rate is constant above the tax-free threshold, so that the advantages of pooling are limited. In many countries, couples with businesses can choose which family member pays the tax on the business income, effectively permitting pooling of this part of household income.

Progressive tax systems often also provide concessions to taxpayers with higher incomes. Most countries provide tax allowances to persons with dependent children, reducing the income subject to tax. However,

in Russia and Ukraine this gain is offset by a reduction in the tax allowance for higher income earners. Tax breaks increase with the number of children, except in Estonia and Georgia. Romania levies an additional tax of 10 percent on people with no dependent children. While it is usually left to the spouses to decide which of them takes advantage of the concessions, in none of the countries surveyed is this option available to cohabiting partners. Also, none allow tax credits for children. Such credits reduce the tax payable by a constant amount, irrespective of income, and so represent a relatively greater benefit to lower income earners.

In many countries, taxpayers are entitled to a tax allowance for low-income spouses that is similar to the allowance for dependent children. This is the case in the Czech Republic, Russia, Tajikistan, and FR Yugoslavia. Only Uzbekistan gives tax concessions to single parents in addition to general concessions for dependent children. In Uzbekistan, single mothers with two or more children under age 16 do not have to pay taxes on income up to four times the minimum wage.

Table 3.4

Main features of maternity leave schemes in selected countries, 1998

	Duration	Value	Eligibility	Changes since 1989
Czech Republic	196 days (259 days for multiple births and for single mothers)	67% of last wage	270 days of health insurance eligibility in last 2 years	1993: cut in replacement rate from 90% to 67%; benefit ceiling cut from 162 to 131 crowns 1994: ceiling raised to 186 crowns, but not indexed
Slovakia	196 days	90% of last wage	270 days of health insurance eligibility in last 2 years	Benefit calculated from maximum daily wage; since 1989 it has gradually risen from 150 to 250 crowns
Poland	112 days for 1st child, 140 days for 2nd, 3rd, etc. child	100% of last wage	Linked to employment	–
Hungary	168 days (28+140)	60-70% of last wage depending on length of employment	180 days of employment in last 2 years	Replacement rates lowered from 65-100% to 60-70% of last wage
FR Yugoslavia	393 days (28+365)	100% of last wage; 80% for 4th child	Linked to employment; reduced benefit available on social assistance basis	1992: leave extended from 270 to 365 days
Albania	365 days (35+330)	First 185 days: 80% of salary in last year, then 50%	Employment record more than 1 year	1994: duration of 2nd part of leave raised from 6 to 12 months
Bulgaria	120-80 days, depending on number of children	100% of last wage; minimum wage for uninsured mothers	Available on both social insurance and social assistance basis	–
Romania	112 days (56+56)	50-85% of last wage, depending on time employed; 94% for 3rd or following child	Linked to full-time employment	–
Estonia	126 days (70+56), or 70+70 in special cases	100% of last wage (average of last 2 months of employment)	Linked to employment	1993: leave extended from 56+56 and 57+70
Lithuania	126 days (70+56)	100% of last wage; 60% of last wage until child is age 1	Linked to employment	1991: benefit indexed to state minimum subsistence level
Latvia	126 days (70+56), linked to prenatal checkups	100% of last wage	Linked to employment	March 1991: period before birth raised from 56 to 70 days
Belarus	126 (70+56) to 140 days, depending on number of children	100% of last wage	Linked to employment	1991: benefit indexed, and period before birth raised from 56 to 70 days
Russia	140 days (70+70)	100% of last wage	Linked to employment	1992: increase in duration from 112 days 1993: extended to women laid off during pregnancy 1995: extended to full-time students 1997: leave extended to 156 days for multiple births
Ukraine	112 days (60+56), 60+70, depending on number of children, health	100% of last wage	Linked to employment	1991: leave raised from 112 to 126 days; increase from 50% to 100% of last wage, depending on length of employment
Armenia	140-80 days	–	Linked to employment	1991: leave raised from 122 to 140 days
Georgia	126 days (70+56)	100% of last wage	Linked to employment	–
Uzbekistan	126 days (70+56)	100% of last wage	Linked to employment	Since 1991, financed from pension fund
Tajikistan	140 days (70+70)	100% of last wage (paid in full, regardless of actual leave used)	Linked to employment	–

Sources: UNICEF (1997a); Posarac (1998); Papp (1998); Kupriyanova (1998); MEG (1998); Marnie (1998); ABW Khujand (1998).

importance of early childhood development. Parental leave in the region is most often available after maternity leave expires. It can be taken by either parent and typically offers time off work and a flat-rate benefit until the child is 2 or 3 years old. In some countries, like Bulgaria, a grandparent can also exercise this leave option. Parental leaves usually provide a guarantee of re-employment and can be used as a tool to reduce the labour force, at least in the short term.

Certainly, these leave options place less demand on government budgets than did the former widespread practice of providing nurseries for infants and toddlers, and many parents prefer staying home with young children, especially given the rising concerns about the quality of public care in the region. However, access to low-cost public childcare is important for parents, especially mothers who are raising children alone, have weak social support networks, or have low incomes and face pressure to return to work soon after childbirth. Kindergartens and pre-schools – usually available for children from age 3 until they enter primary school – not only help parents return to work, but also help children develop cognitive and social skills and prepare for school.

The fact that maternity entitlements – generous by international standards – have remained relatively untouched in the region since transition began indicates that governments recognize the importance of this support. Only a few countries, like the Czech Republic and Hungary, have trimmed benefit entitlements.

However, with the emergence of the private sector, it remains to be seen how maternity and parental leaves will fare. Employers may associate indirect costs (for example replacement workers) with these leaves, and this may fuel discriminatory practices in hiring, promotion and layoffs. The length of leaves may also become an issue. The amount of time off allowed has not been cut back in any country and has even been extended in some. In Russia, for example, the maternity leave has been raised from 16 to 20 weeks since 1992 and, in 1997, was further extended in special cases, such as multiple births and birth problems. Overall, it seems that governments are creating a generous framework for family-related leaves, but that the actual terms are being nego-

tiated at the individual level directly between employers and employees.

This situation puts many parents in a poor bargaining position, especially working women, who are still the primary users of family leaves. One study has found a growing gap since 1989 between parents who are entitled to benefits and those who actually take advantage of the benefits. In the Czech Republic, for example, 23 percent of the maternity leave days permitted by law remained unused in 1993, compared to only 5 percent four years earlier. This was partly due to women returning from leave early. Since maternity benefits are typically delivered through the workplace, the loss of jobs in the region has also affected women's access to these benefits. As a result, countries like Bulgaria or Lithuania have introduced maternity benefits on a social assistance basis as well. In some countries of the former Soviet Union, maternity benefits are, like wages, in arrears, and the value of maternity benefits has frequently eroded with high inflation.

Figure 3.13 compares the share of children looked after by parents on leave and the share of those cared for in nurseries in Poland – two childcare options available after maternity leave expires. The graph reflects a trend seen in many countries: a shift from nursery care to parental leave. The big surge in parental leave around 1991-92 in Poland clearly reflects government efforts to buffer the impact of cutbacks in workplace nurseries by promoting parental leave.

As with maternity leave, extended parental leave can have both positive and negative effects for women. The leave may provide an effective bridge between the workplace and home, but not without consequences for careers and earnings. It is predominantly women who take advantage of parental leave, and there are differences among the women who do. Women with good employment opportunities are less likely to take the full parental leave because the extended absence disrupts their career development. In Poland, more than two-thirds of women with higher education returned to work before the end of their parental leave.

Even though the law creates the basis for equal opportunity in parental leave, male participation remains negligible, often less than 1 percent (although some countries report a slight rise in recent years). Men's relatively higher wages and social expectations as regards gender roles influence this outcome, but laws and public attitudes can also reinforce it. For example, in some countries, like the Czech Republic, legislation makes it easier for women to use parental leave as an extension of maternity leave, whereas men have to pursue a different legal avenue to get parental leave from work. In others, the laws offer women better job protection. In Russia, for example, the law is written specifically to protect women with children under age 3 from dismissal. Fathers are only legally protected when they take parental leave where there is no mother present. Mothers may also have the right to engage in

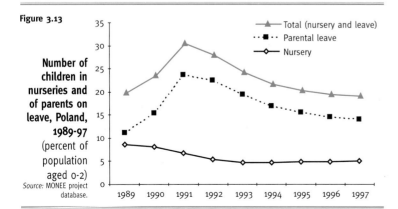

Figure 3.13

Number of children in nurseries and of parents on leave, Poland, 1989-97 (percent of population aged 0-2)

Source: MONEE project database.

Legend:
- Total (nursery and leave)
- Parental leave
- Nursery

part-time work or work at home while receiving leave benefits, but fathers are not permitted this option.

Some observers voice concern that extended parental leave may diminish the chance that a woman will return to the labour market. Again, the potential absences may be viewed by employers as a disincentive to hiring women and, thus, can represent an obstacle to women's economic improvement. Despite legal protection, there is growing evidence of dismissals from work that are related to parental leave. A survey in Hungary showed that about one in 10 women on leave said they could not return to their former employment. Almost one in three said their employers would not want to re-employ them. The survey also found many cases where employers tried to dismiss workers who took parental leave.

In recent years, some countries have restricted parental leave to low-income families, and others have dropped leave programmes entirely. For example, Armenia and Georgia, where extended families are common and the economic losses during transition huge, abolished parental leave in 1994. On the other hand, some countries have recently sought to bolster the value of benefits. As Figure 3.14 shows, the value of the parental leave benefit has eroded considerably during transition in Bulgaria and Russia, though not in Slovakia.

For families with pre-school children, adequate, accessible and affordable childcare is crucial to balancing employment and household responsibilities. Without childcare, one of the parents – typically the woman – has to stay home for a period of years, a circumstance that affects not only immediate household income, but the woman's lifelong career development and earnings. Children undoubtedly benefit greatly from the full-time care of an at-home parent in their early years, but, after age 2 or 3, there are also important social and cognitive developmental benefits associated with group environments outside the parental home, such as daycare or kindergarten.

Still, there has been a post-communist philosophical bent to "de-institutionalize" children and support stay-at-home parenting. For example, in 1993 Hungary introduced "maternity fees" for mothers with three or more children who stay at home with their children until the youngest reaches 8 years of age, and in 1995 the Czech Republic extended parental leave for childcare until the children reach age 4.

As Figure 3.15 presents, enrolment rates in nurseries (children up to age 2) have fallen throughout the region during the transition – most clearly in the Baltics, western CIS, the Caucasus, and Kazakhstan, where enrolments were considerable. In the Czech Republic and Slovakia, nurseries have practically ceased to exist. Many factors have

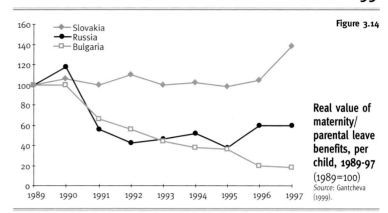

Figure 3.14

Real value of maternity/ parental leave benefits, per child, 1989-97
(1989=100)
Source: Gantcheva (1999).

converged to produce this outcome. The workplace childcare provided by state enterprises has greatly diminished or disappeared, and government policies, such as extended parental leave, and job loss are promoting the idea of stay-at-home parents.

Enrolment rates in kindergartens seem to have been much less affected, as Figure 3.15 shows, although enrolment has declined or is low in the southern part of the region, with the notable exception of Bulgaria and Romania. A recovery in enrolment rates has taken place in most Baltic and Central and Southeastern European countries, despite sharp declines in the number of places available in kindergartens. This is because the overall decrease in fertility has reduced infant and young child populations by 10-50 percent over the transition period. Moreover, in many countries, as Box 3.3 presents, governments have tried to curb rising fees, and local communities have made successful efforts to save kindergartens from closing.

Over 1996-97, kindergarten enrolments stabilized or improved in most countries, but declined further in Moldova, Ukraine, Kazakhstan, Kyrgyzstan, Uzbekistan, and Tajikistan. (See Statistical Annex, Table 7.1.) Current kindergarten enrolment rates reflect a sharper north-south urban-rural division than earlier. Interestingly, however, the changes in enrolment rates do not closely follow the changes in female labour force participation, suggesting that the interplay of household income, family structure, cultural patterns, and policy choices is becoming more important in childcare solutions.

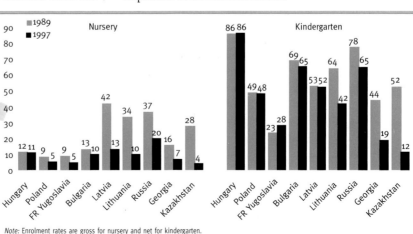

Figure 3.15

Changes in nursery and kindergarten enrolment rates, 1989 and 1997
(percent of children aged 0-2 and 3-5/6)
Sources: Statistical Annex, Table 7.1; MONEE project database.

Note: Enrolment rates are gross for nursery and net for kindergarten.

Box 3.3

Sharing the responsibility for childcare: state, community and family

Every society must answer the question, who pays for childcare and how? The way individuals and communities answer this question is both a cause and a consequence of the balance of gender power in the home and in society. Responsibility for raising children is a fulcrum about which gender equality pivots. Certainly, women have a special and, usually, primary role in raising children; the challenge to progress is to support women in this role without compromising women's equality.

This challenge is particularly acute in the transition countries, where the forces of transformation have upset the former equilibrium among women, work and state-provided childcare. Under communism, childcare was widely available and widely used, particularly in countries where women's participation in the labour force was high. Since the transition began, the availability of public nurseries and kindergartens has decreased; quality has often deteriorated, and user costs have risen.

These conditions mean difficult choices for parents, especially mothers, as they weigh the trade-offs of bleaker job prospects, lower real wages, lower childcare quality, and higher childcare fees in public and new private facilities. (See Table 3.5.) Evidence suggests that households are often unwilling or unable to pay the higher childcare fees in public facilities, creating a chain reaction of dropping demand, empty seats and even less impetus for government to commit further resources. Far fewer can afford higher quality private nurseries and kindergartens. In Hungary in 1997, registered private kindergarten enrolments made up 2 percent of total enrolments, and in Poland 3 percent – less than 2 percent of all children in the 3-6 age group. It is increasingly common for families in Central Europe and western CIS to turn to relatives. This is especially so in the Caucasus, former Yugoslavia and Central Asia, where extended families are still prevalent.

Childcare costs for pre-schoolers are frequently the single highest expenditure on services for families with young children. Often, family decisions come down to a trade-off between the woman's wages and the cost of childcare. Since women's wages are typically significantly lower than men's, it is usually women who give up paid work to stay home. This can be an especially critical decision in lower income and poor families, where the mother's earnings have added importance, and, indeed, may make the difference between low income and poverty for the family. To support gender equality, therefore, policy makers might look at childcare fees as a percentage of women's average wages rather than simply as a percentage of overall average wages.

In response to the difficulties faced by low-income families, some countries have made efforts to contain fees and offer pre-school care based on need. In Kazakhstan, a 1992 decree set user fees in municipal kindergartens at 30 percent of the average per-child food costs in the facilities. A regulation introduced in Russia in 1992 limited user fees to 20 percent of costs and 10 percent for families with three or more children.

Significant numbers of children attend pre-school on a social assistance basis. In Moldova, the families of 18 percent of the children enrolled pay no fees. In FR Yugoslavia, 1996 data show that the fees for 25 percent of the children enrolled were subsidized by up to half of the value of the fee and that the fees of 23 percent were subsidized for more than half this value; overall, parents paid just 15 percent of the average total cost of care per child per month. Nevertheless, many gaps remain in the quality and availability of childcare, and access has become increasingly polarized according to family income level.

Two areas that obviously need development are the status of new private-sector employers in promoting family-friendly workplace policies and programmes and the explicit public policies that encourage the growth of registered home-based childcare services. The one-size-fits-all approach of communism needs to be replaced with a flexible widespread network of childcare options that responds to the diversity emerging in the work and family lives of women and men.

Table 3.5

Monthly fees for public and private nurseries and kindergartens, 1998

	Enrolment rate % (1997)	Public fees % average wage	Public fees % minimum wage	Private fees % average wage
Nurseries				
Romania	2	13	37	65
Estonia	18	2-14	n/a	28-84
Uzbekistan	n/a	8-41	40-200	n/a
Kindergartens				
Czech Republic	83	2-5	6-20	n/a
FR Yugoslavia*	28	25	n/a	120–80
Romania	63	26	79	81
Russia	65	10-14	117-57	no private
Georgia	19	38-47	120-50	118-40

Sources: Hendrichova and Kucharova (1998); Posarac (1998); Zamfir and Zamfir (1998); Papp (1998); Kupriyanova (1998); MEG (1998); Marnie (1998).

Note: n/a = Not available. * Data on fees refer to Belgrade only.

3.4 Conclusions

The role of women in families and of the family in women's lives is one of the defining dimensions of gender equality and human development. This chapter reviews the evidence presented by demographic statistics and sociological surveys with the aim of shaping a portrait of women's changing aspirations and functions related to the family at a time of massive economic transformation. The chapter also examines changes in family-related policies and how they reflect and reinforce social attitudes, public goals and local and individual responses to the competing interests of work and family. The portrait of women and family drawn from the data, though sometimes faint and necessarily incomplete, reveals some noteworthy gaps between women's expressed desires and women's realities.

Certainly, women in the region are diverse in their ambitions and their circumstances. The constraining uniformity of ideology and social policy under communism is fading. In the more open environment of the transition, women and men are becoming more receptive to new ideas and influences, while, at the same time, they are rediscovering their cultural traditions. From this mix, different realities for women are emerging across the region. Divorce rates are higher than marriage rates in Estonia; cohabitation among young couples is more widespread in Slovenia, and single parenthood is rising in Russia. On the other hand, divorce rates are falling in the Caucasus, and marriage and fertility rates are lower but still vigorous in Central Asia. A greater variety of demographic and family behaviour is often appearing within countries as well.

Although the conditions supporting early childbearing have changed drastically during transition, teenage parenthood remains relatively common in most countries. This may simply reflect an ingrained expectation about the appropriate time to have a first child, an expectation many young women hold despite economic and, possibly, personal uncertainty. However, as recent evidence from the Czech Republic shows, teenage girls are increasingly recognizing the personal opportunities lost by following the family formation patterns of earlier generations, especially given current economic conditions in the region. Teenage fertility rates are, however, proving to be more persistent in areas where early childbearing seems to be rooted strongly in ethnic or national culture.

The review of family policies in the region clearly demonstrates that women are less able to count on regular support from the state. Child-related benefits and services represent an implicit and sometimes explicit income support for women, and, with a decline in this support, the gender gap in wages is also being more acutely felt. At the same time, emerging income tax systems do not provide particularly strong incentives for women to withdraw from the labour market and stay at home to raise their young children. Many governments have made considerable efforts to maintain or extend family supports, but both the functions and the resources of the state are weakened, and, therefore, so is the state's capacity to act. Fresh approaches are needed to balance work and childcare responsibilities, especially in the area of workplace policies and programmes in the new private sector and in the area of community-based solutions.

Under communism, the women of the region lived in a unique environment that shaped their choices and decisions about work and family commitments. There was full employment, generous family supports linked to the workplace, and a state with strong pro-natalist goals. However, beyond state-run programmes, there was a glaring absence of organized community or grassroots support for women with children and, in the private realm of the home, little discussion or movement on the gender balance of power and the equitable distribution of family responsibilities. With the retreat of the state from daily life, these societies must now fill in the blanks in the interdependent arrangement of work and the family.

There are a number of opportunities to seize in this new territory, and parts of the inheritance of the past are worth building on. For example, it will pay to maintain the high levels of education and health care enjoyed by women as these are prime determinants of women's and children's welfare and contribution to society. Government still has an important part to play in the work-family balancing act, and the new democratic institutions of the region can develop fresh family policies that are not simply tools to promote women's participation in the labour force, but flexible mechanisms which support a wide range of choices that women and men make about work and family and which, in so doing, enlarge the capacity of individuals to make choices.

To survive the turmoil of the transition, women have drawn on social networks of family and friends, neighbours and acquaintances to keep their households running: trading goods and services, making job connections and soliciting childcare. These spontaneous networks offer a good beginning for the development of organized efforts in civil society to support parents and children. Certainly, since the transition is largely about economic transformation, the new marketplace has a significant part to play in achieving a reasonable equilibrium between work and family. Workplace policies and programmes that enhance the capacity of parents to manage work and family responsibilities – maternity and parental leaves, flexible hours and work arrangements, family leave days, and childcare supports – represent an investment in human resources, including the next generation, and build equal opportunities for women.

It is important that both women and men be given the support they need to make choices about work and family. Just as it is increasingly recognized that women play economic and social roles in society that are equally important to the role they play as mothers, it is being recognized that men have a role to play as fathers that goes beyond their role as breadwinners. The equitable sharing of the responsibility for raising children is not only a fundamental condition of gender equality, it expands the choices of both women and men and must therefore benefit all. ∎

The World Health Organization promotes the concept of good health as "a state of complete physical, mental and social well-being, and not merely the absence of disease or infirmity". This prized state – an important measure of human development – is no less an aspiration of women and men living through the transition than are economic opportunity and political freedom.

In line with the social and economic hardship of the transition, the populations of most countries of the region have experienced a deterioration in health. The bluntest measure of this decline, presented in Chapter 1, is that life expectancy for women and men deteriorated during the first years of transition in most countries, although a recovery has subsequently been observed in some cases. There is also a growing disparity among different geographic areas, within countries, between countries or groups of countries, and between different population groups. In particular, the gap in women's health that existed between Western Europe and Central and Eastern Europe before transition has widened.

Access to good health is a basic element of women's equality in society, and the state of women's health is felt far beyond the well-being of individual women. There are important implications for family and child welfare because key determinants of health, such as education and income, are passed from generation to generation and because women are central figures in household health management, nutrition and care. By extension, women's health also has an important impact on broader society, both in the workplace and in the community. The Platform for Action of the Fourth World Conference on Women, held in Beijing in 1995, states that advancing women's equality in health involves not only addressing the biological differences between women and men, but the unequal access to health care resources and differences in the non-biological determinants that shape health.

Before transition, important investments had been made in health services across the region through the universal health care system. However, the return on that investment was less than might be expected for women's health in most countries of the region. For example, despite an emphasis on care for pregnancy, childbirth and infants, most countries experienced higher maternal mortality rates than those in Western Europe. In general, health awareness was very low across the region. The communist state appropriated the concept of health and defined it as the product of the state's health care system, so that individuals, employers and communities lacked a sense of responsibility for, and the capacity to promote, good health.

The transition has not only weakened the state health system, but triggered changes in the socio-economic factors that shape women's health. Many of the immediate effects are adverse, including lower incomes, increased income disparity and greater social stress. Many countries are becoming more open societies, a shift that can bring both positive and negative changes in health – from improved access to family planning and promotion of healthy lifestyles to increases in the range and intensity of risk-taking behaviours such as drug use or unsafe sex. In most countries, lower levels of public spending limit the capacity of the existing health system to meet demand even if reforms raise quality and efficiency. It is important to realize that, while the health of women and the health of men will be affected, they may be affected in different ways and to different degrees.

One of the most dramatic examples of the different health responses and needs of women and men during the transition has been the mortality crisis (uncovered in earlier Regional Monitoring Reports and updated in Chapter 1) that has affected women and men, but that has been most pronounced among middle-aged men. This is consistent with worldwide patterns that men are more likely to experience premature death and women are more likely to experience sickness and poor health. This disparity simply underscores the reality that women's health issues are different from those of men in a number of ways. Women have particular health needs related to reproductive biology and beyond the reproductive sphere, for instance in terms of mental health. Their health problems tend to start earlier in life and to persist longer into old age. Biological and social factors, including subordination in society, influence women's health throughout their lives and have cumulative effects. Many of the health difficulties faced by women in their reproductive years originate in childhood or adolescence, confirming the importance of considering the health of women throughout the entire life cycle.

This chapter deals with selective aspects of women's health. Section 4.1 starts with the conventional focus on maternal and child health and expands to include reproductive health issues such as abortion and family planning. Section 4.2 reviews the way changes in economic and social determinants during the transition have affected women's health. The Conclusions summarize the challenges to women's health in the region. ■

4.1 Women's Reproductive Health: An Uneven Record

One of the main thrusts in improving the health status of women globally has been to emphasize the whole health of the woman at all ages and stages of life. This life-cycle approach means considering all aspects of female health – physical, mental and social – from birth to old age. Conventionally, medicine and health care have focused on the primacy of a woman's reproductive health and her childbearing years and, more specifically, on pregnancy and infant health. As a result, available data, especially in the transition region, tend to focus on these aspects of women's health. For this reason, the following section covers the more narrow view, but intends to point to a broader perspective which recognizes that women's reproductive health extends well beyond childbearing and is an integral part of women's overall health.

Large variances in maternal health

The overall stability or improvement of infant mortality rates across the region during transition, as presented in Chapter 1, attests to the inherited advantages of good health, education and health services for the mothers. However, during the transition, there has not been an adequate improvement in maternal mortality rates across the region. The level and quality of professional perinatal care have suffered in most countries surveyed, with implications for birth complications and outcomes. There also appear to be increasing differences in pregnancy complications between countries, between regions within countries and between various population groups.

Figure 4.1 presents information on the registered incidence of maternal mortality in the region – a total of about 1,700 deaths from pregnancy-related causes in 1997. The graph shows that 17 of 26 countries reporting document a decrease in the maternal mortality rate between 1989 and 1997. However, in the other nine countries, the rate has increased. Altogether, 17 countries

still have maternal mortality rates above the WHO target for Europe of 15 maternal deaths per 100,000 live births. In 11 countries, the rate is more than twice this target. Altogether, only 11 of the 26 countries have achieved or are about to achieve the goal set in 1990 at the World Summit for Children to halve maternal mortality rates over 1990-2000.

The situation varies significantly by sub-region. The graph clearly shows that maternal mortality is much lower in Central and Eastern Europe, the former Yugoslavia and the Baltics. The rate is generally decreasing and below or around the WHO target for Europe – with the exception of Hungary and Latvia. However, in these two countries the absolute numbers of maternal deaths are relatively small, so the rate can fluctuate greatly from year to year. (For example, the number of maternal deaths in Hungary was 12 in 1996 and 21 in 1997.) In FYR Macedonia, the reduction of the maternal mortality rate might reflect such a fluctuation. However, it should be noted that the share of births attended by professional health care providers rose from 89 percent in 1990 to 96 percent in 1996. In Albania and Romania, high maternal mortality rates in 1989 (49 and 169, respectively) were sharply reduced after the introduction of legal abortion. The rates are, however, still much higher than the WHO target, at 28 and 41 deaths per 100,000 live births, respectively.

The situation in countries of the Commonwealth of Independent States is quite different, with higher maternal mortality rates in most of the countries since transition. Figure 4.2 presents long-term trends in maternal mortality in Russia and Ukraine. It shows that the progress made in the 1980s has stopped or has even been reversed during the transition period of the 90s. As a result, in both countries the mortality rate has stabilized, but remains well above the WHO target for Europe. The trend is also worrying in Tajikistan, where the maternal mortality rate has sharply increased during transition and is about four times higher than this target. Large variations in maternal mortality rates are also observed within countries, particularly where rates are high, such as in the Caucasus and Central Asia. For example, maternal mortality rates in the region of Karakalpakstan, bordering the Aral Sea, in Uzbekistan are significantly higher than in the rest of the country, 120 per 100,000 against a national average of less than 20 in 1994.

Even in some countries where the mortality rate has

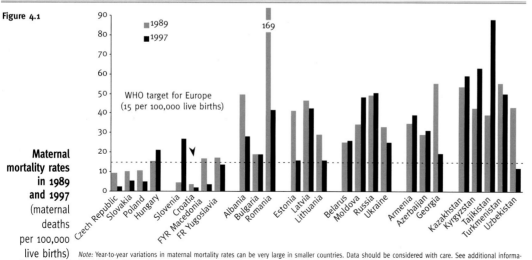

Figure 4.1

Maternal mortality rates in 1989 and 1997 (maternal deaths per 100,000 live births)

Source: Statistical Annex, Table 3.2.

Note: Year-to-year variations in maternal mortality rates can be very large in smaller countries. Data should be considered with care. See additional information in Statistical Annex, Table 3.2. Alternative sources estimate the rate to be 61 in Georgia in 1997. End year is 1995 for Turkmenistan and 1996 for Poland, Slovenia, Croatia, Albania, Tajikistan, and Uzbekistan.

not risen, the incidence of complications during birth is growing. For example, in Belarus, the occurrence of hæmorrhage increased from 190 cases per 10,000 births in 1989 to 280 in 1995. Eclampsia cases rose from 6 per 10,000 births to 14 per 10,000 over the same period. Information for Russia, shown in Figure 4.3, also reveals a dramatic increase in complications, climbing from 23 percent of births in 1989 to as much as 67 percent in 1996. The prevalence of all conditions leading to complications has increased, with the incidence of anæmia growing especially rapidly. The share of births complicated by anæmia rose from 5 to 23 percent over the period. Part of the explanation may be linked to the demographic changes presented in Chapter 3. For instance, in most countries of the former Soviet Union, there is a higher proportion of young mothers, and younger women tend to have less successful birth outcomes, including higher incidence of stillbirth and low birthweight. However, the changes observed are greater than such structural shifts would suggest and point to an actual deterioration in outcomes.

In keeping with the increase in pregnancy and birth complications, the health status of newborns has also deteriorated. The number of stillbirths, low birthweights, congenital anomalies, and problems in the perinatal period has been rising in most of the countries surveyed, particularly in those hard hit during the transition, such as FYR Macedonia, FR Yugoslavia, Bulgaria, and Georgia. In Georgia, the country with the highest rate of stillbirths, the incidence increased from 7 per 1,000 births in 1989 to 18 in 1997.

In particular, the proportion of children born at low birthweight (under 2,500 grams) has been increasing in many countries – with the exception of countries such as Poland, Hungary, or Slovenia. (See Statistical Annex, Table 2.5 for details). A rise in the percentage of children born with a low birthweight may partly reflect improved perinatal and obstetric care that results in fewer stillbirths and more survivors with low weights. It can also reflect a deterioration in maternal health, such as poorer nutrition.

Low birthweight is an important indicator because it raises the probability of infant mortality, has a negative impact on the development of the child, carries financial and emotional stress for the parents, and has resource implications for health services. The situation of babies born to young mothers is of particular concern. For instance, in Bulgaria, the share of children born with low birthweights to women under age 20 increased from 10 percent in 1989 to 14 percent in 1997. Both the level and the deterioration are greater among this age group. Thus, the proportion for women of all ages rose from 7 to 9 percent over the same period. The reasons for this pattern include the fact that younger women tend to lack maturity, have lower socio-economic status and less access to health care, and are likely giving birth to first babies with the attendant higher risks.

Even in the Czech Republic, where there has been a general improvement in birth outcomes, disparity among social groups has been growing, in line with socio-eco-

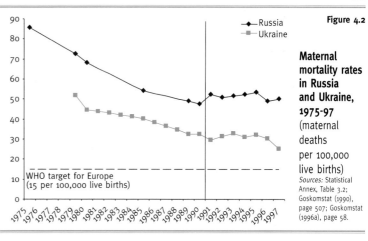

Figure 4.2

Maternal mortality rates in Russia and Ukraine, 1975-97 (maternal deaths per 100,000 live births)
Sources: Statistical Annex, Table 3.2; Goskomstat (1990), page 507; Goskomstat (1996a), page 58.

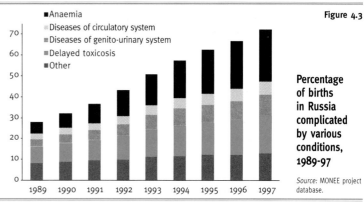

Figure 4.3

Percentage of births in Russia complicated by various conditions, 1989-97
Source: MONEE project database.

nomic changes. Over 1989-97, the mean birthweight in the Czech Republic increased (after an initial decline), while both infant and maternal mortality fell significantly. Figure 4.4 presents the mean birthweight of babies of mothers at various educational levels. It reveals that the differences among mothers with different levels of education are relatively large and have become greater during the transition. Babies born to women with less education showed larger decreases in birthweight during periods of deterioration and smaller increases during periods of improvement. The differences in mean birthweight and in post-neonatal mortality (after the first 27 days of life) were still found to be statistically significant and rising after controlling for other important determinants such as maternal age and the birth order and sex of the child.

Still, in the Czech Republic, the neonatal mortality rate fell over 1989-95, reflecting an improvement in the

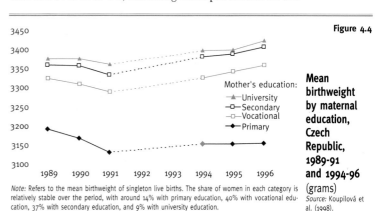

Figure 4.4

Note: Refers to the mean birthweight of singleton live births. The share of women in each category is relatively stable over the period, with around 14% with primary education, 40% with vocational education, 37% with secondary education, and 9% with university education.

Mean birthweight by maternal education, Czech Republic, 1989-91 and 1994-96 (grams)
Source: Koupilová et al. (1998).

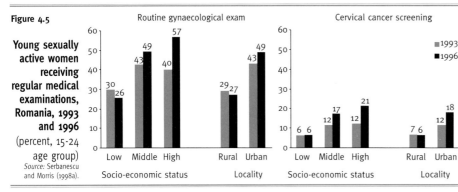

Figure 4.5

Young sexually active women receiving regular medical examinations, Romania, 1993 and 1996
(percent, 15-24 age group)
Source: Serbanescu and Morris (1998a).

by a large representative survey in the Czech Republic in 1993. Up to 10 percent of women were not receiving prenatal care during the first trimester in North Bohemia, compared to only 3 percent in South Bohemia. Similarly, 15 percent of women in North Moravia had not had an ultrasound exam during their pregnancy, compared to 2 percent in South Bohemia.

On the other hand, in Southeastern Europe, Central Asia, the Caucasus, and parts of western CIS and the former Yugoslavia, the initial conditions were usually less adequate, and the situation has deteriorated. This goes against the goal set by the World Summit for Children in 1990 to furnish universal access to prenatal care and to assistance during childbirth.

In Southeastern Europe, evidence indicates a decline in the provision of services for pregnant women. A large 1993 survey in Romania showed substantial inequality in access to prenatal care by age, education and economic status of the mother. The proportion of pregnant women without prenatal care ranged from 10 percent for those with primary education to 2 percent for those with post-secondary education. Both the number of visits and the timing of the first visit correlated with age, education and economic status. Information on changes in access to reproductive health services for young women (aged 15-24) over 1993-96 in Romania is presented in Figure 4.5. It shows an overall improvement in access to routine gynæcological examinations and to cervical cancer screening, but also reveals increasing inequality in access. Women from lower socioeconomic groups and women in rural areas actually had reduced access during a period of general improvement.

In Bulgaria, the proportion of women with no prenatal care was 22 percent in 1996 and 17 percent in 1997, although births were still assisted by trained health professionals. In Albania, birth assistance decreased until 1992, when only 86 percent of births took place with professional attendance, but rose to 91 percent in 1997.

In countries of the former Yugoslavia, the range of services provided to pregnant women has likely diminished in areas where war has caused significant material destruction. In addition, large regional disparities were observed in FR Yugoslavia, especially between the region of strife-torn Kosovo and the rest of the country. Table 4.1 shows that more than one-fourth of deliveries (27.1 percent) were not assisted by professionals in Kosovo, against a national average of 8.3 percent, which is already high compared to neighbouring countries. Women in Kosovo averaged only 0.7 medical visits after birth, compared to a national average of 4.5. Similarly, infant and child mortality rates and the proportion of stunted children were significantly higher than in the rest of the country, while immunization coverage was lower. (These figures pre-date the 1999 conflict.)

In the Caucasus, the situation also appears to have deteriorated, especially in remote rural areas. In Armenia,

ability of the health system to ensure the survival of low birthweight babies. However, regional analysis shows improvements have been much greater in Prague than in the rest of the country, confirming regional imbalances in the quality of neonatal care.

While the health status of women can partly explain changes in birth outcomes, the health system also plays an important role. Maternity care has traditionally been of high standard throughout the region, although emphasis was placed on number of visits, diagnostics and tests rather than on quality, counselling and education. Most women were followed regularly through their pregnancies, and the great majority of births took place in the presence of qualified staff and in health centres.

Evidence suggests that most of the advantages gained before transition in terms of birth care have been maintained, but that there are signs of decline, with important implications for the health of mothers and their children. The situation differs widely across the region.

Countries in Central Europe and the Baltics started with a better situation and have managed to maintain most of their achievements. There are, however, signs of inequality across population groups or regions that raise concerns about setbacks. For instance, big regional variations in the provision of maternity care were highlighted

Table 4.1

Maternal and child health in FR Yugoslavia, 1995-96

	National average	Kosovo
% unattended births (without trained personnel) (1995) a, b	8.3	27.1
Average visits per woman after delivery (1995) c	4.5	0.7
Infant mortality rate (1995) b	16.8	23.6
Under-5 mortality rate (1995) b	19.4	27.7
% children aged 0-5 classified as stunted (1996) d	6.8	13.1
% children fully vaccinated in second year of life (1996) d	65.3	53.0

Sources: a. MONEE project database. b. UNICEF (1997b). c. Posarac (1998). d. IPHS, IPHM and UNICEF (1997).

Note: Children are classified as stunted when their height for age is two standard deviations or more below the median of a reference population. Full vaccination includes BCG, DPT, OPV, and measles vaccination.

the proportion of known home births increased and peaked at 7 percent in 1994 and 1995. Evidence suggests that up to half of deliveries take place at home in some areas of the country. The proportion of infant deaths occurring at home has risen, especially in rural areas, and represents about 30 percent of all infant deaths. The proportion of women without prenatal care has also grown. More than 40 percent of women in the city of Yerevan

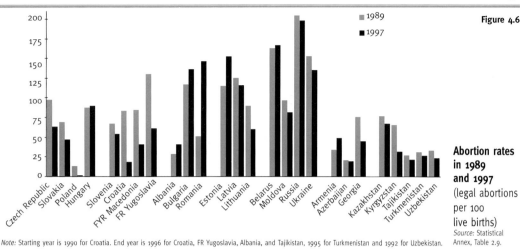

Figure 4.6

■ 1989
■ 1997

Abortion rates in 1989 and 1997 (legal abortions per 100 live births)
Source: Statistical Annex, Table 2.9.

Note: Starting year is 1990 for Croatia. End year is 1996 for Croatia, FR Yugoslavia, Albania, and Tajikistan, 1995 for Turkmenistan and 1992 for Uzbekistan.

and 50 percent of women outside Yerevan are reported to attend their first medical consultation only after the initial trimester of pregnancy. In rural areas, the cost of transportation and health care, poor sanitary conditions and lack of supplies deter women from visiting health centres. The majority of facilities are reportedly in disastrous physical condition and lack drugs and other supplies.

The situation in Central Asia is also showing signs of decline and disparity. For example, in Kazakhstan, the share of women without prenatal care ranges from less than 1 percent in the northeast to up to 14 percent in the south (excluding Almaty). In Kyrgyzstan, the lack of timely transportation is reported to be a major factor. In the remote region of Talas, higher maternal mortality rates are partly attributed to the deterioration of transport facilities. The situation in Tajikistan, where civil war has destroyed health and transportation infrastructure, is particularly worrying, with an estimated 35 percent of infant deaths related to home births, which are often unassisted by professional help.

The care of pregnant women before, during and immediately after birth is fundamental to the health of mothers. A broader approach is also needed to fully address women's reproductive health. Family planning and abortion rates are two wider areas that merit particular attention in the region.

Abortion rates remain very high

Abortion rates in the region are very high relative to those in other industrialized countries. The average legal abortion rate in the region was more than 100 abortions per 100 live births in 1996, compared with an average of 20 abortions per 100 live births in the European Union in 1994. High abortion rates may be partly explained by two inherited conditions. There is a relative lack of promotion of family planning practices in the region, a situation in keeping with the pro-natalist policies pursued in many countries, as Chapter 3 notes. At the same time, universal access to legal abortions was generally guaranteed under the umbrella of basic women's health services. Lack of contraception, combined with the legal availability and

social acceptance of abortion, has contributed to high official rates of abortion.

Abortion rates do, however, vary greatly across countries. Figure 4.6 shows the legal abortion rate in 1989 and 1997 for all transition countries, grouped by geographic sub-region. Rates are particularly high in Southeastern Europe (except Albania), western CIS and the Baltics (except Lithuania). The only countries where the number of legal abortions per 100 live births is around or below the European Union average are Poland (see Box 4.1), Croatia, Azerbaijan, and Tajikistan. In particular, in Russia, there are two abortions for every live birth, that is, about 2.5 million abortions in 1997. Altogether, in seven countries, there were more legal abortions than live births in 1997, and in a further seven countries, there were 50-100 abortions for every 100 births.

The absolute number of legal abortions has declined in every country during the transition. Abortions declined by more than half in nine countries and by 20-50 percent in 10 countries. However, a look at the ratio of abortions to total number of live births shows that the decrease is less pronounced. The abortion rate actually rose in Hungary, Albania, Bulgaria, Romania, Estonia, Belarus, and Armenia. The cases of Poland and Romania are particular because of changes that took place in legislation. (See Box 4.1).

Figure 4.7 presents the legal abortion rate for women of all ages and for women under age 20 in 1997, compared to rates in 1989 (or 1991) for 15 countries. Abortion rates for women under age 20 increased more or decreased less than average, except in Albania, Belarus, Georgia, Azerbaijan, and Kazakhstan. The graph also shows that legal abortion rates for women under 20 have risen in nine of the 15 countries for which data are available in Central Europe, Southeastern Europe and the Baltics. The largest declines are found in the Caucasus and Central Asia.

The high overall numbers of abortions in these countries have important costs. Despite a cultural tolerance for abortion, a large proportion of women who have an abortion experience emotional trauma. Surveys in

Box 4.1

Abortion legislation in the region

In all the countries covered by this Report, with the notable exception of Romania and Albania, abortion was legally permitted before transition. Women were free to have an abortion, irrespective of their health status and on their own initiative (no spousal consent). Often, employed women were even allowed to take a leave day from work for abortion. During the transition, several countries have made adjustments in their abortion laws. Two countries, Romania and Poland, have made major changes.

In Romania, the new abortion law, implemented one day after the fall of the previous regime in 1989, liberalized the very restrictive rules. After an initial spike in the abortion rate – up to 300 abortions per 100 live births, the rate has decreased, but is still high at 150 abortions per 100 live births. As a result of the liberalization, the registered number of maternal deaths caused by abortion declined from 545 in 1989 (out of

a total of 627 maternal deaths) to 51 in 1996, leading to a drop of 76 percent in the maternal mortality rate.

In Poland, since March 1993 (except for the period October 1996 to December 1997), abortion is only permitted in case of severe fœtal damage or serious risk to the life or health of the woman, or when the pregnancy is a result of rape. The practice seems to be even more restrictive than the law, with many legally "eligible" women apparently denied abortions. Polish women are estimated to undergo 40,000-50,000 abortions annually either illegally, or abroad. The official number of legal abortions in 1997 was 3,200. Although covered in the abortion law, the provision of and education on family planning services have not significantly improved. The number of children abandoned in hospitals is also reported to have increased, more than doubling in four districts of the country between 1992 and 1993.

Latvia and Russia show around 70 percent of the women reported feeling depressed after an abortion or experiencing the abortion as psychological trauma.

Abortions also have serious physical complications, especially when the procedure is not performed in safe conditions. Abortions remain one of the leading causes of maternal mortality in the region, accounting for 20-25 percent of all maternal deaths. In Russia, for example, abortions are responsible for 25-30 percent of all maternal deaths, and an estimated 70-90 percent of abortions resulting in maternal death are performed illegally. In Romania, where maternal mortality is still high at 41 deaths per 100,000 live births, over half the maternal deaths follow abortions. In Kazakhstan, 19 percent of maternal deaths in 1995 were due to abortions, almost half of which were performed illegally.

Abortions are also responsible for complications such as infection, hæmorrhage and anæmia, injury to internal organs, and long-term health problems, including chronic pelvic pain and disease, premature delivery, and infertility. In Ukraine, for example, abortions were found

to result in reproductive problems that contributed to sterility in 22 percent of couples and to inflammation of the reproductive organs among 30 percent of the women undergoing the intervention. In Kazakhstan, 20 percent of abortions led to complications, one-third of which required hospitalization. In Romania, 7 to 12 percent of abortions were followed by complications. In Russia, 13 to 17 percent of women had short-term complications – almost half leading to hospitalization, and 3 to 10 percent had long-term complications. The probability of complications increases when abortions are performed illegally. Adolescents are at higher risk of complications after abortion because their reproductive systems are more vulnerable to injury than are those of older women and because they are more likely to undergo illegal abortions.

Abortions, together with sexually transmitted diseases, are considered to be the leading cause of infertility, generating cervical trauma, cervical and uterine adhesions, pelvic infections, and other complications. The prevalence of infertility is relatively high throughout the transition region and increasing in some countries. For instance, the share of infertile women is estimated at 7 to 10 percent of married women in Estonia and Belarus, 15 percent in Moldova, and 10 to 15 percent in both Lithuania and Russia. In a special medical centre in Moscow, four in five of the women treated for secondary infertility had undergone induced abortions. In the Czech Republic in 1993, 13 percent of women who had been married or had cohabited had used infertility services.

The private reasons for abortion are many and include unwanted pregnancy as the result of sexual assault, opposition by the partner, or changes

Figure 4.7

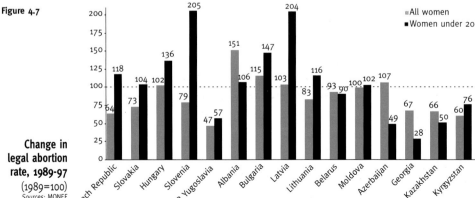

Change in legal abortion rate, 1989-97
(1989=100)
Sources: MONEE project database; Statistical Annex, Table 2.9.

Note: Abortion rate in 1997 (1995 for Albania, 1996 for Slovakia and FR Yugoslavia) relative to abortion rate in 1989 (1991 for countries of the former Soviet Union).

in personal circumstances due to divorce, job loss, displacement, or war. However, the prevalence of abortions in the region has a public dimension, including lack of information and education about reproductive health and contraception and lack of access to affordable, effective birth control options. High abortion rates in the transition countries exact a high price from women's health, a burden that could be greatly alleviated through better access to family planning.

Table 4.2

Contraceptive use at first intercourse

	% women	Year	Type of contraception	Age at time of interview
Czech Republic	27.1	1993	Condoms	15-19
	20.2			20-24
Romania	15.0	1996	Modern methods	15-24, unmarried
	4.8	1993		15-24, unmarried
Moldova	13.5	1997	Modern methods	15-24, unmarried
Russia	30.5	1996	Modern methods	15-24, unmarried
Poland	50.0	1991	All methods	20-24
	49.8			25-29
Latvia	41.8	1995	All methods	18-19
	37.7			20-24
	26.3			25-29

Sources: CSO et al. (1995); Serbanescu and Morris (1998a), (1998b); VCIOM, CDC and USAID (1998); Holzer and Kowalska (1997); Zvidrins, Ezera and Greitans (1998).

Note: Modern methods include birth control pills and IUDs.

Inadequate access to family planning

The Beijing Platform for Action states that "the human rights of women include their right to have control over and decide freely and responsibly on matters related to their sexuality, including sexual and reproductive health" and that women and men have the right to be informed and to have access to "safe, effective, affordable and acceptable methods of family planning of their choice". The universal availability of family planning education and services was also one of the goals set by the 1990 World Summit for Children.

Generally, women throughout the region, in particular young women, have relatively little knowledge of reproductive health issues. Surveys in Central Asia show that only 10 percent of women of reproductive age (15-49) in Uzbekistan in 1996 and 29 percent in Kazakhstan in 1995 knew when the fertile period of their menstrual cycles occurred. In other countries where reproductive awareness is generally higher young women still lacked this basic knowledge. In the Czech Republic in 1993, up to 61 percent of young women aged 15-19 and 41 percent of those 20-24 could not define the most fertile part of the menstrual cycle. In Hungary in 1995, over 40 percent of adolescents could not do so either.

Awareness of various contraceptive methods is usually more widespread, but still not universal. Also, awareness does not automatically entail understanding the proper use of the methods. In a 1993 survey of grade 10 students in St Petersburg, only 25 percent of girls and 35 percent of boys knew that condoms should be used only once; up to 38 percent thought they could be washed and re-used.

The combination of low awareness and inadequate access means use of contraception at first intercourse is low in most of the countries for which information is available. Table 4.2 presents contraceptive use by young women at first intercourse. In Moldova in 1997, less than 14 percent of unmarried women aged 15-24 used modern methods of contraception at first intercourse. However, with the exception of Poland, use of contraceptives seems to have increased during the transition period. For exam-

ple, in Latvia, use of contraception at first intercourse rose from 26 percent to 41 percent in less than a decade (comparing women aged 25-29 and those aged 18-19 at the time of the survey). In Romania, the percentage of unmarried women using contraceptives tripled in three years, from less than 5 percent in 1993 to 15 percent in 1996.

Most young women explained the non-use of contraception by saying they did not expect to have sex, wanted to get pregnant, or did not think they could get pregnant. Lack of access and the cost are rarely mentioned as reasons for non-protection; however, such responses assume an awareness of contraceptives.

In addition to the need for greater awareness and knowledge, access to the full range of modern contraceptive methods is important. This range of access is crucial because different methods suit different groups of users – for physical, philosophical, economic, and socio-cultural

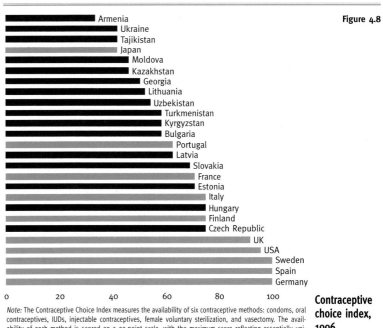

Figure 4.8

Note: The Contraceptive Choice Index measures the availability of six contraceptive methods: condoms, oral contraceptives, IUDs, injectable contraceptives, female voluntary sterilization, and vasectomy. The availability of each method is scored on a 20-point scale, with the maximum score reflecting essentially universal availability. The index converts the total score to a 100-point scale.

Contraceptive choice index, 1996
Source: PAI (1997).

reasons, and, from a health perspective, women need different approaches during their reproductive life cycle.

A Contraceptive Choice Index has been developed by Population Action International to reflect the availability of various means of contraception in a country. The 1996 index, presented in Figure 4.8, reports the availability of six modern contraceptive techniques in countries of the transition region. Choice appears to be less in Central and Eastern Europe and the former Soviet Union than in most Western countries. Availability is lowest in Central Asia, the Caucasus and western CIS.

Efforts have been made in several transition countries to improve access to modern contraceptives. Progress is, however, very slow in most cases. Figure 4.9 presents contraception-use levels for different years and countries. In Russia, there was a slight increase, from around 19 percent in 1991 to 24 percent in 1995 among women aged 15-49. In Belarus, after an initial rise in 1990, the rate declined again to just above pre-transition levels. In Slovenia, administrative data suggest that modern contraceptive prevalence actually declined over transition. A reduction in modern contraception use has also been observed in Lithuania and Poland, where the prevalence of contraception use may have dropped by more than half from 1992 to 1995, possibly as a result of changing values.

Cost and supply may not be major factors in the non-use of contraceptives at first intercourse, as shown in Table 4.2, but they are considerations for sexually active women later on. For instance, in Belarus in 1995, the top reasons given for non-use were fear of side-effects (39 percent), cost (27 percent) and difficulty in purchasing (11 percent). (It is important to note that contraceptive means are often of low quality in the region, which explains the predominance of concerns about side-effects.)

In most countries for which information is available, the prevalence of contraception use varies greatly with education, socio-economic status and place of residence. These variations may partly be linked to cost and availability of birth control, as well as awareness of methods. For example, in Moldova in 1997, less than 40 percent of women with low economic status, aged 15-44, and in marriage or non-marital unions were using modern contraception, compared to almost 60 percent of similar women of high economic status. Data from Kyrgyzstan show that about 10 percent of women with incomplete high school, compared to around 40 percent of women with complete higher education, were using contraception, with use lower in rural than in urban areas.

Figure 4.10 shows information for three countries on the share of sexually active women who use no or only traditional contraception and who need some or better methods. The extent of unmet needs is large. More than 50 percent of women aged 25-34 in Romania have contraception needs; even in the Czech Republic, more than 30 percent of women aged 25-44 have unmet needs for contraception.

In many countries, there are economic incentives to choose abortion over modern contraception methods. For example, in Bulgaria, the cost to the individual for an abortion in 1998 was less than 1 percent of the minimum wage, while modern contraceptives are imported and quite expensive. In some countries, the cost of abortion is subsidized by the state, or women can claim extra sick leave from work for an abortion.

In addition, both physicians and women in the region often have negative perceptions of the quality of modern contraception. Surveys in the 1980s and early 90s showed that very few women considered the birth control pill or intra-uterine devices (IUDs) to be reliable and safe. Two surveys carried out in Russia, in 1982-84 and 1991, showed that less than 20 percent of women considered the pill reliable, safe and convenient. Even among gynæcologists, the pill was found to have a relatively low level of acceptance – only 62 percent considered it safe. As late as the mid-1980s, the Soviet Ministry of Public Health published instructions explicitly warning against the use of oral contraceptives. At times, the negative attitudes of providers towards modern contraception are a factor in the slow progress of contraceptive prevalence, along with high price and limited availability. The shift from abortion to

Figure 4.9

Registered use of modern contraceptives, 1989/90 and 1996/97 (estimated percent of women of fertile age)

Sources: Novák (1998); Shircel (1998); UNICEF (1995a); Tafi (1998); Kupriyanova (1998); Karro (1997).

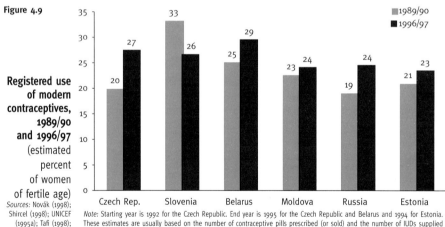

Note: Starting year is 1992 for the Czech Republic. End year is 1995 for the Czech Republic and Belarus and 1994 for Estonia. These estimates are usually based on the number of contraceptive pills prescribed (or sold) and the number of IUDs supplied by the health care system. Estimates of actual use based on surveys often provide different figures. In the case of Slovenia, such surveys suggest that 37% of women of fertile age were actually using modern contraceptives in 1989, and 47% in 1995.

Figure 4.10

Women in need of any or better contraception (percent, includes those using traditional methods)

Sources: Serbanescu and Morris (1998b); IMCC and CDC (1995); CSO et al. (1995).

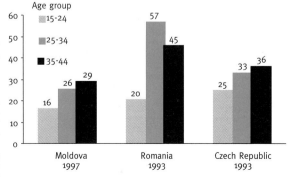

Note: These estimates are based on nationally representative surveys.

family planning calls for the training of physicians to encourage contraception and preventive care and to move away from abortion.

Some countries have taken initiatives to promote the shift from abortion to contraception as a primary means of family planning. For example, in the Czech Republic, the price of an IUD (effective for about two years) or birth control pills (for three months) is kept at around 3 percent of the average monthly wage, while an abortion costs more than 30 percent, except when it is medically required and therefore free. In Estonia, women have to pay half the cost of an abortion, with these funds applied to cutting the costs of contraceptive pills, to reducing the price by 90 percent for women in the first year after birth and for three months after an abortion, and to reducing the price by 50 percent for eligible students.

Public information and promotion campaigns can help improve access to family planning. In many countries, for example, pregnant women are seen regularly by health care providers during their pregnancies, but these visits are not exploited as opportunities to discuss family planning. In three Russian cities in 1996, health workers discussed or offered to discuss contraception with only 34 percent of women giving birth. Even following abortion, only 31 percent of women were offered contraceptive services or counselling.

In most of the countries covered by this Report, sex education is not provided at school. Even in Romania, where sex education is available, the topics of birth control and contraception are not often covered (see Box 4.4): more than 75 percent of teenagers learned about the reproductive system, but less than 25 percent of teenagers were taught about birth control. (Box 4.5 looks at how sex education can lower the risk of unwanted pregnancies and sexually transmitted diseases, or "STDs".) In many countries, non-governmental organizations and associations have implemented information programmes. A student organization at the University of Tirana in Albania provides counselling, contraception and discussion of reproductive health topics. In Uzbekistan, local and international NGOs run a national family planning programme that provides both information and contraception alternatives. Such initiatives are limited in scope and cannot serve large populations. In contrast, the inclusion of sex education in schools reaches all children, including those from ethnic minorities or remote rural areas.

Finally, it is important to recognize that women's reproductive health has dimensions beyond fertility. The registered incidence of breast cancer appears to have increased during the transition period in most of the countries of the region. Part of this increase may be attributed to earlier detection through screening, even though screening is far from universal. For example, in Latvia, the incidence rose from 44 cases per 100,000 individuals in 1989 to 64 in 1996. The registered incidence declined in some countries, including Armenia, Azerbaijan, Tajikistan, Turkmenistan, and Uzbekistan, probably linked to reduced detection. The registered incidence of cervical cancer also fell in these five countries. However, cervical cancer increased in several other countries of the region, in keeping with improved detection. For example, in Bulgaria, the incidence of cervical cancer rose from 16 per 100,000 in 1989 to 23 in 1996. In Romania, the rate increased from 19 to 23 per 100,000 over 1989-94.

The available data suggest that women in the region would benefit from greater awareness, improved detection practices and better medical technology and treatments for these reproductive cancers. The existence of these diseases makes it clear that women's reproductive health embraces more than fertility and is an integral part of women's general health. ■

4.2 Increases in Lifestyle-related Health Risks

Medicine and health policies and programmes throughout the world tend to focus on biological aspects of well-being. Not only do the biological determinants of women's health need broader attention, but so do the social and cultural factors that affect women's health – factors that also have a gender dimension. This section reviews the extent to which women's health may have been exposed to greater risks during the transition because of economic recession, the rising incidence of poverty and overall societal changes. These changes in the social determinants of health have challenged the ability of women to access proper nutrition and health care and to develop and maintain healthy life skills.

Poorer nutrition

Populations in the region face three types of nutritional problems – undernutrition, micronutrient malnutrition, and overnutrition (unbalanced intake of nutrients). In particular, it appears that micronutrient malnutrition is increasing in most countries. This is linked to a constellation of factors, including a drop in food consumption in some countries, a deterioration in the quality of the nutrients consumed, and the disruption of certain nutrition programmes such as the fortification of flour with iron or the distribution of specific food supplements for pregnant women and children. The impact of malnutrition is very important not only in terms of, for example, complications at birth or poor birth outcome (see Figure 4.3), but also in terms of greater risks of illness and death and reduced productivity.

Women are vulnerable to anæmia (iron deficiency) because of needs related to their reproductive biology. Girls' nutritional needs increase at adolescence with puberty and the onset of menstruation, while women have significant needs linked to both menstruation and childbearing. A large proportion of pregnancy complications or poor birth outcomes is a direct consequence of maternal malnutrition. Table 4.3 presents information on the percentage of live births complicated by anæmia in several countries of the former Soviet Union. Such reporting is not available for countries in Central and Eastern Europe, Southeastern Europe and the former Yugoslavia, where the prevalence of anæmia is likely to be lower. However, in light of the changes in nutrition patterns in some of these countries, an erosion in nutritional status can be expected.

A mother's lack of iron also affects the child not only because anæmia increases the risk of hæmorrhage and complications during birth, but also because children born to anæmic mothers are more likely to be anæmic themselves. Anæmic children suffer from listlessness and a lack of concentration, and the onset of puberty may exacerbate the condition in girls.

The situation is particularly acute in Central Asia, where 60 percent of women aged 15-49 in Uzbekistan and just under 50 percent in Kazakhstan suffer some degree of anæmia. The severity of anæmia is higher among pregnant or lactating women. Studies in Kazakhstan point to a decline in the consumption of animal protein, essential vitamins and micronutrients over the last decade. The link between maternal and child anæmia is illustrated by a large health survey carried out in Uzbekistan in 1996. The results show that the anæmia status of children is strongly linked to that of their mothers (at the time of the survey, not at the time of birth): 41 percent of children born to mothers with moderate anæmia suffered severe or moderate anæmia themselves, compared to 15 percent of those born to non-anæmic mothers.

Iron deficiency and other nutritional deficiencies can be addressed in various ways. Nutrition education aimed at changing nutrition behaviour is a very cost-effective way to improve nutritional status. This includes general education for all members of the public, as well as specific information on proper nutrition for ill children and pregnant women. For example, it may be as simple as learning not to drink tea and eat bread at the same time, a common habit in much of the region, because the tea prevents the body from absorbing the iron in the bread. Programmes that fortify common food such as bread with micronutrients or that supply vitamins and minerals separately are also inexpensive ways to reduce deficiencies.

Diets of people in the region have been subject to a variety of influences during transition. Some, such as higher prices and lower availability, may have a negative impact, while others, such as increased health promotion and awareness, may have a positive effect. Overall, evidence on the quality of diets is sparse, but there are signs in Russia of a decrease in the proportion of calories obtained from fat and proteins. Reduced fat consumption may have positive impacts for populations with unhealthily high intakes, but it can have adverse health effects for those who consume too little fat. Reduced protein consumption is also a concern. (See Chapter 1, Box 1.6.)

Worsening nutritional status is revealed by the rise in the proportions of adults who are overweight, obese or underweight. In Russia in 1996, 4 percent of women aged 18-59 were underweight, 28 percent overweight, and 24 percent obese, with underweight being more common among younger women, and overweight and obesity more common among older women. Still, a 1993 Russian survey of young children and their mothers in three cities and the surrounding areas showed a high prevalence of hunger: about 77 percent of the women, 70 percent of the households and 32 percent of the children were classified as hungry. The evidence suggests women may be less well fed than children or other household members. As Box 4.2 discusses, there is evidence that access to health care services has also been compromised.

Increased risk-taking behaviour

The upheaval of transition has created an environment that provides fertile ground for risk-taking behaviours. Increased poverty and social stress, greater travel and migration, changing values, and growing criminality all breed more substance abuse and unsafe sexual behaviour which raises the risk of sexually transmitted diseases.

While substance abuse has been less prevalent among women than men in the past, this pattern is changing across the region. Alcohol consumption and smoking are increasing among women and adolescent girls, raising new health risks. Women also suffer the consequences of men's substance abuse through, for instance, more domestic violence or the death of their partners. STDs pose a greater health risk to women than men. (See Box 4.3.)

It is important to note that some of these phenomena are relatively new to the region, as is the case for drug abuse and certain STDs. The impact of these emerging problems is compounded by the fact that they are occurring in an environment where there is often a lack of awareness, education, infrastructure, and programmes

Table 4.3

Live births complicated by anæmia, 1989-97

(percent)

	1989	1997
Baltics		
Estonia	15	22
Latvia	13	22
Lithuania	6	35
Western CIS		
Belarus	5	18
Moldova	6	27
Russia	5	25
Ukraine	3	24
Caucasus		
Armenia	1	11
Azerbaijan	4	10
Georgia	2	4
Central Asia		
Kazakhstan	11	50
Kyrgyzstan	15	47

Source: MONEE project database.

Note: Data for Armenia refer to the number of women with anæmia before, at, or after birth per 100 live births. The starting year is 1992 for Estonia and 1990 for Lithuania, Armenia and Georgia.

Box 4.2

Deteriorating access to health care

In most countries of the region, poverty and economic hardship have reduced people's access to health care services, often linked to the decline in public spending on health. Households often have to contribute to the cost of drugs and medical supplies in countries where the health system faces shortages. Low wages have caused medical staff to request additional fees for services or to leave public health care, especially in rural areas, in order to set up private practices or take other employment.

This deterioration in medical services may affect women more than men, as women tend to have more contact with the health care system and are usually the managers of family health. The increased requirement to pay for medical services may also affect women disproportionately, since they have been more adversely affected economically during the transition. Single-parent families, most of which are headed by women, are especially vulnerable.

Evidence from various countries points to the increasing practice of informal payments for health services. For example, in Hungary, Bulgaria and Romania, such informal payments are reported to be widespread. In the Czech Republic, patients contributed 11 percent of total health care costs in 1997. There is also evidence that, in general, higher income groups benefit more from public health expenditures. For example, in Bulgaria, the poorest 20 percent of the population received less than 10 percent of public health spending in 1997, while the richest 20 percent received over 30 percent of the total – a gap that has widened since 1995.

In Russia, data from a large household survey for 1994-96 suggest that lack of money is emerging as the main reason for the inability to obtain medication. Table 4.4 shows that, among persons prescribed medication, the share able to comply decreased from 62 percent in 1994 to 45 percent in 1996. Among those unable to obtain medication, cost was the reason given by 48 percent of individuals in 1996 (up from 23 percent in 1994), while unavailability was cited by about 45 percent (down from 76 percent in 1994). Recent

reports note the difficulty the elderly and other groups entitled to free or subsidized drugs have in finding or acquiring medications. Russia's debt to foreign drug companies was estimated in 1998 to have reached US$700 million.

In Moldova, a 1997 representative survey showed that payments are often made for medicine, medical visits and hospital treatments. More than 80 percent of women giving birth had to pay for the professional services provided. The survey also showed half the families interviewed could not buy prescribed medicine,

Table 4.4

Access to prescribed medicines in Russia, 1994-96

When medicine prescribed, % of persons	1994	1995	1996
Able to obtain medicine	62	70	45
Unable to obtain medicine	38	30	55
of which (%)			
because medicine is not available	76	59	45
because of cost	23	32	48
for other reasons (no time, no desire)	2	9	8

Source: Zohoori et al. (1997).

Note: Information is based on the Russia Longitudinal Monitoring Survey, a large nationally representative survey of Russian households.

mainly due to lack of money. Around 40 percent of low-income households had to borrow money or sell assets to cover health expenditures.

Substantial difficulties in acquiring medicines are also reported in the Caucasus and Central Asia. For example, in the Kuba district in Azerbaijan in 1994, 80 percent of households prescribed drugs could not find them. Two-thirds of those who paid for health care had to borrow or sell some goods in order to pay for them, with medicine representing 62 percent of all health care expenditure. For households where a member was ill during the month of the survey, total health care represented, on average, 20 percent of total household expenditure. Evidence from Kazakhstan shows that patient payments for medicines in hospitals made up 25-30 percent of the national health budget in 1996.

---

addressing the issues. Teenagers, though biologically healthy, are especially vulnerable to "social diseases".

The levels of alcohol consumption by adult men and of tobacco use by men and boys in the region have been similar to the prevalence in the West, but, until recently, girls and women smoked and drank relatively less. In particular, adolescent girls in the region used tobacco and alcohol less than their counterparts in Western Europe. Figure 4.11 shows, for selected countries, the percentage

of 15-year-olds who smoke. (Data refer to 1993/94, after the impact of transition had likely been felt already.) This relative advantage for women in the region mitigated against health problems such as lung cancer, which was already soaring among women in Western countries. Since the beginning of the transition, however, a deterioration of this advantage is observed in most of the countries covered in this Report.

WHO expects rising tobacco use to be the single

largest cause of increased disease and death in the region. It is estimated that more than 20 percent of the total adult disease burden will be attributable to tobacco by 2020 in the European part of the region, that is, excluding the

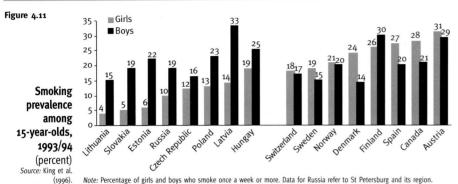

Figure 4.11

Smoking prevalence among 15-year-olds, 1993/94 (percent)
Source: King et al. (1996).

Note: Percentage of girls and boys who smoke once a week or more. Data for Russia refer to St Petersburg and its region.

Caucasus and Central Asia. In a more liberalized marketplace, the concerted targeting of young people, particularly young women, in tobacco advertising and the relatively low price of cigarettes offered by companies to attract new customers are likely to play a pivotal role in the increase in smoking among young women. The absence of control and regulation on sales, advertising or quality standards and the growing influence of media will also conspire to promote smoking by young women. In terms of drinking and smoking, the gap between female teenagers in the region and those in Western countries is, unfortunately, narrowing.

Figure 4.12 presents estimates from surveys carried out in 1990 and 1993/94 in Poland, Hungary and Latvia. It shows increases in the consumption of alcohol and tobacco among teenagers (with the exception of tobacco consumption in Hungary) and the differences by gender. The proportion of girls reporting having been drunk at least twice doubled in Poland, from 9 to 18 percent, but remained well below the proportion of boys. In Latvia, the percentage of girls who smoked weekly also more than doubled over the period. Similar data from Romania reveal that the share of girls aged 18-19 who had smoked rose from 18 to 25 percent over 1993-96.

In terms of the overall population, evidence from some countries in western CIS and the Baltics suggests that

there has been an increase in the consumption of alcohol since the beginning of the transition and often a decline in the quality of the alcohol consumed. The resulting sharp rise in male mortality from alcohol-related diseases can be expected to affect the health of women and children in both direct and indirect ways – through the role model presented to children, the greater stress generated by drunkenness, domestic violence (often associated with drinking), growing poverty (loss of productivity), or the death of a partner or father. In Kiev, street children reported that 63 percent of their fathers and 55 percent of their mothers were abusing alcohol and that 12 percent of their fathers and 8 percent of their mothers were abusing drugs. It is important to note that, although the level of alcohol-related mortality rates is much higher for men than for women in Russia, the increase in the rates since the late 1980s has been similar for both genders, showing that women have not escaped this negative trend. The death rate of adults aged 40-44 due to alcohol-related disease rose fivefold for men over 1987-94 and sixfold for women.

The growth in the incidence of certain STDs in Central and Eastern Europe and the former Soviet Union has also generated attention. The recent rise in HIV infections is staggering. The number of cases recorded jumped from about 30,000 infected persons in 1994 to about 270,000 at the end of 1998. (An estimated 80,000 new infections occurred in 1998 alone.) The biggest increases took place in Belarus, Moldova, Russia, and Ukraine. (Ukraine is currently the country most affected, with the estimated number of carriers soaring from about 1,500 in 1994 to some 110,000 in early 1998.) The transition region risks becoming one of the next areas of burgeoning HIV infections if the epidemic spreads to larger groups in the population.

Intravenous drug use appears to be behind this dramatic surge in the spread of HIV in western CIS, and drug use has been growing rapidly in parts of the region. About 70 percent of all HIV infections in Ukraine over the period 1995-97 occurred among drug users, especially among young people in cities bordering the Black Sea. For example, in the city of Mykolayev, the proportion of intravenous drug users infected with HIV swelled from 2 percent to 57 percent in 1995 alone. Similarly, in Russia, four out of five newly diagnosed infections are among intravenous drug users. Since most drug users are in the 15-24 age group, adolescents and young adults are the most affected. Experience in some Western countries has shown that the spread of HIV can be inhibited through programmes designed to encourage drug users to adopt safer practices. In Poland, initiatives to reduce needle sharing and to encourage sterilization of equipment have lowered the number of new infections among drug users since 1990.

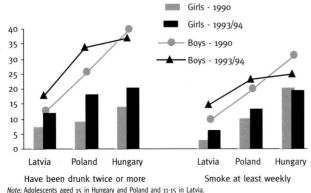

Figure 4.12

Smoking and drinking among adolescents, 1990 and 1993/94 (percent)
Sources: King et al. (1996); King and Coles (1992); Kalnins and Ranka (1996).

Note: Adolescents aged 15 in Hungary and Poland and 11-15 in Latvia.

Box 4.3

Women face higher biological risks of contracting STDs

In addition to social factors that increase the vulnerability of adolescent girls and women to STDs, biological realities place them at higher risk. Women's higher susceptibility to STDs transmitted through unprotected sex is based on biological particulars.

- Female reproductive systems expose a greater surface area of sensitive tissues to a greater variety of pathogens during intercourse. This is especially the case for young women, whose cervical mucus offers less protection from infections. Male-to-female HIV transmission appears to be two to four times as effi-

cient as female-to-male transmission.
- The consequences of STDs are broader for women than men, including pregnancy-related complications, septicæmia, spontaneous abortions, and stillbirths.
- STDs are less likely to produce symptoms in women and are, therefore, harder to diagnose until serious problems arise.

Women STDs also have important implications for children, since they are linked to premature births, low birthweights and congenital infections.

There is an important overlap between drug use and prostitution, and infection is likely to become more widespread among other social groups in the region in the near future. Evidence from the city of Kaliningrad in Russia reveals that about one-third of sex workers are intravenous drug users, while 80 percent of women treated for HIV-related health problems work as prostitutes. The potential growth in the spread of infections through unsafe sex could be dramatic in the region. Again, this is more likely to affect young persons than the rest of the population and women more than men. (See Box 4.3.)

Some countries have also experienced a dramatic resurgence of syphilis, a more familiar disease in the region. This trend is particularly worrying since it indicates that a much broader swath of the population does not practice safer sex, and is, therefore, also exposed to HIV infections.

Syphilis had been practically eradicated in the region by the early 1990s, but the disease is fast re-emerging in many countries, with the exception of Croatia and Poland. The increase may be attributed in part to the collapse of STD management systems, which involved tracing, notifying and treating all infected persons and their partners. Table 4.5 presents the incidence of syphilis for selected countries from each sub-region and for selected countries of the European Union. There is a sharp contrast, with an average incidence of two cases per 100,000 in the European Union, 11 in Central and Eastern Europe and 221 in the former Soviet Union – the last more than 100 times the EU rate. The reported incidence is presented per 100,000 population; computing incidence rates relative only to the population most likely to be sexually active shows significantly higher rates. For example, the incidence rate per 100,000 persons aged 18-59 was 476 in Russia in 1997, meaning almost one adult in 200 became infected with syphilis in that single year.

Rates in Central Europe and the former Yugoslavia are comparable to those in Western Europe, but rates are much higher in Southeastern Europe. Within the former Soviet Union, countries in western CIS and the Baltics have a particularly high incidence, while countries in the Caucasus and Central Asia have a lower incidence, with the exception of Kazakhstan and Kyrgyzstan, where the incidence is similar to western CIS. (See also Statistical Annex, Table 6.4.)

The striking differences among sub-regions are in marked contrast with the situation of the late 1980s, when average sub-regional incidence rates were roughly similar across Europe – two cases per 100,000 in the European Union, six in Central and Eastern Europe and four in the

Table 4.5

Incidence of syphilis, 1997

(newly registered cases per 100,000 population)

Central Europe	Slovakia	3.5
	Hungary	3.0
Former Yugoslavia	Slovenia	1.3
	Croatia	0.4
Southeastern Europe	Bulgaria	87.4
	Romania	31.6
Central and Eastern Europe, average		11.2
Baltics	Latvia	121.8
	Lithuania	84.9
Western CIS	Russia	276.1
	Ukraine	147.7
Caucasus	Armenia	16.7
	Azerbaijan	7.6
Central Asia	Uzbekistan	35.6
	Turkmenistan	54.0
Former Soviet Union, average		220.6
European Union	Spain	2.1
	Italy	0.8
	United Kingdom	2.5
	Netherlands	1.4
European Union, average		1.6

Sources: MONEE project database; WHO (1998) for Croatia, Uzbekistan, Western Europe, and averages.

Note: Data refer to 1996 for Croatia, Romania, Uzbekistan, Western Europe (1995 for the UK), and averages.

Soviet Union in 1989. The sharp jump in the incidence of syphilis is illustrated by Figure 4.13, which presents incidence in seven selected countries for the period 1989-97. In 11 countries of the region, the number of new cases rose more than tenfold over 1990-96. The increase in the rate is higher in the former Soviet Union, particularly in western CIS, the Baltics and Central Asia. Prevalence has been increasing in Bulgaria since 1993. In a number of countries, the rise in the annual number of new cases slowed in 1997.

Breaking down the incidence of syphilis by age and gender underlines the vulnerable position of adolescents and young adults in general and of adolescent girls in particular. In Belarus, where the disease is spreading fast, incidence is significantly higher among the young. Figure 4.14 shows the incidence of syphilis for all teenagers. While the incidence rates follow a similar pattern for women and men who are older (190 new cases per 100,000 for women and 210 for men in 1997), the rate is much higher for female adolescents aged 15-19 than for their male peers. (See Box 4.3.) In 1996, almost 1 percent of females aged 18-19 were infected with syphilis (an incidence rate of 984 per 100,000), compared to 0.3 percent of males the same age. The situation is similar in Moldova and Ukraine, and slightly worse in Russia, where 1.3 percent of girls aged 18-19 were registered as new cases of syphilis in 1997.

At a time when public health services are experiencing greater financial constraints, they are also facing the immediate health demands of more cases of STDs, as well as the long-term health burdens, especially for young people, associated with the diseases. The issue of sexually transmitted diseases needs to be addressed urgently in the region through education campaigns aimed particularly at young people and through better access to reliable means of prevention. Adolescents' knowledge of STDs

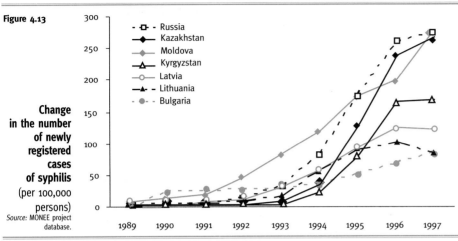

Figure 4.13

Change in the number of newly registered cases of syphilis (per 100,000 persons)
Source: MONEE project database.

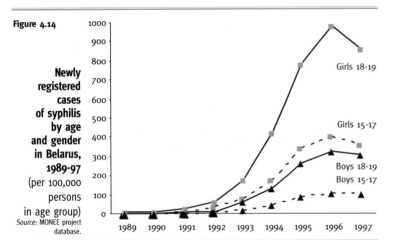

Figure 4.14

Newly registered cases of syphilis by age and gender in Belarus, 1989-97 (per 100,000 persons in age group)
Source: MONEE project database.

Box 4.4

Adolescents' knowledge of STDs

Surveys of adolescents in different countries of the region reveal a lack of knowledge about sexually transmitted diseases and about the means of protection. As in other health areas, lack of information and awareness presents a major barrier to healthy lifestyles among adolescents.

For example, in Romania, general sex education is widely available, with 88 percent of girls and 77 percent of boys aged 15-24 receiving some sex education at school. However, the topics of STDs and AIDS transmission are only rarely discussed – just over one-third of adolescents have received education on these topics, as reported in Figure 4.15. Families do not appear to provide an alternative information source, with parents discussing AIDS prevention with only 28 percent of girls and 16 percent of boys.

The low level of contraception prevalence among young persons, presented in Table 4.2, also points to the lack of knowledge about STDs and their transmission in countries, such as Moldova and Russia, where the incidence of infection is growing.

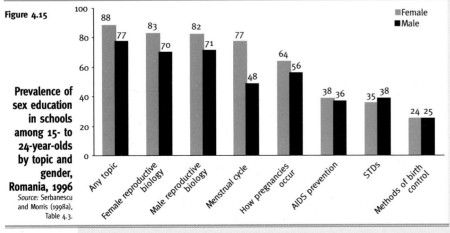

Figure 4.15

Prevalence of sex education in schools among 15- to 24-year-olds by topic and gender, Romania, 1996
Source: Serbanescu and Morris (1998a), Table 4.3.

and of the modes of transmission remains very limited (Box 4.4), and sexual education can help boost awareness (Box 4.5).

Gender dimensions of stress and depression

As set out at the beginning of this chapter, health is not only the absence of disease or infirmity, but a state of physical and mental well-being. Epidemiological and anthropological surveys show gender differences in patterns of psychiatric disorder and psychological distress. It consistently appears that women more frequently experience depression, anxiety and psychological distress, while the prevalence of substance disorders and self-inflicted violence is greater among men. This is consistent with the observation in part of the region of a rise in mortality among men that is linked to alcohol abuse and suicides. The social conditioning of women, including their roles as mothers and caregivers and their greater reliance on social networks, may be a protective factor and may inhibit them from such extreme behaviours as substance abuse, violence and suicide.

Evidence on the emotional and mental health of people in the region before transition is largely absent. A few studies, however, have focused on the topic in recent years. They show that women are particularly at high risk of depression and emotional difficulties. Worsening living conditions in most of the countries of the region suggest this risk has increased during the transition. Certainly, many forms of psychological disorder are significantly influenced by environmental factors.

In 1990, the World Bank and WHO estimated the losses due to premature death and disability for different regions of the world. In the transition region, mental health problems accounted for about 14 percent of the total burden of disease and infirmity, and estimates suggest that the share will climb sharply over the coming decades. Table 4.6 shows the share that different conditions make up in the mental health problems of women and men.

Depressive and post-traumatic stress disorders account for one-third of disability from mental health problems for women, but only for 10 percent for men. On the other hand, substance dependence and self-inflicted injuries account for over 60 percent of the total for men, but for only 18 percent for women. Women also consistently report a lower subjective assessment of their health. Evidence from the region is similar to that from Western Europe, with the proportion of men reporting themselves to be in good health averaging 10 percentage points higher than that of women.

Research in countries around the world points to the social origins of psychological distress for women. Factors which put women at risk include lower social and economic status, physical or sexual abuse, stress generated by the "double burden" of paid and unpaid work, insecurity, isolation, dependence, unemployment and associated loss of support networks, or difficulties in providing for their households. A medical response to psychological distress is sometimes necessary, though largely overlooked by health care systems in the region, but the long-term improvement of women's health and equality requires

---

Box 4.5

Sexual health education lowers risks

Most individuals become sexually active during their teenage years. In addition, "partner turnover" is higher during younger years than later in life, both in terms of casual liaisons and stable, monogamous relationships. Thus, sex occurs with multiple partners even if the cumulative risk is sometimes hidden by the apparent monogamy and commitment of each discrete relationship. Higher risk of unprotected sex among young people is reflected in the disproportionately high rates of STD incidence and unwanted pregnancies among the young. The recent HIV/AIDS epidemic in the region creates new challenges and requires widespread sexual education on historically taboo sexual topics and practices. Sexual health education is needed to ensure healthy and responsible sexuality.

Sexual health education for children and adolescents is debated and often condemned as promoting early or increased sexual activity. A recent thorough review, based on studies carried out mainly in North America and Western Europe, shows that evidence does not support this argument. On the contrary, the survey finds that sex education helps delay first intercourse and protect sexually active young people from HIV, STDs and unwanted pregnancies.

It is important to note that women's decisions on reproductive matters are directly influenced by their partners, whose responsibilities should not be neglected. Young women face particular risks, which arise out of both physical and social vulnerability. (See Box 4.3.) Responsibility for contraception or STD protection is often left to girls and women, while their status does not always give them the power to enforce their choices: a passive sexual role is traditionally prescribed for women; their male partners tend to be older, and girls are more likely than boys to consider their relationships stable and committed and, therefore, not requiring protection. In order to be successful, sex education programmes must also target boys and young men and address the context in which sexual relationships take place. This can help challenge gender roles in terms of sexuality, reproductive health and male-female relationships in general.

Table 4.6

Relative importance of different mental health problems in European transition countries, 1990

(percent of all mental health problems)

	Women	Men
Depressive disorders	25	7
Post-traumatic stress disorder	8	3
Total depressive and post-traumatic stress disorder	33	10
Alcohol and drug dependence	10	39
Self-inflicted injuries	8	25
Total alcohol and drug dependence and self-inflicted injuries	18	64
Alzheimer's and other dementia	27	11
Other	22	15
Total mental health problems	100	100
Mental health problems as a share of total losses	13	14

Source: World Bank (1993).

Note: The countries covered are those of Central and Eastern Europe, Southeastern Europe, the former Yugoslavia, the Baltics, and western CIS (19 countries).

that attention be focused upstream, on the causes of mental health problems.

Differences in subjective feelings between women and men are observed at a young age. Table 4.7 presents the percentage of children aged 15 who report various symptoms and feelings, based on large surveys of children in Central Europe, the Baltics and Russia. Young girls are much more likely than boys to report headaches, stomach aches, and feeling nervous, lonely, low, or depressed. Thus, 20 percent more girls, on average, report headaches, and 15 percent more report feeling depressed. This information is based on self-reported symptoms and feelings. It therefore reflects subjective feelings of health

Table 4.7

The health of 15-year-olds in Central Europe, the Baltics and Russia, 1993/94

(percent)

	Feeling very healthy		Headache		Stomach ache		Feeling nervous		Feeling lonely		Feeling low or depressed	
	Female	Male	Female	Male	Female	Male	Female	Male	Female	Male	Female	Male
Czech Republic	25	32	–	–	–	–	–	–	22	14	–	–
Slovakia	22	40	41	20	25	15	73	57	18	12	25	20
Hungary	16	19	41	19	17	11	61	49	25	14	54	34
Poland	13	25	33	14	13	6	69	51	19	7	29	12
Estonia	10	24	31	19	18	13	54	45	20	11	32	17
Latvia	17	32	36	14	22	9	53	31	25	14	31	17
Lithuania	18	33	42	22	22	10	57	39	29	17	31	17
Russia	14	29	41	19	14	11	54	34	26	15	35	17

Source: King et al. (1996).

Note: For headaches, stomach aches, feeling nervous, or feeling low or depressed, the questions asked whether the child had the characteristic once a week or more over the past six months. For feeling lonely, the question asked whether the child felt lonely very or quite often. Data for Russia refer to St Petersburg and its region.

Table 4.8

Estimated risk of social exclusion in Estonia, 1994

(percent)

Percentage with estimated	Women	Men
Low risk	25	43
Average risk	35	31
High risk	40	26
Total	100	100

Source: NORBALT survey of 4,550 individuals organized by the Estonian Ministry of Social Affairs, the Statistical Office and the Norwegian International Applied Social Research Institute, reported in UNDP (1997a).

Note: The risk of social exclusion is based on 15 indicators of deprivation, isolation and anomy (loss of norms): lack of regular income, reliance on social benefits, poor health, lack of medical insurance, difficulty in meeting housing expenses, lack of labour market participation, living without other adults, feelings of fear in public places or at home, non-participation in associations, no interest in politics, no trust in authorities, no understanding of politics, no faith in democracy, feelings of worthlessness, and lack of plans for the future. Individuals are classified according to the total number of conditions which apply to their situation: 0-6 is "low" risk, 7-9 "average" risk, and 10-15 "high" risk.

and does not necessarily reveal the actual medical/clinical incidence of problems. It still suggests that, irrespective of the actual incidence, girls are more likely to perceive themselves as having problems and, therefore, to have lower subjective perception of their health status.

The survey results emphasize the higher expression of the problems among girls, their different perceptions of their own health, and the impact of their social environments. These girls have yet to face some of the major challenges of life for women, such as raising a family and the cumulative effects of gender bias, but they already suffer a pronounced degree of emotional and mental stress.

A 1994 survey in Estonia evaluated the risk of social exclusion based on measures of deprivation, isolation and anomy (loss of norms). Table 4.8 shows the percentage of women and men who were classified as being at high, average, or low risk of social exclusion. It confirms that women are at greater risk of social exclusion – in other words, of weak participation in society. For example, 40 percent of women, compared to 26 percent of men, were found to be at high risk of social exclusion. The survey finds that this risk is linked to women's lower labour force participation, higher dependence on social assistance, lower capacity to generate income, and the prevalence of women among single parents. This higher risk of exclusion from the mainstream of society may well lead to higher risk of depression and stress.

Further evidence of the emotional difficulties experienced by women comes from a study of the emotional health of pregnant women. Pregnancy is a period with some potential for increased anxiety and depression and decreased emotional well-being. Stressful life events and limited social networks have been found to contribute to the development of emotional disorders during pregnancy. The study, carried out in four municipalities – Avon, England, Yaroslavl, Russia, and Brno and Znojmo, the Czech Republic – over 1990-92, allowed the simultaneous analysis of women's emotional status and the extent of their social networks and support during pregnancy. The level of clinical depression was found to be higher in England than in the Czech Republic or Russia. On the other hand, the average level of non-clinical depression was found to be somewhat higher in the Czech Republic than in England and significantly higher in Russia than in the other two countries, suggesting higher levels of general stress in families and society in the transition region.

Women in Russia and the Czech Republic had lower levels of support than women in England. For example, 30 percent of the British women, but only 18 percent of the Czech women and 8 percent of the Russian women had four or more persons with whom they could discuss "important decisions". Russian and Czech women were less likely than British women to know other pregnant

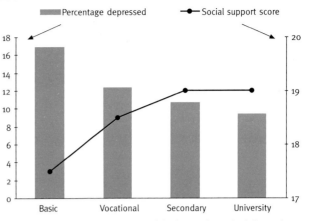

Figure 4.16

Prevalence of depression and level of social support among women in Brno and Znojmo, by education level, 1990-92
Source: Koupilová et al. (1996).

Note: Women are defined as depressed when the Edinburgh Postnatal Depression Scale score is 13 or higher. The social support score is a subjective measure of the amount of support women feel they have from partners, friends and relatives. The sample involved 3,900 women living in Brno and the rural area of Znojmo, the Czech Republic.

women and more likely to doubt whether their neighbours would help out with a difficulty and whether the state would support them in case of problems. In the two Czech centres, where characteristics could be explored by maternal education, clear trends indicated that social support increases and clinical depression decreases with education level. Figure 4.16 presents the prevalence of depression and the "score" of social support from networks among women of different education levels in the Czech Republic.

The higher incidence of clinical depression and depressive disorders among women than men raises a host of questions about the differences between women's and men's health: Is there a biological basis for this gender gap in mental wellness? What are the reasons women and men respond to trauma and stress differently? How much does social and economic inequality influence women's emotional health, and how much does women's mental health affect their ability to participate in society? Most importantly, what range of responses is required?

■

4.3 Conclusions

Overall, women in the region began the transition with relatively good health status and adequate access to basic health services. However, there were some particularly troubling traits in the general health picture of women, including relatively high infant mortality in many countries, high maternal death rates and extremely high abortion rates. The transition period has seen both a depreciation of existing health care assets for women and an inability to improve highly visible health problems such as maternal deaths. Countries with "higher" health status before transition have tended to lose less than those with a "lower" starting point. Within all countries, large and often growing disparities between different socio-economic groups have been noted.

Almost two-thirds of the countries in the region have reported declines in maternal death rates, and one-third have reported increases. Altogether 17 still have maternal mortality rates above the WHO target for Europe. Birth-related complications of all types have increased in many countries, as perinatal care has deteriorated. Abortion rates have long been high by international standards in these countries and have remained high throughout the transition – on average, five times greater than the average in the European Union. These high rates may result from a constellation of factors, including social acceptance of and universal access to medical abortions and lack of promotion of family planning techniques.

Family planning is an important way for women and men to exercise choice and responsibility in their personal lives. Generally, women throughout the region, especially younger women, show relatively poor understanding of reproductive health issues. There is evidence that the range of family planning techniques available is limited and that there are often problems with the availability, price and quality of contraception materials. However, for most countries for which information is available, use of contraception appears to be increasing during transition. The issue of family planning is being raised in a changing environment where fertility rates have plunged and social values are in a state of flux.

The transition period has brought many changes in both the living conditions and the lifestyles of women in the region, factors that are important determinants of health. For many women, these changes have challenged their ability to maintain proper nutrition and healthy behaviours. Evidence shows that populations have experienced micronutrient malnutrition linked to a drop in food consumption in some countries, a deterioration in the quality of the nutrients consumed and the disruption of certain nutrition programmes such as the fortification of bread with iron and the supply of vitamin and mineral supplements to pregnant women and children. Women, in particular, are experiencing more problems with anæmia.

The shifting influences around lifestyle during the transition also include increases in risk-taking behaviour. Alcohol consumption and smoking have risen among women and adolescent girls across the region during the transition period. The prevalence of drug abuse and sexually transmitted diseases, particularly HIV and syphilis, is also rising. Women, especially young women, are both biologically and socially vulnerable to STDs – a situation of major concern given the substantial growth in the sex industry in the region.

Specific dimensions of health, such as mental health, are still largely ignored throughout the region. This is especially troubling for women, as they tend to report more emotional health problems, including stress and depression, than men. In a study of 19 countries in the region, depressive and post-traumatic stress disorders account for one-third of the disabilities from mental health problems for women and only 10 percent for men.

Overall, the health of women is showing the strain of the transition. The system of universal health care, whatever its initial shortcomings, is suffering from the reduced ability of the state to generate revenues. Infant mortality, maternal mortality and abortion rates remain high by international standards. The focus on women's health continues to be related to maternity, and so women's wider health concerns such as violence against women, depression and stress go under-recognized. At the same time, other health issues, particularly those shaped by social and economic factors, have emerged during the transition, including poorer nutrition, rising substance abuse and a higher incidence of STDs. Not only does this increased stress affect women's health directly, but it makes their role as health care managers in their families more difficult. The plunging fertility rates across the region, presented in Chapter 3, also suggest that, since women are making less use of the health care system for pregnancy-related reasons, they may be missing opportunities for more general health care.

A more complete understanding of the health of women requires a more complex understanding than that which underlay the health care system inherited from the communist years. However, it is evident that these curative-driven systems still need to be supported even while health care is being reformed – a step some countries have taken by directing more resources towards the health care system. This survey of women's health in the transition region makes clear that women's health would benefit from a broader approach to health both in terms of biology and in terms of the social determinants that shape health. It is also clear that women's health would benefit from a wider sharing of responsibility and initiative in society.

Under communism, health was considered the domain and the product of the state-run health care system. To improve the health of women in a manner which supports and advances women's equality requires a public policy approach that not only brings a gender lens to the health care infrastructure, but that brings a health perspective to other areas of public policy, including economic policy and social services. There are also many benefits to reap from an emphasis on public education, disease prevention and health promotion. Improving women's health requires the building up in the transition societies of a sense of responsibility and a capacity to contribute to health by individuals, families, communities, civil groups, and businesses. The achievement of optimum individual health is, in the final instance, the outcome of a healthy society.

■

Violence against women and the threat of violence are main barriers to women's empowerment and equal participation in society. However, they often go unnoticed and undocumented and therefore unresolved. When stress and violence increase in society in general, as they have in the transition region, women's safety in the home, workplace and community is often seriously affected.

The UN Declaration on Violence against Women, adopted in 1993, defines violence against women as encompassing "any act of gender-based violence that results in, or is likely to result in, physical, sexual or psychological harm or suffering to women, including threats of such acts, coercion or arbitrary deprivations of liberty, whether occurring in public or private life". Violence against women has particular characteristics and therefore requires particular responses. The gender dimensions of violence are explicit; for example, women are at risk more in their own homes than on the street, and often violence against women takes the form of sexual assault.

Violence is a serious violation of the human rights of women and girls, and it takes a heavy toll on physical and mental health. The World Bank estimates that rape and domestic violence account for 19 percent of the total disease burden among women aged 15-44 in industrialized countries. This means that, for women, one of every five years of healthy life lost because of injury, disease or premature death is attributable to violence.

Despite the official rhetoric of gender equality, there was a notable silence about violence against women under communism. Because of the lack of public discourse, autonomous media and civilian associations, there was little independent space in which to raise the issue. During the transition period, violence against women also appears to have gone largely undocumented as a specific issue, though evidence points to a high incidence in all countries for which some information is available. The changes triggered during the transition can be expected to increase violence of all forms in these societies, including violence against women. Change, however, also offers an historic opportunity to raise the issue and tackle the problem at its roots. The opening up of these countries to democratic practices will allow previously taboo subjects, such as violence against women, to be addressed.

One of the challenges in analysing data on violence in general and on violence against women in particular is the difficulty of measuring the level and degree of violence. Some concepts, such as those of emotional abuse and sexual harassment, are difficult to define and therefore lead to measurement problems. Even when a clear definition is available, some forms of violence frequently go unreported, as is the case with domestic violence. Analysis, therefore, has to combine administrative data with a variety of other information. This supplemental information is often based on small and unrepresentative surveys and should be considered with caution. The quantitative analysis in this chapter combines different types of information and less rigorous data than those provided in other chapters, and the data limitations should be borne in mind.

However, data limitations should not block initiatives to deal with violence against women. Rather, they should prompt a concerted effort to define and identify the forms of violence against women, especially within criminal law, and to improve the collection of data related to violence, especially gender-disaggregated evidence. The Platform for Action signed at the UN Fourth World Conference on Women, held in Beijing in 1995, declared the importance of developing statistical measurements of women's lives as a tool for promoting women's equality. Certainly, in many Western countries where the issue of violence against women has a higher profile, the greatly enhanced collection of data on violence in women's lives has been an essential step in describing the scope and nature of this serious problem and in helping to shape the allocation of efforts and resources to eliminate this social disease.

In this chapter, Section 5.1 reviews the different types of violence women around the world face and the wide-ranging consequences. Section 5.2 presents evidence on the major types of violence women in the region covered by this Report experience in their daily environments. Section 5.3 focuses on new types of violence against women that have arisen during the transition period in some countries – violence against women in war and trafficking of women for sexual exploitation. Section 5.4 looks at the opportunities for addressing violence against women in the region. The Conclusions review the findings of the chapter and the prospects for reducing and preventing violence.

■

5.1 Violence has Many Faces and Many Consequences

Table 5.1

Types of violence against women: a life-cycle approach

Infancy	Female infanticide; emotional, sexual and physical abuse; differential access to food and medical care.
Girlhood	Child marriage; female genital mutilation; sexual and psychological abuse by relatives or strangers; differential access to food and medical care; child prostitution and pornography.
Adolescence	Dating and courtship violence; economically coerced sex; incest; sexual abuse in the workplace; sexual harassment; rape, marital rape; forced prostitution and pornography; trafficking; forced pregnancy.
Reproductive age	Abuse by intimate male partners, marital rape; dowry abuse and murder; partner homicide; psychological abuse; sexual abuse in the workplace; sexual harassment; rape; forced prostitution and pornography; trafficking; abuse of women with disabilities.
Elderly	Sexual, psychological and physical abuse.

Source: Adapted from Heise, Pitanguy and Germain (1994).

Table 5.2

Prevalence of violence against women in the world

Africa	
Tanzania	60% physically abused by partners
Zambia	40% beaten by partners, and another 40% mentally abused
Continent-wide	About two million girls genitally mutilated each year
South Asia	
Sri Lanka	60% beaten
India	More than 5,000 women killed each year over dowries
East Asia and Pacific	
Republic of Korea	38% beaten by partners
Malaysia	39% beaten by partners
Latin America and Caribbean	
Mexico	57% victims of violence in urban areas (44% in rural areas)
Guatemala	49% abused
Colombia	20% physically abused, 33% psychologically abused, 10% raped by their husbands
Industrial countries	
Japan	59% physically abused by partners
United States	40% abused, 31% physically abused
New Zealand	20% physically abused by partners
Canada	25% physically abused by partners
World	An estimated 60 million women are missing from world population statistics due to premature deaths linked to various forms of abuse and violence

Source: Adapted from Heise, Pitanguy and Germain (1994).

Violence against women has many faces around the world. These range from female infanticide and the custom of genital mutilation at puberty to domestic violence in marriage and elder abuse. Table 5.1 presents the different types of violence experienced by women from infancy to old age. Violence against women is distinguished by the fact that, as in domestic abuse and forced prostitution, it is often chronic and prolonged.

A recent international review of evidence offers a chilling picture of high levels of gender violence in many countries. Table 5.2 provides selected data from the survey, illustrating that violence against women is widespread and crosses all cultural, social, economic, class, religious, and regional boundaries. For example, in countries as different as Zambia and Guatemala, Sri Lanka and Japan, the percentage of women abused by their partners is similarly high.

In every country where domestic violence has been studied, it has been found to be a massive problem, with between one-quarter and more than half of women reporting physical abuse by current or former partners. Surveys estimate that 50-60 percent of women who experience physical violence by their partners are also sexually abused by them. An even larger percentage has been subjected to ongoing emotional and psychological abuse.

Certain forms of violence that have cultural and economic roots are not so common in Central and Eastern Europe and the former Soviet Union. For instance, sex-selective abortion, female infanticide and systematic differential access to food or medical care (whereby girls are fed and medically treated less than boys) seem to be non-existent in the region. Available data also indicate there is no significant female "deficit" in population numbers – the "missing millions" phenomenon observed in parts of South and West Asia, China and North Africa, as described in Box 5.1. There are, however, other factors present in much of the transition region that can aggravate already high levels of violence against women, such as alcohol abuse, which is frequently associated with violence. New forms of violence against women in the region include violence against women during and after armed conflicts, which have been numerous since the beginning of transition.

All violence has a lasting impact, but some forms of violence are especially likely to have long-term implications that predispose women to

Box 5.1

The phenomenon of the "missing millions"

The level of violence against women is so extreme in some parts of the world that millions of women are reported to be "missing" from overall population numbers. In the world, an estimated 60 million women are missing from population statistics, that is, there are 60 million fewer women alive than can be expected on the basis of the ratio of females and males at birth and their respective health risks. (See Table 5.2.) This "deficit" phenomenon is observed in several countries on the rim of the Central Asian part of the transition region, including India, Afghanistan, Iran, China, or Pakistan. However, it does not seem to be showing up in the Central Asian countries formerly part of the Soviet Union. Figure 5.1 shows that women in this sub-region outnumber men, the opposite of the situation in neighbouring countries to the south.

Tracking the welfare of children after birth shows no evidence that girls are given less access to food or medical care. Large health surveys of children aged 0-3 in Uzbekistan and Kazakhstan reveal that neonatal, post-neonatal and child mortality rates are lower for girls than for boys. (This is a standard result due to the biological edge in survival that females have over males.) The surveys also show that girls' anthropometric status and anæmia status are better than those of boys.

It is, however, important to note that other forms of violence may be on the rise in Central Asia. Some traditions, revived since independence, may be used to excuse and justify violence against women. The practice of "bride stealing" is reportedly increasing in Kyrgyzstan – 64 bride abductions were recorded in the justice system over 1994-96, and some estimates suggest one in five marriages among ethnic Kyrgyz involves bride stealing, though it is not always involuntary. Young women sometimes have little to say in the choice of a husband and face strong pressure to bear children. If a women does not have a child shortly after marriage, she may feel forced to dissolve the marriage. There also appears to be substantial inconsistency between the legal rights of women in marriage and the de facto enforcement of such rights.

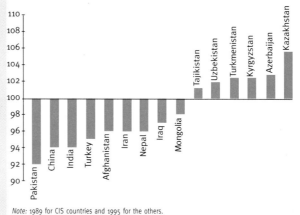

Figure 5.1

The number of women as a percent of the number of men

Sources: CIS from Statistical Annex, Tables 1.1 and 1.2; others from World Bank (1997a).

Note: 1989 for CIS countries and 1995 for the others.

secondary health risks. For example, sexual abuse during childhood can lead to complications during later pregnancies, and violence during childhood or adolescence can increase the risk of suicide, depression, or substance abuse during adulthood. Table 5.3 presents the range of physical and mental health consequences of violence against women, a grim spectrum that runs from chronic depression to immediate death. Many of the mental and physical injuries caused by violence are enduring and impose a heavy burden on women throughout their lives.

The health consequences of violence against women create a ripple effect of losses that acts not only on the victims, but also on their families and children and society at large. Surveys have shown that women victims of violence have lower educational attainment and lower earning capacity and are more likely to become isolated and develop symptoms of depression.

The consequences for children start early. Victims of violence tend to deliver babies with lower birthweights and higher risks of prematurity and complications. Children who are exposed to abuse between their parents are also at risk of being assaulted and of developing emotional and behavioural problems. It is important to note that patterns of violence and abuse pass from one generation to the next, with children who witness or who experience violence more likely to become perpetrators or victims of violence as adults. Also, by negatively affecting

Table 5.3

Health consequences of violence against women

Mental health	Depression
	Fear
	Anxiety
	Low self-esteem
	Sexual dysfunction
	Eating and sleeping disorders
	Obsessive-compulsive disorder
	Post-traumatic stress disorder
	Suicide
Physical health	Death
	Partial or permanent disabilities
	Injury
	Headaches
	Asthma
	Irritable bowel syndrome
	Alcohol or drug abuse
	Destructive health behaviours (smoking, unprotected sex)
Reproductive health	Unwanted pregnancy
	Gynæcological problems
	Sexually transmitted diseases
	Miscarriage
	Low birthweight
	Pelvic inflammatory disease
	Chronic pelvic pain
	Maternal mortality
	Maternal morbidity

the capabilities of its victims, violence against women lowers the economic and psychosocial resources available for the care of children and other household members, including violent partners.

The economic cost to society is also substantial. Violence places a high cost burden on the health care sys-tem for the treatment of the physical and mental health consequences. It reduces the contribution of women at work through lower productivity or more frequent absence from jobs. Violence against women is thus a major barrier to the economic and social development of women.

■

5.2 Violence in the Daily Lives of Women

The transition period has been characterized by many fac-tors that may influence the level of violence against women. The increase in poverty, unemployment, hard-ship, income inequality, stress, and adult mortality and morbidity that is documented in previous chapters sug-gests that there is a rise in violence in society, including violence against women. These factors can also indirectly raise women's vulnerability by encouraging more risk-tak-ing behaviour, more alcohol and drug abuse, the break-down of social support networks, and the economic dependence of women on their partners.

The general level of violence appears to have grown significantly during the transition in most of the countries surveyed. This is in part due to the collapse of regimes that imposed tight controls on any activity or association out-side the home. Weakened public-sector control may con-tribute to a rise in crime rates, including offences such as property crime or violence in the street. The total reported crime rate has more than doubled in seven countries and has soared by more than 50 percent in another six coun-tries of the region during the transition. (See Statistical Annex, Table 9.1.) The sharpest increases have taken place in Central and Southeastern Europe, the Baltics and western CIS. Part of the rise is attributable to the growing prevalence of economic and property crimes. However, a similar trend is observed in violent crimes, particularly in western CIS and the Baltics. (The fourth Regional Monitoring Report pointed out the significant increase in crimes committed by and against young persons.)

Definitions of crimes and capacities to capture data vary greatly from one country to the next. Figure 5.2 therefore presents data on homicides, a form of violence that is commonly recognized as a crime, easily defined and usually reported. The evidence shows that the homicide rate has risen in most of the region during the transition. (It has remained stable in Slovenia, Bulgaria and Uzbekistan and fallen in Croatia, Romania and Turkmenistan.) The homicide rate is much higher and has grown dramatically in the Baltics, western CIS and three Central Asian countries. The sharpest increases have taken place in Tajikistan (almost fourfold) and Estonia (threefold), but the highest level of homicides is found in Russia, with 200 homicides per million inhabitants in 1997, a total of almost 30,000 murders that year. The prevalence of homicides is much higher in the region, especially in the former Soviet Union, than in Western Europe. In 1995, the standardized death rate from homi-cide was about 12 deaths per million inhabitants in the European Union, compared to an average of 30 in Central and Eastern Europe and 219 in the former Soviet Union. The death rate from murders in the former Soviet Union was more than twice the rate in the United States in the mid-1990s, although both were at similar levels in the late 1980s.

The rise in reported crime and homicide, the pinnacle of violent behav-iour, strongly suggests that all kinds of violence have increased in these societies, including violence against women. Strikingly, how-ever, the number of rapes reported has fallen over the period of transition in all countries for which infor-mation is available, with the exception of Estonia, Kazakhstan and Kyrgyzstan. In the context of higher

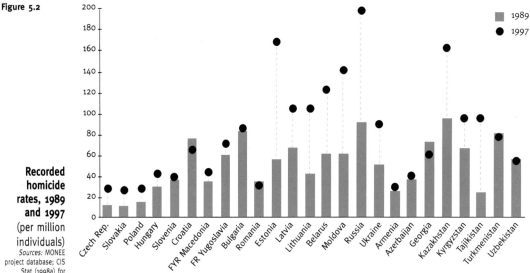

Figure 5.2

Recorded homicide rates, 1989 and 1997 (per million individuals)
Sources: MONEE project database; CIS Stat (1998a) for Tajikistan and Uzbekistan.

Note: Alternative sources show an increase in Georgia (CIS Stat, 1998a). Starting year is 1991 for FYR Macedonia and Bulgaria and 1990 for Georgia and Romania. End year is 1996 for Armenia.

crime rates, particularly rates of violent crime, this decline is conspicuous. It likely reflects a reduced reporting of rape rather than a decrease in the actual number of rapes. This trend therefore merits concern and further investigation.

Comparing the number of rape cases reported and the number of convictions provides another measure of the capacity of law enforcement agencies to investigate and prosecute crimes successfully. Figure 5.3 shows changes since 1989 in the number of recorded homicides, reported rapes and rape convictions in selected transition countries. In all countries, the number of rapes reported rose less or declined more than the number of homicides reported. Comparing the number of rapes reported with the number of convictions, the graph presents two different patterns. In the six countries on the left, the number of convictions for rape fell more than the number of cases reported. (Convictions also decreased in Estonia and Kazakhstan, while the rapes reported increased.) In the case of Hungary, there were 39 percent more homicides, but 14 percent fewer rapes reported and 23 percent fewer rape convictions. For the six countries on the right, in contrast, the number of rape convictions rose more or declined less than the number of rapes reported, indicating the greater success of the authorities in concluding cases.

The under-reporting of sexual assault is not uncommon in most countries of the world. It is generally estimated that the number of rapes (including rapes within marriage) is 5-10 times higher than the number reported. Reported crimes therefore represent only the tip of the iceberg of crime. Low reporting can reflect fear of publicity and fear of damage to the woman's reputation, fear of reprisal, reluctance to repeat and psychologically re-experience the incident, and lack of confidence in the abilities of law enforcement authorities. Various surveys suggest that trust in the ability and capacity of police forces to solve cases is often low.

A survey on crime in Russia shows that cases of crime reported to police are not always processed. It estimated that 15 percent of reported rapes were concealed by law enforcement authorities who did not file or follow up on complaints. Authorities tended to explain such omissions as the result of insufficient manpower or attempts to give the impression of police effectiveness.

The growth in violence – compounded by the general increase in the workload of law enforcement agencies and, often, a decline in the number, quality and motiva-

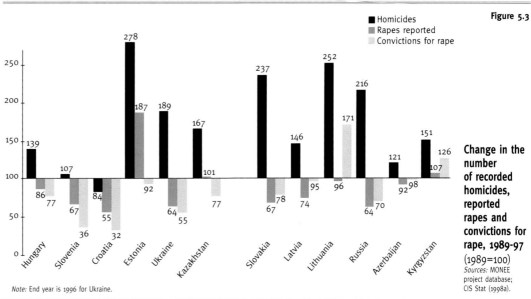

Figure 5.3

Change in the number of recorded homicides, reported rapes and convictions for rape, 1989-97
(1989=100)
Sources: MONEE project database; CIS Stat (1998a).

Note: End year is 1996 for Ukraine.

tion of police staff – raises serious concerns about the capacity of the state to tackle the issue of violence against women. When violence against women that is committed outside the home is not addressed, it can be expected that domestic violence – a complex and largely hidden issue – is even less of a concern for authorities.

Domestic violence revealed

Domestic violence is violence that takes place at home or within the family. It presumes a close relationship between the victim and the offender. It includes emotional abuse and neglect, as well as sexual and physical violence. Although domestic violence can involve both women and men as perpetrators or victims, the focus here is on violence against women.

Domestic violence is not a new phenomenon in Central and Eastern Europe and the former Soviet Union. However, the issue was largely ignored until recent years. Reports surveying human rights conditions in the region characterize the problem of domestic violence as widespread. Authoritative data on domestic violence are, however, generally non-existent. Available crime statistics from official sources are unlikely to capture the extent of this "invisible" form of violence. Ad hoc surveys are often the only reliable sources of information available, but they frequently provide only a snapshot of one place at one time and rely on different concepts and measures. Hence, they cannot be used to draw comparisons across countries or over time. However, survey results in transition countries in most of the sub-regions clearly suggest the problem is not limited to certain areas of the region.

A representative survey of pregnant women carried out in some Western European countries, the Czech Republic and Russia in 1990-92 provides estimates of the levels of violence experienced by pregnant women. Pregnancy appears to be a period of particular vulnerability for women, as their partners react, sometimes violently, to the changes it brings. Figure 5.4 presents survey results for three areas – Avon, United Kingdom, Yaroslavl, Russia, and Brno and Znojmo, the Czech Republic. It shows that 6-7 percent of pregnant women in all three areas reported suffering emotional cruelty by their partners or spouses. Physical abuse was higher in the case of the two transition countries, with almost one in 10

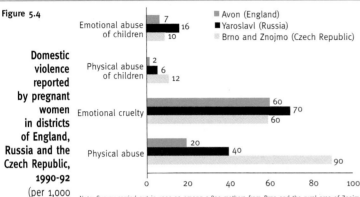

Figure 5.4

Domestic violence reported by pregnant women in districts of England, Russia and the Czech Republic, 1990-92 (per 1,000 women)
Source: Dragonas et al. (1996).

Note: Survey carried out in 1990-92 among 3,830 mothers from Brno and the rural area of Znojmo, the Czech Republic, 5,336 mothers from Yaroslav, Russia, and 12,287 mothers from Avon, England. The samples consisted of all pregnant women who were resident in the survey areas and who were anticipated to deliver within pre-specified dates.

women reporting physical abuse during pregnancy in the Czech centres, and one in 25 in Yaroslavl.

A survey carried out among 2,990 women aged 15-45 in Latvia in 1997 provides evidence on the prevalence of violence against women in the Baltics. Figure 5.5 shows that 7 percent of respondents reported having been victims of sexual violence, 9 percent, of physical violence, and 19 percent, of psychological violence. It is important

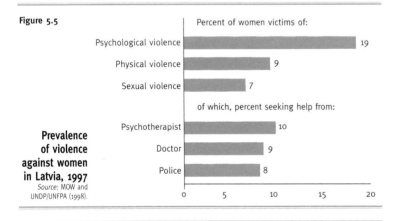

Figure 5.5

Prevalence of violence against women in Latvia, 1997
Source: MOW and UNDP/UNFPA (1998).

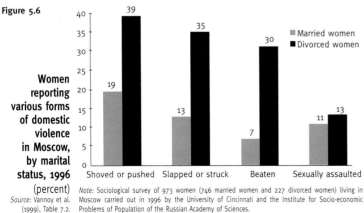

Figure 5.6

Women reporting various forms of domestic violence in Moscow, by marital status, 1996 (percent)
Source: Vannoy et al. (1999), Table 7.2.

Note: Sociological survey of 973 women (746 married women and 227 divorced women) living in Moscow carried out in 1996 by the University of Cincinnati and the Institute for Socio-economic Problems of Population of the Russian Academy of Sciences.

to note that most of these victims did not seek professional help. Only 10 percent visited a psychotherapist, and only 8 percent went to a doctor or the police. This underlines the lack of trust in, and perhaps accessibility of, institutional and social supports.

A 1996 survey of 970 women in Moscow offers a detailed picture of domestic violence in the Russian capital. Figure 5.6 shows that 11 percent of married women and 13 percent of divorced women reported having been sexually abused by their husbands. Divorced women reported a much higher incidence of other forms of abuse. For example, more than 30 percent of divorced women reported having been beaten by their former husbands, while 7 percent of married women reported having been beaten by their spouses. More than half the cases of physical abuse were said to be triggered by the husband's excessive alcohol consumption. The different pattern observed for divorced women suggests that divorces may be motivated by violence in a significant number of cases. This connection has also been noted in Romania, where judges estimated that 60 percent of the cases of divorce in Bucharest involved physical violence and where 23 percent of divorces were filed on the grounds of violence in 1997. Similarly, alcoholism and poor treatment in the family were the reason for more than half the divorces affecting women aged 30-50 in Poland.

In Russia, the number of recorded criminal acts involving women who were victims of jealousy or family conflict increased from around 40,000 in 1994 to 79,000 in 1996. According to the Russian President's Advisor on Women's Issues, 14,000 women are killed by their partners in that country every year. If the figure is reliable, it would mean that about one in six of all deaths of women aged 20-50 and about half of all homicides in Russia in 1997 were caused by domestic violence. (The number of cases of beatings of women by their partners was said to be 36,000 per day.) A comparative analysis of spousal homicide, based on data for 1991, concluded that Russian women are 2.5 times more likely to be murdered by their partners than are American women, who are already two times more likely to be killed by their partners than are women in Western European countries. The analysis also found that the likelihood of murder by an intimate partner is six times higher for women than for men in Russia.

A 1995 survey of 1,500 adolescent girls and boys in Ukraine reveals the scope of physical and sexual abuse of children. Figure 5.7 shows that, among children in mainstream education institutions, the prevalence of rape ranges from 4 percent among students of secondary schools to 9 percent among those attending vocational schools. Other forms of sexual violence are more pervasive, with 11-21 percent of children reporting being subjected to unwanted sexual contact, and 17-27 percent experiencing sexual harassment. (Rates include both girls and boys.) The situation for those adolescents who live in the institutions of the Ministry of the Interior is particularly worrying, with 50 percent of adolescents reporting unwanted sexual contact and as many as 30 percent reporting having been raped.

In Kazakhstan, a sample of 159 women from Almaty, the surrounding region and the region of Jambyl was surveyed in 1997. The sample was small, and the results, presented in Table 5.4, must therefore be seen as merely illustrative. The survey showed that around 3 percent of the women had suffered physical or sexual violence. One woman in eight reported suffering emotional abuse from partners. One-fifth of the women were forbidden by their husbands to see their best friends, and 7 percent were not allowed to see their relatives. Domestic violence by parents and other relatives is also relatively frequent (8 and 6 percent, respectively). Survey respondents said that they were much less likely to report violence to the police if the violence was committed by relatives than if it was committed by strangers (19 percent in the first case versus 37 percent in the second), confirming that there are feelings of shame associated with domestic violence and that there is a desire to keep such violence within the privacy of families. The survey respondents viewed the domestic sphere as the area where discrimination against women is most prominent, followed by the labour market.

Another survey in Central Asia, conducted among 200 women in the Leninabad and Khujand regions of Tajikistan in 1997, suggests that young women are especially at risk of violence. One-fifth of the respondents reported being subjected to physical violence in their families. The situation in Tajikistan appears to be particularly acute due to the low social position of young women.

Sometimes, women in this sub-region resort to violence against themselves, including suicide by self-immolation. In Tajikistan, about 30 women per month are admitted to hospital with severe burns. Suicides of young women have been increasing, mainly among recently married women. In the single district of Khujand, 54 suicide attempts were registered between January 1996 and September 1997. Evidence shows that no action was taken by the local authorities responsible for investigating suicides and attempted suicides. In Uzbekistan, 788 cases of self-immolation were reported to the courts in 1989-91, many of them in the southern regions of Surkhandarya and Kashkadarya.

Other surveys providing evidence on the pervasiveness of domestic violence are summarized in Table 5.5. Again, the results should be considered with care, since the surveys are often not representative of the entire country or population. However, they tend to confirm a high prevalence of domestic violence in all countries of the region, regardless of level of economic development, cultural and religious background, ethnic composition, or geographic location.

The evidence presented here points to a wider problem of violence against women outside the home. Certainly, violence also occurs in other areas and institutions that are part of the daily environment of women.

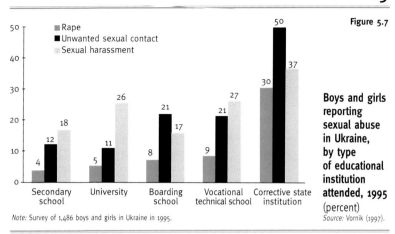

Figure 5.7

Boys and girls reporting sexual abuse in Ukraine, by type of educational institution attended, 1995 (percent)
Source: Vornik (1997).

Note: Survey of 1,486 boys and girls in Ukraine in 1995.

Table 5.4

Women reporting various types of violence in districts of Kazakhstan, 1997

Type of violence	Absolute number	% of total
Sexual violence by partner	4	3
Physical violence by partner	5	3
Emotional violence by partner	21	13
Violence by parents	12	8
Violence by other relatives	9	6
Sexual harassment at work	20	13
Sexual harassment in education	10	6
Total number of women sampled	159	100

Source: Feminist League and UNDP (1997).

Note: Survey carried out among 159 women in Almaty and the regions of Almaty and Jambyl by the Feminist League in 1997. The sample was representative of the population in terms of age, marital status, place of residence, occupation, and number of children.

Vulnerability in the workplace

Violence against women also finds expression in sexual abuse and harassment in the workplace. Chapter 2 reviews the trends and circumstances in the labour markets of the transition region that make women vulnerable to sexual exploitation. Women are more likely to work in lower status positions, increasing the potential for abuse by male supervisors. In the weakened economy, women are vulnerable to sexual threats related to getting or losing a job. The burgeoning grey or illegal economy also exposes women to greater risk of abuse, since working conditions are unregulated, unmonitored and therefore potentially unsafe.

Evidence on sexual abuse in the workplace is piecemeal, but strongly points to a high prevalence throughout the region, from Central Europe to Central Asia. In the former Czechoslovakia, 10 percent of women surveyed in 1991 had personal experience with male superiors who attempted to or did coerce them to engage in sexual acts. More recent evidence in the Czech Republic suggests that about 19 percent of women are victims of sexual harassment. In Russia, 7 percent of the women participating in

Table 5.5

Further evidence on the extent of domestic violence

Central Europe

Czech Republic
- 8% of women clients of consultation centres for family, matrimony and human relations (a non-representative sample of women) reported being exposed to violence. (a)
- 8% of 966 women surveyed by the Universitas agency in 1996 reported having been victims of sexual crimes during the previous five years. (b)

Poland
- 17% of women are estimated by the Public Research Centre to have been beaten by their partners (half of them repeatedly). (c)
- 60% of divorced women surveyed in 1993 by the Centre for the Examination of Public Opinion reported having been hit at least once by their ex-husbands; an additional 25% reported repeated violence. (d)

Former Yugoslavia

Slovenia
- One woman in seven has been a victim of rape, and one family in five experiences domestic violence, according to estimates in a study by the SOS Helpline for Battered Women and Children. (e)

Southeastern Europe

Albania
- 63% of 850 women reported physical or psychological domestic violence, and 20% reported physical domestic violence, according to a survey in 1995. (f)

Romania
- 29% of women treated between March 1993 and March 1994 had been beaten by an intimate partner, according to statistics of the Forensic Hospital, Bucharest. (g)

Baltics

Estonia
- 29% of women aged 18-24 fear domestic violence, and the share rises with age, affecting 52% of women 65 or older, according to a 1994 survey of 2,315 women. (h)

Latvia
- 4% of 853 women reported having been threatened or assaulted, and 3% reported having been sexually abused, according to a 1996 survey by the Criminological Research Centre. (i)

Lithuania
- 20% of women reported having experienced an attempted rape, and 33% reported having been beaten at least once, according to a sociological survey. (j)

Western CIS

Belarus
- 29% of women (and 3% of men) are subject to physical violence by their partners or spouses, research suggests. (k)

Russia (St Petersburg)
- 25% of girls (and 11% of boys) reported unwanted sexual contact, according to a survey of 174 boys and 172 girls in grade 10 (aged 14-17). (l)

Ukraine
- 10-15% of 600 women reported having been raped, and more than 25% reported having been physically abused, according to a survey in Kharkiv. (m)

Caucasus

Azerbaijan
- 26% of women are exposed to domestic violence, and one woman in four reported regular beatings and a ban on leaving the house alone, according to estimates of a UNDP needs assessment survey. (n)

Central Asia

Kyrgyzstan
- Hospital admissions of women who have been injured by family members are on the rise, according to medical records. (o)

Tajikistan
- 23% of 550 women aged 18-40 reported physical abuse, according to a survey. (p)

Sources: a. Foundation ROSA (1997) cited in Hendrichova and Kucharova (1998). b. Hendrichova and Kucharova (1998). c. US Department of State (1998a). d. Daszynska et al. (1998). e. Shircel (1998). f. UNDP (1996a). g. Minnesota Advocates for Human Rights (1995) cited in UN (1996a). h. Sillaste and Purga (1995) cited in Papp (1998). i. CSBL (1998). j. US Department of State (1998b). k. UNDP (1997b). l. Lunin et al. (1995). m. US Department of State (1998c). n. UNDP (1997c). o. US Department of State (1998d). p. UNDP (1997d), chapter 3.

a 1994 survey reported facing discrimination after rebuffing sexual advances by their bosses. A small survey in Kazakhstan (Table 5.4) showed that 13 percent of the women reported being sexually harassed at work.

A large survey carried out in 1996 by the UN Interregional Crime and Justice Research Institute (UNICRI) in 34 countries provides estimates on victimization at work for various Central and Eastern European countries and the former Soviet Union. Figure 5.8 presents estimates of the prevalence of assaults (defined broadly) and the prevalence of sexual incidents involving female workers in 11 countries. (The rates cannot be directly compared between countries because different cultures may perceive the same behaviour differently and because reporting depends on levels of awareness.) The survey shows that, on average, about 3 percent of women were victims of sexual incidents, with rates ranging from less than 1 percent in Russia, Hungary and Albania to more than 10 percent in Romania. A rate of 3 percent may seem low, but it represents hundreds of thousands of individual women whose mental and physical health is at stake and whose basic human rights are violated.

The survey of women in Kazakhstan (Table 5.4) also pointed to the significant problem of sexual abuse in educational institutions: 6 percent of women surveyed reported having been subjected to sexual harassment on application and acceptance into an educational institution. In the case of Ukraine (Figure 5.7), the percentage of abused adolescents was found to be much higher among those living in corrective institutions. Unlike their counterparts in mainstream education facilities, the violence experienced by these children often took place within the confines of the state institutions, a most disturbing situation. UNICEF

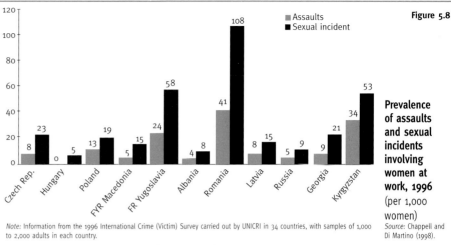

Figure 5.8

Prevalence of assaults and sexual incidents involving women at work, 1996 (per 1,000 women)

Source: Chappell and Di Martino (1998).

Note: Information from the 1996 International Crime (Victim) Survey carried out by UNICRI in 34 countries, with samples of 1,000 to 2,000 adults in each country.

has called attention to sexual abuses, including organized sexual exploitation, of children placed in state institutions in Romania. There are also reports of severe emotional, physical and sexual abuses of children in orphanages in Russia.

■

5.3 New Patterns of Violence against Women

In the unsettled environment of the transition, additional forms of violence have arisen in the region. Armed conflicts in the Balkans, the Caucasus, Russia (Chechnya), Albania, Tajikistan, and Moldova have brought further violence against women both during and after the periods of fighting. Another pernicious phenomenon that has developed is the trafficking of women for the purpose of forced prostitution both within and outside the region.

Armed conflicts and violence against women

In some instances, physical, sexual and psychological violence against women is perpetrated or condoned by the state. In particular, women and children become vulnerable to violence during wars and armed conflicts. Violence against women during conflict and displacement appears to be exacerbated by the general growth in violence and the collapse of order. In addition, during conflict, the concept of masculinity often involves aggressive and misogynist behaviour, whereby women and their bodies are seen as territory to be conquered and possessed in order to increase some men's humiliation or to reward others. Violence against women that takes place during and after armed conflict has chilling characteristics that distinguish it from violence in civilian societies in peacetime.

In a number of conflicts around the world, including some in the transition region, rape has changed from a side-effect of war to an offensive weapon. Rape as an instrument of war is used as a strategy to defeat a whole people, not just their active combatants. Rape is employed

as a tactic to force people to flee their homes and lands; to weaken resistance to aggression by establishing an atmosphere of terror, destroying dignity and pride and undermining community bonds; to promote campaigns of ethnic cleansing by impregnating women of rival groups and holding them until it is too late to safely abort, and, simply, to reward soldiers.

Estimates of the number of women raped as part of a deliberate pattern of abuse during the 1992-95 conflict in Bosnia-Herzegovina, in the former Yugoslavia, vary from 20,000 to 50,000, representing 1-2 percent of the total pre-war female population. Rape as a weapon of war has been internationally condemned, and evidence gathered from the Bosnia-Herzegovina conflict led the UN Commission on Human Rights to pass a resolution placing rape, for the first time, clearly within the framework of war crimes and to call for an international tribunal to prosecute these crimes.

The trauma of wartime rape, both physical and psychological, does not stop with the end of the conflict. Women who have been raped have difficulty returning to "normal" life and are often rejected by their own communities as tainted, for "consorting with the enemy". In addition to the direct gynæcological problems and mental health disorders these rapes generate, the rapes also often result in abortions and the attendant risks to physical and mental health.

On top of the direct threats of violence in a war zone, women face increased risk of violence when fleeing the area of conflict and seeking refuge in other regions or countries. According to estimates by the UN High Commissioner for Refugees, women and children account for more than 75 percent of refugees and displaced persons in the world. In addition to the loss of their homes, property and breadwinning spouses and to the material difficulties generated by their flight, displaced and refugee women encounter sexual violence both during their flight and in the place of asylum from other displaced persons, from members of the local population and from security forces whose task it is to protect them. These women often are forced to trade sex for survival, exchanging sex for food, shelter or "protection". This is especially true for women who head households or who are unaccompanied.

The experience of displacement alone also involves substantial trauma. Information on women's experience in this regard is not available, but a survey of children – the other main demographic group in refugee and displaced populations – can provide an indication of the trauma generated by displacement. Figure 5.9 presents the results of a 1992 survey in Croatia that looked at the average number of traumatic events experienced by each child and the percentage of children with high distress levels among children in four different populations – those mildly exposed to war, those living in a high-risk zone, those displaced within Croatia, and those who had fled Croatia. It shows that, on average, the displaced and refugee children experienced more traumatic events than did the others, even more than the children living in high-risk zones. The displaced and refugee children also suffered a much higher incidence of distress, with one in four displaced children and one in three refugee children classified as exhibiting a high distress level.

Table 5.6 presents UNHCR estimates on the number of refugees and displaced persons in the Caucasus and former Yugoslavia at the end of 1997. Refugees and other populations of concern represented over 8 percent of the total population in the Caucasus and 9 percent in the former Yugoslavia. The current conflict in Kosovo is further swelling the ranks of the refugee and displaced population – by an estimated 600,000 additional refugees and 500,000 additional internally displaced persons by the end of April 1999 – in a region torn by horrendous ethnic hostilities since 1991. Women and children account for 8 of 10 civilians caught up in what has become the single greatest human catastrophe in Europe since the Second World War. The violence and the physical and psychological trauma inflicted especially on women and children in this flagrant violation of human rights are devastating.

Finally, in the long run, even after the end of a conflict and their return to their original places of residence, women and children face additional dire consequences from the environment of violence they have endured. For example, in Croatia, it appears that the weapons made available for the war have not all been recovered and are sometimes now used to perpetrate domestic violence. Calls to hotlines refer to the increasing use of weapons to threaten, control or harm women and children both inside and outside the home. The number of suicides among children and young adults has also risen since the conflict started, with greater resort to firearms. The higher number of suicides is linked to the stress and violence caused by the conflict and to feelings of hopelessness and helplessness during or following the conflict.

Further consequences are likely to emerge even decades after the end of an armed conflict. The trauma experienced by children and

Figure 5.9

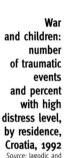

War and children: number of traumatic events and percent with high distress level, by residence, Croatia, 1992
Source: Jagodic and Bunjevac (1995).

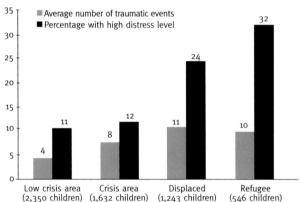

Note: Survey of 5,825 children aged 6-15, November-December 1992. Children in mild crisis areas directly experienced few war activities. Children in crisis areas witnessed extensive warfare and were in the war zone during the survey. Displaced children had fled elsewhere in Croatia. Refugee children had fled to other parts of former Yugoslavia.

Table 5.6

Caucasus and former Yugoslavia: refugees, internally displaced persons and other populations of concern to UNHCR, end-1997

	Refugees	IDPs	Returned refugees	Returned IDPs	Asylum-seekers	Total population of concern
Caucasus						1,418,600
Armenia	219,000	72,000	–	–	–	291,000
Azerbaijan	233,700	551,100	–	69,000	200	854,000
Georgia	200	273,400	–	–	–	273,600
Former Yugoslavia						1,996,400
Slovenia	5,100	–	–	–	–	5,100
Croatia	68,900	79,400	–	2,000	–	150,300
FYR Macedonia	3,500	–	–	–	–	3,500
Bosnia-Herzegovina	40,000	816,000	208,400	223,000	–	1,287,400
FR Yugoslavia	550,100	–	–	–	–	550,100

Source: UNHCR (1998).

Note: IDPs = internally displaced persons. Figures do not take the most recent conflict in FR Yugoslavia into account (for which the number of refugees was estimated at almost 600,000 as of the end of April 1999).

adults will likely give rise to significant mental health problems. This, in turn, will result in destructive behaviours, including violence committed by boys and men. Analysis of the impact of war on children in Croatia helps provide evidence of the extent of the consequences of the conflict. Surveys consistently show that the children are affected in several areas: capacity to study (lack of interest, motivation, concentration, and organization), emotional health (anxiety, fears, passivity, depression, lack of confidence in the future, and withdrawal from peer groups), physical conditioning (sleeping and eating disorders), and behaviour (aggressiveness, negativism, irritability, destructive behaviour, violence, substance abuse, and early sexual activity).

From comparisons of girls and boys, it appears that the experience of girls is more intense in terms of post-traumatic adjustment. They have significantly higher levels of anxiety, depression, sorrow, and psychosomatic symptoms than boys. On the other hand, boys present higher levels of aggressiveness. This aggressiveness is likely to have long-term manifestations, such as violence, including violence against women, years after the actual traumatic event has taken place.

Trafficking in women for the purpose of sexual exploitation

The upheaval of transition has led to a rapid growth in the numbers of women from transition countries involved in the sex industry. It is important to emphasize the potential scale of this particular social problem. Estimates from the Latvian Labour Force Survey and Latvian police suggest that slightly less than 2 percent of employed women were participating in the sex industry in Latvia in the mid-1990s. The negative impact of growing prostitution on the status of women in the transition countries cannot be understated. Prostitution affects perceptions about the role of women in society, places women in positions of economic and physical vulnerability and increases their risk of health problems and violence.

The provision of sex services by women from the transition region is not restricted to the political boundaries of their countries. There is evidence that the share of women from Central and Eastern Europe involved in street prostitution in many of the major cities of Western Europe is growing rapidly. Not infrequently, these women are forced migrants who have been coerced into prostitution through deception, kidnapping, trafficking, and intimidation.

Trafficking in women for the purpose of forced prostitution has reportedly been increasing in Central and Eastern Europe and the former Soviet Union. There is evidence that women from the region have been involved in a new wave of trafficking to Western Europe, the Middle and Far East, and the United States, supplanting, to a great extent, women from Asia and Latin America. Some Central European countries, like the Czech

Republic, Poland and Hungary, are countries both of origin and of destination for this illicit trade.

The International Organization for Migration defines trafficking in women as:

"any illicit transporting of migrant women and/or trade in them for economic or other personal gain. This may include the following elements: facilitating the illegal movement of migrant women to other countries, with or without their consent or knowledge; deceiving migrant women about the purpose of the migration, legal or illegal; physically or sexually abusing migrant women for the purpose of trafficking them; selling women into, or trading in women for the purpose of employment, marriage, prostitution or other forms of profit-making abuse."

Therefore, trafficking in women includes helping women migrate and then directing them into the sex industry.

Little evidence is available on the extent of trafficking in women. However, a few key trends have been well established by experts dealing with the problem. The number of women moving out of Eastern Europe has been rising over the past nine years. Table 5.7 presents some of the available data on the scale and nature of the trafficking in women from Central and Eastern Europe and the former Soviet Union. The evidence is fragmentary, but does provide insight into the issue.

Most of the women from the region affected by trafficking for the purpose of forced prostitution appear to be relatively young and well educated, compared to local and other foreign prostitutes. In Italy, for instance, the majority of the Albanian migrant women are aged 14-18. In the Netherlands, more than 80 percent of the migrant women from Central and Eastern Europe seeking assistance are under the age of 25, and 22 percent are under age 18. In Belgium, it appears that one in five migrant women is under age 19.

The main reasons for the growing prevalence of trafficking from the region are rooted in the adverse economic conditions and lack of opportunities in the countries of origin. Poverty is endemic even in countries carrying out successful market reforms, and women often suffer disproportionately from low income and status in the labour market, as Chapter 2 presents. A survey of prostitutes in Riga in 1995 found that more than 60 percent felt that unemployment had caused them to enter the sex trade. Young persons, especially young women, are at particular disadvantage in the new economic realities of the region; at the same time, they are perhaps most dazzled by the prospects of Western lifestyles, and may be more readily lured into the sex industry. It must be remembered, however, that trafficking in women is also generated by demand from consumer countries.

In the fertile ground of poverty and blunted oppor-

Table 5.7

Evidence on trafficking in women from the region, by country of destination

Austria	● According to the Austrian police, about 3,000 Eastern European prostitutes compete with 600 local prostitutes in Vienna.
	● Victims of trafficking were identified in Austria over the period January 1994-June 1995. The majority, 552 women, came from Central and Eastern Europe, especially from Austria's neighbours (Hungary, Slovakia and the Czech Republic).
Belgium	● The Payoke association reports that the number of migrant women from Central and Eastern Europe and the former Soviet Union involved in the sex industry and seeking assistance more than doubled over 1992-94. Most were from Hungary and Poland.
Israel	● In 1995-97, the authorities deported nearly 1,500 Russian and Ukrainian women.
Italy	● Officials estimate at least 30,000 Ukrainian women are illegally employed in Italy.
	● The number of persons charged with encouraging, exploiting, and aiding and abetting prostitution in Italy rose from 285 in 1990 to 737 in 1994. Among these, 21% came from the transition region (mainly Albania and the former Yugoslavia).
Japan	● According to the Japanese Ministry of Justice, the number of persons from the Soviet Union who entered Japan with an "entertainer" visa was only 378, out of a total of 17,513 visas, in 1989. By 1995, 4,763 Russians had entered Japan as "entertainers" – 22% of the total of 22,060.
Netherlands	● STV, a Dutch association, reports that the number of migrant women from Central and Eastern Europe and the former Soviet Union seeking its assistance related to trafficking tripled over 1992-94. Most were from Ukraine, Russia, the Czech Republic, and Poland.
Switzerland	● The number of visas issued to Russian "dancers" rose from 0 in 1990 to 300 in 1994 and 303 during the last five months of 1995. The number of visas for "dancers" issued to women from Central and Eastern Europe and the former Soviet Union was 616 in 1994.

Sources: IOM (1995), (1996a), (1996b), (1998); Caldwell, Galster and Steinzor (1997); IOM and BMFA (1996); Specter (1998).

Table 5.8

Victims of trafficking: type of work promised and the go-between in recruitment, 1994

Type of work promised		Go-between in recruitment	
Prostitute	27	Family or friends	34
Waitress	21	Street or discothèque	14
Domestic worker	4	Acquaintances	12
Dancer	2	Advertisement	4
Other	19	Travel agency	1
Unknown	35	Unknown	43
Total	108	Total	108

Source: IOM (1995).

Note: Sample of 108 women from Central and Eastern Europe and the former Soviet Union who visited the Foundation against Trafficking in Women (STV) in the Netherlands in 1994.

tunities, trafficking in women prospers mainly because migrants are misinformed or deceived. Evidence suggests that, in many cases, trafficking is organized in response to a demand for migration, under the guise of recruitment for fashion, tourism, or housekeeping agencies. Based on a small sample of 108 women who contacted an NGO in the Netherlands, Table 5.8 shows that only one-fourth understood they would be expected to perform sexual services. The majority had been lured into migration with promises of legitimate jobs, for example as domestic workers or waitresses. It is important to note that women are often directed to intermediaries in this process by relatives, friends, or acquaintances and that the methods of recruiting are much more informal than is commonly thought. Table 5.8 shows that over 30 percent of the women were recruited through family or friends, and another 11 percent through acquaintances.

While most women decide on their own to migrate, many discover too late that they are destined to prostitution. Even those who knew the real purpose of their recruitment are often deceived about working conditions, which sometimes are tantamount to slavery. Whether they end up in prostitution knowingly or unwittingly, these women are at risk of and subjected to physical and emotional violence. They are raped, forced to work long hours in dreadful circumstances, beaten, and threatened. In some cases, they are not even allowed to protect themselves from sexually transmitted diseases, and medical services are rarely available for them.

Women subjected to trafficking are also often deprived of their passports, burdened with heavy debts and victimized by other techniques used to control them. The "irregular" status of these women – without documents, with legal documents that have expired, or with forged documents (to hide the age of young girls, for instance) – means they have little recourse to the authorities of the country of residence. They are therefore vulnerable to violence not only because of the type of work they are forced to do, but also because of their illegal status. When discovered by authorities, migrant women are frequently treated as criminals and illegal immigrants and are eventually deported. They often suffer from detention and harassment by police, with no protection against reprisals from the traffickers if they agree to give evidence in court. This insensitive approach does not encourage victims to cooperate with the police, but, rather, leaves them in the hands of their traffickers, who continue their unsavoury business.

Trafficking is a multifaceted problem that requires a response coordinated among justice, immigration, health, and social service policies and approaches. It calls not only for an integrated approach, but also for international cooperation. ■

5.4 New Opportunities to Prevent Violence

In the transition region, as in the rest of the world, the problem of violence against women, particularly domestic violence, is to a large degree "invisible" – unrecognized, unmeasured and unaddressed. Women around the world face similar barriers to protection from and the prevention of violence. Most violence against women is committed by someone the victim knows – a boyfriend, a partner, a parent, a relative, or a colleague. Often, the violence is considered a private or family affair: the gravity of the offence is minimized, and the victim shamed. Often, the victim is blamed by both relatives and authorities for provoking or bringing the violence upon herself. Often, there is a lack of awareness, sensitivity and support for victims of violence and a lack of alternatives to an abusive environment.

The countries of the transition region have an historic opportunity during this period of reform to implement a broad-based strategy in society to eliminate violence against women. While the law enforcement and justice systems are reformed, there is the opportunity to raise awareness, sensitize processes and change laws. With the opening up of public opinion, there is the opportunity to promote understanding and discussion through education campaigns and the media. With the emergence of new work environments, there is the opportunity to address sexual harassment and abuse in the workplace. The reform of educational curricula affords transition countries the opportunity to promote a sense of responsibility for eliminating and preventing violence, a campaign that can reach everyone, from children to university students. This curriculum reform could be reinforced through youth and outreach programmes and life skills education in conflict resolution, negotiation and decision making.

Recognizing violence against women as a crime

While the recognition of the criminal nature of violence against women is certainly not sufficient to reduce the endemic incidence of this phenomenon, it is important to make such violence a punishable offence. Lack of recognition of specific forms of violence against women as crimes symptomizes a lack of commitment on the part of the state to tackle the problem. For example, domestic violence against women is not specifically prohibited by law in Armenia, Bulgaria, or Georgia. Marital rape is not recognized as a crime in Albania, Azerbaijan (where no form of spousal abuse is recognized as criminal), Croatia, FYR Macedonia, Romania, Tajikistan, Ukraine, and FR Yugoslavia. In Slovenia, domestic physical violence is not considered criminal in cases of "light" injury – a definition that includes "fractured nose, rib, light contusions and punched-out teeth". In Russia, the new 1997 criminal code does not distinguish domestic violence from other forms of violence.

The lack of recognition of the criminal nature of violence against women is also of concern in terms of non-domestic violence. For example, in Hungary, Poland and Romania, the law does not specifically address sexual harassment in the workplace. In addition, the status of women subjected to trafficking is often unclear in national legislation, and these women are frequently treated as law-breakers rather than as victims. Even in some countries where specific forms of violence against women are recognized as crimes, the laws are rarely enforced. In Estonia, for example, the criminal code condemns the sexual abuse of a person who is materially dependent or a subordinate in the workplace, but no cases were prosecuted under this provision in 1996-97. In Russia, the *St Petersburg Times* reports, not a single case of sexual harassment went to court between 1993 and 1996.

Sometimes, legal process is effectively inaccessible for victims of violence. In Croatia, prosecution for "minor" sexual violence is at the woman's expense; in Bulgaria, women must pay for the prosecution unless the victim is permanently injured or killed; in Romania, witnesses are required for the prosecution of rape; in Russia, the victim's lawyer cannot take part in the trial, though the state provides a lawyer for the offender, and domestic violence tends to be prosecuted only in cases of murder, grave physical injury, suicide, or similar circumstances.

There are many steps that can be taken to make it easier for victims of violence to come forward and participate in the judicial process. Victims could receive free legal assistance and be provided protection from unnecessary publicity. The legal process, including questioning, could become more sensitive to the distress of the plaintiff, as well as to the service of justice. This may mean avoiding unwarranted confrontations between the victim and the accused and permitting or providing an advocate for the victim in the investigation process. Means of establishing facts should be developed, for example by allowing health workers to provide evidence.

The various forms of violence against women, including abuse by partners and psychological abuse, need to be clearly defined and explicitly covered in the criminal codes and civil laws of the countries in the region. All countries have ratified the Convention on the Elimination of All Forms of Discrimination against Women, and the international committee reviewing country reports on CEDAW implementation in the region has repeatedly called attention to the need for steps to recognize and eliminate gender violence. This recognition in law reflects and reinforces public values and gives authorities and victims an important tool for holding offenders responsible for their violent behaviour.

More support from authorities is needed

Placing violence against women in a legal framework needs to be followed by enforcement and active support from authorities. This is especially true in the complex case of domestic violence, which presents particular challenges to all parties involved. Agencies and groups active on the issue of violence against women have repeatedly called upon law enforcement authorities in the transition region to increase support for the victims of domestic violence. In some criminal justice systems, the bias against victims appears to be pervasive on the part of police officers, doctors, prosecutors, and judges. This bias translates into the rejection of complaints, mistreatment, delayed referrals, the inaccessibility of doctors, abusive examinations, reluctance to investigate, invasions of privacy, failure to protect the victims, and dismissal of cases prior to trial.

For example, in Albania, the group Minnesota Advocates for Human Rights found that more than 50 percent of the 70 cases of domestic violence appearing before the Tirana District Court in 1994 were set aside because women were persuaded to withdraw their complaints. The Russian crime survey referred to earlier revealed that police forces sometimes conceal crimes by refusing to file a complaint.

Health professionals can also take a more active role in supporting women victims of violence. It appears that women are often reluctant to use medical facilities because of the lack of compassion and understanding of medical staff and because of the shame frequently associated with domestic violence. For example, more than three-quarters of the young Tajik women interviewed in a 1997 survey in Leninabad said they would not approach medical institutions about violence under any circumstances. Evidence from Latvia (see Figure 5.5) shows that women are unlikely to ask health workers for help. In Hungary, a sociological survey revealed that ethnic Roma women face cultural barriers when contacting health professionals.

This lack of trust in and support by authorities is illustrated by surveys of the women who called a hotline in Belgrade during 1991-93 and in 1995. Women victims of violence were asked whether they had contacted various institutions and whether they were satisfied with the services offered. Their answers are reported in Figure 5.10, which shows that the share of women contacting institutions decreased over the period under study: 24 percent contacted police in 1991-93, but only 12 percent in 1995. The graph also shows that satisfaction levels with police, social workers and doctors were very low. Only 5 percent of the victims were satisfied with the police response in 1991-93, and 3 percent in 1995. Satisfaction with other institutions was even lower: 3 percent for social workers and 2 percent for doctors in both periods surveyed.

Part of the problem is that professionals dealing with women victims of violence often do not benefit from any special training. Police officers, doctors and social workers do not receive such training in most of the countries for which information is available, including the Czech Republic, Bulgaria, Romania, Russia, Ukraine, Georgia, Uzbekistan, and Tajikistan (with the exception of social workers in Romania and Russia, doctors in Russia, and police officers in the Czech Republic). The reform of curricula in institutions of higher education offers transition countries the possibility to include training programmes for recognizing and thwarting violence against women.

Professionals whose work brings them into contact with victims of violence – police officers, social workers and health care professionals, including doctors, community health workers and birth attendants – should be trained to recognize and acknowledge violence and to deal effectively with victims and perpetrators of violence. Police officers should be obligated to register the complaints and carry out the investigations without delay, and health workers should be required to collect accurate and complete documentation on the violence for use as legal evidence. Authorities should also be made responsible for respecting the victims' privacy, referring the victims to specialized services without delay, providing immediate support and protection for the victims as required (removal of the perpetrators from the home, help in finding alternative housing, medical and psychological assistance), and providing psychological assistance, treatment and rehabilitation for the offenders. In countries in conflict, additional

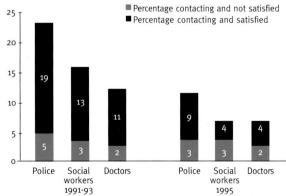

Figure 5.10

Women victims of violence: contact and satisfaction with institutions, Belgrade

Sources: 1991-93 data: Mrsevic and Hughes (1997); 1995 data: Posarac (1998).

Note: Survey of women who contacted the SOS Hotline for Women and Children Victims of Violence in Belgrade. Sample sizes were 770 women in 1991-93 and 2,035 women in 1995.

health workers, including women from refugee and host communities, should be trained to address the particular issues raised by war and displacement.

Developing escape routes from abusive environments

Women in the region face a lack of alternatives for escaping from a violent home environment or from abuse in the workplace. Particularly acute in the region is the shortage of housing and, during the transition, the growth in the economic dependence of women on their partners and the increase in the vulnerability of women in the labour market.

Alternative accommodation has been a key policy intervention for responding to domestic violence in many Western European countries, for example the 1977 and 1996 Housing Acts in the UK. In the transition region, shelters for victims of violence are rare and usually full and must turn women away. It is relatively common for couples to continue sharing the same home after their divorce due to the lack of housing, an arrangement which can lead to domestic violence. Analysis of the calls made to a hotline in Belgrade (Figure 5.10) showed that more than 28 percent of the women said lack of housing was one of the reasons they did not leave a violent partner. Another 25 percent of the women cited economic reasons, while 23 percent said they were afraid of the reaction of their partners.

There are many initiatives that can help victims of violence leave abusive environments: removing the partner from the shared home so the victim can stay in her home until a formal separation can be implemented, enforcing rights under family law, providing effective support in finding alternative housing, and helping women become financially independent.

A support network needs to be developed for victims of violence, including assistance through the legal system and assistance in finding ways to leave a violent situation. The fourth Regional Monitoring Report documented the poor legacy of the transition countries in terms of social and family support services, including counselling, support groups and temporary shelters. The transition societies simply lack this array of tools for prevention and intervention, leaving little choice between ignoring an emerging problem and responding with extreme measures at a later acute stage. As a result, shel-

ters, hotlines, crisis centres, legal aid centres, and other support mechanisms for women victims of violence have been largely unavailable until recently. In addition, the breakdown of many formal associations to which women belonged before the transition, such as trade unions, women's organizations and local branches of the communist party, has reduced the protection and support social networks may provide. The drop in the participation of women in the labour force, highlighted in Chapter 2, could also increase their isolation.

It is important to provide avenues for women to address sexual harassment and abuse in the workplace. Again, this calls for a legal framework, workplace policies, training, awareness among human resource professionals, supervisors and managers, and mechanisms of recourse for victims and of discipline for offenders.

The emerging civil societies in the transition countries have a large part to play in overcoming the lack of support for women subjected to violence. The number of NGOs and associations established to address the issues of violence against women is on the rise. These organizations have started setting up hotlines, crisis centres, shelters, and legal aid centres in most countries of the region. They have also initiated campaigns to raise public awareness and to lobby authorities, as well as providing training for health workers, police officers and other law enforcement staff. In some Western European countries, NGOs have organized assistance for women from the transition region who have been victims of trafficking.

The efforts of individuals and grassroots groups to break the silence surrounding violence against women in the region have often been innovative and hard-fought. Frequently, this work involves a heavy investment of personal resources in a context of restricted access to materials and funding and, sometimes, strong opposition from both public authorities and criminal organizations.

Despite the important efforts of grassroots organizations, the impact of their achievements has been limited. For instance, support is direly lacking in some countries and some geographical regions, especially rural areas. Even in urban areas, where most initiatives have taken place, the scarce resources of most of these organizations do not allow them to meet the needs of all victims of violence. Their activities are also hampered by prevailing attitudes, which tend to overlook or to tolerate violence against women. ∎

5.5 Conclusions

Violence against women is one of the broadest violations of human rights in the contemporary world and a substantial barrier to women's equality. Studies from different parts of the globe confirm that it is pervasive and persistent at all levels of society; yet gender-related violence remains largely invisible. Women do not speak about the

violence out of shame and fear, and the public, often through a misbegotten sense of what is private, turns away its gaze. Even when the violence cannot be ignored, social attitudes tend to hold the victim at least partly to blame.

This chapter looks at the many forms of gender-related violence around the world and then attempts to provide a portrait of the violence against women in Central and Eastern Europe and the former Soviet Union both before and since the onset of transition. The analysis finds that, under communism, violence against women was largely ignored and undocumented. Data and evidence have remained fragmentary during the transition, although there are reasons to believe that violence against women in its many forms has increased. The unsettling changes of the transition have been accompanied by a spreading sense of lawlessness and an alarming growth in crime, including homicides, in most parts of the region. The expanding culture of violence in many countries must surely have exposed women to even greater risks during these years of profound social upheaval.

Analysis shows a high incidence of domestic violence – which presumes an intimate relationship between the victim and the offender and includes emotional abuse and neglect, as well as sexual and physical violence – in all countries for which information is available. Domestic violence is not limited to particular geographic sub-regions. It is therefore surprising to find that reported rapes have fallen (or increased less than homicides) in all transition countries for which information is available. It is reasonable to conclude that this trend indicates reduced reporting of rape rather than a drop in actual cases. It is not uncommon for sexual assaults to go unreported, but this particular trend in the transition region merits concern, if not alarm. This is especially disquieting because, if the reporting of cases of rape is down, it is even more unlikely that the criminal nature of domestic violence will be recognized. Indeed, evidence shows that violence against women is sometimes not treated seriously by the criminal justice system, and domestic violence is often not even considered a crime. Documentation also indicates that women victims of violence simply do not receive adequate support from health professionals, police officers, prosecutors, judicial authorities, and social service workers.

Particularly disturbing is the eruption of new forms of violence against women during the transition. The use of violence against women, rape and forced pregnancy as weapons of war in ethnic conflicts in the region is horrific. Women and children in war zones are facing the trauma of displacement, and women refugees are particularly vulnerable to sexual exploitation and abuse. This Report documents another tragic form of displacement, the heinous practice of trafficking in women for the purposes of sexual exploitation – one more aspect of a burgeoning sex industry which exposes more women to higher risks of violence.

What does the future hold and what is to be done? As Chapters 1 and 2 point out, though economic recovery is under way in many countries of the region, the employment prospects and real incomes of many people, especially women, remain strained, if not bleak. This is a source of stress on families and raises the chances that women and children will be assaulted and abused in their homes. At the same time, as earlier chapters describe, the government capacity for maintaining public services such as health care, housing, family benefits, and childcare has often significantly declined, thereby removing valuable means and avenues of support and intervention in favour of women victims of violence.

Experience around the world suggests that leadership in dealing with gender-related violence frequently comes from the grassroots – from women's groups, non-governmental organizations and, often, the ranks of the victims of violence themselves. The involvement of communities is an effective way to foster discussion and action to halt family violence. Responsibility and accountability can be promoted by participation in the design and establishment of support services for victims of violence. As Chapter 6 discusses, these frontline and on-the-ground efforts by women to become agents of social change are vital in establishing women's equality and in the development of societies where not only economic and political rights, but also the basic human right of security of person are promoted.

However, given the pervasive nature of violence against women and the attitudes and behaviours that sustain it, leadership and active participation at every level in every society are required to address this issue. The transition countries have an historic opportunity to break the silence by adapting the best practices from around the world for eliminating and preventing violence against women and by creating new approaches to contribute to this global effort. The state may have a reduced role in the transition societies, but it is still compelled under international agreements to act convincingly to confront the issue of violence against women.

In the transition countries, governments have substantial opportunities to effect change as they reform the major social institutions – the workplace, the justice system, education, health care, social services, as well as the cultivation of civil society and public discourse. They have the opportunity to outlaw violence against women, to establish processes of justice that respect the victims, to prosecute and punish offenders, to provide rehabilitation services, to develop early-warning systems and interventions related to domestic violence, to cultivate violence-free environments and attitudes in schools, to raise awareness and change attitudes through media campaigns, and to make violence against women a public health issue. In the rapidly growing private sector, business and labour interests both have a role to play in creating safe workplaces for women through policies and practices dealing with sexual harassment, exploitation and abuse on the job.

Violence against women takes many forms and calls for a range of measures – curative and preventive, immediate and long term. The pervasive and persistent nature of this violation of women's human rights requires an equally broad response aimed at changing the mindset of individuals and influencing the criminal justice system and the development of public policy.

■

6 Women as Agents of Change

One of the great expectations people have of the transition to democratic governments and market economies in the region is the increased opportunity for citizens to participate in and benefit from a society of their own making. In a society that values equality, this requires the representative involvement of constituents at all levels and in all fields of decision making so as to ensure that people have a voice in the decisions which affect them and that the decisions taken are more well informed and therefore more effective.

In the international arena, there is a growing recognition that women's representative participation in decision making is a fundamental condition of women's equality and a hallmark of an inclusive society that values and capitalizes on the contributions of all its members. The 1979 UN Convention on the Elimination of All Forms of Discrimination against Women specifically requires states to promote women's equal representation in the formulation and implementation of government policy, women's equal access to employment and promotion opportunities, and women's equal participation in non-governmental organizations and associations. The Platform for Action of the Fourth World Conference on Women, held in Beijing in 1995, states that the equal participation of women and men in decision making strengthens democracy and promotes its proper functioning.

There is often an impression that women enjoyed a particular prominence under communism both in the workplace and in political life. The reality, however, was that men dominated in the decisive positions in government, the party and state enterprises. There were quotas for the representation of women in elected bodies, but this exercise was largely cosmetic, as the representatives were, in fact, appointed, and the bodies had little real power. The ideological promise of gender equality under communism went unfulfilled, as did the assurance of self-government and national sovereignty.

With national autonomy restored and cultural traditions revived, there is concern that, in some areas, a revitalization of pre-communist patriarchal values might stifle the voices of women. There is also a broader risk that during the transition women's interests will be subordinated to, rather than integrated into, national agendas for change.

The disintegration of Soviet control in the transition region has created a host of new frontiers – economic, political and social – and a multitude of new possibilities. Some observers are asking, however, whether equality of opportunity, including a meaningful role for women as agents of change, will grow in the new ideological and economic spaces being created. Difficult features of the political and social topography in the transition region must be negotiated in order for women to increase their claim on this territory.

In the command-and-control environment of the communist countries, the vast majority of people were disempowered. There was little opportunity for women and men to participate in genuine decision making at any level or in any area of life. This was true in government, the workplace and social organizations and even in personal lifestyle decisions such as whether to buy health insurance or a particular piece of property or how to save for retirement.

Now, there is the challenge and the opportunity in these countries for women not only to aspire to decision-making positions at the top of society's institutions, but to build decision making and participation in institutions from the ground up – in families and communities, in local governments and the workplace. The meaningful representation of women at the pinnacles of economic and political power implies the existence of a power base which is well anchored.

This chapter explores the participation of women in decision making in the transition countries – in government and business, in the family and civil society. The impact of the transition on women has in many ways inhibited their capacity to participate in public life. Women across the region tend to face higher unemployment, lower real income, a gender gap in wages, loss of formal childcare supports, increased violence, and a deterioration in health.

However, women in the region have also demonstrated resilience and initiative in this unsettled environment. They have ably leveraged their flexibility and exploited social networks in their efforts to help themselves and their families survive the shocks of transition. The social resources and skills that women exercise at this immediate and intimate level are valuable building blocks for their increased participation in civic, economic and political life.

Section 6.1 examines the representation of women at the top levels of government and business across the region. Section 6.2 explores women's participation in local politics, non-governmental organizations and small business enterprises. Section 6.3 looks at avenues for women's increased participation at all levels of decision making in society. The Conclusion summarizes the findings and points to the need for more active measures to empower women as agents of change.

∎

6.1 Women as Political and Economic Leaders

Each child should be able to dream of becoming the leader of his or her country. This pinnacle of aspiration means that every other position of authority and decision making is also accessible. Boosting the representation of women in decision making at all levels of government raises the chances that girls will believe they, too, can eventually have a say.

When government is truly representative of the society it serves, its decisions will also fully serve society. For example, if more women are involved in decision making, this may result in more family-friendly policies because of women's primary responsibilities for children.

However, experience shows that women have to make up a sizeable proportion of any decision-making group in order to reach a "critical mass" and represent their unique priorities and concerns and become a genuine and effective voice for substantive change.

Compared to Western countries, the communist countries of Europe and the Soviet Union were quick to grant women legal rights and favour important attainments for them in employment, education, health care, and childcare. However, the socialist state also claimed control over the issue of gender equality. As in the case of many other areas, the politics of gender equality was suppressed, and there was little public discourse to shape and advance women's equality and a fairer sharing of power, including in the household. In effect, women were unable to exercise ownership over women's issues. Public discussion was monopolized by official ideology.

Women in national politics

The communist legacy in the representation of women in politics must also be overcome. The former governments featured "elected" parliaments, but all candidates were designated by the ruling communist party. In this system, quotas ensured seats for women, but little power for them. The highest share of women "elected" to parliament was 34 percent – in Romania under the dictatorship of

Ceauçescu. In reality, women were picked to fill the "workers and peasants" quotas as well – killing two political birds with one stone – and were rarely "re-elected". The real power remained with the male-dominated "nomenklatura".

The token representation of women in public life is well illustrated by a biting description referring to Albania. "Women were often seen on platforms at solemn meetings, serving the same function as the potted plants – decoration."

Real power was held by the communist party. Though women did have the formal right to belong to the highest organ of the party – the political committee, their participation in this top body never exceeded 5 percent in any country during the 1960s and 70s. In 1989, there were no women on the political committees of the USSR, Czechoslovakia and Bulgaria and only two women of the 15 members in Hungary, two of the 16 in Poland, and two of the 21 in Romania.

Under communism, civil institutions were limited because the state did not tolerate free association among citizens. Social, political and economic change was usually initiated by the party. Civil associations, such as youth groups, were often supplanted by state-sponsored and state-controlled organizations. There was also little incentive to form interest groups since the authorities were not democratically elected and therefore were not accountable to the people.

With the introduction of democratic multi-party elections, the number of women in national parliaments has been drastically reduced across the region. Partly this is the outcome of the abolishment of quotas for women in elected bodies. Figure 6.1 clearly illustrates the effect of political liberalization on the representation of women in Central Europe, where democratic elections first took place. At the outset of transition, the share of women elected to parliaments plunged from 23-30 percent to less than 10 percent in Poland, Hungary and Czechoslovakia.

Recent experience indicates that women who engage in political competition have less chance than their male colleagues of being elected. In the 1998 elections in Hungary, women made up 14 percent of the candidates, but won only 8 percent of the seats in parliament. The lower success rate obviously discourages women from participating and political parties from backing them. This pattern is also evident in Southeastern Europe. In Bulgaria in 1990, for example, almost 12 percent of the candidates to the national assembly were women, but less than 9 percent of the members were women.

However, observers agree that women elected in the new democratic parliaments are involved in politics in their own right, and the

Figure 6.1

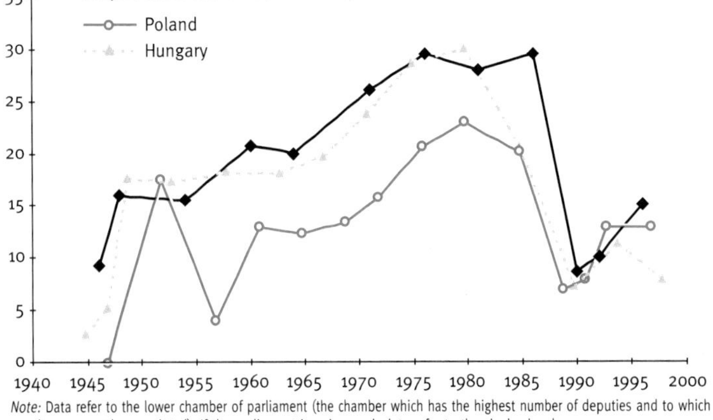

Share of women in parliament, 1945-98 (percent)
Source: IPU (1995).

Note: Data refer to the lower chamber of parliament (the chamber which has the highest number of deputies and to which members cannot be appointed). If the parliament is unicameral, data refer to the single chamber.

Box 6.1

Women in politics and child welfare: the case of the Nordic countries

The Nordic countries – Denmark, Finland, Iceland, Norway, and Sweden – stand out among the nations of the world for both their strong social welfare policies and their significant representation of women in parliament.

The Nordic countries are widely regarded as progressive and committed to social justice and equality. They are characterized by high levels of women's participation in the labour force: around 85 percent for women aged 25-49 in 1996, compared to an average of 71 percent in the 15 countries of the European Union (which includes Denmark, Finland and Sweden). They also exhibit a relatively high proportion of part-time work among women (except in Finland): 45 percent in Norway, 40 percent in Sweden and 35 percent in Denmark in 1996, compared to an average of 32 percent in the EU (with shares below 20 percent in countries such as Greece, Spain, Italy, or Portugal).

A UNICEF study exploring convergence and divergence in child welfare indicators in the EU shows that, in the 1990s, the Netherlands and the three Nordic countries which belong to the EU have the lowest under-5 mortality rates and the lowest share of births to 16-year-olds. The proportion of children living in poverty in Denmark (5 percent) is by far the lowest in the EU, where the proportion is a two-digit figure in all non-Nordic countries.

Many factors have been put forward to explain the egalitarian and social welfare model of development in the Nordic countries. One is related to economic development. Rapid growth in the 1950s and 60s and a high demand for labour caused a massive shift of women from the household economy to the paid labour mar-

ket. Since the late 1960s, the welfare state has, in effect, taken on both some of the traditional male role of economic provider and some of the female role of childcare provider. Women, in turn, have become the premier client group of the welfare state not only as parents, but likewise as paid state employees. Indeed, the labour market in the Nordic countries is highly segregated by gender, and the state remains a primary employer of women, despite a reduction in public expenditures during the economically troubled 1990s.

The Nordic countries are rather small in population and relatively homogeneous ethnically, making it easier for society as a whole to share and embrace similar values, including those around gender equality. This homogeneity also renders the job of the state more straightforward, and the state has long played an active role in the economy and in society in these countries. Most importantly, citizens have viewed the state positively, an important element for the success of progressive policies.

It appears that the high levels of women's participation in Nordic society is the result of a virtuous circle. To begin with, the strong tradition of social solidarity mitigates against sharp disparity among population groups, including women and men. The state, in turn, promotes gender equality, both as governor and as employer. Progressive public policies resonate strongly with the values of citizens, thereby reinforcing the cultivation of an environment of equality in the daily lives of people. This means not only that there is a sympathy between government and citizens, but that the cycle of adjustments required to reach equality is self-perpetuating.

---

lower share may therefore be more credible and effective than the mandatory high numbers of the past. Figure 6.1 also shows an encouraging upward trend after the initial drop in the number of women elected, with the exception of a sharp fall in Hungary after the 1998 elections.

In the West, the Nordic countries have led the way with a consistently high representation of women in parliament. (See Box 6.1.) This is the fruit of progressive attitudes and of voluntary quotas applied by political parties for their own candidates. After 1998 elections, the Netherlands and Germany joined the ranks of the Nordic nations among countries with women making up more than 30 percent of the members of parliament.

Figure 6.2 reports trends in the percentage of women parliamentarians in OECD countries. It must be emphasized that there is no uniform pattern in OECD countries. At present, the shares range from lows in Japan (less than 5 percent) and Turkey (below 3 percent) to Sweden (more than 40 percent), with the highest share in the world.

Although the figure shows a definite upward trend, progress has often not been smooth. For example, the 1997 victory of the Labour Party in the United Kingdom doubled the proportion of women parliamentarians to 18 percent. Though commitment to women's representation

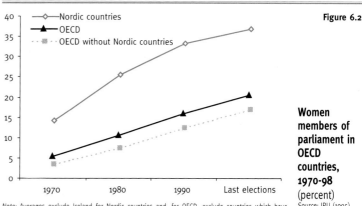

Figure 6.2

Women members of parliament in OECD countries, 1970-98 (percent)

Source: IPU (1995), (1999).

Note: Averages exclude Iceland for Nordic countries and, for OECD, exclude countries which have become members in the 1990s. See also note to Figure 6.1.

is most frequently associated with left-wing and liberal political parties, the 1996 right-wing coalition in Spain raised the share of women parliamentarians by one-third, bringing the proportion to a noteworthy high of 24 percent.

A comparison between Figure 6.2 (where separate blue lines show the women's share of parliamentary seats for Nordic countries and non-Nordic OECD countries) and Figure 6.1 reveals an interesting parallel. While, before transition, the share of women deputies in the Central European communist countries followed the numeric pattern of Nordic countries, after the fall of communism the ratios of women appear similar to the non-Nordic OECD average. In the Czech Republic and Poland, the proportion of women who won in the last elections (15 and 13 percent, respectively) is higher than in Italy (11 percent, 1996), France (11 percent, 1997), or the US (12 percent, 1996).

In the former Soviet Union, the significant decrease in the number of women parliamentarians began with reforms instituted by Gorbachev in the 1980s. In the 1989

elections, quotas were partially lifted, and the share of women deputies halved, falling from 31 percent in 1984 to 16 percent. Figure 6.3 shows the results of the last elections in the Baltic and CIS countries. The Baltic countries are all at the top, with 17-18 percent of parliamentarians being women. The western CIS countries are in the middle or the lower half of the spread. The highest rate in the entire region – slightly more than 18 percent – has been noted in Turkmenistan, where there is only one political party represented in parliament; the lowest rate – 1 percent – has also been reported from a Central Asian country, Kyrgyzstan.

There is some evidence that in the countries of the former Soviet Union, women also have less chance than men of winning a free political competition. In 1996, in Lithuania, a country with a high number of women parliamentarians, women made up 20 percent of candidates, but only 17-18 percent of those elected. Box 6.2 looks at three countries to cast some light on the attitudes of people towards women in politics.

Political parties are a crucial part of the new civil society in the region, but they are no exception in terms of gender inequity. Women usually make up a smaller share of party members than men, and the representation of women on party executive committees is invariably less than their share in the membership. In Hungary in 1992, for example, women made up 25 percent of the membership, but less than 5 percent of the executive of the Hungarian Democratic Forum, which led the coalition government after the first democratic elections. The same was true of political parties in Slovenia, where in 1998, for instance, women constituted 60 percent of the membership of the Christian Democrats, but accounted for less than 20 percent of the leadership positions. This unwritten, but common practice discourages the active participation of women in politics by limiting their potential,

Figure 6.3

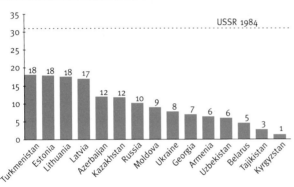

Women elected in countries of the former Soviet Union, last elections
(percent)
Sources: IPU (1995), (1999); Papp (1998); UNDP (1997b).

Note: Data refer to 1994 for Uzbekistan and Turkmenistan, 1995 for Azerbaijan, Kazakhstan, Russia, Georgia, Armenia, Tajikistan, and Kyrgyzstan, 1996 for Lithuania and Belarus, 1998 for Latvia, Moldova and Ukraine, and 1999 for Estonia. See also note to Figure 6.1.

Box 6.2

Public attitudes towards women in politics: Lithuania, Poland and the Czech Republic

Public opinion polls from the region reveal that people are generally supportive of a greater role for women in politics, although there is a clear gender difference in attitudes. However, neither women, nor men show much support for compulsory measures to raise participation by women in political life.

A public opinion poll carried out in Lithuania in 1994 found that only 28 percent of women and 18 percent of men believed women should participate more in politics. Yet, the majority of respondents also did not feel that greater representation by women would lead to a deterioration in economic and political decision making. Indeed, they even felt it might result in improvement in some areas, such as health care. The major obstacle to women's greater participation in politics was seen to be their family commitments.

In Poland, 50 percent of women and 28 percent of men surveyed in 1997 did not agree with the statement that men are more well suited to politics than women. A random sample of 1,000 people found that almost 60 percent of men voted only for male candidates; a pattern followed by less than half of the women respondents.

In the Czech Republic, survey respondents in 1998 cited tradition and family commitments as important factors inhibiting a larger political role for women. Almost half thought that men "do not let [women] in" politics or claimed politics was a hard or dirty job unfit for women. One-third of the respondents believed women were less assertive than men. Still, two-thirds said women were insufficiently represented in political life.

thereby perpetuating a cycle of inequality: if women are unable to acquire leadership experience they will remain less likely to become elected leaders.

Imposed quotas are a discredited strategy in these former communist countries, but there is pressure for pro-active measures by government to promote gender equality in politics. In Russia, it is being debated whether the law on equal opportunity should authorize the imposition of quotas among all elected posts. The deputy speaker of the Senate in Poland, a woman, told the UN Status of Women Commission that all democratic countries should have a law requiring equal gender status in order to surmount existing barriers like gender stereotypes and traditions within political parties. The law would mandate a parity threshold whereby no fewer than 30-40 percent and no more than 60-70 percent of elected positions would be held by each gender. There are political parties in a number of Western democracies that have voluntarily adopted such balancing mechanisms for their own candidates – a positive measure arguably quite different in spirit and outcomes from the quota system of the communist governments since it has been generated from the bottom up within the parties.

Women's low share of senior government posts

It is one thing for women to be elected to parliament and another for them to rise to senior decision-making positions such as cabinet minister, deputy minister or secretary of state. Table 6.1 reports the proportion of women in top government jobs across the region and compares this to the average for OECD countries. (Once again, the Nordic countries stand out, with more than 20 percent women ministers on average and with Finland and Sweden above 30 percent.) The representation of women among top government decision makers is low in the transition countries.

In 1996, in only four countries (Slovakia, Croatia, Latvia, and Kyrgyzstan) did women make up more than 10 percent of government ministers, and only Slovakia was close to the OECD average. In nine countries (including Estonia, Lithuania and the Czech Republic), there were no women ministers in 1996. (Even in Latvia, there were no women in the first two cabinets formed after independence.) In Hungary, after the 1998 elections, there was only one woman in the cabinet.

Women ministers can shape decision making, but can also act as important role models in society. Adding the shares of women in sub-ministerial positions – deputy ministers, secretaries of state and their deputies – gives a statistically more positive picture of women's presence in government decision making across the region. Figure 6.4 presents the share of women, by sub-region, among all senior government positions (also see the last column in Table 2.1) and, for comparison, shows the Nordic and non-Nordic OECD averages.

The gap between Central and Eastern Europe and

Table 6.1

Senior government positions occupied by women, 1996

(percent)

	Ministerial level	Sub-ministerial level	Total
Central Europe	7.2	11.4	10.7
Czech Republic	0.0	12.6	10.6
Slovakia	15.0	15.7	15.6
Poland	8.3	10.1	9.8
Hungary	5.6	7.1	6.9
Former Yugoslavia	7.0	15.8	13.2
Slovenia	9.1	19.7	16.9
Croatia	11.5	21.1	19.0
FYR Macedonia	8.7	25.0	20.0
Bosnia-Herzegovina	0.0	4.6	2.8
FR Yugoslavia	5.9	8.7	7.3
Southeastern Europe	3.4	11.4	9.9
Albania	5.3	14.0	11.8
Bulgaria	4.8	16.2	14.6
Romania	0.0	4.1	3.3
Baltic States	3.7	14.2	13.1
Estonia	0.0	16.8	14.3
Latvia	11.1	19.0	17.6
Lithuania	0.0	6.8	7.3
Western CIS	1.9	4.7	3.8
Belarus	5.3	7.0	6.6
Moldova	0.0	7.0	4.3
Russia	2.4	2.6	2.6
Ukraine	0.0	2.2	1.7
Caucasus	2.6	4.8	4.2
Armenia	0.0	2.9	2.1
Azerbaijan	7.7	6.9	7.1
Georgia	0.0	4.7	3.4
Central Asia	4.5	3.5	4.2
Kazakhstan	2.6	1.7	2.1
Kyrgyzstan	10.5	12.0	11.4
Tajikistan	3.7	3.9	3.8
Turkmenistan	3.1	0.0	2.2
Uzbekistan	2.6	0.0	1.3
OECD	16.8	13.8	14.6
Nordic	33.1	19.0	22.3
others	13.5	12.8	13.1

Source: Computed from UN (1997b).

Note: Regional values are unweighted averages. Ministerial level positions refer to ministers or equivalent positions. Sub-ministerial level positions refer to deputy or assistant ministers or equivalent, secretaries of state or permanent secretaries or equivalent, and deputies of state or directors of government or equivalent. OECD does not include countries which have become members in the 1990s. Nordic excludes Iceland.

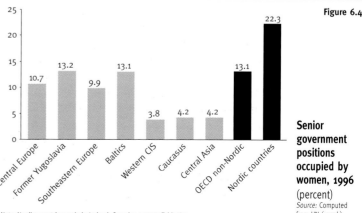

Note: Nordic countries exclude Iceland. See also note to Table 6.1.

Figure 6.4

Senior government positions occupied by women, 1996 (percent) *Source:* Computed from UN (1997b).

the three CIS sub-regions is clear. Unlike Central and Eastern Europe, all CIS sub-regions and most CIS countries fall far below the non-Nordic OECD average. In Russia, Ukraine and Uzbekistan, the first, second and fourth most populous countries in the entire region, the share of women in senior government positions is strikingly low. (The averages do obscure the fact that the ratios in Bosnia-Herzegovina and Romania, both around 3 percent, are more in line with the CIS countries than with Eastern Europe and that Kyrgyzstan, with a relatively high share, stands out in Central Asia.)

There seems to be no statistically significant relationship in the transition countries between the proportion of women in parliament and the representation of women in senior government positions. (There also appears to be little association between rates of female labour force participation and women's presence in top government posts.) Kyrgyzstan, with a relatively high share of women in senior government positions (11 percent), has a low proportion of elected female deputies – 1 percent in one chamber and 5 percent in the other. In Kazakhstan, by contrast, the proportion of women in parliament almost doubled, from 7 percent in 1990 to 13 percent in 1995, but representation in top posts remained slim. In the Baltics, Lithuania has a high percentage of women deputies, but a low share of women in government decision-making positions.

The link between women's share among legislators and senior government positions is stronger for OECD countries (correlation coefficient = 0.45, compared to 0.06 in the transition region). This may be explained by the fact that in OECD countries there has been a steady (although non-linear) growth in the numbers of women parliamentarians in the last 50 years, and this process has created a stronger precedent for the attainment of government positions by women. Hopefully, the transition countries will not take such a long road to fairer representation for women.

Overall, there has been little vocal demand for increased political participation for women, and even some women politicians have claimed that, because of the transition crisis, this is not an appropriate time to deal with women's issues. In 1990, the Czech ambassador to the UN, a woman, said "feminism is a flower on democracy"; in other words, a stable democratic system must be in place before issues of women's equality can be addressed. Nonetheless, women's equality might be more solidly integrated into the foundations of a developing democracy. Yet, as some commentators note, the political transformation promised by transition has so far built upon, rather than levelled, existing gender inequality.

Women also appear to have lost ground during the transition in another important area of public leadership: the judiciary. In Kyrgyzstan, women held 31 percent of the positions in the justice system in 1985, but only 8 percent

a decade later. In Moldova, there were 13 women judges on the Supreme Court in 1990, but only seven in 1994. Not only are these posts prestigious, but judicial decisions affect the political, economic and social life of a nation. The influence of the judiciary is bound to grow in the newly democratic societies of the region, and it is important that women be represented equitably in these centres of influence. Similarly, women are poorly represented in top positions in foreign affairs and international relations. Moldova, for example, has no female ambassadors.

Women in top economic positions

A role in high-level economic decision making is as important to women's participation in society as is equitable representation in political bodies. Leaders in business and industry help set the direction of economic policy and development and are part of the power elite in any country; there is often an overlap and career interplay between top economic and political positions. Economic leaders include the executives of national public bodies dealing with economic matters, senior managers of enterprises, senior managers of international and regional financial institutions, and the leaders of trade unions and professional and business organizations.

Women's low representation in key economic positions under communism more genuinely reflected their lack of influence in decision making than did their share among parliamentarians and in other government bodies. Women directors at large state enterprises were rare. In Hungary in the mid-1980s, for example, almost 90 percent of top managers were men. Women managers tended to have positions in sectors of lower strategic importance (where women were often over-represented among employees, such as in retail trade, hotels and restaurants, and the textile industry).

Available evidence suggests that men have preserved their dominance in key economic decision-making positions during the transition. Women make up the majority of public-sector employees, but are scarce at senior levels. In the Czech Republic in 1997, only 7 percent of the directors of state-owned enterprises were women. Much of the new private sector in the region consists of former state enterprises that have been privatized. A sample of directors of large private organizations and companies in the Czech Republic found a ratio of one woman to every 10 men (with women earning on average 63 percent of the salary of their male colleagues, pointing to further male advantage). In Russia, almost half of the women managers are employed in retail trade and in the hotel and restaurant industry, but even in these sectors women account for only one-fourth of the managerial posts. Box 6.3 presents one possible explanation for women's low share of top decision-making positions: gender stereotyping that acts as a powerful invisible barrier to women's upward mobility.

Box 6.3

Gender stereotypes limit women's potential

Managers have to be aggressive to succeed; women are not aggressive by nature: therefore, women cannot succeed as managers.

Stereotypes and the exclusionary logic that goes with them are so commonplace, they usually go unnoticed and, so, unchallenged and unchecked. The stereotype described above demonstrates how narrow definitions (in this case, of both managers and women) can lead to seemingly logical – but actually flawed – conclusions. In this example, the stereotype puts limits not only on the participation of women in management, but on the styles of management available as well.

Stereotypes affect women's aspirations and self-image and promote a biased evaluation of their actions and capabilities, thus confining the opportunities and potential of women. Such thinking is an extremely powerful barrier to women's access to decision-making positions.

Women in politics typically endure more public scrutiny stemming from stereotypes. Their physical appearance and family status and private relationships are referred to more frequently by commentators, factors often ignored for male candidates. The effect of these comments is to undermine women as serious political representatives. In an interview with Radio Free Europe/Radio Liberty in December 1995, Irina Khakamada, one of Russia's most well known women politicians, said that women in politics are subject to discrimination and, to succeed, are required to be "stronger and cleverer" than men. Women parliamentarians in Romania complain they are not taken seriously by male colleagues and that their speeches are received with scorn.

One of the most effective ways to counter stereotypes is to give prominence to role models, that is, individuals whose stature and accomplishments successfully challenge pre-conceived labels. It is crucial that role models be held up to view and receive attention. Expectations greatly influence outcomes. If girls and women and men and boys believe that women can participate in the highest levels of decision making, this will happen.

Women in the region have been, in some ways, in a good position to benefit from the economic liberalization of the transition. They are not only educated and experienced in the workplace, but are concentrated in fields of study and business with strong growth potential. Still, men have often been able to leverage their advantages under the old economic system to their profit in the new marketplace, entering the more promising professions and occupying top-level posts. In Russia, the share of women employed in sectors of the economy where the pay prospects have improved with marketization – trade, credit and financial institutions, insurance, the hotel and restaurant industry – shrank by 15-17 percent between 1990 and 1996. (This did not happen in all countries. For example, in Romania during the same period, women maintained their share of employment in financial, banking and insurance services.)

It is generally difficult to find internationally comparable data on the gender distribution of high-level economic managers in the region. Figure 6.5 offers some statistics from the region and a few Western countries using the International Labour Organization's ISCO-88 definition of "legislative, senior official and manager posts". This definition embraces occupations in which decision making constitutes a major part of the job activity. Although countries do not necessarily consider such positions in the same way, broadly speaking this classification

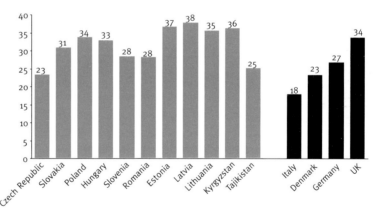

Figure 6.5

Share of women in legislative, senior official and manager posts, 1997
(percent)
Sources: ILO (1998); Bauer, Green and Kuehnast (1997); ABW Khujand (1998).

Note: Data refer to Major Group 1 of the International Standard Classification of Occupations (ISCO-88). Data refer to 1994 for Kyrgyzstan, 1995 for Italy and 1996 for Estonia.

covers all persons with managerial responsibilities: according to data, about 3-7 percent of the workforce.

Several conclusions may be drawn from Figure 6.5. First, although the ratios show variance, the overall situation of women within this wider pool of business and public service decision makers compares favourably with that in the West. Poland, Slovakia and Hungary have relatively more female managers than Germany (although the Czech Republic has fewer); the three Baltic countries have more than Denmark or the UK; Slovenia, Romania and even Tajikistan have more women in this broadly defined decision-making position than Italy. There are hardly any data on the extent to which these gender ratios were different pre-transition (as most countries shifted to the ISCO-88 definition after several years of transition). In Estonia, the Czech Republic and Hungary some erosion

Box 6.4

The glass ceiling: invisible barriers to women's upward mobility

The "glass ceiling" is a term coined in the 1970s to describe the invisible matrix of attitudinal and organizational prejudices that keep women out of top jobs. In the 1990s, it has been joined with the term "glass walls" to describe the gender bias that confines to less strategic and, therefore, less important areas those women who do become senior managers.

It was assumed that, once women had the same education, experience, abilities, and career ambitions as men and had entered the same fields, they could rise up the workplace ladder in the same way as men. In fact, the ascent of women to the top jobs has not been easy. Research shows that, when all else is equal, women are still heavily under-represented in senior positions. In the absence of obvious barriers that they can identify and set out to overcome, women have said that they feel like they have come up against a "glass ceiling" – invisible and seemingly impenetrable.

The term illustrates well that the obstacles preventing women from attaining decision-making positions are often non-explicit and, therefore, hard to challenge formally or informally. These obstacles may consist of the sheer prevalence of men in the ranks, unwritten rules, traditions and codes of conduct, the cumulative effect of years of networking, and long- and strongly held views about the appropriate roles for women and men in society.

In the West, more direct efforts are being made today to promote the rise of women up the ladder in both the public and private sectors. At the same time, in the 1990s significant numbers of women executives and women on the executive track have decided to leave organizations to set up their own businesses. Women's entrepreneurship seems particularly strong in North America: according to some reports, for example, women are now starting 1,600 businesses in the US per day, twice the rate among men.

seems to have occurred in women's relative status; in Slovakia, Slovenia and Romania data for 1993-94 imply some recent improvement.

Second, it is also clear from a comparison of these data and the low ratios at the very highest ranks of political and economic leadership that women do have a relatively stronger position at lower levels of the economic decision-making ladder (including top positions in mid-sized firms and small enterprises); even in countries where this share is smaller, the gender balance seems more equitable at middle levels of decision making than at top levels. Moreover, women in many transition countries appear to have an equal or stronger position than men in the next rung down in the ILO classification system – the "professionals". For example, half of all professionals in Romania are women, two-thirds in Slovakia, and 70 percent in Lithuania.

These positions – either already shaping decisions even if mostly at lower levels, or close to the key decision makers – provide a substantial base from which women can chip away at the "glass ceiling" that keeps them from top jobs (see Box 6.4) or, alternatively, gain the experience they need to become heads of their own businesses.

∎

6.2 Women's Participation in the New Civil Societies

Decisions about development in democratic countries are not taken solely by top-level political and economic leaders. They are also shaped by civil society, including lower level administrators, entrepreneurs, households as economic actors, special interest groups, trade unions, social movements, non-governmental organizations (NGOs), and the news media.

Experience shows that a strong civil society can provide a sound foundation for economic and political development in the transition countries. How women participate in this process is vital for women's well-being and, no doubt, for the success of the transition itself. Just as participation in local politics and NGOs can help women develop political and social power, the acknowledgement and cultivation of women's work in the household economy and small entrepreneurship can help establish a broad base of economic power.

Women in local government

Democracy is new in much of the region, but where data are available they show that women are consistently more well represented in local governments than in national governments. (See Figure 6.6.) There are many reasons for this greater success, not least of which may be that local politics is literally closer to home. Women may be more likely to participate because it is easier to combine family responsibilities with local political work, and issues tend to have a more immediate impact on families and their communities. The lower cost of local political campaigns means women can afford to compete more readily and political parties may be more willing to invest the smaller sums in women candidates. There is also evidence that the belief that politics is a tough business unsuitable for women may not extend to local government, perhaps because this is seen more as a community activity. Local media may sometimes be less inclined to play up the gender angle in politics and more inclined to portray female candidates as individuals in the community.

In all but two of the 11 countries for which data are available, the proportion of women elected to local governments is higher than that of women elected to national parliaments. In Latvia, the share of women in local councils is about 40 percent, more than double that in the national parliament. The difference is also great in Hungary, Bulgaria and Moldova. In Romania and Azerbaijan, the proportion of women elected to local governments is slightly less than the success rate of women in national elections.

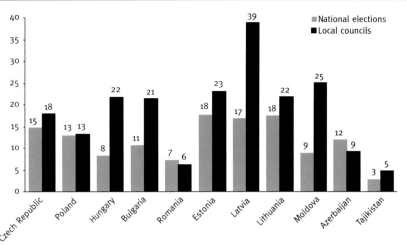

Figure 6.6

Share of women elected to local councils and national parliaments (percent)

Sources: IPU (1999); Novák (1998); Daszynska et al. (1998); Lakatos (1998); Tzvetkova-Anguelova (1998); NCS (1998); Kask et al. (1998); CSBL (1998); LDS (1998); Tafi (1998); Gardashkhanova (1998); ABW Khujand (1998).

Note: National and local data refer, respectively, to 1998 and 1996 in the Czech Republic, 1997 and 1994 in Poland, 1998 and 1994 in Hungary, 1997 and 1995 in Bulgaria, 1996 and 1997 in Romania, 1999 and 1996 in Estonia, 1998 and 1997 in Latvia, 1996 and 1997 in Lithuania, 1998 and 1994 in Moldova, 1995 and latest elections in Azerbaijan, and 1995 and 1998 in Tajikistan.

The high share of women elected to local bodies in many countries is especially significant because, during transition, countries are moving away from the heavily centralized governments of the communist era. Local governments are becoming more and more responsible for the provision of public services, such as education and social care, though the economic recession accompanying transition has left many of them with few resources. Indeed, local governments have often been put on the frontline of the transition crisis in that they have been given the responsibilities but not the resources to provide public services. The vigorous participation of women in local politics is proof that women are intensely interested in taking up decision-making positions.

Data on the number of female mayors are less encouraging, underlining the continuing exclusion of women from top political jobs even at the local level. In Hungary, Bulgaria and Estonia, 10-13 percent of mayors are women (including the major of Tallinn, Estonia's capital); in the Czech Republic and Moldova somewhat less, and only 2-4 percent in Romania and Lithuania. In Russia, only one of 89 regional governments (that is, oblasts, republics, or autonomous districts) has a woman governor.

Women in grassroots movements

Civil organizations are an indispensable part of democratic societies and constitute an increasingly powerful "third" sector that balances and acts in partnership with the public and private sectors. In almost all transition countries, political liberalization has encouraged the formation of NGOs, social movements, grassroots groups, and media organizations; the long-standing repression of autonomous civil associations has largely evaporated. The number of NGOs is growing in the transition region, filling the space left by the retreating state and fulfilling the desire for a civil society.

In today's world, civil associations are important incubators for leadership and are becoming bodies of consequence in society. They are therefore major vehicles in which women can gain experience, build skills and exercise influence. In Western democracies, a broad-based women's movement has been the primary force in advancing women's equality, in part by putting and keeping equality issues on the public and political agenda.

Under communism, the state appropriated women's organizations and representation and turned the concept of the active promotion of gender issues into an empty, imposed ideology. This may explain the signs in the region that both women and men are disenchanted with the words "feminism" and "gender equality" and have even developed "an allergy to feminism". However, as an observer has noted, top women decision makers in Poland may eschew the label "feminist" and yet still act as advocates and role models of equality for women. (A backlash against the term "feminist" has also emerged in Western countries during economically troubled years.)

The distaste in the region for gender equality as a political concept raises an obstacle to the public discussion of women's rights. Still, a range of initiatives has sprung up to move beyond the communist women's associations which were frequently accused of poorly representing the political interests of women. One remarkable initiative is the Women's Party in Russia that gained 8 percent of the seats in the 1993 elections to the Duma. In the following elections, however, the party failed to pass the 5 percent threshold. Women's parties have also been created in other countries, for example in former Czechoslovakia, but none has gained political representation. In Western democracies, women's political parties are rare. Instead, equality issues have tended to be incorporated into the platforms of mainstream political parties.

For many countries, the Fourth World Conference on Women, held in Beijing in 1995, was a catalyst for the organization and mobilization of new women's groups and organizations advocating women's equality – fresh alternatives to discredited national women's organizations inherited from the communist state. This UN Conference relied firmly on the promotion of NGO participation before, during and after the conference so as to make NGOs an effective partner in the conference discussions and outcomes.

The Beijing Conference also acted as a catalyst for the new governments of the transition countries, stimulating recognition of and action on women's equality issues. For example, in Latvia and Lithuania, the process of collecting data to be presented at the conference helped establish official national machinery to promote the improved status of women. Contact with Western academics has encouraged the creation of gender studies programmes at universities. Women have also been active in the establishment of their own business associations.

Table 6.2 presents the results of an inquiry carried out in 10 transition countries for this Report on the numbers and main focus of women's organizations in the region.

The range of issues serving as the focus of NGO activities is often quite similar across the region, with four prominent areas of interest: political concerns and rights, the promotion of business and professional activities, social services such as health care and education, and activism against violence against women and domestic abuse. There is, however, substantial variation in the strength and autonomy of the NGOs.

International and Western NGOs have been active in the region, especially in Central and Eastern Europe, starting projects and supporting the formation of local associations, notably self-help groups, hotlines and shel-

ters for battered women that deal openly with the problems of domestic violence and sexual abuse. In Poland in 1997, there were reportedly 73 women's organizations and informal groups, including six religious associations, eight research centres and six political groups attached to political parties or trade unions (where women are said to have a strong presence). In FYR Macedonia, 154 of the 271 registered NGO activists are women.

Women's NGOs are numerous in Russia, but appear to be less vigorous in other CIS countries. Established under Gorbachev in the 1980s in an effort to stimulate discussion and debate, many women's groups have continued to develop autonomously since transition. For instance, housing groups have grown out of neighbourhood committees. Women of Russia and the Free Association of Feminist Organizations and Independent Women's Fora are examples of umbrella groups which have emerged in the 1990s. Women are active in ethnocultural affairs. For instance, the International Women's Organization for Keeping and Developing the Culture of Turkic Nations was recently founded in Moscow. Women's business organizations are also becoming more active. In 1998 the Confederation of Businesswomen of Russia jointly organized a major conference, "Women and Management", with the International Institute of St Petersburg. In 1992, among women's groups, a "Group of Gender Expertise" of 15 independent experts was established within the highest legislative body of the Russian Federation.

In Ukraine, observers have been more sceptical of women's groups and the Women's Party in Ukraine, arguing that these organizations are isolated from each other and from the great majority of Ukrainian women and that they have failed to challenge prevalent patriarchal values and attitudes. However, some of the newly formed women's organizations also appear to have high numbers of members, which is a reason for optimism.

NGOs are often unregulated in the transition countries. This has meant that commercial businesses sometimes masquerade as not-for-profit organizations. Legislation and regulation are needed to define the differences between businesses and NGOs, so as not to discourage the growth of these important civic actors.

Given the history of oppression of associations of citizens in the former communist countries and the current economic problems in the region, the development of this sector has been modest. However, the emergence of women's groups is positive, as is the fact that governments do consult such groups on new policies and legislation. The challenge now is to promote and support the growth of these new and necessarily tentative

Table 6.2

Women's non-governmental organizations in 10 countries, 1997-98

	Estimated number	Areas of activity
Czech Republic	Unknown	Politics, social issues (education, refugees), health care, anti-violence, minorities, environment.
FR Yugoslavia	Unknown	Anti-violence, marriage issues.
Bulgaria	Unknown	Charity, family planning, legislative lobbying groups.
Romania	50	Women's equality, health care, education, professional groups, social issues.
Estonia	160	Politics, education, business interests, rural women.
Russia	600	Politics, education, health care, anti-violence, business interests.
Ukraine	70	Politics, social services (health care, anti-poverty), anti-violence, business interests, environment.
Georgia	43	Not reported.
Tajikistan	Unknown	Women's rights, health care, anti-violence, professional groups.
Uzbekistan	Unknown	Health care, education, anti-violence, professional groups, business interests, media, gender research.

Sources: Hendrichova and Kucharova (1998); Posarac (1998); Noncheva (1998); Zamfir and Zamfir (1998); Papp (1998); Kupriyanova (1998); Libanova, Makarova and Poznyak (1998); MEG (1998); ABW Khujand (1998); Marnie (1998).

beginnings. For example, grassroots women's groups are typically the first to address violence against women. The Crisis Centre for Women in Moscow responds to about 200 calls per month and also carries out media campaigns and public education, despite limited and fragile financial resources. The initiative of such NGOs should be matched with action by many other actors in society, including government and business.

Women's participation in new private business

The creation of new private-sector businesses – rather than the often disappointing privatization process of state enterprises – has been the driving force behind the growing number of enterprises, improvements in labour productivity and much of the economic recovery in the "successful" transition countries. It is also evident from the data that women are less likely than men to be private-sector employees, self-employed or entrepreneurs. Still, there is now a significant block of women business owners in the region.

Figure 6.7 presents the share of women among entrepreneurs in nine countries from the region, showing that about one-quarter of all entrepreneurs are women. This is consistent with the share in many developed market economies: across Western Europe, women entrepreneurs head 20-30 percent of small and medium enterprises. The available data cover a range of concepts and activities. In Slovakia (26 percent) and Lithuania (29 percent), the definition covers founders and managers of new enterprises (small family ventures and big firms alike, though obviously most entrepreneurs run smaller firms). The Czech data (22 percent) refer to self-employed persons who have employees. For many countries the data simply refer to persons who are "employers".

Enterprises are important engines of economic growth in the region, and women's ownership of businesses, no matter how big or how small, is an important form of economic decision making. The seeding and cultivation of women-led businesses represent an effective strategy for building the economy and supporting women's equality.

Entrepreneurial activities reflect risk-taking behaviour. The decision to start up a business can be prompted either by an entrepreneurial spirit, or by the more negative motivators of economic crisis and reduced employment prospects.

The mass collapse of former job, wage and career prospects at state enterprises has placed many families in a desperate situation. Despite the poor traditions, the meagre experience and the limitations on family assets that could help in setting up and financing an independent enterprise, venture, or farm, the economic crisis has generated a wide range of coping activities across the region. Many of these strategies, as Box 6.5 details, have remained within the household economy, but a substantial number of them has involved the creation of small independent enterprises, which, not infrequently, have

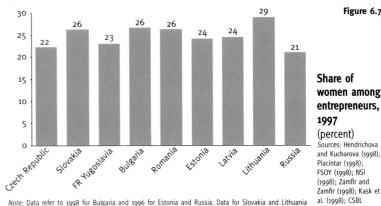

Figure 6.7

Share of women among entrepreneurs, 1997
(percent)
Sources: Hendrichova and Kucharova (1998); Placintar (1998); FSOY (1998); NSI (1998); Zamfir and Zamfir (1998); Kask et al. (1998); CSBL (1998); LDS (1998); Kupriyanova (1998).

Note: Data refer to 1998 for Bulgaria and 1996 for Estonia and Russia. Data for Slovakia and Lithuania refer to the share of women among the total number of proprietors starting new businesses. Data for FR Yugoslavia refer to owners of private firms.

grown into medium-size businesses.

In established market economies micro-entrepreneurship is particularly important to women who have limited access to power through conventional employment, such as women who face barriers because of education, age, ethnicity, or rural residence. In the transition region, women's entrepreneurship has taken varied routes. In Kazakhstan, interviews with 100 women working in the Almaty wholesale and street trade in 1996 found that 52 percent had higher education, all but 2 percent had completed secondary school, and three-quarters had worked as professionals at one time. Most of the women interviewed also held regular jobs. In Kyrgyzstan, where economic reforms resulted in a significant economic shock, but also, in recent years, a more robust economic recovery, women with higher education are reported to be more likely than men with higher education to set up businesses and to focus on new technology enterprises such as copy centres and computer shops.

The biggest problem women often face is lack of access to credit. In Kazakhstan, for example, none of the women surveyed had received a bank loan, and many had been obliged to raise money from friends and family. In Lithuania, entrepreneurs cite lack of access to financing as their main problem, though this is only slightly more true among women business owners (85 percent) than among men (83 percent). In Western countries with long-established market economies, lack of access to credit is recognized as the biggest barrier to new businesses.

Women face particular obstacles to establishing and developing their own businesses. Women entrepreneurs may have good ideas, much insight into pent-up consumer demands and strong local networks, but they often lack business experience, training, capital, and influential connections in other organizations. They also still have substantial family responsibilities and may work in family businesses without direct compensation or much decision-making power. Women who do start businesses tend to have small enterprises. To support women as economic agents, there must be efforts to finance and otherwise encourage women-run businesses.

Box 6.5

Networks of women at the economic grassroots

Women in the transition region remain under-represented at senior levels of economic decision making, including in public and private enterprises. However, there is evidence of a groundswell of paid and unpaid, formal and informal work among women of the region that has the potential to enhance the economic opportunities for women at the grassroots.

While women may be under-represented in the suites in office towers, they are involved in an extensive layer of less visible economic activity that blankets the region – from making ends meet in the household to improving productivity on the farm or running a lively street stall. Women may end up in these activities because they find themselves out in the economic cold, but these activities nonetheless are an opportunity for women to build a power base that can increase their participation in decision making within the household, the community and the economy.

At the most basic level, women have played a central and distinctive role in economic survival during the transition. At the household level, women's coping strategies have required a mix of increasing income, reducing expenditures and borrowing. A project called the "Social Costs of Economic Transformation in Central Europe" has surveyed five countries and found that most households relied on a defensive approach for survival in the first half of the 1990s – cutting spending, bargain hunting, repairing instead of replacing appliances, household maintenance, and household food production. The next most common strategy was to attempt to raise income through extra work and the production of commodity goods. Since women spend substantially more time than men in household work and management, they have been more likely to take the initiative in devising strategies for household coping.

The pressing need to feed families has placed women in the trenches of economic development during transition, and they have drawn on the strength of their family and friendship networks to succeed. Women have used their social skills and networks to adapt strategies for household economic survival to the new economic environment of transition. Local studies suggest that, in both urban and rural areas, women have adapted to the exigencies of the transition by taking on

a "third burden" of household survival activities in addition to their double burden of unpaid household work and a paying job. Detailed qualitative studies in St Petersburg, for example, show it has been women who have made the essential connections in family and friendship networks that have resulted in the procurement of goods and services and in finding employment.

Women have also used their networking skills in urban kiosk-trading. One observer has noted that economic givens such as price, debt and profit have a different value in the context of these female-dominated networks in which social solidarity and mutual support often take priority over economic rationale, particularly in moments of conflict. It is also reported that women and men street vendors in Russia are viewed quite differently. The men are seen as profiteers who are out to exploit ordinary people and who undermine economic regeneration in the process. The women are seen as fair dealers who are compelled to trade because they must support their families or pay for the education of their children. In Kyrgyzstan and to a lesser extent in Kazakhstan, women have become prominent in the rapidly expanding informal "bazaar economy" and in the "shuttle tours" to import goods to sell at a profit, as Chapter 2 notes. Trips to neighbouring countries aimed at securing goods that are hard to obtain locally are estimated to yield US\$500-3,000 per trip in countries where the average annual wage income is less than US\$1,000. Middle-aged women, who are seen as less likely to be challenged by custom officials and less likely to drink or gamble away their profits, reportedly predominate in this type of commerce.

Women's cooperation is even more pronounced in rural areas, where women trade in "social capital" to improve the operation of small-scale agricultural production. For example, rural women have been primarily responsible for the intensification of production on small plots, assuring their own subsistence and frequently also that of urban relatives, as well as providing surplus for sale. Women have organized cooperative agricultural activities to tend the increasing number of cattle at pasture and to share responsibilities as production grows. In many countries, this intensification yields an impressive amount of agricultural output from a relatively tiny portion of the cultivated land.

6.3 Building Blocks and Ladders to Women's Success

The transition has been expected to expand the opportunities available to the people of the region, women and men alike. However, gender equality of opportunity has not flourished and, in some areas, has even diminished. Much undeniably remains to be done to build up civil

society and to cultivate an environment of gender equality in the region.

At its 39th session in March and April 1995, the UN Commission on the Status of Women discussed a series of general policy recommendations to help promote women's equal representation in decision making. With regard to vertical discrimination, the commission recommended that the civil service set an example by promoting women to high ranks and that organizations:

- increase transparency in the selection for top posts;
- use gender-fair criteria, as well as affirmative action incentives;
- promote training in management skills;
- encourage the development of female networks.

With regard to horizontal discrimination, it recommended that organizations:

- encourage the recruitment of women in post-secondary business education through subsidies and quotas;
- promote training in management skills;
- encourage "mentoring" by senior women;
- promote credit programmes targeted at women entrepreneurs, including the provision of incentives to financial institutions to support credit programmes aimed at women.

These guidelines are clearly relevant to the situation of women in the transition countries. In particular, there is a tremendous opportunity in the region to adopt and adapt such initiatives and practices in order to cultivate women's equal participation from the ground up. Some basic building blocks of women's empowerment are already in place in the transition environment. From this foundation, ladders of access must be raised to enable women to move on to higher levels of decision making and more political and economic participation.

Education and training

The importance of education to progress is evident in its inclusion, along with economic output and health, in the Human Development Index (described in Chapter 1). An investment in human capital through education and training is critical to improving economic productivity in the transition countries, especially in the context of the increasingly knowledge-driven world markets. Similarly, education for women represents a direct investment in the ability of women to participate in society, especially in decision-making positions. Although there are several pathways to power, in democratic countries education is the broadest avenue.

Fortunately, the transition countries have a legacy of good education systems for both girls and boys, and no evidence of a systematic gender gap at any level of education has appeared since the transition began. Tertiary education is especially important so that women can move

into positions of political, economic and social leadership, and enrolment rates have mostly risen during transition. As Table 7.5 in the Statistical Annex shows, the proportion of women in tertiary education grew or remained stable in all countries of the region with the exception of Kyrgyzstan, Tajikistan and Turkmenistan. The share is at or above 50 percent in 21 of the 27 transition countries and around 45 percent in two others.

As Figure 6.8 confirms, women tend to be well represented in fields common for senior decision makers, such as law and business administration. The diagram shows that in all 12 countries for which data are available female enrolment was higher – in several countries much higher – than male enrolment in commercial tertiary education in 1997. Overall, women had an advantage also in law studies, although here the picture is more mixed: in the Czech Republic, Lithuania, Belarus, and Moldova more men were enrolled than women. It is important to note that during the transition both disciplines have been much preferred by students, and enrolment has increased, often many times over. Therefore, young women have managed to maintain their high share in these areas of study despite a very competitive environment. This is very encouraging.

The gender distribution among business administration students is only slightly different from that in Western countries such as Sweden and the United Kingdom. However, the trends are somewhat opposite: in the West more women are entering the traditional male preserve of business studies; in the transition region the absolute numbers are rising for both women and men, but at times more rapidly for men in a field which, under communism, was dominated by women and was little valued.

Government machinery

The Platform for Action of the UN Fourth World Conference on Women makes it clear that the state is crucial to the effort to advance women's equality through the development of "national machineries" for the advancement

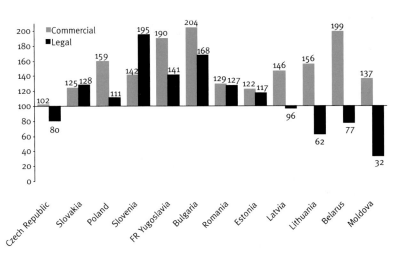

Figure 6.8

Women in tertiary education in commercial and business administration and law, 1997 (female enrolment as a percent of male enrolment)
Source: MONEE project database.

Note: Data refer to 1996 for FR Yugoslavia.

of women. In the former communist countries, there may be an "allergy" to state intervention in general and to the imposition of "equality from above" in particular, but government agencies that promote equal opportunity among citizens are a legitimate feature of democratic societies. In other words, government has an essential role to play in building and maintaining a culture of equality in the nation.

The fact that a significant number of governments in the transition region have submitted national reports on the status of women in compliance with the UN Convention on the Elimination of All Forms of Discrimination against Women is a positive sign (see Chapter 1, Section 1.4). The participation of these national machineries in such an international milieu and in relevant conferences is important for the exchange of information – including information on best practices – and the reinforcement of commitments to progress in women's equality.

The basic unit of a national machinery for improving the status of women is a central office or department within government with the mandate to coordinate the development of public policy so that a gender perspective is mainstreamed into all areas of public affairs. Such an office not only ensures that the needs and concerns of the half of the citizenry consisting of women are integrated into government laws, policies and programmes, but provides government leadership on women's issues, works in partnership with other levels of government and civilian actors, and supports the activities of non-governmental women's groups and equality-seeking organizations.

Since the collapse of communism in the region, existing mechanisms have evolved and new mechanisms have been established to monitor women's issues. In Hungary, for example, a year after the Fourth World Conference on Women, an equal opportunities secretariat for women was created within the Ministry of Labour. Although agencies have been established in many other countries as well, an investigation in 10 countries (Table

Table 6.3

Equal opportunity agencies or ministry sections in 10 countries

	Special agency or ministry section (year)
Czech Republic	Special agency (1998)
FR Yugoslavia	No
Bulgaria	No
Romania	Ministry section
Estonia	Special agency (1996)
Russia	Special agency (1993)
Ukraine	Special agency (1996)
Georgia	No
Tajikistan	No
Uzbekistan	Ministry section

Sources: Hendrichova and Kucharova (1998); Posarac (1998); Noncheva (1998); Zamfir and Zamfir (1998); Papp (1998); Kupriyanova (1998); Libanova, Makarova and Poznyak (1998); MEG (1998); ABW Khujand (1998); Marnie (1998).

6.3) found that in four of these countries there is still no government agency to promote gender issues.

To be effective, national machineries clearly require political will, legal clout and adequate resources. Moreover, only tight collaboration with civil organizations and dialogue among all relevant players – government, business, trade unions, religious organizations, political parties, women's NGOs – can create an environment in which women are empowered.

Promoting women's ventures and small enterprises

Government and international agencies can play a crucial role in supporting women as agents of change by encouraging the development of small- and medium-sized enterprises in the transition countries. Women have established or own about one-quarter of the new businesses in the region – a promising start, given the newness of entrepreneurial freedom and the high-risk environment for small businesses.

The region has an historical deficit in small- and medium-sized enterprises (especially in consumer- and service-related fields). However, as recent experience shows, such businesses have become the spark plugs of new economic growth in Western countries. Because of the involvement of women as small-scale entrepreneurs, efforts to promote the development of small businesses in the transition countries could broaden women's access to economic decision making and power.

The revitalization of economies in the transition region can be accelerated if support is offered to the new small-enterprise sector in general and to women in particular. Such investments would pay off in terms not only of gender equality, but of fresh approaches to business as well. While women entrepreneurs have much in common with men entrepreneurs, they may envision different business opportunities, structure business differently (for example so as to accommodate family responsibilities), have different aspirations for growth, and even have non-traditional business goals and operating practices.

The number of women who are managers and professionals in the transition region – relatively more than in many Western countries – shows that women stand out because of their strong potential as owners of new businesses. They therefore represent a good target for policies and programmes that aim to promote the growth of the small-business sector. Nonetheless, a survey carried out for this Report in 10 transition countries shows that public programmes promoting female entrepreneurship have been set up in only three of the countries (Russia, Romania and Estonia). In the other seven countries (the Czech Republic, Bulgaria, FR Yugoslavia, Ukraine, Georgia, Tajikistan, and Uzbekistan), no dedicated government programmes seem to exist to support the effort of women to engage in private economic activity.

Box 6.6

Micro-credits targeting disadvantaged women

Micro-credit programmes have become widespread as a development tool in the last decade, expanding greatly through the interest and involvement of international agencies. The underlying principle of empowerment is that it is better for the poor to have a chance to sustain themselves rather than being obliged to rely on charity.

In Central Europe, a tradition of credit unions has been reinvigorated by emigrant communities which are now helping to re-establish this type of member-driven financial institution in their home countries. In Central Asia, the economic crisis, the closure of state farms and the continued existence of centralized banking systems have prompted the creation of small-business financing associations sponsored by international institutions such as the Asian Development Bank.

Micro-credit or micro-finance entails not-for-profit organizations putting small-business loans into the hands of target groups whose credit needs are not served by regular financial institutions. Often banks do not supply this sort of credit because operational costs make small loans unprofitable or because borrowers are unable to provide collateral or proof of ability to repay. Borrowers may also find it difficult to deal with banks because of physical distance in rural areas or because bank procedures are inhibiting, for example, to poorly literate indi-

viduals. Micro-credit is available only upon approval of a business plan and, so, excludes consumer loans.

Micro-credit programmes also aim at the alleviation of poverty by sustaining farmers, self-employment and small entrepreneurship. Typically, in a rural context, micro-credit is made available to poor landless peasants and is tied to the agricultural production cycle. The most well known micro-credit scheme is the Grameen Bank of Bangladesh, which serves about two million landless villagers, 95 percent of whom are women, and has a remarkably high debt-recovery rate of 98 percent. Targeting women is particularly important because women usually have less access to resources and must bear full responsibility for child-rearing. Targeting poor women thus helps alleviate poverty among children.

A recent UN report states that,

"many micro-credit programmes have targeted one of the most vulnerable groups in society – women who live in households that own little or no assets. By providing opportunities for self-employment, many studies have concluded that these programmes have significantly increased women's security, autonomy, self-confidence and status within the household."

Much time, pressure and public leadership have also been necessary in many Western countries before financial institutions have begun to respond to the banking needs of small businesses. For example, the legislative mandate of the Business Development Bank of Canada, wholly owned by the Canadian government, was amended in 1995 to focus on supporting small businesses and targeting particular groups of entrepreneurs, including women. Studies have concluded that many micro-businesses and a majority of unincorporated or home-based businesses do not fit conventional loan models. (Research has also found that women-owned businesses pose no special risk of financial difficulty.)

Experience in established market economies demonstrates that women's initiatives are also crucial in

this area. An example is offered by Mama Cash, an independent women's financial institution which was set up in the Netherlands in 1983. Among other services, it provides advice on drafting business plans and gaining access to credit; it offers to act as guarantor for half of the loan made by a commercial bank to a female entrepreneur, and it cosponsors a "mentorship" programme with an association of experienced women entrepreneurs.

In many countries, a variety of innovative programmes has been developed in recent decades to help women overcome systemic barriers to entrepreneurship, especially obstacles to financing. Not infrequently, micro-credit schemes target disadvantaged groups of women (Box 6.6).

∎

6.4 Conclusions

The transition is about change – the deep and wide-reaching transformation of social, political, cultural, and economic life in the 27 countries of Central and Eastern Europe and the former Soviet Union. The best-case scenario for human development holds that women, representing more than half of the population of the region, must be fully empowered as agents of this change. One of

the great political lessons of the 20th century is that one community of people cannot adequately represent the interests of another community, no matter how sincere their intentions, no matter how concerted their efforts. Such is the case with the rich and the poor, one ethnic group and another, the developed and the developing nations. And such is the case with women and men.

Women are the best able to espouse their own interests, and the whole of society is more effectively served if all its constituents are equitably represented in the processes of change and decision making.

Under communism, the voices of most women and men were not heard. The state and the party were the only sanctioned agents of change. During the transition, the voices of women have not been heard adequately, but there are significant building blocks in place to promote women's participation. The share of women in national parliaments has dropped substantially across the region – from the 30 percent or so imposed by quotas under communism to somewhere between 4 and 14 percent in most countries. Although these shares are low and fall far short of a representative "critical mass", it can be argued that, unlike the women selected under communism's quota system, the women now serving are genuine political representatives of their communities. Women have enjoyed significantly better success in getting elected to local governments, which are not only important platforms for effecting community-oriented change, but a meaningful base from which women can expand their political power.

Pro-active measures are clearly necessary to increase the awareness of gender discrimination and to provide instruments for the promotion of women's participation in politics. Still, considering the historical context, caution is needed in the application of rigid quotas in political bodies and public administration. A combination of public and private pressure – from ordinary citizens and NGOs, business associations and business leaders, governments and international organizations – seems to deliver more lasting results. A strategy based on this approach, which is built on dialogue and partnership, seems to fit best with the new political cultures emerging in democratic countries in the region.

There is a strong case to be made that the full inclusion of women in positions of power is economically efficient, as well as socially just: the equal participation of women in decision making substantially broadens the pool of human resources which are the foundation of the economy. So far in the transition, women are not well represented in the privatization of large-scale enterprises in the former socialist countries, and they are less likely than men to work in the private sector or in their own businesses.

However, there are still some important basics that can be built upon. Women in the region are well educated, a resource that can be leveraged in the new economies. Small enterprises are vital engines of economic growth and innovation, and women in the region have demonstrated interest and ability in establishing micro-enterprises – initiatives that need to be sustained and encouraged.

Governments and business both have an interest in the development of strong civilian institutions that can act as partners in community and national life. The establishment and growth of women's groups and equality-seeking organizations are an essential part of a revitalized civil society in the region. International NGOs and other agencies can support this process by supplying resources, funding and support for the efforts of the women of the transition region. Women from many professional areas elsewhere – parliamentarians, business leaders, educators, rights advocates – can extend their embrace to include the women of the transition region, who, in turn, can contribute to the global community of women.

There is evidence that women's NGOs are spreading across the region. The findings of this Report highlight the fact that the main concerns of groups – political and legal issues, the promotion of business and professional activities, social services such as health care and education, and the elimination of violence against women – are fundamentally important to the human rights of women and the advancement of women's equality in the region.

The advancement of women to decision-making positions will not necessarily be a spontaneous outcome of political or economic reform. It requires an environment in which women are encouraged and supported in their efforts, in which women have equitable access to resources and opportunities, and in which pro-active policies and practices are pursued by governments, business and civilian institutions. It is clear that women's concerns will not be addressed in the political sphere without the active participation of women, from the grassroots and local governments to national political and economic leadership.

There is an important role for the international community to play in the advancement of gender equality in the transition countries, as well as in the development of market economies and democratic governments. In particular, for UNICEF this will involve promoting and supporting the implementation of international conventions that focus on the rights of women and children. Envisioning a world where girls and women are fully active agents of change means planning a change for the better. It is not hard to argue that equality is a hallmark of human development, a goal all people would wish for themselves, their communities and their countries.

■

Statistical Annex

The data in the Statistical Annex are taken from various sources. The great majority are provided by the central statistical offices participating in the MONEE project. In some cases additional calculations have been made to derive figures which are comparable among countries, for example enrolment rates in education. Other sources are given in the table notes when relevant. The phrase "MONEE project database" given as the source to a number of tables and graphs in the main text usually refers to data provided by central statistical offices. (The data are not necessarily consistent with those found in other UNICEF publications, which sometimes rely on non-national sources.) The Glossary, which follows the Statistical Annex, offers descriptions of some of the indicators used.

A menu-driven database called "TransMONEE 4.0", which includes all the data in the Statistical Annex, together with a substantial amount of additional data, can be downloaded free of charge from UNICEF ICDC via the Internet. Windows 3.1 and Windows95/NT versions are available,

both of which contain the same set of data. (The Windows95/NT version has an interface containing more advanced features.) The database allows the user to extract a profile of economic and social indicators for a single country or to compare a single indicator across sub-regions, countries and time-periods. Data can be converted into index form or expressed as rates of change. Data can also be outputted as a table or graph and can be exported to different file formats, for example for further use in a spreadsheet package.

For more details and instructions for downloading and installing the database, see the UNICEF ICDC website at: http://www.unicef-icdc.org. The database can also be downloaded through the European University Institute (Italy) at ftp://datacomm.iue.it/unicef/. To access an interactive version of the database, see the website of the Centre for Europe's Children, Glasgow University, UK. The address is: http://eurochild.gla.ac.uk.

1. Population 110
   1.1 Total population
   1.2 Female population
   1.3 Child population, age 0-17
   1.4 Child population, age 0-4
   1.5 Youth dependency ratio
   1.6 Elderly dependency ratio
   1.7 Rate of natural population increase
   1.8 Net external migration

2. Natality 114
   2.1 Crude birth rate
   2.2 Teenage birth rate
   2.3 Share of births to mothers under age 20
   2.4 Share of births to unmarried mothers
   2.5 Share of low-weight births
   2.6 Total fertility rate
   2.7 Average age of mothers at first birth
   2.8 Number of abortions
   2.9 Abortion rate

3. Child and maternal mortality 119
   3.1 Infant mortality rate
   3.2 Maternal mortality rate
   3.3 Under-5 mortality rate
   3.4 Age 5-19 mortality rate
   3.5 Age 5-19 female mortality rate due to accidents, poisoning
      or violence excluding suicide
   3.6 Age 5-19 male mortality rate due to accidents, poisoning
      or violence excluding suicide
   3.7 Age 5-19 female suicide rate
   3.8 Age 5-19 male suicide rate

4. Life expectancy and adult mortality 123
   4.1 Crude death rate
   4.2 Female life expectancy at birth
   4.3 Male life expectancy at birth
   4.4 Age 20-39 female mortality rate
   4.5 Age 20-39 male mortality rate
   4.6 Age 40-59 female mortality rate
   4.7 Age 40-59 male mortality rate
   4.8 Age 60+ mortality rate

5. Family formation 127
   5.1 Crude marriage rate
   5.2 Average age of women at first marriage
   5.3 Average age of men at first marriage
   5.4 Crude divorce rate
   5.5 General divorce rate
   5.6 Number of children involved in divorce

6. Health 130
   6.1 DPT immunization rate
   6.2 Polio immunization rate
   6.3 Measles immunization rate
   6.4 Incidence of sexually transmitted diseases
   6.5 Individuals registered with HIV

7. Education 133
   7.1 Kindergarten enrolments
   7.2 Basic education enrolments
   7.3 General secondary enrolments
   7.4 Tertiary enrolments
   7.5 Women enrolled in tertiary education
   7.6 Public expenditures on education

8. Child protection 136
   8.1 Children in infant homes
   8.2 Gross adoption rate

9. Crime indicators 137
   9.1 Registered total crime rate
   9.2 Total sentencing rate

10. Economic indicators 138
   10.1 Real GDP growth
   10.2 Annual percent change in GDP
   10.3 Share of the agricultural sector in GDP
   10.4 Foreign direct investment
   10.5 General government balance
   10.6 General government expenditure
   10.7 Annual inflation rate
   10.8 Real wages
   10.9 Employment growth
   10.10 Annual registered unemployment rate
   10.11 Registered unemployed women
   10.12 Distribution of earnings: Gini coefficient
   10.13 Income distribution: Gini coefficient

4ª bozza – 16 giugno 1999

1.1 Total population (beginning of year de facto population, thousands)

	1980	1985	1989	1990	1991	1992	1993	1994	1995	1996	1997	1998
Czech Republic[a]	10,320	10,336	10,360	10,362	10,305	10,313	10,326	10,334	10,333	10,321	10,309	10,299
Slovakia[a]	4,991	5,162	5,264	5,288	5,272	5,296	5,314	5,336	5,356	5,368	5,379	5,388
Poland[a]	35,578	37,203	37,885	38,038	38,183	38,309	38,418	38,505	38,581	38,609	38,639	38,660
Hungary[a]	10,708	10,579	10,589	10,374	10,355	10,337	10,310	10,277	10,246	10,212	10,174	10,135
Slovenia[a b]	1,801	1,973	1,996	1,996	2,000	1,999	1,994	1,989	1,989	1,990	1,987	1,985
Croatia[a c d e]	4,588	4,702	4,762	4,773	4,781	4,782	4,734	4,705	4,712	4,681	4,663	4,668
FYR Macedonia[d e f]	1,909	—	—	—	2,035	2,047	2,063	2,009	1,957	1,975	1,989	2,003
Bosnia-Herzegovina[e]	—	—	4,435	4,478	4,518	—	—	3,885	3,484	3,197	3,167	3,294
FR Yugoslavia[a g]	9,842	10,209	10,445	10,500	10,558	10,434	10,469	10,503	10,535	10,568	10,594	10,614
Albania[a d e]	2,671	2,957	3,182	3,250	3,266	3,224	3,172	3,166	3,198	3,241	3,281	3,315
Bulgaria[a]	8,862	8,961	8,987	8,767	8,669	8,595	8,485	8,460	8,427	8,385	8,341	8,283
Romania[a]	22,201	22,725	23,112	23,211	23,192	22,811	22,779	22,748	22,712	22,656	22,582	22,526
Estonia[a h]	1,469	1,529	1,566	1,572	1,570	1,562	1,527	1,507	1,492	1,476	1,462	1,454
Latvia[a h]	2,512	2,579	2,666	2,673	2,668	2,657	2,606	2,566	2,530	2,502	2,480	2,458
Lithuania[a h]	3,413	3,545	3,675	3,708	3,736	3,747	3,736	3,724	3,718	3,712	3,707	3,704
Belarus[h i]	9,622	9,969	10,152	10,211	10,212	10,233	10,298	10,319	10,297	10,264	10,236	10,204
Moldova[h i j]	3,987	4,195	4,335	4,359	4,364	4,357	4,346	4,350	4,346	4,332	4,318	3,651
Russia[h]	138,483	143,033	147,022	147,662	148,164	148,326	148,295	147,997	147,939	147,609	147,137	146,739
Ukraine[h i]	49,953	50,858	51,452	51,584	51,690	51,802	51,989	51,860	51,474	51,079	50,639	50,245
Armenia[g h i]	3,074	3,317	3,288	3,515	3,578	3,649	3,708	3,739	3,753	3,767	3,780	3,792
Azerbaijan[h i]	6,114	6,622	7,021	7,115	7,120	7,230	7,301	7,364	7,420	7,469	7,508	7,565
Georgia[h i]	5,053	5,264	5,401	5,414	5,422	5,420	5,405	5,391	5,375	5,373	5,381	5,395
Kazakhstan[h i]	14,832	15,739	16,185	16,314	16,382	16,519	16,516	16,442	16,151	15,981	15,861	15,642
Kyrgyzstan[h i]	3,593	3,976	4,254	4,335	4,390	4,452	4,469	4,430	4,451	4,512	4,574	4,635
Tajikistan[d e h i]	3,899	4,493	5,109	5,258	5,407	5,541	5,639	5,712	5,781	5,846	5,912	5,983
Turkmenistan[h i]	2,826	3,189	3,545	3,611	3,703	3,798	3,895	4,002	4,435	4,518	4,605	4,681
Uzbekistan[d e h i]	15,758	17,926	19,905	20,368	20,880	21,371	21,820	22,232	22,616	22,971	23,305	23,626

a. 1980, 1985: mid-year population.
b. To 1992 de jure citizens of former Yugoslavia w/permanent residence in Slovenia. Since 1992 permanent residents of Slovenia.
c. 1980, 1985, 1989: CBSC (1996).
d. 1990-92: based on US Census Bureau (1997).
e. 1993-98: based on US Census Bureau (1997).
f. 1980: refers to 1981.
g. 1998: ICDC estimate.
h. 1989: census.
i. 1980, 1985: CIS Stat (1997).
j. 1998: excludes Transdniestr.

1.2 Female population (beginning of year, thousands)

	1980	1985	1989	1990	1991	1992	1993	1994	1995	1996	1997	1998
Czech Republic[a]	5,304	5,320	5,327	5,326	5,304	5,307	5,312	5,315	5,313	5,305	5,297	5,290
Slovakia[a]	2,538	2,621	2,687	2,701	2,699	2,713	2,724	2,736	2,747	2,754	2,760	2,766
Poland[b c]	17,982	—	19,418	19,498	19,577	19,648	19,710	19,758	19,803	19,823	19,843	19,859
Hungary[b]	5,521	—	5,482	5,390	5,383	5,377	5,367	5,354	5,342	5,328	5,311	5,293
Slovenia	—	—	1,028	1,028	1,030	1,029	1,027	1,025	1,025	1,022	1,018	1,017
Croatia[d]	—	—	—	—	2,466	2,465	2,464	2,427	2,430	2,414	2,404	2,405
FYR Macedonia[d]	—	—	—	—	—	—	—	999	977	986	994	1,001
Bosnia-Herzegovina[d]	—	—	2,224	2,245	2,264	—	—	1,966	1,773	1,635	1,623	1,688
FR Yugoslavia[b e f]	11,341	—	5,252	5,281	5,310	5,259	5,278	5,295	5,312	5,328	5,341	5,351
Albania[d g]	—	—	—	1,585	1,607	1,616	1,623	1,639	1,661	1,685	1,707	1,726
Bulgaria[h]	4,437	4,515	4,547	4,444	4,399	4,366	4,316	4,308	4,297	4,281	4,263	4,238
Romania[b j]	10,934	—	11,709	11,761	11,752	11,597	11,588	11,579	11,569	11,548	11,519	11,499
Estonia[b c j]	787	—	834	837	836	831	813	803	796	788	781	777
Latvia[b c j]	1,351	—	1,427	1,430	1,425	1,420	1,395	1,375	1,357	1,343	1,332	1,320
Lithuania[b c j]	1,792	—	1,936	1,953	1,967	1,973	1,968	1,963	1,961	1,959	1,958	1,957
Belarus[b c j k]	5,111	5,316	5,402	5,428	5,425	5,431	5,461	5,471	5,490	5,473	5,458	5,443
Moldova[b c j k l]	2,085	2,210	2,272	2,283	2,283	2,278	2,272	2,273	2,270	2,262	2,254	1,903
Russia[b c j k]	74,202	76,439	78,308	78,550	78,744	78,784	78,712	78,524	78,452	78,320	78,108	77,916
Ukraine[b c j k]	26,993	27,438	27,707	27,739	27,766	27,798	27,870	27,786	27,568	27,353	27,116	26,903
Armenia[b c f k]	1,559	1,695	—	1,805	1,843	1,880	1,912	1,928	1,936	1,943	1,948	1,954
Azerbaijan[b c j k]	3,093	3,393	3,597	3,641	3,644	3,697	3,728	3,752	3,775	3,793	3,806	3,835
Georgia[b c j k]	2,654	2,778	2,839	2,841	2,843	2,839	2,829	2,821	2,812	2,810	2,813	2,818
Kazakhstan[b c j k]	7,609	8,144	8,345	8,403	8,430	8,495	8,490	8,450	8,303	8,213	8,152	8,039
Kyrgyzstan[b c j k]	1,815	2,043	2,178	2,217	2,241	2,269	2,272	2,245	2,257	2,286	2,316	2,346
Tajikistan[b c d k]	1,926	2,263	—	—	—	—	—	2,870	2,905	2,938	2,972	3,008
Turkmenistan[b c j k]	1,406	1,621	1,796	1,831	1,876	1,923	1,971	2,023	2,237	2,273	2,322	2,359
Uzbekistan[b c d k]	7,833	9,087	—	—	—	—	—	11,223	11,415	11,593	11,761	11,923

a. 1980: census. 1980, 1985: CSO (1998).
b. 1980: census, UN (1993a).
c. 1980: refers to 1979.
d. 1993-98: based on US Census Bureau (1998).
e. 1980: refers to former Yugoslavia in 1981.
f. 1998: ICDC estimate.
g. 1990-92: based on US Census Bureau (1997).
h. 1980, 1985: NSI (1997).
i. 1980: refers to 1977.
j. 1989: census.
k. 1985: CIS Stat (1998a).
l. 1998: excludes Transdniestr.

1.3 Child population, age 0-17 (beginning of year, thousands)

	1980	1985	1989	1990	1991	1992	1993	1994	1995	1996	1997	1998
Czech Republic	3,818	3,659	2,804	2,780	2,727	2,679	2,611	2,543	2,467	2,386	2,302	2,226
Slovakia	–	–	1,615	1,613	1,595	1,584	1,563	1,543	1,514	1,479	1,442	1,404
Poland	11,619	12,130	11,352	11,350	11,319	11,275	11,175	11,032	10,857	10,645	10,418	10,166
Hungary	3,759	3,629	2,648	2,611	2,587	2,560	2,497	2,422	2,358	2,297	2,238	2,183
Slovenia	558	588	511	506	500	490	481	470	459	452	438	425
Croatia[a]	–	–	–	–	–	1,118	1,086	1,073	1,059	1,034	1,015	1,002
FYR Macedonia[a]	–	–	–	–	–	589	589	586	582	581	578	576
Bosnia-Herzegovina[a]	–	–	–	–	–	–	–	1,018	867	756	726	745
FR Yugoslavia[b]	–	–	2,923	2,916	2,907	2,846	2,822	2,795	2,767	2,743	2,716	2,685
Albania[a]	–	–	1,248	1,253	1,262	1,264	1,265	1,273	1,285	1,296	1,304	1,305
Bulgaria	3,306	3,109	2,273	2,188	2,138	2,083	2,000	1,954	1,901	1,844	1,791	1,731
Romania	7,349	7,590	6,661	6,635	6,543	6,398	6,235	6,069	5,900	5,723	5,553	5,398
Estonia	–	538	415	416	414	408	393	382	372	362	352	343
Latvia	831	877	681	681	678	674	656	639	623	609	594	577
Lithuania	1,294	1,312	1,000	1,000	1,003	1,003	994	982	971	959	945	930
Belarus	–	–	2,777	2,800	2,793	2,783	2,784	2,764	2,723	2,673	2,618	2,558
Moldova[c]	1,749	1,833	1,420	1,439	1,439	1,432	1,415	1,403	1,387	1,366	1,339	1,132
Russia	49,577	51,349	40,048	40,174	40,082	39,881	39,458	38,823	38,260	37,570	36,718	35,846
Ukraine	17,615	17,778	13,317	13,325	13,257	13,183	13,136	12,973	12,705	12,449	12,151	11,839
Armenia[b]	–	–	–	1,243	1,272	1,290	1,301	1,298	1,283	1,265	1,243	1,219
Azerbaijan	3,471	3,537	2,700	2,741	2,755	2,810	2,839	2,859	2,868	2,863	2,878	2,900
Georgia	2,102	2,111	1,589	1,585	1,579	1,576	1,553	1,525	1,493	1,464	1,432	1,400
Kazakhstan	–	–	6,062	6,074	6,049	6,074	6,035	5,966	5,820	5,716	5,605	5,462
Kyrgyzstan	–	–	1,850	1,888	1,911	1,940	1,955	1,950	1,952	1,971	1,984	1,991
Tajikistan[a]	–	–	2,555	2,595	2,675	2,745	2,790	2,819	2,840	2,854	2,863	2,869
Turkmenistan	–	–	1,663	1,689	1,729	1,769	1,809	1,854	2,073	2,106	2,131	2,144
Uzbekistan[a]	–	–	9,458	9,577	9,808	10,014	10,186	10,323	10,423	10,487	10,520	10,534

a. 1989-92: based on US Census Bureau (1997). 1993-98: based on US Census Bureau (1998).
b. 1998: ICDC estimate.
c. 1998: excludes Transdniestr.

1.4 Child population, age 0-4 (beginning of year, thousands)

	1980	1985	1989	1990	1991	1992	1993	1994	1995	1996	1997	1998
Czech Republic	815	693	663	655	642	639	632	622	602	570	532	502
Slovakia	479	–	426	416	401	394	386	378	367	350	332	317
Poland	3,238	3,423	3,145	3,009	2,884	2,799	2,711	2,620	2,540	2,430	2,316	2,218
Hungary	803	635	622	617	614	615	612	605	599	586	565	544
Slovenia	146	142	128	125	122	117	112	106	102	100	97	96
Croatia[a]	–	–	–	–	–	270	262	258	252	246	245	246
FYR Macedonia[a]	–	–	–	–	–	156	156	154	154	157	157	156
Bosnia-Herzegovina[a]	–	–	–	–	–	–	–	227	171	129	118	130
FR Yugoslavia[b]	–	–	806	789	779	765	744	726	710	696	684	679
Albania[a]	401	–	–	383	386	388	387	385	379	371	363	355
Bulgaria	700	591	591	569	543	515	482	460	435	409	390	366
Romania	1,998	1,727	1,794	1,811	1,763	1,615	1,507	1,397	1,281	1,225	1,191	1,168
Estonia	109	118	122	121	119	113	104	94	85	77	72	67
Latvia	173	193	208	205	200	192	178	162	148	134	121	109
Lithuania	259	277	295	294	292	290	279	266	251	236	220	205
Belarus	727	–	819	813	793	757	727	678	630	585	547	509
Moldova[c]	377	417	438	433	420	400	379	357	338	318	299	245
Russia	10,663	11,586	12,032	11,730	11,300	10,624	9,759	8,841	8,192	7,585	7,090	6,749
Ukraine	3,653	3,821	3,791	3,714	3,616	3,474	3,343	3,146	2,950	2,773	2,596	2,442
Armenia[b]	321	–	–	382	383	379	371	355	331	302	273	247
Azerbaijan	697	793	862	875	875	894	896	884	859	818	822	829
Georgia	430	458	466	458	450	443	424	397	366	330	296	276
Kazakhstan	–	–	1,917	1,899	1,855	1,816	1,753	1,665	1,577	1,495	1,407	1,307
Kyrgyzstan	–	–	617	624	625	624	618	599	580	573	556	533
Tajikistan[a]	–	–	929	939	958	963	948	922	888	844	801	772
Turkmenistan	–	–	565	573	583	588	598	605	668	658	648	624
Uzbekistan[a]	–	–	3,297	3,313	3,333	3,322	3,281	3,222	3,141	3,031	2,912	2,802

a. 1989-92: based on US Census Bureau (1997). 1993-98: based on US Census Bureau (1998).
b. 1998: ICDC estimate.
c. 1998: excludes Transdniestr.

1.5 Youth dependency ratio (ratio of 0-17 population to 18-59 population)

	1989	1990	1991	1992	1993	1994	1995	1996	1997	1998
Czech Republic	48.9	48.3	47.5	46.3	44.6	42.9	41.1	39.2	37.4	35.8
Slovakia	56.1	55.7	55.1	54.2	52.9	51.6	49.9	48.1	46.3	44.4
Poland	54.0	53.8	53.6	53.1	52.4	51.3	50.1	48.7	47.3	45.7
Hungary	44.4	45.0	44.6	44.2	42.8	41.3	39.9	38.7	37.6	36.5
Slovenia	43.4	42.9	42.3	41.5	40.8	39.9	38.9	38.1	36.9	35.6
Croatia[a]	–	–	–	39.9	39.2	39.2	38.7	38.1	37.6	37.1
FYR Macedonia[a]	–	–	–	49.3	49.0	50.6	52.2	51.5	50.8	50.2
Bosnia-Herzegovina[a]	–	–	–	–	–	43.6	41.6	39.6	38.5	37.8
FR Yugoslavia[b]	49.0	48.7	48.6	48.7	48.2	47.6	47.0	46.4	45.8	45.0
Albania[a]	–	71.9	72.3	74.5	77.2	78.5	78.6	78.1	77.4	76.4
Bulgaria	45.1	44.6	44.2	43.4	42.1	41.1	40.0	38.8	37.7	36.3
Romania	51.5	51.1	50.4	50.5	49.0	47.4	45.8	44.2	42.8	41.4
Estonia	46.8	46.9	46.8	46.5	45.8	45.0	44.1	43.3	42.4	41.5
Latvia	44.7	44.7	44.7	44.9	44.7	44.2	43.6	43.0	42.3	41.4
Lithuania	47.7	47.2	47.2	46.9	46.7	46.4	46.0	45.4	44.8	44.0
Belarus	48.4	48.7	48.9	48.7	48.5	48.0	47.2	46.3	45.4	44.3
Moldova[c]	59.9	60.9	60.9	60.5	59.9	58.9	58.0	57.0	55.7	55.8
Russia	47.5	47.7	47.7	47.5	47.0	46.0	45.0	44.0	43.0	42.1
Ukraine	46.1	46.3	46.1	45.6	45.1	44.3	43.3	42.7	42.0	41.4
Armenia[b]	–	64.7	65.6	65.4	65.0	64.1	62.8	61.3	59.7	58.1
Azerbaijan	71.6	72.1	72.7	73.3	73.8	73.9	73.5	72.8	72.8	72.8
Georgia	52.3	52.3	52.3	52.3	51.8	50.9	49.7	48.7	47.6	46.4
Kazakhstan	70.1	69.8	69.2	68.7	68.1	67.2	66.4	65.6	64.5	63.7
Kyrgyzstan	89.9	90.4	90.5	90.5	91.4	92.2	91.3	90.5	89.4	87.8
Tajikistan[a]	–	111.0	111.8	112.2	112.1	111.6	110.7	109.4	107.8	105.8
Turkmenistan	100.4	99.4	99.2	98.7	98.2	97.5	98.4	97.8	96.3	94.5
Uzbekistan[a]	–	101.3	101.2	100.8	100.1	99.1	97.6	95.8	93.8	91.8

a. 1989-92: based on US Census Bureau (1997). 1993-98: based on US Census Bureau (1998).
b. 1998: ICDC estimate.
c. 1998: excludes Transdniestr.

1.6 Elderly dependency ratio (ratio of 60+ population to 18-59 population)

	1989	1990	1991	1992	1993	1994	1995	1996	1997	1998
Czech Republic	31.8	31.8	32.0	31.9	31.6	31.3	31.0	30.6	30.2	29.9
Slovakia	26.8	27.0	26.9	27.0	27.0	26.9	26.7	26.5	26.2	26.0
Poland	26.1	26.6	27.1	27.4	27.7	27.8	27.9	28.1	28.2	28.2
Hungary	33.3	33.8	34.1	34.2	34.0	33.8	33.7	33.5	33.2	33.1
Slovenia	26.0	26.4	27.1	27.7	28.4	29.0	29.5	30.0	30.3	30.7
Croatia[a]	–	–	–	30.8	31.7	32.8	33.5	34.3	35.1	35.7
FYR Macedonia[a]	–	–	–	22.0	22.6	22.9	23.1	23.6	23.9	24.2
Bosnia-Herzegovina[a]	–	–	–	–	–	22.8	25.5	28.0	29.2	29.4
FR Yugoslavia[b]	26.0	26.8	27.8	29.8	30.6	31.2	31.8	32.3	32.7	33.0
Albania[a]	–	14.6	14.9	15.5	16.3	16.8	17.0	17.2	17.4	17.6
Bulgaria	33.3	34.3	35.1	35.6	36.5	37.0	37.5	37.7	37.7	37.5
Romania	27.2	27.7	28.3	29.5	30.0	30.3	30.6	30.8	31.1	31.4
Estonia	29.7	30.2	30.7	31.3	32.3	32.6	32.7	33.1	33.7	34.4
Latvia	30.3	30.8	31.3	31.8	32.8	33.3	33.4	33.8	34.3	35.0
Lithuania	27.6	28.0	28.6	28.4	29.0	29.6	30.1	30.4	30.8	31.4
Belarus	28.5	29.0	30.0	30.3	31.0	31.1	31.2	31.4	31.9	32.4
Moldova[c]	23.1	23.5	23.7	23.7	24.0	23.9	23.7	23.7	23.8	24.2
Russia	26.7	27.6	28.5	29.1	29.5	29.3	28.9	29.0	29.4	30.3
Ukraine	32.1	32.8	33.5	33.6	33.4	32.7	32.3	32.4	33.0	34.2
Armenia[b]	–	18.2	19.0	19.6	20.2	20.6	20.9	21.3	21.9	22.6
Azerbaijan	14.6	14.9	15.2	15.3	16.0	16.4	16.7	17.0	17.0	17.1
Georgia	25.5	26.4	27.3	27.6	28.5	28.9	29.2	30.1	31.2	32.4
Kazakhstan	17.0	17.6	18.3	18.2	18.2	17.9	17.8	17.8	18.1	18.6
Kyrgyzstan	16.9	17.2	17.3	17.2	17.6	17.3	16.9	16.6	16.7	16.7
Tajikistan[a]	–	13.9	14.2	14.3	14.4	14.5	14.6	14.7	14.8	14.9
Turkmenistan	13.6	13.1	13.3	13.2	13.3	13.0	12.1	12.0	11.9	11.8
Uzbekistan[a]	–	14.1	14.3	14.3	14.3	14.3	14.1	14.0	14.0	14.1

a. 1989-92: based on US Census Bureau (1997). 1993-98: based on US Census Bureau (1998).
b. 1998: ICDC estimate.
c. 1998: excludes Transdniestr.

1.7 Rate of natural population increase
(birth rate minus death rate, per thousand population; excludes changes due to migration)

	1980	1985	1989	1990	1991	1992	1993	1994	1995	1996	1997
Czech Republic	4.2	2.8	0.1	0.2	0.5	0.2	0.3	-1.0	-2.1	-2.1	-2.1
Slovakia	—	—	5.0	4.9	4.6	4.1	3.9	2.9	1.7	1.7	1.3
Poland	9.6	7.9	4.9	4.2	3.8	3.2	2.7	2.6	1.3	1.2	0.9
Hungary	0.4	-1.6	-2.0	-1.9	-1.6	-2.6	-3.2	-3.0	-3.2	-3.7	-3.8
Slovenia	5.8	3.1	2.5	2.0	1.2	0.4	-0.1	0.1	0.1	0.1	-0.3
Croatia[a b c]	4.0	2.3	0.7	0.7	-0.6	-1.0	-0.5	-0.1	0.0	0.7	0.8
FYR Macedonia[b c]	13.9	12.1	—	—	10.0	8.5	8.3	9.3	8.2	7.9	6.6
Bosnia-Herzegovina[c d]	—	—	8.3	8.5	—	—	0.5	1.5	4.3	5.2	5.0
FR Yugoslavia[e]	8.6	6.8	5.3	5.5	4.9	3.4	3.3	3.1	3.2	2.5	2.0
Albania[c f g]	20.1	20.4	18.8	19.5	18.3	18.0	15.8	16.9	16.8	15.6	—
Bulgaria	3.5	1.4	0.7	-0.3	-1.6	-2.1	-2.9	-3.8	-5.0	-5.3	-6.9
Romania	7.6	4.9	5.4	3.0	1.1	-0.1	-0.5	-0.8	-1.5	-2.4	-1.8
Estonia	2.7	2.8	3.8	1.9	-0.2	-1.3	-3.9	-5.2	-4.9	-3.8	-4.0
Latvia	1.3	2.2	2.5	1.2	0.1	-1.3	-4.7	-6.8	-6.8	-5.8	-5.9
Lithuania	4.7	5.4	4.9	4.7	4.2	3.4	0.5	-1.0	-1.0	-1.0	-0.8
Belarus[h]	6.1	5.9	5.0	3.3	1.8	1.2	-1.0	-1.8	-3.1	-3.6	-4.6
Moldova[h i]	9.7	10.6	9.8	8.1	6.1	5.9	4.6	2.5	0.9	0.5	0.9
Russia	4.9	5.3	4.0	2.4	0.8	-1.4	-5.0	-6.0	-5.6	-5.2	-5.1
Ukraine[h]	3.5	2.9	1.9	0.6	-0.7	-1.8	-3.4	-4.6	-5.8	-6.0	-6.1
Armenia[h]	18.2	19.8	15.9	16.6	15.3	12.3	8.6	7.2	6.5	6.2	5.4
Azerbaijan[h]	17.2	18.2	19.7	19.9	20.5	18.1	16.8	14.3	12.6	10.9	11.4
Georgia[h]	9.1	9.8	8.3	8.8	8.0	4.8	—	3.0	3.5	3.7	2.8
Kazakhstan[g h]	15.9	17.1	15.7	14.3	13.3	12.1	9.7	8.9	6.7	5.5	4.6
Kyrgyzstan[g h]	21.2	23.9	23.4	22.5	22.3	21.6	18.5	16.4	17.9	16.2	14.7
Tajikistan[i k]	28.9	33.0	32.3	32.6	32.9	25.6	24.3	21.3	22.8	16.9	19.2
Turkmenistan[h k]	26.0	27.9	27.2	27.2	26.4	26.9	25.2	23.1	22.6	17.0	15.1
Uzbekistan[i k]	26.4	30.2	26.9	27.6	28.3	26.6	24.9	22.8	23.4	21.1	19.7

a. 1980, 1985: CBSC (1996).
b. Population data, 1991-92: US Census Bureau (1997).
c. Population data, 1993-97: US Census Bureau (1998).
d. 1993-97: Federation of B-H.
e. 1980, 1985: FSOY (1996).
f. Population data, 1989-92: US Census Bureau (1997).
g. Birth rate based on live births.
h. 1980, 1985: CIS Stat (1997).
i. 1997: population data exclude Transdniestr.
j. 1980-95: CIS Stat (1997).
k. 1996-97: CIS Stat (1998b).

1.8 Net external migration (immigrants minus emigrants, thousands)

	1980	1985	1989	1990	1991	1992	1993	1994	1995	1996	1997
Czech Republic	-1.3	-1.0	1.5	0.6	2.9	11.8	5.5	9.9	10.0	10.1	12.1
Slovakia	—	—	—	0.1	1.2	2.0	1.8	4.8	2.8	2.3	1.7
Poland	-21.2	-18.9	-24.4	-15.8	-15.9	-11.6	-15.5	-19.0	-18.2	-13.1	-11.8
Hungary	—	—	23.9	22.6	17.3	10.8	13.3	13.1	13.2	12.1	7.9
Slovenia[a]	—	—	2.4	2.2	-3.1	-0.4	1.4	0.9	2.5	6.5	2.4
Croatia	—	—	—	—	1.4	39.5	48.5	23.3	26.6	34.6	33.8
FYR Macedonia	—	—	—	—	—	-0.6	3.2	3.0	1.7	1.2	1.0
Bosnia-Herzegovina	—	—	—	—	—	—	—	—	—	—	—
FR Yugoslavia	—	—	—	—	—	—	—	—	—	—	—
Albania	—	—	—	—	—	—	—	—	—	—	—
Bulgaria	—	—	-217.6	-87.6	-46.5	-67.7	-64.4	-62.7	-50.5	-64.5	—
Romania	-24.7	-27.2	-41.4	-96.9	-42.6	-29.4	-17.2	-16.3	-21.2	-19.5	-13.3
Estonia	—	6.5	0.2	-4.0	-8.0	-33.8	-13.8	-7.6	-8.2	-5.7	-2.5
Latvia	4.4	10.9	1.2	-0.5	-10.8	-46.9	-27.9	-18.8	-10.5	-7.3	-4.8
Lithuania	8.9	13.8	1.3	-8.8	-8.9	-22.2	-13.1	-2.6	-1.8	-0.9	0.1
Belarus[b]	14.4	0.3	25.9	-19.6	30.4	66.0	37.9	-3.3	-0.2	9.4	14.7
Moldova[b c]	5.6	-3.8	—	—	—	-5.8	-4.6	-5.0	-4.0	-12.7	—
Russia	63.4	267.2	115.3	183.8	16.7	252.9	440.3	809.6	502.5	343.5	349.0
Ukraine	7.9	22.5	-108.9	-139.3	-180.4	290.1	49.6	-143.2	-94.8	-131.2	-82.1
Armenia	-19.1	-36.3	17.8	40.8	23.0	-6.3	-20.9	-19.1	-7.8	-6.4	-8.5
Azerbaijan	-8.4	-15.4	2.1	-10.5	-18.5	-32.6	-21.2	-22.8	-21.8	-25.4	-11.3
Georgia	-5.5	-5.5	-14.9	-39.0	-44.0	-41.6	-30.3	-31.5	-20.2	-11.7	-0.5
Kazakhstan[b]	-62.7	-92.6	-93.4	-130.9	-48.9	-179.3	-222.1	-414.4	-238.5	-175.5	-261.4
Kyrgyzstan[b]	-7.9	-19.8	-16.0	-41.9	-33.8	-77.5	-120.6	-51.1	-18.9	-11.7	-6.7
Tajikistan[d]	-8.6	-2.6	-20.5	-60.3	19.0	-142.3	-2.2	-51.8	-38.2	—	—
Turkmenistan[b]	-4.8	-9.0	—	-0.9	2.4	-7.7	2.6	-11.6	-12.3	-25.9	-16.6
Uzbekistan[e]	-31.7	-48.9	-97.9	-179.6	-95.9	-74.7	-54.0	-138.9	-89.0	-50.3	—

a. 1989-94: migration of Slovenian citizens only.
b. 1980, 1985: CIS Stat (1997).
c. 1996: CIS Stat (1998c).
d. 1980-94: CIS Stat (1997). 1995: CIS Stat (1998c).
e. 1980-96: CIS Stat (1997).

2.1 Crude birth rate (live births per thousand population)

	1980	1985	1989	1990	1991	1992	1993	1994	1995	1996	1997
Czech Republic[a b 1]	16.4	14.7	12.4	12.6	12.5	11.8	11.7	10.3	9.3	8.8	8.8
Slovakia[a b 1]	16.4	14.7	15.2	15.2	14.9	14.1	13.8	12.4	11.5	11.2	11.0
Poland[i]	19.5	18.2	14.9	14.4	14.3	13.4	12.9	12.5	11.2	11.1	10.7
Hungary[b 1]	14.0	12.4	11.8	12.1	12.3	11.8	11.4	11.3	11.0	10.3	9.9
Slovenia[c 1]	15.7	13.1	11.7	11.2	10.8	10.0	9.9	9.8	9.5	9.4	9.1
Croatia[d 1]	14.9	13.3	11.7	11.6	10.8	9.8	10.4	10.3	10.7	11.5	11.9
FYR Macedonia[e 1]	21.0	19.2	17.0	16.6	17.1	16.2	15.6	17.2	16.3	15.8	14.8
Bosnia-Herzegovina[f 1]	17.3	16.8	15.0	14.9	—	—	—	—	—	14.7	—
FR Yugoslavia[g 1]	17.6	16.3	14.8	14.7	14.5	13.5	13.4	13.1	13.3	13.0	12.4
Albania[b h]	26.5	26.2	24.4	25.1	23.7	23.6	21.5	22.7	22.4	21.0	—
Bulgaria[b 2]	14.6	13.4	12.6	12.1	11.1	10.4	10.0	9.4	8.6	8.6	7.7
Romania[b 1]	18.0	15.8	16.0	13.6	12.0	11.4	11.0	10.9	10.4	10.2	10.5
Estonia[b 3]	15.0	15.5	15.5	14.2	12.3	11.7	10.0	9.5	9.1	9.0	8.7
Latvia[b 4]	14.1	15.4	14.6	14.2	13.0	12.0	10.3	9.5	8.6	7.9	7.6
Lithuania[b 4]	15.2	16.5	15.1	15.3	15.0	14.3	12.7	11.4	11.1	10.5	10.2
Belarus[i 5]	16.0	16.5	15.1	13.9	12.9	12.5	11.4	10.7	9.8	9.3	8.8
Moldova[i j 6]	19.8	21.5	18.9	17.7	16.5	16.0	15.2	14.3	13.0	12.0	15.6
Russia[7]	15.9	16.6	14.7	13.4	12.1	10.7	9.3	9.5	9.2	8.9	8.6
Ukraine[6]	14.8	15.0	13.4	12.7	12.2	11.5	10.7	10.1	9.6	9.2	8.8
Armenia[i 8]	22.7	24.1	21.6	22.5	21.5	19.2	15.8	13.6	13.0	12.8	11.6
Azerbaijan[i 6]	25.2	26.6	25.7	25.7	26.5	25.0	23.8	21.6	19.3	17.3	17.5
Georgia[i k 5]	17.6	18.5	16.9	17.1	16.4	13.4	11.4	10.6	10.5	10.0	9.7
Kazakhstan[i 6]	23.9	25.1	23.4	22.1	21.5	20.4	19.1	18.8	17.2	15.9	14.8
Kyrgyzstan[i 6]	29.6	32.0	30.6	29.5	29.3	28.8	26.2	24.8	26.2	23.8	22.2
Tajikistan[l m 6]	37.0	40.0	38.7	38.8	38.9	32.2	33.1	28.2	28.6	22.0	25.0
Turkmenistan[m 6]	34.3	36.0	34.9	34.3	33.7	34.1	33.3	30.7	28.4	24.0	21.6
Uzbekistan[l m 6]	33.9	37.4	33.3	33.7	34.5	33.1	31.5	29.4	29.8	27.3	25.5

2.2 Teenage birth rate (live births per thousand women aged 15-19)

	1989	1990	1991	1992	1993	1994	1995	1996	1997
Czech Republic	44.9	44.7	46.7	44.7	42.9	32.6	24.9	20.1	18.0
Slovakia	46.8	45.5	50.2	47.4	45.7	38.3	32.4	30.5	28.6
Poland	30.9	31.5	32.2	29.3	27.2	25.5	22.0	21.1	19.5
Hungary	41.3	40.1	38.6	36.1	34.5	34.1	31.8	29.9	28.0
Slovenia	27.2	24.6	21.1	19.4	16.1	14.3	13.3	11.1	9.2
Croatia	—	—	—	—	—	—	—	—	—
FYR Macedonia	—	—	—	—	—	—	—	—	—
Bosnia-Herzegovina	38.3	38.2	—	—	—	—	—	—	—
FR Yugoslavia	42.8	41.1	39.2	35.5	35.3	34.0	32.2	30.2	—
Albania	—	—	—	—	—	—	—	—	—
Bulgaria	75.2	72.7	72.7	70.5	67.3	60.8	53.5	51.2	45.1
Romania	59.9	51.8	50.2	48.0	47.7	45.7	42.6	40.5	41.4
Estonia	48.2	50.0	47.8	50.1	43.0	38.6	36.0	33.4	29.4
Latvia	44.5	50.0	51.1	48.3	43.7	33.7	29.6	25.5	21.2
Lithuania	36.8	41.6	46.9	47.1	42.7	40.9	39.7	36.4	32.1
Belarus	39.7	43.5	44.9	45.6	43.3	42.5	39.0	35.8	33.1
Moldova	56.2	57.8	61.6	62.1	65.7	65.1	61.7	53.1	47.7
Russia	52.1	55.1	54.3	50.8	46.8	48.7	44.6	38.9	35.9
Ukraine	55.3	58.8	59.8	59.8	57.7	56.2	54.3	50.8	45.7
Armenia	62.7	70.0	76.6	82.5	77.0	68.0	56.2	53.3	43.4
Azerbaijan	28.2	27.1	31.2	35.8	39.3	41.7	40.7	37.0	43.2
Georgia[a]	58.6	60.2	61.0	52.7	—	61.7	58.2	51.9	46.6
Kazakhstan	47.9	52.4	54.6	52.1	52.8	54.3	49.3	44.1	38.4
Kyrgyzstan	44.4	46.3	50.9	55.4	59.3	55.2	56.3	54.4	46.1
Tajikistan	—	—	—	—	—	—	—	—	—
Turkmenistan	21.8	24.1	25.9	27.3	31.4	27.7	24.2	—	—
Uzbekistan	—	—	—	—	—	—	—	—	—

2.3 Share of births to mothers under age 20 (percent of total live births)

	1989	1990	1991	1992	1993	1994	1995	1996	1997
Czech Republic	13.6	14.1	15.5	16.2	15.8	13.5	11.0	9.0	7.7
Slovakia	11.9	12.0	14.0	14.3	14.3	13.4	12.3	11.7	11.0
Poland	7.4	8.0	8.5	8.4	8.3	8.2	8.0	7.8	7.6
Hungary	12.3	12.3	12.3	12.4	12.6	12.5	11.5	11.0	10.2
Slovenia	8.2	7.8	7.0	7.0	5.9	5.4	5.1	4.3	3.6
Croatia	8.4	7.9	7.8	7.2	6.5	6.2	5.7	5.6	5.1
FYR Macedonia	11.1	10.8	10.5	10.4	11.5	10.9	11.0	10.0	10.1
Bosnia-Herzegovina	10.4	10.4	10.4	—	—	—	—	—	—
FR Yugoslavia	10.6	10.3	10.0	9.8	9.9	9.8	9.0	8.6	8.4
Albania	—	—	—	—	—	—	—	—	—
Bulgaria	20.9	21.4	23.5	24.6	24.9	23.7	22.6	21.1	20.4
Romania	15.1	15.2	16.9	17.4	18.4	17.9	17.3	16.5	16.0
Estonia	10.5	12.0	13.2	14.7	14.8	14.1	13.7	12.9	12.0
Latvia	10.3	11.7	12.7	12.9	13.5	11.4	11.2	10.5	9.3
Lithuania	8.9	9.8	11.2	11.7	11.7	12.4	12.4	12.0	11.0
Belarus	9.2	11.0	12.3	12.9	13.4	14.1	14.3	14.0	14.1
Moldova	11.1	12.8	15.1	15.9	17.7	18.9	19.8	18.6	17.9
Russia	11.8	13.9	15.4	16.5	17.7	18.2	17.5	16.1	15.6
Ukraine	14.1	16.1	17.3	18.3	18.9	19.5	19.9	19.5	18.4
Armenia	11.3	12.5	14.5	17.6	20.0	20.8	18.3	18.1	16.5
Azerbaijan	5.0	4.7	5.2	6.3	7.2	8.4	9.3	9.5	11.0
Georgia[a]	12.9	12.8	13.5	14.4	—	22.0	21.1	19.7	18.4
Kazakhstan	8.7	10.0	10.9	11.2	12.2	13.0	13.0	12.6	12.0
Kyrgyzstan	6.9	7.6	8.5	9.3	10.9	10.9	10.6	11.3	10.4
Tajikistan[b]	5.1	—	—	—	8.0	—	—	—	—
Turkmenistan	3.2	3.6	3.9	4.0	4.7	4.5	4.3	—	—
Uzbekistan[b]	6.3	—	—	—	10.7	—	—	—	—

a. 1992-97: excludes Abkhazia and Tskhinvali.
b. 1989: Goskomstat (1990). 1993: CIS Stat (1995a).

2.4 Share of births to unmarried mothers (percent of total live births)

	1989	1990	1991	1992	1993	1994	1995	1996	1997
Czech Republic	7.9	8.6	9.8	10.7	12.7	14.5	15.6	16.9	17.8
Slovakia	7.2	7.6	8.9	9.8	10.6	11.7	12.6	14.0	15.1
Poland	6.1	6.5	6.9	7.5	8.5	9.0	9.5	10.2	11.0
Hungary	12.4	13.1	14.1	15.6	17.6	19.4	20.7	22.6	25.0
Slovenia	23.2	24.5	26.4	27.7	28.0	28.8	29.8	31.9	32.7
Croatia	6.6	7.0	7.5	7.7	7.7	7.6	7.5	7.1	7.3
FYR Macedonia	7.0	7.1	7.0	7.3	8.1	8.5	8.2	8.2	8.9
Bosnia-Herzegovina	6.9	7.4	—	—	—	—	—	—	—
FR Yugoslavia	12.4	12.7	13.6	14.0	15.8	16.0	16.4	17.8	19.1
Albania	—	—	—	—	—	—	—	—	—
Bulgaria	11.4	12.4	15.5	18.5	22.1	24.5	25.7	28.1	30.0
Romania	—	—	—	—	17.0	18.3	19.7	20.7	22.2
Estonia	25.2	27.1	31.1	34.0	38.2	40.9	44.1	48.1	51.6
Latvia	15.9	16.9	18.4	19.6	23.0	26.4	29.9	33.1	34.8
Lithuania	6.7	7.0	7.0	7.9	9.1	10.9	12.8	14.3	16.5
Belarus	7.9	8.5	9.4	9.8	10.9	12.1	13.5	14.9	16.2
Moldova	10.4	11.0	11.8	11.6	11.2	12.3	13.3	14.6	—
Russia	13.5	14.6	16.0	17.1	18.2	19.6	21.1	23.0	25.3
Ukraine	10.8	11.2	11.9	12.1	13.0	12.8	13.2	13.6	15.2
Armenia	7.9	9.3	10.9	12.3	14.0	15.3	15.2	22.3	25.8
Azerbaijan	2.5	2.6	3.7	4.4	5.0	5.2	5.8	6.8	7.5
Georgia[a]	17.7	18.2	18.7	21.8	—	28.4	29.2	30.9	33.4
Kazakhstan	12.0	13.2	13.4	13.4	13.4	14.5	15.7	17.6	21.0
Kyrgyzstan	12.7	13.0	13.9	13.2	16.7	16.8	18.5	21.1	24.1
Tajikistan[b]	7.0	6.9	—	—	9.2	—	—	—	—
Turkmenistan	3.5	4.4	4.6	3.5	4.2	4.3	4.6	—	—
Uzbekistan[b]	4.2	4.4	—	—	3.8	—	—	—	—

a. 1992-97: excludes Abkhazia and Tskhinvali.
b. 1989-90: CE (1993). 1993: CIS Stat (1995a).

2.5 Share of low-weight births (births under 2,500 grams as percent of total live births)

	1989	1990	1991	1992	1993	1994	1995	1996	1997
Czech Republic	6.0	6.3	6.7	6.5	6.4	6.1	6.2	6.2	6.3
Slovakia	5.6	5.8	6.1	6.5	6.4	6.4	6.5	—	—
Poland	7.9	8.4	8.3	8.1	8.1	7.2	6.7	6.4	6.1
Hungary	9.2	9.3	9.3	9.0	8.6	8.6	8.2	8.3	8.4
Slovenia	5.9	5.0	5.3	5.8	5.5	5.4	5.2	5.2	5.2
Croatia	—	—	—	—	—	—	—	—	—
FYR Macedonia	—	—	—	—	—	5.1	5.3	5.3	5.1
Bosnia-Herzegovina	—	—	—	—	—	—	—	—	—
FR Yugoslavia	—	—	—	—	—	4.9	5.3	5.3	5.0
Albania	6.5	6.5	6.3	5.8	5.6	5.7	5.5	5.4	—
Bulgaria	6.9	7.2	8.3	8.4	8.3	8.4	8.6	9.1	9.2
Romania	7.3	7.1	7.9	8.2	10.9	8.6	8.8	8.9	9.2
Estonia	—	—	—	4.3	3.8	4.5	4.3	4.2	4.2
Latvia	—	—	4.6	5.0	5.1	5.0	4.8	5.1	5.0
Lithuania	—	—	—	—	—	—	—	—	—
Belarus	4.2	4.3	4.3	4.3	4.6	4.9	5.0	4.9	5.0
Moldova	7.1	5.6	5.6	5.5	5.5	5.8	6.1	5.8	6.0
Russia	5.6	5.6	5.6	5.8	6.2	6.2	6.1	6.0	6.2
Ukraine	—	—	—	—	—	—	—	—	—
Armenia	6.8	6.5	6.7	7.7	7.4	6.5	7.4	7.5	6.8
Azerbaijan	5.6	5.2	4.9	5.2	5.4	5.5	5.7	4.4	4.5
Georgia[a]	5.3	4.9	8.6	5.8	6.0	6.6	6.2	7.1	7.0
Kazakhstan	5.0	5.0	6.0	5.3	5.6	6.1	5.7	6.0	5.6
Kyrgyzstan	—	—	—	—	—	—	—	—	—
Tajikistan	—	—	—	—	—	—	—	—	—
Turkmenistan	3.9	4.5	4.2	4.0	4.6	4.2	3.9	—	—
Uzbekistan	—	—	—	—	—	—	—	—	—

a. 1992-97: excludes Abkhazia and Tskhinvali.

2.6 Total fertility rate (births per woman)

	1980	1985	1989	1990	1991	1992	1993	1994	1995	1996	1997
Czech Republic[a b]	2.15	2.06	1.87	1.89	1.86	1.72	1.67	1.44	1.28	1.19	1.17
Slovakia[a b]	2.15	2.06	2.08	2.09	2.05	1.98	1.92	1.66	1.52	1.47	1.43
Poland[b]	2.28	2.33	2.05	2.04	2.05	1.93	1.85	1.80	1.61	1.60	1.50
Hungary[b]	1.92	1.83	1.78	1.84	1.86	1.77	1.69	1.64	1.57	1.46	1.38
Slovenia[b]	2.11	1.72	1.52	1.46	1.42	1.34	1.34	1.32	1.29	1.28	1.25
Croatia	—	—	1.63	1.63	1.53	1.48	1.52	1.47	1.58	1.67	1.69
FYR Macedonia[b]	2.45	2.31	2.09	2.06	2.30	2.18	2.16	2.08	1.97	1.90	—
Bosnia-Herzegovina[c]	1.88	1.89	1.70	1.70	—	—	—	—	—	—	—
FR Yugoslavia[d]	2.30	2.20	2.06	2.08	2.08	1.91	1.91	1.85	1.88	1.83	1.74
Albania[b]	3.62	3.26	2.96	3.03	—	—	—	—	—	—	—
Bulgaria[b]	2.05	1.95	1.90	1.81	1.65	1.54	1.45	1.37	1.23	1.24	1.09
Romania[b]	2.45	2.26	2.20	1.84	1.57	1.52	1.44	1.41	1.34	1.30	1.32
Estonia[e]	2.02	2.12	2.21	2.05	1.79	1.69	1.45	1.37	1.32	1.30	1.24
Latvia[e]	1.88	2.07	2.05	2.02	1.86	1.73	1.51	1.39	1.25	1.16	1.11
Lithuania[e]	2.00	2.10	1.98	2.00	1.97	1.89	1.69	1.52	1.49	1.42	1.39
Belarus[e f]	2.01	2.07	2.03	1.91	1.80	1.75	1.61	1.51	1.39	1.31	1.23
Moldova[e f]	2.39	2.66	2.46	2.39	2.26	2.21	2.10	1.95	1.76	1.67	—
Russia[e]	1.87	2.05	2.01	1.89	1.73	1.55	1.39	1.40	1.34	1.28	1.23
Ukraine[e]	1.95	2.10	1.90	1.90	1.70	1.70	1.60	1.50	1.40	1.30	1.30
Armenia[e f]	2.31	2.47	2.61	2.62	2.58	2.35	1.97	1.70	1.63	1.60	1.45
Azerbaijan[e]	3.22	2.90	2.79	2.77	2.89	2.74	2.70	2.52	2.29	2.06	2.07
Georgia[e]	2.21	2.26	2.13	2.20	2.15	1.79	—	—	—	—	—
Kazakhstan[e f g]	2.90	3.03	2.88	2.72	2.63	2.49	2.34	2.25	2.15	2.07	2.00
Kyrgyzstan[e f]	4.07	4.14	3.81	3.69	3.67	3.62	3.30	3.14	3.31	2.99	2.79
Tajikistan[e f h i]	5.64	5.50	5.08	5.05	5.01	4.13	4.25	3.66	3.77	3.19	3.63
Turkmenistan[e f j]	4.93	4.66	4.27	4.17	4.09	4.14	4.03	3.88	3.40	3.20	2.88
Uzbekistan[e f g h]	4.81	4.64	4.02	4.07	4.17	4.00	3.81	3.55	3.59	3.39	3.17

a. 1980, 1985: Czechoslovakia.
b. 1980, 1985: CE (1993).
c. CE (1993).
d. 1980 (which refers to 1975), 1985: FSOY (1996).
e. 1980: refers to 1980-81. 1985: refers to 1984-85.
f. 1980, 1985: Goskomstat (1988).
g. 1991-97: ICDC estimates.
h. 1989: CE (1993).
i. 1993-97: ICDC estimates.
j. 1992-97: ICDC estimates.

2.7 Average age of mothers at first birth (years)

	1989	1990	1991	1992	1993	1994	1995	1996	1997
Czech Republic	22.5	22.4	22.2	22.2	22.3	22.5	22.9	23.3	23.7
Slovakia	22.0	21.0	21.1	21.1	21.3	21.5	—	—	—
Poland[a]	23.0	23.0	22.9	22.6	22.6	22.7	22.8	22.9	23.1
Hungary	22.6	22.5	22.5	22.6	22.6	22.7	22.9	23.2	23.4
Slovenia	23.7	23.9	24.2	24.3	24.7	24.8	25.1	25.3	25.6
Croatia	24.2	24.3	24.4	24.5	24.7	24.8	25.0	25.1	25.2
FYR Macedonia	23.3	23.3	23.4	23.4	23.3	23.5	23.5	23.7	23.7
Bosnia-Herzegovina	23.6	—	—	—	—	—	—	—	—
FR Yugoslavia	23.9	24.0	24.1	24.2	24.1	23.8	23.9	24.7	24.2
Albania	—	—	—	—	—	—	—	—	—
Bulgaria	22.0	22.1	22.0	22.0	22.1	22.3	22.2	22.4	22.7
Romania	22.5	22.4	22.2	22.3	22.4	22.5	22.7	22.9	23.1
Estonia	23.0	22.9	22.7	22.7	22.7	22.8	23.0	23.2	23.4
Latvia	22.9	22.7	22.6	22.5	22.5	22.9	23.0	23.1	23.5
Lithuania	—	22.9	22.7	22.6	22.7	22.7	22.8	22.9	23.4
Belarus	23.1	22.9	22.9	22.8	22.8	22.8	22.9	23.0	23.0
Moldova	—	—	—	—	—	—	—	—	—
Russia	23.1	22.9	22.8	22.8	22.6	22.5	22.6	22.8	22.9
Ukraine	—	—	—	—	—	—	—	—	—
Armenia	22.7	22.8	22.5	22.2	22.0	22.0	22.5	22.2	22.3
Azerbaijan	23.8	23.8	24.0	24.0	23.9	23.9	23.8	24.0	23.5
Georgia	23.7	23.7	23.7	23.6	—	23.4	23.5	23.6	23.8
Kazakhstan	22.6	22.4	22.4	22.4	22.3	22.1	22.2	22.3	22.5
Kyrgyzstan	22.3	22.2	22.2	22.9	21.9	21.9	21.9	21.9	22.0
Tajikistan	—	—	—	—	—	—	—	—	—
Turkmenistan	—	—	—	—	—	—	—	—	—
Uzbekistan	—	—	—	—	—	—	—	—	—

a. Median age.

2.8 Number of abortions (thousands)

	1989	1990	1991	1992	1993	1994	1995	1996	1997
Czech Republic	126.5	126.1	120.1	109.3	85.4	67.4	61.6	60.0	57.0
Slovakia	56.3	56.2	53.1	49.5	45.6	41.3	35.9	30.9	27.8
Poland	82.1	59.4	30.9	11.6	1.2	0.9	0.6	0.5	3.2
Hungary	108.2	108.0	107.0	103.1	91.1	90.0	92.2	91.4	89.8
Slovenia	15.9	14.7	14.0	13.3	12.2	11.3	10.8	10.2	9.7
Croatia	—	46.7	40.3	34.9	31.2	26.0	20.0	12.3	10.0
FYR Macedonia	30.4	21.9	23.2	19.9	18.5	16.5	15.8	14.2	12.1
Bosnia-Herzegovina	—	—	—	—	—	—	—	—	—
FR Yugoslavia	201.7	195.7	157.5	142.3	119.3	119.2	96.9	84.1	—
Albania	23.4	26.1	30.4	27.7	33.4	31.3	32.3	27.7	22.1
Bulgaria	132.0	144.6	138.4	132.9	107.4	97.6	97.1	98.6	86.9
Romania	192.5	992.3	866.9	691.9	585.8	530.2	502.8	456.2	347.1
Estonia	28.2	29.4	29.4	28.4	25.6	22.5	20.5	19.5	19.2
Latvia	—	—	38.8	34.3	31.3	26.8	25.9	24.2	21.8
Lithuania	—	—	40.8	41.0	35.2	30.4	31.3	27.8	22.7
Belarus	250.9	254.7	235.3	234.3	212.7	207.7	188.7	169.9	148.9
Moldova	80.0	68.6	58.8	61.8	55.2	50.4	49.5	46.0	37.1
Russia	4,427.7	4,103.4	3,608.4	3,436.7	3,244.0	3,060.2	2,766.4	2,652.0	2,498.1
Ukraine	1,058.4	1,019.0	957.0	932.3	861.0	798.5	740.2	687.0	596.7
Armenia	26.1	25.3	27.2	28.0	27.9	30.6	30.7	31.3	21.4
Azerbaijan	39.0	24.6	34.0	31.8	33.9	33.3	28.6	28.4	25.2
Georgia[a]	68.9	61.1	59.4	50.7	45.1	49.0	43.5	31.9	23.4
Kazakhstan	295.3	278.3	358.5	346.4	290.7	261.8	224.1	194.2	156.8
Kyrgyzstan	87.2	73.8	66.4	59.4	52.7	49.3	42.5	34.1	31.6
Tajikistan[b c]	54.5	52.7	51.7	47.0	39.9	35.7	—	28.3	—
Turkmenistan	39.1	35.7	35.5	37.0	32.9	33.5	33.8	31.9	33.8
Uzbekistan[b]	226.3	214.4	—	168.3	—	—	—	—	—

a. 1992-97: excludes Abkhazia and Tskhinvali.
b. 1989-90: CE (1993). 1992: CIS Stat (1995b).
c. 1991, 1993-94, 1996: UNDP (1997d).

2.9 Abortion rate (per hundred live births)

	1989	1990	1991	1992	1993	1994	1995	1996	1997
Czech Republic	98.6	96.5	92.8	89.8	70.6	63.3	64.1	66.3	62.8
Slovakia	70.3	70.2	67.6	66.4	62.2	62.2	58.4	51.4	47.0
Poland	14.6	10.8	5.6	2.3	0.3	0.2	0.1	0.1	0.8
Hungary	87.8	85.9	84.1	84.7	77.9	77.9	82.3	86.8	89.5
Slovenia	67.7	65.9	65.0	66.3	61.4	58.2	56.9	54.4	53.5
Croatia	—	84.2	77.8	74.3	64.4	53.5	39.8	22.9	18.1
FYR Macedonia	84.7	61.8	66.5	59.7	57.0	49.2	49.2	45.1	40.9
Bosnia-Herzegovina	—	—	—	—	—	—	—	—	—
FR Yugoslavia	130.5	126.2	103.5	101.1	84.6	86.6	68.9	61.1	—
Albania	29.6	31.8	39.3	36.8	49.4	43.4	44.8	40.6	—
Bulgaria	117.6	137.5	144.3	149.1	127.3	122.8	134.9	136.5	135.4
Romania	52.1	315.3	314.9	265.7	234.3	214.9	212.5	197.2	146.5
Estonia	116.2	131.8	152.2	157.7	168.7	158.3	151.3	146.4	151.7
Latvia[a]	125.8	—	112.1	108.7	117.1	110.5	120.1	122.5	115.6
Lithuania[a]	89.8	—	72.5	76.4	74.2	71.6	75.9	71.2	60.0
Belarus	163.5	179.2	178.2	183.1	181.2	187.8	186.5	177.4	166.2
Moldova	97.3	89.0	81.6	88.7	83.5	81.1	87.7	88.7	81.5
Russia	204.9	206.3	201.1	216.5	235.2	217.3	202.8	203.3	198.3
Ukraine	153.2	155.1	151.7	156.2	154.4	153.1	150.2	147.1	134.8
Armenia	34.7	31.6	34.9	39.6	47.3	59.8	62.8	65.1	48.8
Azerbaijan	21.5	13.4	17.9	17.5	19.4	20.8	20.0	21.9	19.1
Georgia[b]	75.6	65.9	66.7	69.9	73.3	85.4	77.2	59.5	45.0
Kazakhstan	77.5	76.9	101.5	102.6	92.1	85.7	81.2	76.7	67.5
Kyrgyzstan	66.3	57.3	51.3	46.3	45.1	44.8	36.2	31.6	31.0
Tajikistan[c d]	27.2	25.6	24.3	26.2	21.4	22.0	—	21.8	—
Turkmenistan	31.3	28.5	28.1	28.2	25.1	25.8	26.6	—	—
Uzbekistan[c]	33.8	31.0	—	23.7	—	—	—	—	—

a. 1989: Goskomstat (1990).
b. 1992-97: excludes Abkhazia and Tskhinvali.
c. 1989-90: CE (1993). 1992: CIS Stat (1995b).
d. 1991, 1993-94, 1996: UNDP (1997d).

3.1 Infant mortality rate (per thousand live births)

	1980	1985	1989	1990	1991	1992	1993	1994	1995	1996	1997
Czech Republic[a b 1]	18.4	14.0	10.0	10.8	10.4	9.9	8.5	7.9	7.7	6.0	5.9
Slovakia[a b 1]	18.4	14.0	13.5	12.0	13.2	12.6	10.6	11.2	11.0	10.2	8.7
Poland[i]	25.5	22.0	19.1	19.3	18.2	17.3	16.1	15.1	13.6	12.2	10.2
Hungary[b 1]	23.2	20.4	15.7	14.8	15.6	14.1	12.5	11.5	10.7	10.9	9.9
Slovenia[b 1]	15.3	13.0	8.2	8.4	8.2	8.9	6.8	6.5	5.5	4.7	5.2
Croatia[b 1]	20.6	16.6	11.7	10.7	11.1	11.6	9.9	10.2	9.0	8.0	8.2
FYR Macedonia[b 1]	54.2	43.4	36.7	31.6	28.2	30.6	24.1	22.5	22.7	16.4	15.7
Bosnia-Herzegovina[b c 1]	31.5	25.1	18.4	15.3	14.6	20.6	22.7	13.8	13.2	12.5	12.7
FR Yugoslavia[b d 1]	33.9	33.7	29.3	22.8	20.9	21.7	21.9	18.4	16.8	15.0	14.3
Albania[b]	50.3	30.1	30.8	28.3	32.9	30.9	33.2	35.7	34.0	25.8	—
Bulgaria[b 2]	20.2	15.4	14.4	14.8	16.9	15.9	15.5	16.3	14.8	15.6	17.5
Romania[b 1]	29.3	25.6	26.9	26.9	22.7	23.3	23.3	23.9	21.2	22.3	22.0
Estonia[b 3]	17.1	14.1	14.8	12.4	13.4	15.8	15.8	14.5	14.8	10.4	10.1
Latvia[b 4]	15.3	13.0	11.1	13.7	15.6	17.4	15.9	15.5	18.5	15.8	15.3
Lithuania[b 4]	14.5	14.2	10.7	10.3	14.3	16.5	15.6	13.9	12.4	10.1	10.3
Belarus[b 5]	16.2	14.6	11.8	11.9	12.1	12.3	12.5	13.2	13.3	12.5	12.4
Moldova[b 6]	35.0	30.8	20.4	19.0	19.8	18.4	21.5	22.6	21.2	20.2	20.0
Russia[b 7]	22.0	20.8	17.8	17.4	17.8	18.0	19.9	18.6	17.6	17.4	17.2
Ukraine[b 6]	16.6	15.9	13.0	12.8	13.9	14.0	14.9	14.5	14.4	14.3	14.0
Armenia[b 8]	26.2	24.7	20.4	18.3	18.0	18.9	17.8	14.7	14.2	15.5	15.4
Azerbaijan[b 6]	30.3	29.2	26.2	23.0	25.3	25.5	28.2	25.2	23.3	19.9	19.6
Georgia[b e 5]	25.4	23.9	19.6	15.8	13.8	12.4	18.3	16.7	13.1	17.4	17.3
Kazakhstan[b 6]	32.7	30.1	25.6	26.3	27.3	25.9	28.1	27.1	27.0	25.4	24.9
Kyrgyzstan[b 6]	43.3	41.6	32.2	30.0	29.7	31.5	31.9	29.1	28.1	25.9	28.2
Tajikistan[f g 6]	58.1	46.8	43.2	40.7	40.6	45.9	47.0	40.6	30.9	31.8	27.9
Turkmenistan[f g 6]	53.6	52.4	54.7	45.2	47.0	43.6	45.9	46.4	42.2	39.6	37.5
Uzbekistan[f g 6]	47.0	45.3	37.7	34.6	35.5	37.4	32.0	28.2	26.0	24.2	22.8

a. 1980, 1985: Czechoslovakia.
b. 1980, 1985: CE (1993).
c. 1992-97: deaths in Federation of B-H only.
d. 1980, 1985: Serbia.
e. 1992-97: excludes Abkhazia and Tskhinvali.
f. 1980-96: CIS Stat (1997).
g. 1997: CIS Stat (1998b).

Birth concepts:
1 WHO.
2 National concept.
3 1980-91: Soviet. 1992-97: WHO.
4 1980-90: Soviet. 1991-97: WHO.
5 1980-93: Soviet. 1994-97: WHO.
6 Soviet concept.
7 1980-92: Soviet. 1993-97: WHO.
8 1980-94: Soviet. 1995-97: WHO.

3.2 Maternal mortality rate (per hundred thousand live births)

	1980	1985	1989	1990	1991	1992	1993	1994	1995	1996	1997
Czech Republic[a b]	9.2	8.0	9.3	8.4	13.1	9.9	11.6	6.6	2.1	5.5	2.2
Slovakia[a b]	9.2	8.0	10.0	6.3	14.0	1.3	12.3	6.0	8.1	5.0	5.1
Poland[a]	11.7	11.1	10.6	12.8	12.8	9.9	11.7	11.0	9.9	4.9	—
Hungary[a]	20.9	26.1	15.4	20.7	12.6	9.9	18.8	10.4	15.2	11.4	20.9
Slovenia[a]	13.4	15.5	4.3	0.0	4.6	5.0	10.1	10.3	5.3	26.6	—
Croatia	—	—	3.6	1.8	7.7	4.3	10.3	10.3	12.0	1.9	10.8
FYR Macedonia	—	—	16.7	11.3	11.5	9.0	6.2	11.9	21.8	0.0	3.4
Bosnia-Herzegovina	—	—	—	—	—	—	—	—	—	—	—
FR Yugoslavia[a c]	17.8	16.4	16.8	11.0	13.1	8.5	17.7	13.1	12.1	7.3	13.7
Albania	45.2	57.6	49.5	37.7	29.7	25.2	16.2	40.2	33.3	27.8	—
Bulgaria[a]	21.1	12.6	18.7	20.9	10.4	21.3	14.2	12.6	19.5	19.4	18.7
Romania[a]	132.1	137.4	169.4	83.6	66.5	60.3	53.2	60.4	47.8	41.1	41.4
Estonia[d]	27.0	46.6	41.2	31.4	31.1	22.2	33.0	56.4	51.6	0.0	15.8
Latvia[a]	25.3	30.2	46.2	23.7	31.8	41.2	29.9	57.7	37.0	40.4	42.5
Lithuania	27.0	22.2	28.7	22.9	19.6	20.5	12.6	16.5	17.0	12.8	15.9
Belarus[d]	29.1	17.0	24.8	21.8	31.1	21.1	20.4	19.0	13.8	21.9	25.7
Moldova[d]	64.1	49.8	34.1	44.1	26.4	37.3	33.2	17.7	12.4	40.5	48.3
Russia[a]	68.0	54.0	49.0	47.4	52.4	50.8	51.6	52.3	53.3	48.9	50.2
Ukraine[d]	44.8	40.4	32.7	32.4	29.8	31.3	32.8	31.3	32.3	30.4	25.1
Armenia[d]	27.0	22.4	34.6	40.1	23.1	14.2	27.1	29.3	34.7	20.8	38.7
Azerbaijan[a]	38.7	41.1	28.6	9.3	10.5	17.6	34.4	43.8	37.0	44.1	31.0
Georgia[d]	25.7	22.5	54.9	20.5	10.1	5.5	—	—	33.7	18.4	19.2
Kazakhstan[d]	55.6	47.9	53.3	55.0	48.1	57.2	49.4	48.4	57.6	52.9	59.0
Kyrgyzstan[d]	49.4	42.8	42.6	62.9	55.6	49.9	44.5	42.7	44.3	31.5	62.7
Tajikistan[d e f]	94.2	59.1	38.9	—	—	69.6	74.0	—	58.0	—	—
Turkmenistan[d]	40.8	56.8	55.2	42.3	45.9	58.8	44.2	46.3	49.6	—	—
Uzbekistan[d e g]	46.3	48.6	42.8	—	—	30.1	24.1	17.3	18.9	12.0	—

a. 1980, 1985: UN (1986), (1992).
b. 1980, 1985: Czechoslovakia.
c. 1980, 1985: former Yugoslavia.
d. 1980, 1985: Goskomstat (1991a).
e. 1989: Goskomstat (1990). 1992: CIS Stat (1995b). 1993: CIS Stat (1995a).
f. 1995: CIS Stat (1998c).
g. 1994-96: UNDP (1997e).

3.3 Under-5 mortality rate (per thousand live births)

	1989	1990	1991	1992	1993	1994	1995	1996	1997
Czech Republic	11.8	12.4	12.1	11.6	10.1	10.2	9.5	7.8	7.6
Slovakia	15.8	14.1	15.4	14.7	12.7	13.2	13.1	12.2	10.7
Poland	22.0	22.0	20.4	19.8	18.2	17.3	15.6	14.1	11.9
Hungary	18.0	16.8	17.6	15.9	14.6	13.5	12.5	12.7	11.8
Slovenia	10.3	10.2	10.0	10.6	8.4	8.2	6.7	6.1	6.3
Croatia	13.7	12.5	12.6	14.0	12.0	11.8	10.4	9.3	9.5
FYR Macedonia	40.3	34.9	31.6	34.4	26.9	25.8	25.3	19.0	18.5
Bosnia-Herzegovina	21.1	17.2	18.5	—	—	—	—	—	—
FR Yugoslavia	33.8	26.2	24.1	24.6	24.9	21.5	19.4	17.6	16.5
Albania	45.5	41.5	44.5	46.9	49.7	44.7	37.0	30.6	—
Bulgaria	18.3	18.7	21.4	20.6	19.6	20.9	19.0	19.8	23.5
Romania	34.9	35.7	30.8	30.5	30.3	29.7	26.2	27.5	26.4
Estonia	18.9	17.2	17.6	21.0	20.1	17.4	20.0	12.3	13.0
Latvia	15.2	18.1	20.5	22.2	22.2	20.1	23.3	20.7	18.5
Lithuania	14.3	13.5	17.4	20.0	19.0	18.4	16.2	13.2	13.2
Belarus	15.4	15.8	16.2	16.0	16.2	16.8	17.4	16.5	16.0
Moldova	27.1	25.2	25.0	24.5	27.6	28.8	27.4	26.5	25.6
Russia	22.8	22.3	23.2	23.7	26.4	23.9	23.4	22.0	21.7
Ukraine	17.6	17.3	18.5	18.7	19.9	19.6	19.9	19.4	18.9
Armenia	27.1	23.8	22.6	24.2	24.2	21.4	19.9	19.5	19.5
Azerbaijan	45.6	40.5	40.1	41.7	44.4	45.2	43.2	39.3	37.5
Georgia[a]	24.9	19.9	17.9	17.0	—	21.8	17.0	20.4	19.0
Kazakhstan	34.8	35.0	35.6	34.2	38.1	36.2	38.5	35.2	34.6
Kyrgyzstan	47.3	41.8	38.7	42.4	46.8	43.9	40.8	37.8	44.0
Tajikistan[b]	—	—	—	—	81.7	—	—	—	—
Turkmenistan	77.8	64.1	64.2	60.3	67.6	70.3	67.9	—	—
Uzbekistan[b]	—	—	—	—	48.1	—	—	—	—

a. 1992-97: excludes Abkhazia and Tskhinvali.
b. 1993: CIS Stat (1995a).

3.4 Age 5-19 mortality rate (per thousand relevant population)

	1989	1990	1991	1992	1993	1994	1995	1996	1997
Czech Republic	0.33	0.35	0.38	0.37	0.37	0.37	0.39	0.33	0.32
Slovakia	0.36	0.37	0.38	0.34	0.33	0.35	0.34	0.32	0.35
Poland	0.41	0.40	0.41	0.39	0.36	0.37	0.36	0.35	0.36
Hungary	0.41	0.44	0.39	0.40	0.35	0.35	0.36	0.32	0.29
Slovenia	0.39	0.35	0.36	0.36	0.33	0.44	0.38	0.35	0.34
Croatia[a]	—	—	0.57	0.61	0.47	0.36	0.42	0.37	0.34
FYR Macedonia[a]	—	—	0.36	0.38	0.38	0.38	0.29	0.32	0.34
Bosnia-Herzegovina[a]	0.31	0.27	—	—	—	—	—	—	—
FR Yugoslavia	0.38	0.40	0.40	0.44	0.39	0.33	0.32	0.33	0.33
Albania[a]	0.64	0.64	0.68	0.64	0.62	0.61	0.56	0.53	—
Bulgaria	0.50	0.53	0.51	0.52	0.50	0.51	0.48	0.49	0.53
Romania	0.64	0.60	0.57	0.53	0.55	0.61	0.63	0.65	0.65
Estonia	0.74	0.73	0.65	0.68	0.67	0.67	0.66	0.52	0.57
Latvia	0.79	0.85	0.79	0.75	0.77	0.67	0.70	0.51	0.61
Lithuania	0.66	0.58	0.68	0.60	0.62	0.62	0.54	0.51	0.44
Belarus	0.54	0.52	0.58	0.57	0.51	0.56	0.54	0.48	0.50
Moldova[b]	0.68	0.60	0.66	0.72	0.65	0.70	0.63	0.57	0.53
Russia	0.69	0.69	0.74	0.76	0.83	0.81	0.88	0.80	0.73
Ukraine	0.59	0.57	0.62	0.61	0.62	0.65	0.65	0.61	0.57
Armenia	0.45	0.38	0.29	0.36	0.41	0.55	0.38	0.36	0.33
Azerbaijan	0.52	0.48	0.56	0.94	0.94	1.12	0.72	0.59	0.58
Georgia[c]	0.44	0.42	0.42	0.44	—	0.34	0.28	0.21	0.24
Kazakhstan	0.71	0.73	0.79	0.78	0.84	0.79	0.79	0.75	0.75
Kyrgyzstan	0.65	0.67	0.59	0.64	0.63	0.62	0.64	0.61	0.61
Tajikistan[d]	0.65	—	—	—	—	—	—	—	—
Turkmenistan	0.74	0.75	0.71	0.69	0.82	0.78	0.72	—	—
Uzbekistan[d]	0.65	—	—	—	—	—	—	—	—

a. Population data, 1989-92: US Census Bureau (1997), 1993-97: US Census Bureau (1998).
b. 1997: population data exclude Transdniestr.
c. 1992-97: deaths exclude Abkhazia and Tskhinvali.
d. 1989: Goskomstat (1990).

3.5 Age 5-19 female mortality rate due to accidents, poisoning or violence excluding suicide
(per hundred thousand relevant population)

	1989	1990	1991	1992	1993	1994	1995	1996	1997
Czech Republic	6.1	10.1	10.1	10.9	10.0	12.3	12.0	8.2	8.7
Slovakia	8.9	10.8	8.9	9.3	8.7	7.0	9.4	—	—
Poland	9.8	10.2	11.8	10.0	9.2	10.8	9.6	9.7	—
Hungary	9.9	11.7	10.5	10.5	8.1	8.4	8.2	9.1	7.7
Slovenia	11.7	13.2	9.0	11.5	6.3	14.7	12.9	6.6	7.3
Croatia[a]	—	—	15.8	20.4	14.5	11.7	16.7	14.2	7.6
FYR Macedonia[a]	—	—	6.6	3.7	6.2	8.8	—	9.7	4.2
Bosnia-Herzegovina[a]	5.2	4.5	—	—	—	—	—	—	—
FR Yugoslavia	8.5	7.9	7.5	8.1	4.6	6.3	5.7	6.3	7.1
Albania[a]	7.7	3.1	—	9.4	9.5	—	—	—	—
Bulgaria	10.8	12.9	10.7	13.5	11.3	10.3	10.3	11.1	9.3
Romania	14.5	16.8	16.5	14.4	14.6	15.8	14.3	15.7	14.9
Estonia	24.8	18.7	18.6	21.3	17.9	20.4	15.5	16.3	14.7
Latvia	24.1	19.2	23.2	25.2	22.8	20.2	27.1	16.3	20.2
Lithuania	23.4	20.6	23.4	21.4	22.0	21.7	19.0	17.5	12.5
Belarus	14.6	13.3	18.7	17.1	14.8	13.9	15.4	15.7	16.6
Moldova[b]	—	16.1	21.4	19.0	12.7	12.1	9.2	15.7	14.1
Russia	21.0	19.7	22.2	23.0	26.1	26.2	27.9	25.7	23.3
Ukraine	—	17.3	18.6	—	16.6	18.3	17.2	17.5	16.5
Armenia	23.5	10.6	11.1	8.1	4.8	4.0	6.2	3.4	4.6
Azerbaijan	9.2	9.2	10.5	13.5	13.1	10.9	6.6	7.3	8.7
Georgia[c]	8.1	8.4	7.2	8.1	—	4.9	5.0	3.5	2.8
Kazakhstan	15.7	21.0	23.2	20.8	24.2	18.5	19.5	19.1	24.0
Kyrgyzstan	12.1	18.6	18.1	16.6	11.1	14.1	12.1	11.6	12.5
Tajikistan	—	—	—	—	—	—	—	—	—
Turkmenistan	15.5	19.6	19.8	15.7	20.4	19.1	13.4	—	—
Uzbekistan	—	—	—	—	—	—	—	—	—

a. Population data, 1989-92:
US Census Bureau (1997), 1993-97:
US Census Bureau (1998).
b. 1997: population data exclude
Transdniestr.
c. 1992-97: deaths exclude Abkhazia
and Tskhinvali.

3.6 Age 5-19 male mortality rate due to accidents, poisoning or violence excluding suicide
(per hundred thousand relevant population)

	1989	1990	1991	1992	1993	1994	1995	1996	1997
Czech Republic	21.6	23.7	26.2	28.8	28.4	26.7	26.4	25.2	23.8
Slovakia	21.5	22.3	24.8	24.4	21.3	23.8	23.0	—	—
Poland	29.6	30.6	29.7	29.1	25.4	26.9	25.8	22.6	—
Hungary	27.9	30.7	26.7	28.4	20.8	22.6	21.2	18.2	15.5
Slovenia	30.3	25.9	32.8	24.1	23.9	37.2	23.5	28.3	24.6
Croatia[a]	—	—	62.8	68.3	47.3	33.0	35.4	30.3	21.2
FYR Macedonia[a]	—	—	15.7	15.7	15.5	16.1	13.0	11.9	13.6
Bosnia-Herzegovina[a]	19.0	15.9	—	—	—	—	—	—	—
FR Yugoslavia	17.9	19.5	24.2	28.1	17.1	17.2	14.1	15.4	17.3
Albania[a]	22.1	7.7	—	31.5	24.7	—	—	—	—
Bulgaria	29.1	32.6	28.5	31.2	30.0	33.7	27.5	18.2	23.3
Romania	40.1	40.8	41.4	35.9	37.8	38.3	37.1	36.1	33.7
Estonia	70.8	74.6	63.8	58.7	54.2	65.1	65.3	37.0	55.4
Latvia	68.0	74.9	77.1	73.3	72.5	57.9	63.5	55.0	53.1
Lithuania	55.5	51.0	62.9	57.4	50.7	51.9	41.5	43.2	33.4
Belarus	44.9	42.5	49.9	44.3	38.2	47.2	41.4	38.7	41.1
Moldova[b]	—	32.2	40.1	52.9	35.9	39.9	35.4	41.3	35.1
Russia	59.4	59.5	65.2	65.4	72.3	68.5	78.4	67.2	58.6
Ukraine	—	46.0	48.4	—	46.3	49.6	47.9	43.9	39.3
Armenia	27.2	31.3	20.8	32.6	39.2	70.5	31.9	36.2	28.7
Azerbaijan	25.8	26.6	27.8	93.3	87.4	114.3	25.0	26.7	22.6
Georgia[c]	33.1	29.1	26.4	36.2	—	22.7	17.8	13.4	9.7
Kazakhstan	43.0	55.2	58.3	55.8	56.1	53.4	49.5	48.4	43.6
Kyrgyzstan	32.9	41.1	38.2	38.8	38.0	33.0	31.1	31.1	29.0
Tajikistan	—	—	—	—	—	—	—	—	—
Turkmenistan	35.9	40.6	38.2	36.2	39.3	33.2	32.2	—	—
Uzbekistan	—	—	—	—	—	—	—	—	—

a. Population data, 1989-92:
US Census Bureau (1997), 1993-97:
US Census Bureau (1998).
b. 1997: population data exclude
Transdniestr.
c. 1992-97: deaths exclude Abkhazia
and Tskhinvali.

3.7 Age 5-19 female suicide rate (per hundred thousand relevant population)

	1989	1990	1991	1992	1993	1994	1995	1996	1997
Czech Republic	0.8	1.2	1.1	0.6	1.3	1.2	2.1	1.3	1.0
Slovakia	1.4	1.2	0.9	0.8	1.4	0.8	1.5	—	—
Poland	0.7	1.0	0.9	1.0	0.9	1.1	1.1	1.2	—
Hungary	2.2	2.9	1.3	2.0	2.5	1.5	0.9	1.3	1.9
Slovenia	2.3	1.9	2.4	2.4	1.9	2.0	2.5	3.5	2.1
Croatiaᵃ	—	—	1.0	1.7	0.7	0.9	0.7	0.5	0.2
FYR Macedoniaᵃ	—	—	1.2	1.2	1.7	2.1	3.4	1.3	2.5
Bosnia-Herzegovinaᵃ	2.0	1.5	—	—	—	—	—	—	—
FR Yugoslavia	1.2	2.0	1.2	0.9	1.4	1.5	1.6	1.3	1.9
Albaniaᵃ	0.4	0.8	—	1.2	0.6	—	—	—	—
Bulgaria	2.5	2.0	2.1	2.0	1.9	2.4	2.5	2.1	2.6
Romania	1.8	1.3	1.1	1.0	1.0	1.0	1.1	0.8	1.0
Estonia	2.4	1.2	1.8	4.3	3.1	5.6	1.9	3.1	2.6
Latvia	4.1	3.3	1.1	1.5	1.9	1.9	2.3	1.9	3.0
Lithuania	2.2	1.7	1.2	2.7	1.7	4.0	2.5	2.2	2.5
Belarus	1.4	1.2	1.4	1.7	1.6	1.6	1.6	1.8	2.1
Moldovaᵇ	—	1.8	2.1	2.4	2.9	2.0	1.2	2.4	0.9
Russia	2.3	2.3	2.4	2.6	3.0	3.3	3.5	3.0	3.3
Ukraine	1.9	1.6	1.8	2.1	1.7	1.9	2.0	1.6	1.8
Armenia	0.0	0.2	0.0	0.0	0.2	0.4	0.6	0.2	—
Azerbaijan	0.3	0.2	0.3	0.3	0.4	0.2	0.0	0.1	0.3
Georgiaᶜ	0.2	0.2	0.6	0.5	—	0.2	0.5	0.0	0.3
Kazakhstan	3.8	3.8	3.7	4.0	5.2	4.0	3.5	3.6	4.8
Kyrgyzstan	3.0	2.7	3.3	2.7	1.7	1.3	3.8	1.1	1.6
Tajikistan	—	—	—	—	—	—	—	—	—
Turkmenistan	1.9	2.4	2.6	2.1	1.9	1.9	0.8	—	—
Uzbekistan	—	—	—	—	—	—	—	—	—

a. Population data, 1989-92: US Census Bureau (1997), 1993-97: US Census Bureau (1998).
b. 1997: population data exclude Transdniestr.
c. 1992-97: deaths exclude Abkhazia and Tskhinvali.

3.8 Age 5-19 male suicide rate (per hundred thousand relevant population)

	1989	1990	1991	1992	1993	1994	1995	1996	1997
Czech Republic	3.6	3.4	5.9	5.1	5.1	6.1	7.0	6.0	5.8
Slovakia	3.3	3.2	5.2	2.4	3.5	4.8	4.7	—	—
Poland	3.7	3.8	4.4	4.4	5.2	5.3	6.0	6.1	—
Hungary	6.4	6.0	5.6	7.9	5.9	7.1	6.8	5.3	4.5
Slovenia	4.5	3.6	4.9	5.9	11.5	9.3	8.5	7.7	7.9
Croatiaᵃ	—	—	1.0	1.6	1.8	2.0	1.2	0.4	1.3
FYR Macedoniaᵃ	—	—	2.4	5.5	7.0	4.3	1.6	3.6	4.4
Bosnia-Herzegovinaᵃ	4.7	7.8	—	—	—	—	—	—	—
FR Yugoslavia	2.4	2.7	2.0	3.4	3.3	2.7	3.5	3.9	3.2
Albaniaᵃ	0.6	—	—	2.0	2.4	—	—	—	—
Bulgaria	5.4	5.4	5.0	5.6	6.9	5.5	5.7	5.4	6.0
Romania	2.6	3.1	2.5	3.1	3.2	3.0	3.3	3.5	3.3
Estonia	13.2	8.7	8.7	9.4	13.1	9.6	10.2	8.5	9.8
Latvia	6.8	8.2	9.2	11.8	11.5	10.9	8.7	8.7	7.0
Lithuania	7.7	5.5	8.6	7.9	9.3	10.3	11.0	10.4	12.1
Belarus	4.4	4.3	5.5	8.6	6.0	7.3	8.4	7.2	7.1
Moldovaᵇ	—	3.3	4.5	5.1	6.0	5.5	3.8	4.3	4.7
Russia	7.4	8.9	9.3	9.7	11.8	13.0	13.4	13.0	13.4
Ukraine	5.0	5.1	5.2	5.3	6.5	6.8	7.1	6.8	6.5
Armenia	1.4	1.2	0.8	0.6	0.7	0.7	0.5	0.5	0.5
Azerbaijan	0.6	0.9	0.8	1.1	1.0	0.2	0.2	0.3	0.3
Georgiaᶜ	1.1	2.1	0.9	1.5	—	0.6	0.9	0.8	1.2
Kazakhstan	9.0	8.7	10.3	11.6	13.5	10.6	11.7	12.2	12.7
Kyrgyzstan	6.1	5.4	5.1	5.7	5.8	5.2	5.2	3.7	4.9
Tajikistan	—	—	—	—	—	—	—	—	—
Turkmenistan	2.7	4.8	4.5	6.5	5.2	3.7	4.3	—	—
Uzbekistan	—	—	—	—	—	—	—	—	—

a. Population data, 1989-92: US Census Bureau (1997), 1993-97: US Census Bureau (1998).
b. 1997: population data exclude Transdniestr.
c. 1992-97: deaths exclude Abkhazia and Tskhinvali.

4.1 Crude death rate (per thousand population)

	1980	1985	1989	1990	1991	1992	1993	1994	1995	1996	1997
Czech Republic[a b]	12.2	11.9	12.3	12.5	12.1	11.7	11.4	11.4	11.4	10.9	10.9
Slovakia[a b]	12.2	11.9	10.2	10.3	10.3	10.1	9.9	9.6	9.8	9.5	9.7
Poland	9.9	10.3	10.1	10.2	10.6	10.3	10.2	10.0	10.0	10.0	9.8
Hungary[b]	13.6	14.0	13.8	14.1	14.0	14.4	14.6	14.3	14.2	14.0	13.7
Slovenia	9.9	10.0	9.4	9.3	9.7	9.7	10.0	9.7	9.5	9.4	9.5
Croatia[b c d e]	10.9	11.1	11.0	10.9	11.5	10.8	10.8	10.5	10.8	10.9	11.1
FYR Macedonia[b d e f]	7.1	7.1	6.9	6.9	7.3	7.8	7.5	8.1	8.3	8.1	8.3
Bosnia-Herzegovina[b e g]	6.4	6.7	6.8	6.5	—	—	—	—	—	5.4	5.0
FR Yugoslavia[b h]	9.2	9.8	9.5	9.3	9.7	10.1	10.2	10.0	10.2	10.6	10.5
Albania[b d e]	6.4	5.8	5.6	5.6	5.4	5.6	5.7	5.8	5.6	5.4	—
Bulgaria[b]	11.1	12.0	12.0	12.5	12.8	12.6	12.9	13.2	13.6	14.0	14.7
Romania[b]	10.4	10.9	10.7	10.6	10.9	11.6	11.6	11.7	12.0	12.7	12.4
Estonia	12.3	12.7	11.8	12.4	12.6	13.0	14.0	14.8	14.1	12.9	12.7
Latvia	12.8	13.2	12.2	13.0	13.1	13.5	15.2	16.4	15.5	13.8	13.6
Lithuania	10.5	11.1	10.3	10.7	11.0	11.1	12.4	12.5	12.2	11.6	11.1
Belarus[i]	9.9	10.6	10.2	10.7	11.2	11.4	12.5	12.6	13.0	13.0	13.4
Moldova[i]	10.1	10.9	9.2	9.7	10.5	10.2	10.7	11.8	12.2	11.6	10.6
Russia[i]	11.0	11.3	10.7	11.2	11.4	12.2	14.4	15.6	14.9	14.1	13.7
Ukraine[i]	11.3	12.1	11.7	12.2	12.9	13.4	14.3	14.8	15.5	15.3	15.0
Armenia[i]	5.6	6.1	6.0	6.2	6.5	7.0	7.4	6.6	6.6	6.6	6.3
Azerbaijan[i]	7.0	6.8	6.2	6.0	6.2	7.1	7.2	7.4	6.8	6.4	6.2
Georgia[i j]	8.5	8.7	8.7	8.5	8.6	8.6	—	7.7	7.0	6.4	7.0
Kazakhstan[k]	8.0	8.0	7.8	7.9	8.2	8.3	9.5	9.8	10.5	10.4	10.2
Kyrgyzstan[i]	8.4	8.1	7.3	7.0	7.0	7.2	7.8	8.4	8.2	7.6	7.5
Tajikistan[d e i l]	8.1	7.0	6.5	6.2	6.1	6.6	8.7	7.0	5.9	5.1	5.8
Turkmenistan[m]	8.3	8.1	7.7	7.0	7.3	7.2	7.9	7.6	7.0	7.0	6.5
Uzbekistan[d e i l]	7.5	7.2	6.3	6.1	6.2	6.5	6.6	6.6	6.4	6.2	5.8

a. 1980, 1985: Czechoslovakia.
b. 1980, 1985: CE (1993).
c. 1989, 1990: CBSC (1996).
d. Population data, 1991-92: US Census Bureau (1997).
e. Population data, 1993-96: US Census Bureau (1998).
f. 1989, 1990: CE (1993).
g. 1996-97: deaths in Federation of B-H only.
h. 1980, 1985: Serbia.
i. 1980, 1985: Goskomstat (1990).
j. 1992-97: deaths exclude Abkhazia and Tskhinvali.
k. 1980, 1985, 1989: Goskomstat (1990).
L. 1997: CIS Stat (1998b).
m. 1996-97: CIS Stat (1998b).

4.2 Female life expectancy at birth (years)

	1980	1985	1989	1990	1991	1992	1993	1994	1995	1996	1997
Czech Republic[a b]	74.0	74.7	75.4	76.0	75.7	76.1	76.4	76.6	76.9	77.3	77.5
Slovakia[a b]	74.0	74.7	75.2	75.4	75.2	76.2	76.7	76.5	76.3	76.7	76.7
Poland[b]	75.4	75.3	75.5	75.5	75.3	75.7	76.0	76.1	76.4	76.6	77.0
Hungary[b]	72.7	73.1	73.8	73.7	73.8	73.7	73.8	74.2	74.5	74.7	75.1
Slovenia	75.4	75.3	76.7	77.3	77.4	77.3	77.3	77.4	76.8	78.3	78.6
Croatia[c d]	74.2	—	—	—	76.0	—	—	—	75.7	—	—
FYR Macedonia[c]	71.9	—	—	—	74.4	—	—	74.0	—	—	—
Bosnia-Herzegovina[c d]	72.9	—	—	—	—	—	—	—	75.1	—	—
FR Yugoslavia[e]	72.8	—	73.8	74.3	74.6	74.4	74.5	74.5	74.7	74.6	—
Albania[b]	72.2	73.9	75.5	75.4	75.4	74.3	74.3	75.6	74.3	—	—
Bulgaria[b]	73.6	—	75.1	74.8	74.7	74.5	74.6	74.9	74.9	74.6	74.4
Romania[b]	71.8	72.8	72.4	72.7	73.1	73.2	73.2	73.3	73.4	73.1	73.0
Estonia[f g]	74.0	75.0	74.7	74.6	74.8	74.7	73.8	73.1	74.3	75.5	76.0
Latvia[f g]	73.9	74.5	75.2	74.6	74.8	74.8	73.8	72.9	73.1	75.7	74.9
Lithuania[f g]	75.0	75.0	76.3	76.2	76.1	76.0	75.0	74.9	75.2	76.1	76.8
Belarus[h]	75.6	77.2	76.4	75.6	75.5	75.4	74.4	74.3	74.3	74.4	74.3
Moldova[h]	68.8	68.6	72.3	71.8	71.0	71.9	71.1	69.8	69.7	70.4	70.3
Russia[h]	73.0	73.3	74.5	74.3	74.3	73.8	71.9	71.2	71.7	72.5	72.8
Ukraine[h]	74.0	74.0	75.0	75.0	75.0	74.0	73.0	73.2	72.7	73.0	73.0
Armenia[h]	75.7	75.7	74.7	75.2	75.6	75.5	74.4	74.9	75.9	76.2	77.3
Azerbaijan[f g]	71.8	73.1	74.2	74.8	74.5	73.9	73.9	73.9	72.9	73.8	74.6
Georgia[f g]	74.8	75.1	75.7	76.1	—	—	—	—	—	—	—
Kazakhstan[h]	71.9	72.5	73.1	72.7	72.4	72.3	70.8	70.4	69.5	70.0	70.2
Kyrgyzstan[h]	70.1	70.2	72.4	72.6	72.7	72.2	71.7	70.7	70.4	71.0	71.4
Tajikistan[h i]	68.6	70.8	71.7	71.9	73.2	—	—	—	71.2	—	—
Turkmenistan[h]	67.8	68.1	68.4	69.7	69.3	—	—	—	67.5	67.7	67.5
Uzbekistan[h i]	70.7	70.8	72.1	72.4	—	—	—	—	—	—	—

a. 1980, 1985: Czechoslovakia.
b. 1980, 1985: UN (1986), (1992).
c. 1980 (which refers to 1980-81): CE (1993). 1989: refers to 1989-90.
d. 1980 (which refers to 1990-95): UN (1997a).
e. 1980 (which refers to Serbia in 1980-81): CE (1993).
f. 1980 (which refers to 1979-80): Goskomstat (1991a).
g. 1985 (which refers to 1985-86): Goskomstat (1991b).
h. 1980, 1985: CIS Stat (1997).
i. 1989-91: CIS Stat (1997).
j. 1995: CIS Stat (1998c).

4.3 Male life expectancy at birth (years)

	1980	1985	1989	1990	1991	1992	1993	1994	1995	1996	1997
Czech Republic[a b]	66.8	67.3	68.1	67.5	68.2	68.5	69.3	69.5	70.0	70.4	70.5
Slovakia[a b]	66.8	67.3	66.8	66.6	66.8	67.6	68.4	68.3	68.4	68.8	68.9
Poland[b]	66.9	66.9	66.7	66.5	66.1	66.7	67.4	67.5	67.6	68.1	68.5
Hungary[b]	65.5	65.1	65.4	65.1	65.0	64.6	64.5	64.8	65.3	66.1	66.4
Slovenia	67.4	67.9	68.8	69.4	69.5	69.5	69.4	69.6	70.3	70.3	71.0
Croatia[c d]	66.6	—	66.8	—	68.6	—	—	—	67.1	—	—
FYR Macedonia[c]	68.3	—	70.1	—	70.1	—	—	69.6	—	—	—
Bosnia-Herzegovina[c d]	67.9	—	69.7	—	—	—	—	—	69.5	—	—
FR Yugoslavia[e]	68.1	—	68.7	69.1	69.0	68.6	69.1	69.1	69.9	69.9	—
Albania[b]	67.7	68.5	69.6	69.3	69.3	68.5	68.5	69.5	68.5	—	—
Bulgaria[b]	68.4	—	68.6	68.1	68.0	68.0	67.7	67.3	67.1	67.1	67.2
Romania[b]	66.5	66.8	66.5	66.6	66.6	66.6	66.1	65.9	65.7	65.3	65.2
Estonia[f g]	64.0	65.0	65.7	64.6	64.4	63.5	62.5	61.1	61.7	64.5	64.5
Latvia	63.6	65.5	65.3	64.2	63.9	63.3	61.6	60.7	60.8	63.3	64.1
Lithuania[f g]	65.0	66.0	66.9	66.6	65.3	64.9	63.3	62.8	63.6	65.0	65.9
Belarus[h]	65.9	67.4	66.8	66.3	65.5	64.9	63.8	63.5	62.9	63.1	62.9
Moldova[h]	62.4	62.0	65.5	65.0	64.3	63.9	64.3	62.3	61.8	62.9	62.9
Russia[h]	61.5	62.3	64.2	63.8	63.5	62.0	58.9	57.6	58.3	59.8	60.9
Ukraine[h]	64.6	64.8	66.0	66.0	66.0	64.0	64.0	62.8	61.8	61.0	62.0
Armenia[h]	69.5	69.8	69.0	68.4	68.9	68.7	67.9	68.1	68.9	69.3	70.3
Azerbaijan[f g]	64.2	65.3	66.6	67.0	66.3	65.4	65.2	65.2	65.2	66.3	67.4
Georgia[f g]	67.1	67.4	68.1	68.7	—	—	—	—	—	—	—
Kazakhstan[h]	61.6	62.6	63.9	63.3	62.7	62.5	60.3	60.0	58.4	58.5	59.0
Kyrgyzstan[h]	61.1	64.1	64.3	64.2	64.6	64.2	62.9	61.6	61.4	62.3	62.6
Tajikistan[h i j]	63.7	65.3	66.8	66.8	67.6	—	—	—	65.5	—	—
Turkmenistan[h]	61.1	61.1	61.8	62.9	62.3	—	—	—	61.8	61.9	62.1
Uzbekistan[h i]	64.0	64.3	66.0	66.1	—	—	—	—	—	—	—

a. 1980, 1985: Czechoslovakia.
b. 1980, 1985: UN (1986), (1992).
c. 1980 (which refers to 1980-81): CE (1993). 1989: refers to 1989-90.
d. 1995 (which refers to 1990-95): UN (1997a).
e. 1980 (which refers to Serbia in 1980-81): CE (1993).
f. 1980 (which refers to 1979-80): Goskomstat (1991a).
g. 1985 (which refers to 1985-86): Goskomstat (1991b).
h. 1980, 1985: CIS Stat (1997).
i. 1989-91: CIS Stat (1997).
j. 1995: CIS Stat (1998c).

4.4 Age 20-39 female mortality rate (per thousand relevant population)

	1989	1990	1991	1992	1993	1994	1995	1996	1997
Czech Republic	0.62	0.65	0.65	0.66	0.64	0.58	0.57	0.52	0.54
Slovakia	0.68	0.73	0.69	0.65	0.65	0.60	0.58	0.54	0.57
Poland	0.76	0.77	0.81	0.74	0.71	0.69	0.68	0.63	0.61
Hungary	1.16	1.17	1.19	1.21	1.25	1.11	1.00	0.91	0.81
Slovenia	0.69	0.61	0.60	0.64	0.70	0.70	0.60	0.63	0.51
Croatia[a b]	—	—	0.76	0.72	0.63	0.66	0.61	0.58	0.59
FYR Macedonia[a b]	—	—	0.66	0.62	0.64	0.57	0.73	0.67	0.67
Bosnia-Herzegovina	0.62	0.54	—	—	—	—	—	—	—
FR Yugoslavia	0.76	0.70	0.75	0.73	0.77	0.73	0.67	0.71	0.71
Albania	0.73	0.67	0.65	0.69	0.70	0.66	0.67	0.60	—
Bulgaria	0.79	0.86	0.78	0.84	0.83	0.86	0.81	0.81	0.86
Romania	1.13	1.01	0.99	0.95	0.98	0.94	0.95	0.96	0.93
Estonia	1.00	0.95	0.92	0.94	1.06	1.66	1.20	0.99	0.79
Latvia	1.03	1.02	1.00	1.12	1.33	1.43	1.28	1.08	1.12
Lithuania	0.96	0.87	0.91	0.90	1.03	1.13	1.10	1.02	0.98
Belarus	0.85	0.83	0.93	0.95	0.98	1.00	1.07	1.04	1.09
Moldova[c]	1.10	1.09	1.22	1.15	1.20	1.27	1.29	1.27	1.11
Russia	1.02	1.04	1.11	1.28	1.58	1.74	1.72	1.56	1.46
Ukraine	0.90	0.94	1.00	1.07	1.12	1.24	1.37	1.33	1.26
Armenia	0.85	0.80	0.72	0.78	0.76	0.71	0.65	0.65	0.63
Azerbaijan	0.89	0.85	0.91	1.19	1.15	1.25	1.20	1.14	1.06
Georgia[d]	0.83	0.80	0.77	0.81	—	0.71	0.70	0.56	0.67
Kazakhstan		1.19	1.22	1.29	1.34	1.56	1.60	1.75	1.79	1.85
Kyrgyzstan	1.30	1.35	1.40	1.41	1.44	1.58	1.66	1.61	1.46
Tajikistan[e]	1.39	—	—	—	—	—	—	—	—
Turkmenistan	1.51	1.41	1.54	1.56	1.56	1.55	1.47	—	—
Uzbekistan[e]	1.30	—	—	—	—	—	—	—	—

a. Population data, 1991-92: US Census Bureau (1997).
b. Population data, 1993-97: US Census Bureau (1998).
c. 1997: population data exclude Transdniestr.
d. 1992-97: deaths exclude Abkhazia and Tskhinvali.
e. 1989: Goskomstat (1990).

4.5 Age 20-39 male mortality rate (per thousand relevant population)

	1989	1990	1991	1992	1993	1994	1995	1996	1997
Czech Republic	1.58	1.77	1.68	1.69	1.59	1.58	1.51	1.38	1.38
Slovakia	2.01	2.16	2.11	2.12	1.83	1.75	1.71	1.61	1.70
Poland	2.48	2.61	2.71	2.55	2.29	2.33	2.31	2.10	2.13
Hungary	2.89	3.06	3.00	3.20	3.19	2.99	2.70	2.23	2.09
Slovenia	2.07	1.67	2.07	2.08	2.21	2.02	1.64	1.62	1.74
Croatia[a][b]	—	—	4.77	3.95	2.66	1.97	2.33	1.77	1.60
FYR Macedonia[a][b]	—	—	1.21	1.13	1.29	1.23	1.18	1.10	1.07
Bosnia-Herzegovina	1.47	1.50	—	—	—	—	—	—	—
FR Yugoslavia	1.50	1.55	2.00	1.93	1.62	1.45	1.38	1.37	1.44
Albania	1.15	1.30	1.64	1.80	2.17	2.27	2.19	2.02	—
Bulgaria	1.95	2.04	1.94	2.08	2.19	2.24	2.10	1.90	1.93
Romania	2.34	2.36	2.30	2.49	2.42	2.52	2.57	2.51	2.46
Estonia	2.98	3.46	3.68	4.06	4.44	5.39	4.78	3.54	3.73
Latvia	3.41	3.59	3.95	4.45	5.30	6.08	5.41	4.20	3.71
Lithuania	3.20	3.20	3.86	3.73	4.34	4.73	4.27	3.88	3.65
Belarus	3.01	3.19	3.37	3.77	4.00	4.21	4.31	4.28	4.33
Moldova[c]	3.21	3.29	3.54	4.39	3.35	3.84	3.98	3.66	3.03
Russia	3.84	4.01	4.27	5.11	6.46	7.15	6.95	6.22	5.58
Ukraine	3.16	3.27	3.59	3.98	4.04	4.49	4.99	4.85	4.45
Armenia	1.70	1.91	1.99	2.80	2.70	3.00	1.91	1.68	1.55
Azerbaijan	1.75	1.97	2.04	4.11	3.56	4.68	2.59	2.44	2.26
Georgia[d]	2.29	2.26	2.45	3.03	—	2.56	2.20	1.70	1.73
Kazakhstan	3.43	3.46	3.69	3.83	4.63	4.70	5.47	5.76	5.54
Kyrgyzstan	3.08	3.21	3.27	3.01	3.52	3.87	4.07	3.70	3.76
Tajikistan[e]	1.77	—	—	—	—	—	—	—	—
Turkmenistan	2.62	2.57	2.48	2.55	2.79	2.62	2.50	—	—
Uzbekistan[e]	2.16	—	—	—	—	—	—	—	—

a. Population data, 1991-92: US Census Bureau (1997).
b. Population data, 1993-97: US Census Bureau (1998).
c. 1997: population data exclude Transdniestr.
d. 1992-97: deaths exclude Abkhazia and Tskhinvali.
e. 1989: Goskomstat (1990).

4.6 Age 40-59 female mortality rate (per thousand relevant population)

	1989	1990	1991	1992	1993	1994	1995	1996	1997
Czech Republic	4.06	3.93	3.89	3.67	3.49	3.40	3.53	3.28	3.36
Slovakia	4.24	4.44	4.39	4.05	3.88	3.65	3.61	3.42	3.66
Poland	4.49	4.41	4.44	4.27	3.98	3.90	3.83	3.71	3.67
Hungary	5.87	5.78	5.72	5.99	6.07	5.83	5.74	5.27	5.41
Slovenia	3.94	3.50	3.84	3.63	3.61	3.52	3.33	3.39	3.14
Croatia[a][b]	—	—	4.16	3.79	3.68	3.55	3.51	3.57	3.48
FYR Macedonia[a][b]	—	—	3.55	3.56	3.52	3.94	3.69	3.77	3.90
Bosnia-Herzegovina	4.32	3.86	—	—	—	—	—	—	—
FR Yugoslavia	4.26	4.13	4.23	4.43	4.47	4.41	4.23	4.32	4.40
Albania[a][b]	2.41	2.30	2.50	2.43	2.32	2.34	2.26	2.08	—
Bulgaria	4.16	4.19	4.18	4.19	3.94	4.06	4.14	4.13	4.42
Romania	4.98	4.93	4.86	5.07	5.10	5.19	5.27	5.36	5.19
Estonia	4.91	4.52	5.08	4.82	5.51	6.37	5.70	4.92	4.94
Latvia	5.02	5.12	5.11	5.56	6.56	7.57	7.31	5.61	5.21
Lithuania	4.58	4.60	4.93	4.81	5.45	5.80	5.76	5.18	4.58
Belarus	4.58	4.83	4.85	5.07	5.50	5.52	5.66	5.44	5.39
Moldova[c]	7.14	7.08	7.65	6.69	6.89	7.70	8.07	7.41	6.45
Russia	4.99	5.04	5.06	5.51	6.82	7.71	7.17	6.41	5.79
Ukraine	4.76	4.83	5.10	5.33	5.78	6.14	6.63	6.47	6.08
Armenia	4.06	4.14	3.90	4.15	4.01	3.51	3.69	3.82	3.30
Azerbaijan	4.77	4.78	4.89	5.26	5.33	5.36	4.94	4.66	4.45
Georgia[d]	4.13	3.96	3.97	3.95	—	3.43	2.98	2.68	2.66
Kazakhstan	5.58	5.40	5.34	5.56	6.45	6.86	7.51	7.42	7.11
Kyrgyzstan	5.65	5.54	6.08	5.77	6.09	7.00	7.43	6.51	5.75
Tajikistan[e]	5.56	—	—	—	—	—	—	—	—
Turkmenistan	6.47	6.24	6.31	6.38	7.03	6.70	6.35	—	—
Uzbekistan[e]	5.75	—	—	—	—	—	—	—	—

a. Population data, 1989-92: US Census Bureau (1997).
b. Population data, 1993-97: US Census Bureau (1998).
c. 1997: population data exclude Transdniestr.
d. 1992-97: deaths exclude Abkhazia and Tskhinvali.
e. 1989: Goskomstat (1990).

4.7 Age 40-59 male mortality rate (per thousand relevant population)

	1989	1990	1991	1992	1993	1994	1995	1996	1997
Czech Republic	9.40	10.05	9.27	9.06	8.38	8.31	8.09	8.03	8.09
Slovakia	12.31	12.47	11.78	11.31	10.63	9.85	9.71	9.22	9.41
Poland	11.83	11.87	12.38	11.76	10.82	10.47	10.59	10.01	9.88
Hungary	13.98	14.29	14.46	15.56	15.87	15.73	15.24	14.14	13.80
Slovenia	9.63	9.19	8.83	8.51	8.98	8.31	7.82	7.41	7.52
Croatia[a b]	—	—	10.84	10.08	9.26	8.73	8.51	8.25	8.44
FYR Macedonia[a b]	—	—	6.17	6.60	6.56	7.32	7.37	7.33	7.07
Bosnia-Herzegovina	11.97	10.54	—	—	—	—	—	—	—
FR Yugoslavia	8.58	8.33	8.87	8.76	8.47	8.23	8.06	8.08	8.13
Albania[a b]	4.93	4.55	4.89	4.94	4.94	4.78	4.53	4.25	—
Bulgaria	10.07	10.03	9.63	10.47	10.93	11.19	11.20	10.88	11.16
Romania	10.52	10.94	10.98	11.95	12.34	12.67	13.16	13.33	13.20
Estonia	12.13	13.54	14.37	14.51	16.89	19.75	18.62	15.36	14.88
Latvia	13.15	14.28	15.06	16.49	20.56	23.68	21.51	16.69	15.30
Lithuania	12.27	12.89	13.63	14.20	16.70	17.84	17.60	15.42	13.65
Belarus	12.78	13.02	13.56	14.12	16.08	16.21	17.05	16.49	16.26
Moldova[c]	12.00	12.76	13.37	12.43	12.84	15.46	16.09	14.72	12.91
Russia	13.87	14.35	14.42	16.49	21.09	24.11	22.35	19.69	17.36
Ukraine	12.33	13.10	14.14	15.27	16.17	17.38	19.53	19.11	17.89
Armenia	8.72	9.38	9.65	9.35	9.90	8.95	8.90	8.48	7.40
Azerbaijan	10.49	10.85	11.49	11.79	11.95	11.99	11.45	10.76	9.87
Georgia[d]	9.95	9.90	9.94	9.46	—	8.17	7.98	7.19	6.58
Kazakhstan	13.18	13.32	13.46	13.80	16.55	17.31	19.75	19.78	18.60
Kyrgyzstan	12.10	12.32	12.10	12.07	13.75	16.42	16.12	14.22	13.42
Tajikistan[e]	8.41	—	—	—	—	—	—	—	—
Turkmenistan	11.92	11.64	12.79	11.32	13.73	13.17	11.88	—	—
Uzbekistan[e]	10.03	—	—	—	—	—	—	—	—

a. Population data, 1989-92: US Census Bureau (1997).
b. Population data, 1993-97: US Census Bureau (1998).
c. 1997: population data exclude Transdniestr.
d. 1992-97: deaths exclude Abkhazia and Tskhinvali.
e. 1989: Goskomstat (1990).

4.8 Age 60+ mortality rate (per thousand relevant population)

	1989	1990	1991	1992	1993	1994	1995	1996	1997
Czech Republic	57.68	57.54	55.17	53.00	52.32	51.90	52.23	49.91	49.63
Slovakia	52.85	53.02	53.03	51.50	51.01	49.64	50.92	49.39	49.56
Poland	50.69	50.71	51.86	49.96	50.05	48.65	48.04	48.01	46.68
Hungary	55.82	56.30	55.50	56.40	56.86	55.54	55.34	55.61	54.14
Slovenia	45.64	45.47	46.28	45.52	46.17	43.92	42.98	41.54	41.74
Croatia[a b]	—	—	47.09	44.49	44.59	43.04	43.31	43.46	44.08
FYR Macedonia[a b]	—	—	40.68	43.39	41.12	45.91	46.95	45.40	46.42
Bosnia-Herzegovina	44.16	42.34	—	—	—	—	—	—	—
FR Yugoslavia	46.47	44.79	44.68	45.69	45.72	44.25	44.91	46.33	45.64
Albania[a b]	43.57	43.44	39.78	39.75	38.91	39.36	39.94	39.63	—
Bulgaria	50.36	51.12	52.15	49.75	50.02	50.37	51.79	53.21	55.44
Romania	49.87	49.05	50.28	51.84	50.58	50.13	50.55	53.20	51.07
Estonia	51.60	53.76	52.84	53.60	55.73	55.50	52.86	50.33	48.46
Latvia	51.43	54.27	52.91	52.48	56.65	59.59	56.23	52.09	51.49
Lithuania	46.80	48.04	47.52	47.70	51.99	50.71	49.20	47.30	45.67
Belarus	44.94	47.20	48.61	47.92	52.10	52.18	53.13	52.92	53.88
Moldova[c]	47.50	50.69	54.95	53.18	56.53	61.33	—	60.16	55.42
Russia	47.62	48.77	48.60	49.89	56.76	60.26	57.76	55.57	54.61
Ukraine	47.80	49.34	51.60	52.84	56.64	58.29	59.65	58.23	56.88
Armenia	37.81	39.01	41.29	43.59	46.07	39.39	40.76	39.95	37.86
Azerbaijan	41.25	39.37	40.32	43.16	44.37	43.90	43.93	42.43	41.75
Georgia[d]	42.45	40.61	40.58	40.35	—	34.97	31.19	27.56	30.21
Kazakhstan	47.34	46.94	48.37	49.56	55.59	58.71	60.74	59.76	57.63
Kyrgyzstan	44.93	43.81	44.54	46.52	50.62	56.67	55.23	52.66	51.25
Tajikistan	—	—	—	—	—	—	—	—	—
Turkmenistan	47.70	46.69	50.18	50.45	55.24	55.76	54.20	—	—
Uzbekistan	—	—	—	—	—	—	—	—	—

a. Population data, 1989-92: US Census Bureau (1997).
b. Population data, 1993-97: US Census Bureau (1998).
c. 1997: population data exclude Transdniestr.
d. 1992-97: deaths exclude Abkhazia and Tskhinvali.

5.1 Crude marriage rate (number of marriages per thousand mid-year population)

	1980	1985	1989	1990	1991	1992	1993	1994	1995	1996	1997
Czech Republic[a b]	7.7	7.7	7.8	8.8	7.0	7.2	6.4	5.7	5.3	5.2	5.6
Slovakia[a b]	7.7	7.7	6.9	7.7	6.2	6.4	5.8	5.3	5.1	5.1	5.2
Poland[b]	8.6	7.2	6.7	6.7	6.1	5.7	5.4	5.4	5.4	5.3	5.3
Hungary[b]	7.5	6.9	6.4	6.4	5.9	5.5	5.3	5.3	5.2	4.8	4.6
Slovenia[b]	6.5	5.4	4.9	4.3	4.1	4.6	4.5	4.2	4.1	3.8	3.8
Croatia[c d e]	7.3	6.6	6.1	5.8	4.5	4.6	4.9	5.1	5.2	5.3	5.3
FYR Macedonia[d e f]	8.5	8.1	—	—	7.7	7.4	7.4	8.1	8.0	7.1	7.1
Bosnia-Herzegovina[b e g]	8.6	8.1	7.8	6.7	—	—	—	—	3.0	4.5	4.9
FR Yugoslavia[h]	7.6	6.9	6.6	6.2	5.9	6.1	5.9	5.7	5.7	5.4	5.3
Albania[b e i]	8.1	8.5	8.6	8.9	7.6	8.3	8.2	8.8	8.4	8.5	—
Bulgaria[b]	7.9	7.4	7.1	6.9	5.7	5.2	4.7	4.5	4.4	4.3	4.2
Romania[b]	8.2	7.1	7.7	8.3	8.0	7.7	7.1	6.8	6.8	6.6	6.5
Estonia	8.8	8.4	8.1	7.5	6.6	5.7	5.1	4.9	4.7	3.8	3.8
Latvia	9.8	9.3	9.2	8.8	8.4	7.2	5.6	4.5	4.4	3.9	3.9
Lithuania	9.2	9.7	9.4	9.8	9.2	8.0	6.4	6.3	6.0	5.5	5.1
Belarus[j]	10.1	9.9	9.6	9.7	9.3	7.8	8.0	7.3	7.5	6.2	6.8
Moldova[j k]	11.5	9.7	9.2	9.4	9.1	9.0	9.1	7.8	7.6	6.0	7.6
Russia	10.6	9.7	9.4	8.9	8.6	7.1	7.5	7.3	7.3	5.9	6.3
Ukraine	9.3	9.6	9.5	9.3	9.5	7.6	8.2	7.7	8.4	6.0	6.8
Armenia	10.4	9.9	7.8	8.0	7.8	6.2	5.8	4.6	4.2	3.8	3.3
Azerbaijan[j]	9.8	10.5	10.2	10.3	10.4	9.5	8.2	6.4	5.8	5.2	6.2
Georgia[l]	10.0	8.4	7.1	6.8	7.0	5.0	4.5	4.1	4.0	3.6	3.2
Kazakhstan[j]	10.6	10.1	10.1	10.0	10.1	8.9	8.8	7.5	7.2	6.4	6.5
Kyrgyzstan[j]	10.7	10.1	9.7	10.0	10.6	9.2	8.3	5.9	6.0	5.8	5.8
Tajikistan[e i m]	10.7	10.5	9.2	9.5	10.3	8.4	9.6	6.8	5.5	—	—
Turkmenistan[j]	9.8	9.8	9.8	10.2	10.8	11.1	10.7	8.8	8.1	7.3	7.1
Uzbekistan[e i m]	10.9	11.0	10.0	10.5	12.8	10.9	10.2	7.9	7.5	7.4	7.7

a. 1980, 1985: Czechoslovakia.
b. 1980, 1985: CE (1993).
c. 1980, 1985, 1989-90: CBSC (1996).
d. Population data, 1991-92: US Census Bureau (1997).
e. Population data, 1993-97: US Census Bureau (1998).
f. 1980, 1985, 1989-90: CE (1993).
g. 1995-97: Federation of B-H.
h. 1980, 1985: FSOY (1996).
i. Population data, 1989-92: US Census Bureau (1997).
j. 1980, 1985: CIS Stat (1997).
k. 1997: population data exclude Transdniestr.
l. 1992-97: marriages exclude Abkhazia and Tskhinvali.
m. Marriages: CIS Stat (1998a).

5.2 Average age of women at first marriage (years)

	1989	1990	1991	1992	1993	1994	1995	1996	1997
Czech Republic	21.2	21.1	21.4	21.6	21.7	22.0	22.4	22.8	23.3
Slovakia	22.9	22.7	21.3	21.7	21.1	21.3	—	—	—
Poland[a]	21.7	21.6	21.7	21.7	21.8	21.9	22.0	22.2	22.4
Hungary	21.4	21.5	21.5	21.6	21.7	22.0	22.2	22.6	23.5
Slovenia	23.5	23.8	24.0	24.2	24.7	24.9	25.2	25.4	25.6
Croatia	23.5	23.6	23.7	24.1	24.1	24.4	24.5	24.7	25.1
FYR Macedonia[b]	22.6	22.8	—	—	—	—	—	—	—
Bosnia-Herzegovina[b]	22.9	23.3	—	—	—	—	—	—	—
FR Yugoslavia	23.2	23.6	23.8	23.8	24.0	23.8	24.0	24.2	24.3
Albania	22.8	22.6	22.2	22.2	22.3	—	—	—	—
Bulgaria	21.5	21.4	21.5	21.6	21.9	22.3	22.6	23.1	23.4
Romania	22.1	22.0	22.0	22.1	22.2	22.4	22.8	22.8	22.9
Estonia	22.5	22.5	22.4	22.4	22.9	23.4	23.6	23.8	24.1
Latvia	22.2	22.2	22.2	22.4	22.5	22.5	22.8	23.2	23.6
Lithuania	—	—	—	—	22.2	22.3	22.4	22.6	22.8
Belarus	22.3	22.0	21.9	21.8	21.7	21.7	21.7	21.9	22.1
Moldova	22.0	21.0	21.0	21.0	21.0	21.0	22.0	22.0	22.0
Russia	22.9	22.6	22.5	22.5	22.4	22.4	22.6	22.7	—
Ukraine	21.5	21.6	21.6	—	—	—	—	—	—
Armenia	22.3	22.3	22.0	21.9	21.8	21.7	21.9	22.1	22.7
Azerbaijan	22.8	23.2	22.9	22.7	22.3	22.3	22.9	22.6	22.6
Georgia	24.5	24.2	23.9	23.7	—	23.2	23.7	23.8	24.5
Kazakhstan	22.4	22.3	22.2	22.1	21.6	20.8	21.0	22.2	22.4
Kyrgyzstan	21.9	21.7	21.7	21.4	21.2	21.2	21.4	21.5	21.7
Tajikistan[c]	22.1	—	—	—	—	—	—	—	—
Turkmenistan[c]	23.6	—	—	—	—	—	—	—	—
Uzbekistan[d]	22.3	—	—	21.0	21.0	20.5	20.2	—	—

a. Median age.
b. 1989-90: CE (1993).
c. 1989: CE (1993).
d. UNDP (1997e).

5.3 Average age of men at first marriage (years)

	1989	1990	1991	1992	1993	1994	1995	1996	1997
Czech Republic	23.8	23.5	24.2	24.2	24.4	24.7	25.0	25.4	26.0
Slovakia	25.6	25.4	23.8	24.2	23.6	23.8	—	—	—
Poland[a]	24.2	24.0	24.0	24.0	24.1	24.2	24.3	24.3	24.5
Hungary	24.2	24.2	24.2	24.3	24.4	24.7	25.0	25.2	26.5
Slovenia	26.4	26.6	26.8	27.1	27.6	27.7	27.9	28.2	28.5
Croatia	26.7	26.9	27.0	27.2	27.3	27.6	27.8	28.1	28.4
FYR Macedonia	—	—	—	—	—	—	—	—	—
Bosnia-Herzegovina	—	—	—	—	—	—	—	—	—
FR Yugoslavia	26.9	27.5	27.7	27.6	27.8	27.4	27.6	27.8	27.9
Albania	26.7	26.7	26.7	26.6	26.7	—	—	—	—
Bulgaria	24.7	24.6	24.7	24.9	25.2	25.7	26.0	26.3	26.5
Romania	25.3	25.0	25.0	25.2	25.4	25.6	26.0	26.0	26.2
Estonia	24.6	24.6	24.5	24.7	25.2	25.6	25.7	26.1	26.3
Latvia	24.3	23.9	23.9	24.1	24.3	24.3	25.0	25.1	25.7
Lithuania	—	—	—	—	24.1	24.2	24.4	24.5	24.6
Belarus	24.1	23.9	23.8	23.7	23.6	23.7	23.7	24.0	24.2
Moldova	24.0	22.0	23.0	23.0	23.0	23.0	24.0	24.0	24.0
Russia	24.9	24.7	24.7	24.6	24.5	24.7	24.8	25.0	—
Ukraine	23.8	23.7	23.5	—	—	—	—	—	—
Armenia	25.5	25.5	25.6	25.6	25.8	26.1	26.3	26.5	26.8
Azerbaijan	25.7	26.2	26.2	25.9	25.9	24.2	26.5	26.6	26.8
Georgia	27.6	27.5	27.0	27.0	—	25.2	27.2	27.4	28.3
Kazakhstan	24.6	24.5	25.0	24.4	24.0	24.1	24.6	24.7	24.9
Kyrgyzstan	24.5	24.4	24.4	24.2	24.0	24.2	24.4	24.7	24.9
Tajikistan	—	—	—	—	—	—	—	—	—
Turkmenistan	—	—	—	—	—	—	—	—	—
Uzbekistan	—	—	—	—	—	—	—	—	—

a. Median age.

5.4 Crude divorce rate (number of divorces per thousand mid-year population)

	1980	1985	1989	1990	1991	1992	1993	1994	1995	1996	1997
Czech Republic[a b]	2.2	2.2	3.0	3.1	2.8	2.8	2.9	3.0	3.0	3.2	3.2
Slovakia[a b]	2.2	2.2	1.6	1.7	1.5	1.5	1.5	1.6	1.7	1.7	1.7
Poland[b]	1.1	1.3	1.2	1.1	0.9	0.8	0.7	0.8	1.0	1.0	1.1
Hungary[b]	2.6	2.8	2.4	2.4	2.4	2.1	2.2	2.3	2.4	2.2	2.5
Slovenia[b]	1.2	1.3	1.1	0.9	0.9	1.0	1.0	1.0	0.8	1.0	1.0
Croatia[c d e]	1.2	1.1	1.1	1.1	1.0	0.8	1.0	1.0	0.9	0.8	0.8
FYR Macedonia[d e f]	0.5	0.4	—	—	0.2	0.3	0.3	0.3	0.4	0.4	0.5
Bosnia-Herzegovina[e g h]	0.6	0.7	0.5	0.4	—	—	—	—	0.1	0.1	0.2
FR Yugoslavia[i]	1.2	1.2	1.2	1.0	0.8	0.7	0.7	0.7	0.8	0.7	0.7
Albania[b e i]	0.8	0.9	0.8	0.8	0.7	0.7	0.7	0.7	0.7	0.6	0.4
Bulgaria[b]	1.5	1.6	1.4	1.3	1.3	1.1	0.9	0.9	1.3	1.2	1.1
Romania[b]	1.5	1.4	1.6	1.4	1.6	1.3	1.4	1.7	1.5	1.6	1.5
Estonia	4.2	4.0	3.8	3.7	3.7	4.3	3.8	3.7	5.0	3.9	3.6
Latvia	5.0	4.5	4.2	4.0	4.2	5.5	4.0	3.3	3.1	2.4	2.5
Lithuania	3.2	3.2	3.3	3.4	4.1	3.7	3.7	3.0	2.8	3.0	3.1
Belarus[k]	3.2	3.1	3.4	3.4	3.7	3.9	4.4	4.3	4.1	4.2	4.6
Moldova[k l]	2.8	2.7	2.9	3.0	3.2	3.4	3.3	3.2	3.4	3.1	2.5
Russia	4.2	4.0	4.0	3.8	4.0	4.3	4.5	4.6	4.5	3.8	3.8
Ukraine	3.6	3.6	3.8	3.7	3.9	4.3	4.2	4.0	3.9	3.8	3.7
Armenia	1.1	1.2	1.2	1.2	1.1	0.9	0.8	0.9	0.7	0.7	0.6
Azerbaijan	1.2	1.2	1.6	2.0	1.5	1.3	0.9	0.8	0.8	0.7	0.8
Georgia[m]	1.3	1.2	1.4	1.4	1.4	0.9	0.6	0.6	0.5	0.4	0.4
Kazakhstan[k]	2.6	2.6	2.8	2.7	3.0	3.0	2.8	2.6	2.4	2.5	2.3
Kyrgyzstan[k]	1.8	1.7	1.9	1.8	2.0	1.8	1.6	1.2	1.3	1.4	1.4
Tajikistan[e j n]	1.5	1.5	1.5	1.4	1.4	1.2	0.9	0.8	0.7	—	—
Turkmenistan	1.4	1.5	1.4	1.4	1.6	1.5	1.4	1.5	1.3	1.5	1.3
Uzbekistan[e j n]	1.4	1.4	1.5	1.5	1.6	1.5	1.2	1.1	0.9	0.9	0.9

a. 1980, 1985: Czechoslovakia.
b. 1980, 1985: CE (1993).
c. 1980, 1985, 1989-90: CBSC (1996).
d. Population data, 1991-92: US Census Bureau (1997).
e. Population data, 1993-97: US Census Bureau (1998).
f. 1980, 1985, 1989-90: CE (1993).
g. 1980, 1985, 1991: CE (1993).
h. 1992-97: Federation of B-H.
i. 1980, 1985: FSOY (1996).
j. Population data, 1989-92: US Census Bureau (1997).
k. 1980, 1985: CIS Stat (1997).
l. 1997: population data exclude Transdniestr.
m. 1992-97: divorces exclude Abkhazia and Tskhinvali.
n. Divorces: CIS Stat (1998a).

5.5 General divorce rate (number of divorces per hundred marriages)

	1980	1985	1989	1990	1991	1992	1993	1994	1995	1996	1997
Czech Republic[a][b]	28.6	28.6	38.6	35.2	40.8	38.6	45.8	52.9	56.7	61.4	56.2
Slovakia[a][b]	28.6	28.6	22.7	21.9	24.1	23.8	26.5	30.8	32.7	34.2	32.7
Poland[a]	12.8	18.1	18.5	16.6	14.5	14.7	13.4	15.2	18.4	19.4	20.8
Hungary[a]	34.7	40.6	37.3	37.5	39.9	37.9	41.3	43.3	46.5	46.2	53.3
Slovenia[a]	18.5	24.1	22.1	21.8	22.4	21.6	21.7	23.1	19.2	26.5	26.6
Croatia[c]	16.0	17.4	18.6	19.6	22.6	16.6	20.3	19.3	17.4	14.7	17.4
FYR Macedonia[a]	5.9	4.9	5.8	4.7	3.2	3.8	4.1	3.9	4.5	5.0	7.3
Bosnia-Herzegovina[a][d]	7.0	8.6	6.1	5.9	5.6	—	—	—	3.0	2.2	3.3
FR Yugoslavia[e]	15.3	17.5	17.5	16.5	14.2	11.2	11.9	11.7	13.2	13.9	14.1
Albania[a]	9.9	10.6	9.5	9.2	9.0	8.9	8.7	7.6	8.6	6.9	—
Bulgaria[a]	19.0	21.6	20.0	19.0	22.6	21.1	18.3	21.1	29.0	28.0	26.9
Romania[a]	18.3	19.7	20.2	17.1	20.2	16.8	19.3	25.7	22.7	23.7	23.6
Estonia[a]	47.7	47.6	46.8	49.1	55.8	74.9	74.3	76.0	106.4	102.5	94.5
Latvia[a]	51.0	48.4	45.9	45.7	49.6	77.0	70.4	72.7	70.6	62.8	63.0
Lithuania[a]	34.8	33.0	35.5	35.1	44.5	46.4	58.6	47.4	46.1	55.4	60.5
Belarus[f]	32.0	31.6	35.3	35.3	39.9	50.0	54.5	58.3	54.7	67.7	67.8
Moldova[f]	24.5	27.3	31.1	32.2	35.0	37.7	36.7	40.9	44.6	51.5	45.9
Russia[f]	39.7	41.3	42.1	42.4	46.8	60.7	59.9	63.0	61.9	64.9	59.8
Ukraine[f]	39.2	37.4	39.6	39.9	40.7	56.5	51.2	52.0	45.9	62.8	54.6
Armenia[f]	10.5	11.2	15.2	15.4	13.8	13.7	14.3	20.1	17.2	18.3	18.5
Azerbaijan[f]	11.8	11.2	15.9	19.2	14.4	13.8	10.9	13.3	13.1	14.5	12.4
Georgia[f][g]	13.4	14.7	19.2	21.2	19.5	18.2	13.3	14.1	12.5	11.8	13.3
Kazakhstan[f]	24.2	25.9	27.5	26.4	29.3	33.8	31.0	33.9	33.4	39.5	35.1
Kyrgyzstan[f]	17.2	17.0	19.7	18.0	19.0	19.7	19.9	21.2	22.3	25.1	24.6
Tajikistan[h]	14.3	14.6	15.9	14.7	13.4	13.9	9.8	11.3	13.5	—	—
Turkmenistan	13.8	15.0	14.2	13.2	14.4	13.7	13.3	17.5	18.0	22.4	19.4
Uzbekistan[h]	13.0	13.0	14.9	13.8	12.3	13.9	12.0	13.8	12.4	11.8	—

a. 1980, 1985: computed from crude divorce and marriage rates.
b. 1980, 1985: Czechoslovakia.
c. 1980, 1985: CBSC (1996).
d. 1992-97: Federation of B-H.
e. 1980, 1985: FSOY (1996).
f. 1980, 1985: CIS Stat (1997).
g. 1992-97: excludes Abkhazia and Tskhinvali.
h. CIS Stat (1998a).

5.6 Number of children involved in divorce (thousands)

	1989	1990	1991	1992	1993	1994	1995	1996	1997
Czech Republic	34.7	35.2	32.0	31.1	32.5	33.1	32.8	34.7	33.3
Slovakia	10.9	13.5	10.3	9.7	9.7	10.3	6.8	7.0	—
Poland	50.1	45.1	35.8	33.5	28.4	32.8	40.6	42.2	44.6
Hungary[a]	26.1	26.1	25.4	22.9	22.9	23.3	24.9	21.0	24.9
Slovenia	2.1	2.0	1.9	2.0	2.0	2.0	1.5	2.0	1.9
Croatia	6.6	6.7	6.3	4.6	5.9	5.8	5.5	4.7	5.0
FYR Macedonia	—	—	—	—	—	—	—	—	—
Bosnia-Herzegovina	—	—	—	—	—	—	—	—	—
FR Yugoslavia	7.0	6.3	4.9	4.1	4.2	4.5	5.0	4.7	4.6
Albania	2.3	2.5	2.1	—	2.1	1.2	1.4	1.2	0.9
Bulgaria	14.1	12.7	12.0	10.3	7.8	7.0	9.3	8.6	8.1
Romania	30.6	27.7	30.5	23.6	21.6	32.8	27.2	26.8	26.9
Estonia[a]	5.3	5.3	5.4	6.2	5.1	4.8	7.0	5.6	5.1
Latvia[a]	9.7	9.6	10.0	13.7	9.2	8.1	7.7	5.6	5.8
Lithuania	11.6	12.0	15.2	13.8	13.3	11.5	11.0	12.1	12.2
Belarus	31.6	31.6	35.9	38.8	45.0	42.9	40.5	42.3	45.5
Moldova	10.6	11.6	12.9	14.3	13.5	12.2	13.0	—	—
Russia	479.1	466.1	522.2	569.1	593.8	613.4	588.1	463.5	454.5
Ukraine	155.9	158.5	170.7	186.7	184.7	—	—	—	—
Armenia	3.5	3.6	3.2	2.7	2.8	3.0	2.2	2.3	2.2
Azerbaijan	7.5	9.9	8.0	6.5	4.8	4.0	2.5	2.2	3.6
Georgia[a][b]	4.5	4.4	4.5	1.9	—	1.6	1.5	1.0	0.9
Kazakhstan	41.1	40.5	45.8	47.4	43.6	39.2	37.1	39.3	36.4
Kyrgyzstan	7.8	7.0	8.3	7.1	6.5	5.1	5.8	6.6	6.8
Tajikistan[c]	7.0	—	—	—	4.9	—	—	—	—
Turkmenistan	4.7	4.8	6.2	6.0	5.8	6.2	6.5	—	—
Uzbekistan[c]	25.8	—	—	—	—	—	—	—	—

a. Only children from the marriage.
b. 1992-97: excludes Abkhazia and Tskhinvali.
c. CIS Stat (1995a).

6.1 DPT immunization rate (percent of children under 2 immunized against diphtheria, pertussis and tetanus)

	1989	1990	1991	1992	1993	1994	1995	1996	1997
Czech Republic	99.0	99.0	99.0	99.0	99.0	98.0	96.0	98.0	98.0
Slovakia	99.1	99.4	99.7	99.3	99.1	98.9	99.1	—	—
Poland[a b]	—	90.1	88.9	88.0	89.0	89.5	90.5	91.7	—
Hungary[c]	99.9	99.9	99.9	99.9	99.9	99.9	99.9	99.8	99.8
Slovenia	97.4	97.1	97.3	97.8	98.1	98.1	95.8	96.2	91.9
Croatia	—	—	—	—	—	—	—	—	—
FYR Macedonia	93.7	94.4	92.5	95.4	89.6	87.7	95.2	92.5	96.6
Bosnia-Herzegovina	—	93.0	—	—	—	—	—	—	—
FR Yugoslavia	89.2	84.0	79.0	84.2	84.6	85.0	89.0	91.2	94.0
Albania	—	—	77.6	94.0	95.8	96.3	97.1	98.1	98.6
Bulgaria[d]	99.5	99.5	99.4	97.9	97.7	93.3	94.8	95.1	94.2
Romania	79.3	75.5	77.3	86.8	97.6	97.6	98.3	98.0	—
Estonia[b c e]	—	—	—	—	53.9	57.8	63.2	68.7	67.8
Latvia[b c]	81.1	83.5	82.8	83.5	78.8	72.4	71.8	73.7	74.2
Lithuania[d]	81.9	78.4	74.9	87.2	86.8	87.2	97.3	92.1	92.0
Belarus[c]	93.8	92.4	87.7	88.1	89.4	89.5	93.9	97.7	96.7
Moldova[c]	84.0	81.0	81.0	84.0	87.0	86.0	96.0	97.7	97.9
Russia[b c]	82.7	68.5	68.7	72.6	79.2	88.1	92.7	95.1	87.5
Ukraine[c f]	79.2	78.8	65.5	82.7	95.6	91.5	97.7	98.6	98.5
Armenia[c g]	81.5	82.3	83.0	85.2	85.3	86.0	98.0	86.0	88.5
Azerbaijan[c]	90.8	92.1	92.2	82.0	89.5	94.0	95.9	95.8	94.5
Georgia[h i]	82.1	41.4	73.8	54.1	53.2	100.0	52.0	97.3	99.3
Kazakhstan[d g]	84.8	84.2	82.7	85.3	81.6	84.4	92.9	95.0	99.0
Kyrgyzstan[c g j]	—	—	78.1	88.5	64.4	85.3	93.1	97.7	98.1
Tajikistan	—	—	—	—	—	—	—	—	—
Turkmenistan[b c k]	78.4	82.2	80.9	84.1	72.8	89.7	92.6	93.6	98.6
Uzbekistan[c g l]	—	—	84.1	83.2	49.2	66.8	87.8	95.7	—

a. 3-year-olds.
b. Diphtheria and tetanus.
c. 1-year-olds.
d. 1- to 2-year-olds.
e. Vaccination and revaccination.
f. 1989-90, 1995-97: diphtheria only.
g. Diphtheria only.
h. Number of vaccinations of children of all ages divided by 0-1 population (may overestimate the rate). 1992-97: excludes Abkhazia and Tskhinvali.
i. A 1996 survey on DPT3 found 75% among 0- to 5-year-olds and 40% among 0- to 1-year-olds (MOHG and UNICEF, 1996).
j. A 1995 survey on DPT3 found 74% among children 12-23 months old (MOHK and UNICEF, 1995).
k. A 1995 survey on DPT3 found 80% among children 12-23 months old (MOHT and UNICEF, 1995).
l. UNDP (1997e).

6.2 Polio immunization rate (percent of children under 2 immunized)

	1989	1990	1991	1992	1993	1994	1995	1996	1997
Czech Republic	99.0	99.0	99.0	99.0	99.0	98.0	98.0	98.0	99.0
Slovakia	98.8	99.0	99.2	98.6	98.6	98.6	98.6	—	—
Poland[a]	—	90.1	88.6	87.9	88.9	89.3	90.4	91.6	—
Hungary	98.5	98.6	98.6	98.6	99.9	99.9	99.9	99.8	99.7
Slovenia	96.5	96.8	97.6	98.3	98.5	98.5	96.8	97.2	91.0
Croatia	—	—	—	—	—	—	—	—	—
FYR Macedonia	94.4	94.3	93.5	93.8	93.7	90.7	94.7	94.4	97.4
Bosnia-Herzegovina	—	94.0	—	—	—	—	—	—	—
FR Yugoslavia	88.8	80.7	80.5	84.5	82.6	84.4	89.6	91.1	94.0
Albania	—	—	82.5	87.0	97.5	97.2	97.8	99.6	99.1
Bulgaria[b]	99.7	99.7	99.0	98.8	97.0	93.9	96.8	95.4	95.9
Romania	89.4	80.5	83.5	92.3	90.7	91.0	94.2	96.8	—
Estonia[c d]	—	—	—	—	44.7	50.8	52.1	58.3	57.5
Latvia[c]	83.6	85.6	84.1	94.9	80.9	59.3	76.3	73.7	73.4
Lithuania	86.6	77.1	79.0	88.2	86.3	87.7	89.3	92.6	94.8
Belarus[c]	90.0	89.2	89.4	89.9	90.5	92.4	96.1	97.9	98.3
Moldova[c]	92.0	91.0	89.0	93.0	97.0	94.0	97.0	98.6	98.4
Russia[c]	68.6	69.4	71.5	69.0	82.2	87.5	91.6	96.8	91.4
Ukraine[c]	80.5	81.3	86.3	90.1	91.1	96.3	97.5	98.9	98.2
Armenia[c]	93.1	93.3	91.8	91.9	91.9	92.0	93.0	97.0	94.6
Azerbaijan[c]	96.8	95.7	97.5	96.2	94.2	93.6	98.0	97.3	98.3
Georgia[e f]	98.0	47.4	100.0	67.3	83.9	100.0	63.0	99.3	100.0
Kazakhstan[g]	85.6	85.0	83.7	86.5	68.7	57.9	93.1	94.2	97.0
Kyrgyzstan[c h]	—	—	80.9	91.5	69.4	84.6	96.3	94.2	99.1
Tajikistan	—	—	—	—	—	—	—	—	—
Turkmenistan[c i]	83.7	92.2	91.1	90.9	91.8	94.4	96.7	95.6	99.2
Uzbekistan[c j]	—	—	89.1	85.3	45.9	79.0	98.1	96.5	—

a. 3-year-olds.
b. 1- to 2-year-olds.
c. 1-year-olds.
d. Vaccination and revaccination.
e. Number of vaccinations of children of all ages divided by 0-1 population (may overestimate the rate). 1992-97: excludes Abkhazia and Tskhinvali.
f. A 1996 survey on OPV3 found 77% among 0- to 5-year-olds and 41% among 0- to 1-year-olds (MOHG and UNICEF, 1996).
g. 1989-93: 1- to 2-year-olds. 1994-97: 0- to 2-year-olds.
h. A 1995 survey on OPV3 found 67% among children 12-23 months old (MOHK and UNICEF, 1995).
i. A 1995 survey on OPV3 found 83% among children 12-23 months old (MOHT and UNICEF, 1995).
j. UNDP (1997e).

6.3 Measles immunization rate (percent of children under 2 immunized)

	1989	1990	1991	1992	1993	1994	1995	1996	1997
Czech Republic	99.0	98.0	98.0	97.0	98.0	97.0	96.0	97.0	98.0
Slovakia	98.9	98.5	98.0	96.2	97.9	97.8	97.4	—	—
Poland[a]	—	94.6	93.5	94.9	95.3	95.6	96.1	96.7	—
Hungary	99.9	99.7	99.9	99.8	99.8	99.8	99.9	99.8	99.8
Slovenia	90.8	92.3	90.6	90.3	89.7	91.1	92.6	91.6	94.7
Croatia	—	—	—	—	—	—	—	—	—
FYR Macedonia	93.7	93.6	92.8	52.9	97.8	86.0	96.7	91.0	97.8
Bosnia-Herzegovina	—	—	—	—	—	—	—	—	—
FR Yugoslavia[b]	90.7	83.0	75.5	81.8	84.9	80.8	86.0	90.1	91.9
Albania	—	—	80.5	87.0	76.2	81.2	91.0	91.7	95.1
Bulgaria[c d]	99.6	99.6	97.8	92.2	87.9	93.3	96.4	95.1	93.8
Romania	86.2	93.0	87.6	90.8	90.2	90.1	93.3	93.8	—
Estonia[c e]	—	—	—	—	60.2	64.1	65.1	71.5	76.6
Latvia[f]	89.4	89.1	89.4	68.4	78.7	66.4	75.5	78.6	80.1
Lithuania	92.2	98.0	85.7	98.0	91.8	92.7	93.7	96.3	95.9
Belarus[f]	96.7	96.2	94.9	93.7	95.6	96.6	92.8	96.4	97.6
Moldova[g]	95.0	94.0	93.0	92.0	92.0	95.0	98.0	98.4	98.9
Russia[g]	82.0	81.1	78.7	82.6	88.2	91.3	94.1	95.3	91.1
Ukraine[g]	87.9	88.7	60.9	90.3	94.3	95.5	97.1	92.4	97.8
Armenia[f]	94.5	94.8	80.7	77.4	82.1	95.0	96.0	89.0	91.5
Azerbaijan[f]	87.6	83.3	70.1	66.3	27.8	91.3	97.0	98.5	96.6
Georgia[h i]	82.0	42.0	76.3	16.1	65.5	91.9	50.8	97.0	100.0
Kazakhstan[j]	93.0	95.1	91.4	90.2	91.0	71.7	95.4	96.6	97.0
Kyrgyzstan[g k]	—	—	94.1	94.0	93.0	88.6	97.1	98.0	98.0
Tajikistan	—	—	—	—	—	—	—	—	—
Turkmenistan[f l]	67.0	79.6	62.6	76.0	85.1	90.2	91.9	93.8	99.6
Uzbekistan[m]	—	—	83.9	84.1	82.2	20.9	60.3	98.2	—

a. 3-year-olds.

b. 1989-90: combined with parotitis and rubella.

c. 1- to 2-year-olds.

d. Combined with parotitis and rubella.

e. Vaccination and revaccination.

f. 1-year-olds.

g. 2-year-olds.

h. Number of vaccinations of children of all ages divided by 0-1 population (may overestimate the rate). 1992-97: excludes Abkhazia and Tskhinvali.

i. A 1996 survey found 51% among 0- to 5-year-olds (MOHG and UNICEF, 1996).

j. 2- to 3-year-olds.

k. A 1995 survey found 74% among children 12-23 months old (MOHK and UNICEF, 1995).

l. A 1995 survey found 66% among children 12-23 months old (MOHT and UNICEF, 1995).

m. UNDP (1997e).

6.4 Incidence of sexually transmitted diseases
(newly registered cases of syphilis and gonorrhoea per hundred thousand population)

	1989	1990	1991	1992	1993	1994	1995	1996	1997
Czech Republic	60	63	71	73	47	31	23	16	15
Slovakia[a]	31	38	38	37	26	15	11	7	7
Poland	27	27	20	15	13	10	8	7	—
Hungary	45	48	44	37	27	25	23	21	19
Slovenia	0	0	0	0	0	0	1	1	5
Croatia[b]	11	9	7	5	4	3	2	1	—
FYR Macedonia[c]	—	—	6	4	1	2	2	1	1
Bosnia-Herzegovina	6	4	—	—	—	—	—	—	—
FR Yugoslavia[d]	9	4	4	8	10	9	8	5	5
Albania	—	—	—	—	—	—	—	—	—
Bulgaria	52	67	72	66	47	44	44	48	46
Romania	20	23	26	26	26	29	35	32	—
Estonia	132	132	154	192	256	263	264	232	210
Latvia[e]	106	104	101	136	298	364	388	351	265
Lithuania	—	81	87	115	169	205	200	179	139
Belarus	109	102	107	142	196	243	314	337	303
Moldova[f]	128	117	110	152	195	234	275	281	280
Russia	142	133	136	183	264	289	351	402	390
Ukraine	86	79	79	105	136	177	208	226	208
Armenia	41	33	30	20	37	45	47	55	44
Azerbaijan	25	13	12	18	22	25	37	26	22
Georgia	76	—	55	47	41	35	39	36	64
Kazakhstan	110	109	118	134	152	148	256	352	360
Kyrgyzstan[g]	—	219	234	246	231	248	295	363	386
Tajikistan	—	—	—	—	—	—	—	—	—
Turkmenistan	37	37	37	32	37	46	59	70	88
Uzbekistan	—	—	—	—	—	—	—	—	—

a. Total cases.

b. Population data, 1989-90: CBSC (1996), 1991-92: US Census Bureau (1997), 1993-97: US Census Bureau (1998).

c. Population data, 1991-92: US Census Bureau (1997), 1993-97: US Census Bureau (1998).

d. Population data, 1997: ICDC estimate.

e. Includes chlamydial infection and anogenital herpes.

f. 1997: population data exclude Transdniestr.

g. Includes trichomoniasis.

6.5 Individuals registered with HIV (newly registered cases)

	1989	1990	1991	1992	1993	1994	1995	1996	1997
Czech Republic	—	—	—	143	170	208	248	—	63
Slovakia	12	3	5	2	5	11	8	4	8
Poland	—	—	559	482	385	423	539	661	—
Hungary	36	40	55	61	56	65	81	63	71
Slovenia	6	2	5	5	3	4	14	3	7
Croatia	3	9	11	6	14	16	15	16	—
FYR Macedonia	2	1	1	—	3	4	—	3	—
Bosnia-Herzegovina	—	—	—	—	—	—	—	—	—
FR Yugoslavia	33	56	61	88	70	84	97	89	67
Albania	—	—	—	—	—	—	—	—	—
Bulgaria[a]	6	10	12	18	24	34	—	—	—
Romania	—	—	—	—	—	—	—	—	—
Estonia	0	0	0	1	0	1	3	7	3
Latvia	—	—	2	1	2	3	1	8	3
Lithuania	1	8	1	5	4	10	10	12	31
Belarus	12	14	12	21	10	5	8	1,021	653
Moldova	—	1	0	2	3	4	7	47	404
Russia[b]	—	441	81	87	108	156	189	1,525	4,399
Ukraine[c]	—	—	—	—	—	—	1,499	5,422	8,934
Armenia	—	—	—	—	—	—	—	2	—
Azerbaijan	—	—	—	3	—	3	—	2	11
Georgia	1	3	1	6	—	1	2	8	18
Kazakhstan	—	2	1	1	2	0	5	46	429
Kyrgyzstan	—	—	—	—	—	—	—	1	2
Tajikistan	—	—	—	—	—	—	—	—	—
Turkmenistan	—	—	—	—	—	—	—	—	—
Uzbekistan	—	—	—	—	—	—	—	—	—

a. Total registered cases.
b. 1990: total cases registered in 1987-90.
c. Includes cases of AIDS.

7.1 Kindergarten enrolments (net rates, percent of relevant population)

	1989	1990	1991	1992	1993	1994	1995	1996	1997
Czech Republic[a]	89.8	89.8	89.8	83.3	84.9	86.6	88.7	88.5	83.0
Slovakia[a]	91.5	83.7	75.7	78.1	78.0	74.6	70.2	75.2	—
Poland[b]	48.7	47.1	43.9	42.6	42.7	44.3	45.3	46.8	47.9
Hungary[a]	85.7	85.3	86.1	86.9	87.1	86.2	87.0	86.5	86.1
Slovenia[b c]	56.3	56.6	55.8	56.2	60.3	62.8	65.1	66.7	66.2
Croatia[b d]	29.4	29.4	19.1	20.0	—	26.1	31.0	30.9	—
FYR Macedonia[b d]	—	26.2	24.4	25.3	25.5	26.9	28.0	—	—
Bosnia-Herzegovina	—	—	—	—	—	—	—	—	—
FR Yugoslavia[b]	24.1	23.8	21.9	20.5	21.8	24.6	26.3	28.1	29.2
Albania[a d]	43.1	44.1	36.3	26.8	26.5	26.5	—	—	—
Bulgaria[b]	63.9	63.9	55.9	57.4	56.2	57.5	61.6	62.6	58.8
Romania[b]	63.3	54.3	51.9	53.3	50.2	55.2	58.4	55.1	52.8
Estonia[b]	62.2	67.4	60.5	53.7	56.0	58.8	63.2	67.1	70.4
Latvia[b]	52.8	44.8	37.0	28.3	32.6	39.9	47.1	50.8	52.1
Lithuania[b]	63.9	58.6	63.9	39.1	30.1	34.5	36.2	40.0	41.6
Belarus[b]	63.1	63.3	62.5	58.0	58.3	61.0	62.3	64.0	66.9
Moldova[e f]	62.8	61.4	58.7	42.4	36.6	35.1	32.3	32.1	31.5
Russia[b g]	69.3	66.4	63.9	56.8	57.4	56.2	55.5	55.0	56.0
Ukraine[b]	65.1	62.3	61.0	57.5	54.7	52.0	48.2	44.9	41.6
Armenia[b]	65.2	60.5	60.4	51.9	45.3	39.1	31.4	32.4	—
Azerbaijan[b]	20.8	19.7	18.9	18.0	18.1	15.5	14.6	13.5	13.1
Georgia[b]	43.8	42.7	39.1	30.2	26.9	19.0	19.6	21.0	20.4
Kazakhstan[b]	52.2	52.7	52.0	45.9	40.9	30.7	24.6	—	11.7
Kyrgyzstan[e]	31.3	30.3	26.7	23.3	13.4	8.8	7.7	8.2	7.0
Tajikistan[d e g]	16.7	15.4	14.1	11.5	11.5	11.1	8.2	7.7	—
Turkmenistan[e]	36.0	35.0	35.0	34.0	34.0	32.0	26.0	22.0	21.0
Uzbekistan[d e g]	38.5	38.8	38.1	34.2	33.0	30.7	27.9	22.7	—

a. 3- to 5-year-olds.
b. 3- to 6-year-olds.
c. Refers to gross rates in public schools.
d. ICDC estimates. Population data, 1989-92: US Census Bureau (1997), 1993-97: US Census Bureau (1998).
e. 1- to 6-year-olds.
f. 1992-97: enrolments exclude Transdniestr.
g. Enrolments: CIS Stat (1998a).

7.2 Basic education enrolments (gross rates, percent of relevant population)

	1989	1990	1991	1992	1993	1994	1995	1996	1997
Czech Republic[a]	97.6	98.6	98.7	99.2	99.1	99.5	99.4	99.2	99.1
Slovakia[a]	96.8	97.2	98.0	99.8	99.5	97.0	96.5	96.3	—
Poland[b c]	97.9	97.5	97.3	97.1	97.2	97.1	97.2	97.4	98.0
Hungary[d]	99.0	99.2	99.2	99.2	99.1	99.1	99.1	99.2	99.2
Slovenia[c]	96.1	97.1	96.8	97.6	97.8	96.7	97.3	99.8	99.8
Croatia[c e]	96.0	94.0	81.0	79.0	85.0	89.0	88.0	89.0	—
FYR Macedonia[c f]	—	89.4	87.1	86.2	86.2	86.8	86.5	86.9	—
Bosnia-Herzegovina	—	—	—	—	—	—	—	—	—
FR Yugoslavia[b c g]	95.3	95.0	94.4	72.7	74.3	72.5	71.6	72.7	71.8
Albania[d f]	90.8	90.7	88.5	85.9	86.6	87.6	—	—	—
Bulgaria[c]	98.4	98.6	97.3	95.1	94.0	94.3	93.7	93.6	94.0
Romania[c]	93.6	89.5	89.4	89.6	90.3	91.4	92.6	93.9	95.0
Estonia[h i]	96.2	94.9	93.6	92.3	91.7	91.2	92.2	92.8	93.7
Latvia[h i]	95.8	96.4	95.2	90.9	89.4	89.0	89.5	90.3	90.7
Lithuania[c]	94.0	93.0	92.6	92.8	91.9	92.2	93.2	93.6	95.8
Belarus[h]	95.8	94.9	94.2	94.2	93.7	93.6	94.1	93.8	94.1
Moldova[c i j]	95.8	95.6	94.4	80.3	80.0	79.3	79.8	79.3	78.8
Russia[h i]	93.0	93.6	94.4	93.3	91.9	90.7	91.3	91.4	90.8
Ukraine[h i]	92.8	92.3	91.5	91.1	90.4	90.6	90.8	91.2	90.7
Armenia[c i]	95.5	94.6	91.6	91.1	86.4	82.2	81.4	82.8	82.9
Azerbaijan[h i]	89.5	90.5	90.5	91.3	92.4	94.2	94.4	95.4	96.6
Georgia[h k]	95.2	95.3	92.4	83.3	82.4	80.7	79.8	80.7	—
Kazakhstan[h i]	93.9	93.1	92.7	91.7	91.5	90.9	90.5	90.0	89.2
Kyrgyzstan[h]	92.5	91.8	90.6	90.3	89.7	89.0	89.1	89.3	89.2
Tajikistan[f h i]	94.1	94.0	94.2	89.6	85.1	86.4	86.6	85.0	85.5
Turkmenistan[h i]	94.3	94.9	92.5	91.7	92.0	91.8	83.9	83.2	83.1
Uzbekistan[f h i]	92.2	91.1	87.9	87.5	87.9	88.6	—	89.0	89.7

a. 6- to 14-year-olds.
b. Net rates.
c. 7- to 14-year-olds.
d. 6- to 13-year-olds.
e. 1991-96: some areas not reported; estimated rate 95%.
f. ICDC estimates. Population data, 1989-92: US Census Bureau (1997), 1993-97: US Census Bureau (1998).
g. 1992-97: enrolments exclude ethnic Albanians in Kosovo.
h. 7- to 15-year-olds.
i. ICDC estimates.
j. 1992-97: enrolments exclude Transdniestr.
k. 1992-96: enrolments exclude Abkhazia and Tskhinvali.
l. Enrolments: CIS Stat (1998a).

7.3 General secondary enrolments[a] (gross rates, percent of 15-18 population)

	1989	1990	1991	1992	1993	1994	1995	1996	1997
Czech Republic	15.9	16.1	15.6	15.9	16.5	17.6	18.8	18.8	—
Slovakia	15.6	16.0	16.4	17.1	18.0	19.0	20.0	20.9	21.5
Poland	21.0	21.7	23.3	24.9	26.4	28.1	29.7	30.5	31.9
Hungary	19.7	19.8	19.5	19.5	19.2	20.0	21.2	22.3	23.6
Slovenia	—	—	—	—	19.5	20.1	20.5	21.4	—
Croatia[b c]	—	—	—	8.8	13.9	18.0	18.5	18.7	—
FYR Macedonia[b]	—	—	—	—	—	15.9	17.4	18.1	18.7
Bosnia-Herzegovina	—	—	—	—	—	—	—	—	—
FR Yugoslavia	—	—	—	—	—	12.4	12.8	12.9	13.5
Albania[b]	20.0	21.9	26.3	29.5	29.9	29.3	30.5	—	—
Bulgaria	30.7	29.9	29.4	29.3	29.6	31.3	31.7	31.4	30.6
Romania	3.8	11.6	16.4	17.8	18.4	19.3	19.8	20.4	20.6
Estonia	37.3	36.3	36.7	37.0	39.4	43.5	43.7	43.9	44.6
Latvia	22.1	21.2	20.3	20.3	24.7	26.7	28.7	30.3	32.4
Lithuania	34.7	34.2	32.8	30.6	30.4	32.9	34.8	38.6	39.5
Belarus	27.5	26.6	26.0	25.2	24.2	24.9	24.9	26.8	28.3
Moldova[d]	29.0	26.6	22.6	17.1	17.1	17.6	18.1	19.4	18.9
Russia	23.6	24.4	24.7	23.6	22.6	22.3	23.4	23.4	28.7
Ukraine	25.8	25.2	24.2	—	22.7	23.4	24.0	25.5	27.4
Armenia	35.9	34.3	32.5	31.3	31.2	30.7	29.1	29.6	30.4
Azerbaijan	33.3	33.5	34.5	32.8	28.9	27.0	25.8	28.1	32.2
Georgia[e f]	40.2	39.7	34.4	26.4	23.0	21.8	24.0	—	—
Kazakhstan	30.4	31.7	32.3	31.0	28.4	27.0	25.5	24.8	26.5
Kyrgyzstan	—	36.6	36.7	36.0	32.5	28.6	27.3	28.8	32.4
Tajikistan[b e]	41.5	40.7	37.7	29.7	26.8	25.3	23.6	22.3	22.5
Turkmenistan[e]	39.0	39.7	37.5	34.9	35.2	35.6	34.4	—	—
Uzbekistan[b e]	37.5	37.7	36.5	31.0	28.0	27.8	—	27.0	28.6

a. Typically, 2- to 4-year programmes. In countries w/2-year programmes, coverage may be underestimated.
b. ICDC estimates. Population data, 1989-92: US Census Bureau (1997), 1993-97: US Census Bureau (1998).
c. End of school year.
d. 1992-97: number of students excludes Transdniestr.
e. Enrolments: CIS Stat (1998a).
f. 1992-95: enrolments exclude Abkhazia and Tskhinvali.

7.4 Tertiary enrolments[a] (gross rates, percent of 18-22 population)

	1989	1990	1991	1992	1993	1994	1995	1996	1997
Czech Republic	12.7	13.6	13.1	13.3	13.6	14.2	15.0	16.6	17.3
Slovakia	13.2	13.8	13.3	14.2	14.4	15.0	15.6	16.8	17.6
Poland[b c]	11.6	12.4	13.0	14.3	15.7	17.0	18.1	19.7	20.6
Hungary[c]	13.9	14.2	14.8	15.7	16.8	18.5	20.7	22.9	23.8
Slovenia[d]	18.2	19.3	21.8	21.6	22.9	23.4	24.7	25.7	—
Croatia[e]	—	—	13.9	14.3	16.0	16.5	16.6	17.2	—
FYR Macedonia[e]	—	—	14.4	14.4	12.6	11.3	—	—	—
Bosnia-Herzegovina	—	—	—	—	—	—	—	—	—
FR Yugoslavia[f]	17.1	16.9	15.8	13.7	14.8	14.5	14.9	16.5	—
Albania[g]	4.8	5.8	6.0	5.9	5.2	4.6	—	—	—
Bulgaria[h]	16.4	18.8	18.7	19.8	20.9	23.0	26.0	27.3	27.1
Romania[i]	8.8	10.1	11.0	12.2	13.1	13.4	13.2	18.6	18.7
Estonia[c]	—	14.2	14.1	13.8	14.3	15.6	16.9	18.6	21.3
Latvia[c]	15.2	15.5	15.6	15.9	15.8	16.4	18.5	22.8	24.6
Lithuania[c]	17.7	17.2	15.6	13.7	13.3	13.1	13.9	15.4	18.2
Belarus[j]	16.5	16.7	16.6	17.0	16.1	17.3	17.8	18.7	19.5
Moldova[j]	11.6	11.7	11.4	10.8	10.3	10.8	11.9	12.5	13.5
Russia[j]	16.6	16.9	17.1	17.0	16.4	16.1	16.9	17.6	18.7
Ukraine[j]	15.3	15.3	15.2	15.1	14.5	16.0	16.8	17.9	20.1
Armenia[j]	16.5	17.0	16.8	15.0	12.3	10.2	13.2	11.5	—
Azerbaijan[j]	8.1	8.6	9.2	8.6	8.5	8.7	11.0	—	12.3
Georgia	14.3	16.4	15.7	13.4	12.7	13.7	12.1	13.6	14.4
Kazakhstan[j]	12.9	13.0	13.4	13.1	12.7	12.6	12.5	12.9	13.4
Kyrgyzstan[j]	10.9	10.8	10.4	9.7	9.7	10.8	11.8	12.9	15.2
Tajikistan[e j]	9.0	9.4	9.4	9.3	8.6	9.2	—	9.4	8.9
Turkmenistan[j]	8.1	8.0	7.9	7.4	7.4	—	7.3	—	—
Uzbekistan[e j]	9.1	9.5	9.4	8.7	7.4	6.3	5.4	5.0	5.0

a. ICDC calculations based on the number of full-time tertiary students unless otherwise noted.
b. Based on 19-24 age group.
c. 1997: preliminary estimates.
d. Excludes advanced degree programmes; includes part- and full-time students.
e. Population data, 1989-92: US Census Bureau (1997), 1993-97: US Census Bureau (1998).
f. 1992-97: number of students excludes ethnic Albanians in Kosovo.
g. Laporte and Ringold (1997).
h. Includes part- and full-time students. 19-25 age group.
i. 1996-97: includes students in private universities.
j. Enrolments: CIS Stat (1998a).

7.5 Women enrolled in tertiary education (percent of total number of students)

	1989	1990	1991	1992	1993	1994	1995	1996	1997
Czech Republic	44.4	45.9	46.5	49.2	48.2	43.6	45.0	41.8	44.7
Slovakia	45.7	46.9	47.1	46.8	47.2	47.5	47.3	47.3	47.7
Poland	51.3	50.2	50.3	51.5	53.3	54.9	56.0	56.6	56.6
Hungary	49.1	48.6	47.9	49.8	50.3	50.0	—	52.9	54.4
Slovenia	52.8	59.3	54.3	57.5	57.6	58.0	59.6	57.5	57.0
Croatia	50.1	50.8	50.8	51.1	51.4	52.9	53.6	54.8	—
FYR Macedonia	48.6	48.9	51.7	50.6	51.7	52.8	54.0	54.4	54.4
Bosnia-Herzegovina	49.8	51.0	52.9	51.7	51.2	50.6	52.3	43.4	51.5
FR Yugoslavia	47.5	48.3	52.4	53.8	55.1	55.3	54.8	55.1	55.5
Albania	51.3	51.3	51.9	50.6	53.2	52.7	53.8	56.6	55.8
Bulgaria	51.7	48.7	51.1	55.2	56.9	58.9	60.7	60.1	59.8
Romania[a]	48.3	47.2	46.0	46.7	46.6	47.1	67.4	49.9	49.9
Estonia	49.7	49.3	48.2	50.1	51.0	51.7	52.0	53.0	54.7
Latvia	—	—	—	—	53.7	55.8	57.4	59.5	54.7
Lithuania	53.3	51.9	52.7	53.1	55.2	54.7	56.2	56.3	57.7
Belarus	53.1	52.3	52.9	51.1	51.8	52.1	52.7	52.9	54.5
Moldova	—	—	55.5	53.9	55.4	54.9	54.7	54.8	55.0
Russia	51.9	50.5	50.4	50.5	51.5	52.9	54.3	55.2	55.7
Ukraine[b]	—	—	50.3	—	50.9	50.2	49.9	49.8	—
Armenia	46.4	45.9	47.6	48.7	52.1	50.2	51.1	55.5	50.4
Azerbaijan	41.7	37.9	35.5	38.4	41.9	43.6	43.8	42.3	41.0
Georgia	49.4	48.0	45.4	47.9	49.7	46.0	54.9	52.5	50.4
Kazakhstan[b]	—	—	51.2	51.5	51.6	52.6	52.9	52.2	—
Kyrgyzstan	53.6	51.2	53.6	53.5	54.4	51.9	52.0	51.3	50.7
Tajikistan[b]	—	—	33.6	31.0	28.0	27.5	—	25.8	—
Turkmenistan	42.4	41.4	40.0	38.2	38.2	37.2	36.4	36.2	35.1
Uzbekistan[b]	—	—	40.2	39.3	39.3	39.6	38.9	39.4	—

a. 1996-97: includes students in private universities.
b. CIS Stat (1998c).

7.6 Public expenditures on education[a] (percent of GDP)

	1989	1990	1991	1992	1993	1994	1995	1996	1997
Czech Republic	4.0	4.1	4.1	4.5	5.2	5.4	5.3	5.3	4.7
Slovakia	—	5.1	5.6	6.0	5.2	4.4	5.1	5.0	—
Poland	—	4.8	5.1	5.4	5.4	5.3	5.2	5.4	5.5
Hungary	5.7	5.8	6.3	6.6	6.5	6.4	5.5	4.9	4.3
Slovenia	—	—	4.8	5.5	5.8	5.5	5.8	5.8	—
Croatia	—	—	—	—	—	—	—	—	—
FYR Macedonia	—	5.9	6.8	5.4	6.0	5.7	5.7	5.9	5.4
Bosnia-Herzegovina	—	—	—	—	—	—	—	—	—
FR Yugoslavia	—	—	—	—	—	—	—	—	—
Albania[b]	4.0	4.2	5.0	4.2	3.3	3.2	3.8	3.2	—
Bulgaria	—	5.0	5.1	6.1	5.7	4.8	4.0	3.2	4.0
Romania[c]	2.2	2.8	3.6	3.6	3.3	3.1	3.4	3.5	—
Estonia	—	—	—	6.1	7.1	6.7	7.1	7.3	—
Latvia	5.8	4.8	4.2	4.6	6.1	6.1	6.9	5.8	5.8
Lithuania[d]	—	4.5	—	—	4.6	5.6	5.6	5.4	5.8
Belarus	—	—	4.6	5.3	6.0	5.8	5.5	6.1	6.6
Moldova	—	—	—	7.8	6.0	7.4	7.7	9.4	8.9
Russia[e]	—	3.7	3.6	3.6	4.0	4.5	3.6	3.8	4.2
Ukraine	—	—	—	—	—	—	—	—	—
Armenia	—	—	7.5	8.9	5.2	2.5	3.3	2.0	1.7
Azerbaijan	—	—	6.9	6.7	7.6	4.9	3.5	3.7	3.6
Georgia	—	6.1	6.4	4.0	0.6	0.5	0.9	1.2	1.3
Kazakhstan[f]	—	—	—	2.1	3.9	3.0	3.2	—	—
Kyrgyzstan	7.5	8.0	1.3	1.0	4.2	6.1	6.6	5.2	5.2
Tajikistan	—	—	—	—	—	—	—	—	—
Turkmenistan[c]	—	—	—	—	4.0	2.1	1.7	1.9	—
Uzbekistan	—	—	—	—	—	—	—	—	—

a. GDP data: EBRD (1998).
b. 1989-96: Laporte and Ringold (1997).
c. Current expenditures.
d. 1990: Mockiene, Klepaciene and Jackunas (1997).
e. 1990-91: UNESCO (1997).
f. 1992-95: ADB and UNESCO (1995).

8.1 Children in infant homes (per hundred thousand 0-3 population)

	1989	1990	1991	1992	1993	1994	1995	1996	1997
Czech Republic	533.0	509.0	492.0	460.5	455.8	466.7	498.7	517.7	533.2
Slovakia	191.7	170.7	170.5	206.2	215.3	238.3	240.2	272.6	—
Poland	179.7	190.9	196.9	193.5	193.2	—	—	—	—
Hungary	504.6	390.1	376.6	390.5	396.7	385.0	382.5	384.2	374.0
Slovenia	40.8	28.7	27.6	25.8	40.1	34.3	23.9	—	—
Croatia[a][b]	—	—	—	61.4	—	57.1	—	70.7	—
FYR Macedonia[a][b]	—		51.3	140.8	64.3	81.0	85.6	63.6	194.3
Bosnia-Herzegovina	—	—	—	—	—	—	—	—	—
FR Yugoslavia	—	48.2	—	43.8	—	52.6	—	73.0	—
Albania[b]	—	—	—	—	—	56.9	75.2	77.7	84.4
Bulgaria	873.8	861.8	863.7	923.4	1,009.9	1,084.2	1,089.0	1,205.8	1,263.1
Romania	—	597.1	604.5	653.8	750.3	1,074.0	887.7	938.9	944.3
Estonia[c]	149.9	148.9	154.5	168.4	181.2	185.8	213.1	244.4	261.4
Latvia	528.2	497.4	461.1	488.5	575.4	661.0	737.1	803.4	877.2
Lithuania	275.6	202.7	216.2	218.5	245.4	215.7	254.4	296.4	312.6
Belarus	169.4	164.7	162.6	168.6	184.2	205.9	223.6	241.6	287.0
Moldova[d]	183.5	175.0	182.0	172.2	182.1	198.1	195.8	217.7	248.3
Russia	203.8	203.5	209.2	226.2	250.7	278.8	306.0	346.1	334.1
Ukraine	—	—	—	—	160.9	177.5	200.1	223.0	—
Armenia[e]	13.2	11.6	10.8	13.2	12.5	13.9	15.3	17.9	—
Azerbaijan	35.5	34.3	32.8	26.3	27.0	27.5	25.2	25.1	28.3
Georgia	75.7	70.7	57.6	36.1	41.5	33.8	39.7	64.9	56.4
Kazakhstan	122.6	119.1	121.0	111.9	132.3	147.2	169.8	197.5	211.2
Kyrgyzstan	—	—	47.2	47.5	42.4	50.7	48.8	52.3	50.6
Tajikistan[a][b][f]	92.1	87.3	74.9	67.4	59.1	—	—	—	—
Turkmenistan	62.4	61.3	53.9	48.1	47.8	42.0	45.0	30.9	35.5
Uzbekistan[a][f]	180.8	183.7	173.5	179.3	—	—	—	—	—

a. Population data, 1989-92: US Census Bureau (1997).
b. Population data, 1993-97: US Census Bureau (1998).
c. 0- to 7-year-olds.
d. 1997: population data exclude Transdniestr.
e. 0- to 5-year-olds.
f. Number of children in infant homes: CIS Stat (1997).

8.2 Gross adoption rate (adoptions per hundred thousand 0-3 population)

	1989	1990	1991	1992	1993	1994	1995	1996	1997
Czech Republic	104.2	96.7	103.6	93.7	92.7	111.8	137.1	134.8	160.0
Slovakia	114.6	122.4	126.7	119.3	148.1	140.6	182.9	196.6	179.4
Poland	149.7	157.4	150.3	139.2	133.8	127.7	128.0	136.6	137.8
Hungary	198.4	195.3	206.9	188.0	183.1	190.5	201.0	227.6	208.7
Slovenia	153.3	135.1	149.8	131.2	121.6	161.8	93.2	101.3	74.4
Croatia[a][b]	—	—	47.2	54.9	106.0	150.8	88.0	92.3	80.0
FYR Macedonia[a][b]	—	—	204.4	166.4	159.3	153.0	140.1	164.6	156.7
Bosnia-Herzegovina	—	—	—	—	—	—	—	—	—
FR Yugoslavia	—	—	—	—	—	—	—	—	—
Albania[b]	—	—	—	—	—	22.6	28.6	39.9	21.6
Bulgaria	588.7	577.9	551.3	557.0	542.5	603.2	639.1	668.1	725.0
Romania	—	—	—	—	—	—	264.3	243.4	107.9
Estonia	—	—	—	309.9	418.0	417.0	436.6	471.1	422.3
Latvia	356.0	362.2	415.7	426.8	356.5	354.4	360.6	400.2	466.3
Lithuania	—	—	—	147.7	53.5	152.1	116.9	240.1	258.1
Belarus	—	—	—	—	45.7	65.3	55.7	57.4	48.5
Moldova[c]	—	—	—	—	—	109.2	131.9	134.7	148.2
Russia	129.9	141.1	152.5	178.6	215.6	252.4	225.5	213.9	263.4
Ukraine	217.2	201.1	235.6	243.3	269.0	327.9	341.3	231.3	—
Armenia	178.2	102.5	71.2	61.1	57.8	166.5	217.2	96.5	—
Azerbaijan	99.8	86.4	73.5	63.7	52.4	74.9	60.2	71.7	64.4
Georgia	—	—	—	—	—	—	—	45.3	—
Kazakhstan	—	—	—	—	—	—	—	—	—
Kyrgyzstan	—	—	—	—	—	—	—	—	—
Tajikistan	—	—	—	—	—	—	—	—	—
Turkmenistan	—	—	—	—	—	—	—	—	—
Uzbekistan	—	—	—	—	—	—	—	—	—

a. Population data, 1991-92: US Census Bureau (1997).
b. Population data, 1993-97: US Census Bureau (1998).
c. 1997: population data exclude Transdniestr.

9.1 Registered total crime rate (per hundred thousand population)

	1989	1990	1991	1992	1993	1994	1995	1996	1997
Czech Republic	1,166	2,099	2,745	3,345	3,858	3,604	3,637	3,822	3,917
Slovakia	879	1,323	1,668	1,980	2,744	2,576	2,137	1,850	1,716
Poland	1,442	2,318	2,265	2,297	2,217	2,351	2,526	2,324	2,568
Hungary	2,150	3,291	4,256	4,332	3,895	3,795	4,908	4,572	5,066
Slovenia	2,002	1,919	2,113	2,709	2,223	2,193	1,919	1,840	1,872
Croatia[a]	1,185	1,123	971	1,325	1,547	1,191	1,034	1,066	926
FYR Macedonia[b]	—	—	797	1,224	1,174	1,204	1,178	1,264	1,102
Bosnia-Herzegovina[c]	48	39	—	—	11	12	18	26	30
FR Yugoslavia	1,175	1,144	1,174	1,293	1,656	1,512	1,268	1,238	1,202
Albania[d]	—	—	—	—	—	—	—	160	194
Bulgaria	672	772	2,062	2,630	2,599	2,639	2,452	2,337	2,896
Romania	208	422	606	635	964	1,043	1,309	1,422	1,601
Estonia	1,220	1,515	2,027	2,671	2,450	2,384	2,667	2,410	2,810
Latvia	1,112	1,299	1,575	2,351	2,043	1,609	1,556	1,534	1,493
Lithuania	846	995	1,202	1,513	1,619	1,576	1,637	1,835	2,046
Belarus	653	741	796	941	1,002	1,167	1,282	1,241	1,257
Moldova[e]	940	986	1,021	901	853	858	885	805	1,002
Russia	1,099	1,244	1,466	1,861	1,890	1,779	1,865	1,781	1,632
Ukraine	626	716	784	926	1,039	1,107	1,252	1,214	1,168
Armenia[f]	241	342	363	441	350	265	270	331	326
Azerbaijan	212	217	218	309	247	251	268	234	218
Georgia[g]	326	364	518	447	409	328	293	269	258
Kazakhstan	833	906	1,057	1,216	1,250	1,238	1,145	1,156	1,032
Kyrgyzstan	595	680	725	985	955	927	915	872	809
Tajikistan[h]	316	317	337	452	433	248	250	228	222
Turkmenistan	483	509	514	466	398	351	331	324	313
Uzbekistan[h]	420	427	419	433	409	328	294	285	285

a. Population data, 1989-90: CBSC (1996), 1991-92: US Census Bureau (1997), 1993-97: US Census Bureau (1998).

b. Population data, 1991-92: US Census Bureau (1997), 1993-97: US Census Bureau (1998).

c. 1993-97: for crime data Federation of B-H only, for population data US Census Bureau (1998).

d. Population data: US Census Bureau (1998).

e. 1992-97: crime data exclude Transdniestr. 1997: population data exclude Transdniestr.

f. Crime data, 1997: CIS Stat (1998a).

g. Crime data, 1989: CIS Stat (1998a).

h. Crime data, CIS Stat (1998a). Population data: 1989-92: US Census Bureau (1997), 1993-97: US Census Bureau (1998).

9.2 Total sentencing rate (per hundred thousand population)

	1989	1990	1991	1992	1993	1994	1995	1996	1997
Czech Republic	557	183	271	301	340	503	532	562	580
Slovakia	581	258	433	446	482	476	482	492	416
Poland[a]	—	384	—	528	562	624	710	733	—
Hungary	617	460	635	751	724	763	838	817	867
Slovenia	696	552	473	441	404	376	233	258	310
Croatia[b]	859	934	665	520	602	581	482	542	511
FYR Macedonia[c]	—	—	415	395	406	425	452	373	—
Bosnia-Herzegovina	—	—	—	—	—	—	—	—	—
FR Yugoslavia	475	428	365	317	368	371	398	398	416
Albania	—	—	—	—	—	—	—	—	—
Bulgaria[d]	186	116	125	114	76	103	127	179	239
Romania	255	160	265	303	366	421	448	460	496
Estonia	208	225	252	326	414	485	540	579	621
Latvia	278	268	277	346	436	443	389	419	517
Lithuania	204	211	244	349	437	470	494	458	488
Belarus[e]	238	292	321	357	462	518	572	604	566
Moldova[f]	218	239	275	273	305	350	336	313	349
Russia[g]	297	363	401	446	535	625	701	754	690
Ukraine[e]	175	202	210	222	294	339	415	476	471
Armenia[g]	126	110	122	136	172	188	167	179	187
Azerbaijan	100	99	107	97	147	165	187	171	168
Georgia[h]	156	138	122	69	130	154	132	157	142
Kazakhstan	249	296	345	402	530	553	579	534	550
Kyrgyzstan[i]	160	197	201	245	337	323	393	386	426
Tajikistan[h,j]	99	108	113	80	108	126	110	—	—
Turkmenistan[k]	155	178	200	203	—	—	—	—	—
Uzbekistan[h,l]	135	156	180	192	—	—	—	—	—

a. Adults sentenced by courts of first instance: GUS (1994), (1997).

b. Population data, 1989-90: CBSC (1996), 1991-92: US Census Bureau (1997), 1993-97: US Census Bureau (1998).

c. Population data, 1991-92: US Census Bureau (1997), 1993-96: US Census Bureau (1998).

d. Excludes white-collar crime.

e. Crime data, 1989: CIS Stat (1998a).

f. 1992-97: crime data exclude Transdniestr. 1997: population data exclude Transdniestr.

g. Crime data, 1997: CIS Stat (1998a).

h. Crime data, 1989-96: CIS Stat (1998a).

i. Crime data, 1989-90: CIS Stat (1998a).

j. Population data, 1989-92: US Census Bureau (1997), 1993-95: US Census Bureau (1998).

k. Convictions.

l. Population data, 1989-92: US Census Bureau (1997).

10.1 Real GDP growth[a] (index, 1989 = 100)

	1989	1990	1991	1992	1993	1994	1995	1996	1997	1998
Czech Republic[b]	100.0	98.8	87.5	84.6	85.1	87.8	93.4	97.0	98.0	97.0
Slovakia	100.0	97.5	83.3	77.9	75.0	78.6	84.1	89.6	95.4	100.2
Poland	100.0	88.4	82.2	84.3	87.6	92.1	98.6	104.6	111.8	117.6
Hungary	100.0	96.5	85.0	82.4	81.9	84.3	85.5	86.6	90.4	94.6
Slovenia	100.0	95.3	86.8	82.0	84.3	88.8	92.5	95.3	98.9	102.9
Croatia	100.0	92.9	73.3	64.7	59.5	63.1	67.3	71.4	76.0	79.2
FYR Macedonia	100.0	90.1	79.2	62.5	56.8	55.8	55.1	55.5	56.4	59.2
Bosnia-Herzegovina	—	—	—	—	—	—	—	—	—	—
FR Yugoslavia[c]	100.0	92.1	81.4	58.7	40.6	41.7	44.2	46.8	50.3	—
Albania	100.0	90.0	65.1	60.4	66.2	72.4	78.8	86.0	80.0	87.2
Bulgaria[d]	100.0	90.9	80.3	74.4	73.3	74.6	76.2	67.9	63.2	65.7
Romania	100.0	94.4	82.2	75.0	76.1	79.1	84.7	88.0	82.2	78.1
Estonia	100.0	91.9	79.4	68.1	62.0	60.8	63.4	65.9	73.4	77.1
Latvia	100.0	102.9	92.2	60.0	51.1	51.5	51.0	52.7	56.2	58.4
Lithuania	100.0	95.0	89.6	70.5	59.1	53.3	55.1	57.6	60.9	62.8
Belarus	100.0	97.0	95.8	86.6	80.1	70.0	62.7	64.4	71.1	74.7
Moldova	100.0	97.6	80.5	57.1	56.4	38.8	37.6	34.6	35.1	34.4
Russia[e]	100.0	97.0	92.2	78.8	71.9	62.8	60.2	58.1	58.6	55.7
Ukraine	100.0	96.6	85.4	73.7	63.2	48.7	42.7	38.5	37.2	37.2
Armenia[e]	100.0	94.5	78.3	37.1	31.6	33.3	35.6	37.7	38.9	41.2
Azerbaijan	100.0	100.0	99.3	76.9	59.1	47.5	41.9	42.4	44.9	47.9
Georgia[e]	100.0	84.9	67.4	37.2	27.8	24.6	25.2	27.8	30.9	33.7
Kazakhstan	100.0	99.6	86.7	84.1	76.4	66.8	61.3	61.6	62.8	63.5
Kyrgyzstan	100.0	103.0	97.9	79.3	66.6	53.3	50.4	54.0	57.5	59.8
Tajikistan	100.0	98.4	91.4	64.9	57.8	46.8	41.0	39.2	39.9	41.0
Turkmenistan	100.0	102.0	97.2	92.1	82.8	67.3	61.8	56.8	42.0	44.1
Uzbekistan	100.0	101.6	101.1	89.9	87.8	84.1	83.4	84.7	86.7	88.5

a. EBRD (1998). 1997: estimates. 1998: projections.
b. 1990-93: in constant 1984 prices.
c. UNECE (1998).
d. 1989-93: includes holding gain.
e. 1990 (which refers to net material product): UNECE (1998).

10.2 Annual percent change in GDP[a]

	1989	1990	1991	1992	1993	1994	1995	1996	1997	1998
Czech Republic[b]	4.5	-1.2	-11.5	-3.3	0.6	3.2	6.4	3.9	1.0	-1.0
Slovakia	1.0	-2.5	-14.6	-6.5	-3.7	4.9	6.9	6.6	6.5	5.0
Poland	0.2	-11.6	-7.0	2.6	3.8	5.2	7.0	6.1	6.9	5.2
Hungary	0.7	-3.5	-11.9	-3.1	-0.6	2.9	1.5	1.3	4.4	4.6
Slovenia	-0.5	-4.7	-8.9	-5.5	2.8	5.3	4.1	3.1	3.8	4.0
Croatia[c]	-1.6	-7.1	-21.1	-11.7	-8.0	5.9	6.8	6.0	6.5	4.2
FYR Macedonia	1.9	-9.9	-12.1	-21.1	-9.1	-1.8	-1.2	0.8	1.5	5.0
Bosnia-Herzegovina	—	—	-20.0	—	—	—	32.0	45.8	38.5	30.0
FR Yugoslavia[d]	1.2	-7.9	-11.6	-27.9	-30.8	2.7	6.0	5.9	7.5	—
Albania	9.9	-10.0	-27.7	-7.2	9.6	9.4	8.9	9.1	-7.0	9.0
Bulgaria[e]	-1.9	-9.1	-11.7	-7.3	-1.5	1.8	2.1	-10.9	-6.9	4.0
Romania	-5.8	-5.6	-12.9	-8.8	1.5	3.9	7.1	3.9	-6.6	-5.0
Estonia	6.6	-8.1	-13.6	-14.2	-9.0	-2.0	4.3	4.0	11.4	5.0
Latvia	7.4	2.9	-10.4	-34.9	-14.9	0.6	-0.8	3.3	6.5	4.0
Lithuania	1.6	-5.0	-5.7	-21.3	-16.2	-9.8	3.3	4.7	5.7	3.0
Belarus[f]	8.2	-3.0	-1.2	-9.6	-7.6	-12.6	-10.4	2.8	10.4	5.0
Moldova[f]	8.8	-2.4	-17.5	-29.1	-1.2	-31.2	-3.0	-8.0	1.3	-2.0
Russia[g]	1.6	-3.0	-5.0	-14.5	-8.7	-12.7	-4.1	-3.5	0.8	-5.0
Ukraine[f]	5.0	-3.4	-11.6	-13.7	-14.2	-23.0	-12.2	-10.0	-3.2	0.0
Armenia[g]	8.4	-5.5	-17.1	-52.6	-14.8	5.4	6.9	5.8	3.1	6.0
Azerbaijan[f]	-8.8	0.0	-0.7	-22.6	-23.1	-19.7	-11.8	1.3	5.8	6.7
Georgia[g]	-3.5	-15.1	-20.6	-44.8	-25.4	-11.4	2.4	10.5	11.0	9.0
Kazakhstan[f]	-0.1	-0.4	-13.0	-2.9	-9.2	-12.6	-8.2	0.5	2.0	1.0
Kyrgyzstan[f]	4.6	3.0	-5.0	-19.0	-16.0	-20.0	-5.4	7.1	6.5	4.0
Tajikistan[f]	-6.4	-1.6	-7.1	-29.0	-11.0	-18.9	-12.5	-4.4	1.7	3.0
Turkmenistan[f]	-7.0	2.0	-4.7	-5.3	-10.0	-18.8	-8.2	-8.0	-26.0	5.0
Uzbekistan[f]	3.1	1.6	-0.5	-11.1	-2.3	-4.2	-0.9	1.6	2.4	2.0

a. 1989: UNECE (1998). 1990-98: EBRD (1998). 1997: estimates. 1998: projections.
b. 1990-93: in constant 1984 prices.
c. 1989: gross material product.
d. 1989-97: UNECE (1998).
e. 1989-93: includes holding gain.
f. 1989: net material product.
g. 1989-90 (which refer to net material product): UNECE (1998).

10.3 Share of the agricultural sector in GDP[a] (percent)

	1989	1990	1991	1992	1993	1994	1995	1996	1997
Czech Republic[b]	9.9	8.4	6.0	6.1	6.5	3.8	5.3	5.1	4.8
Slovakia[b]	9.9	—	—	6.2	6.6	7.4	5.6	5.2	4.8
Poland	12.9	7.4	6.8	6.7	6.6	6.2	6.4	6.0	—
Hungary	13.7	—	8.5	7.2	6.6	6.7	7.2	—	—
Slovenia	4.4	4.7	5.2	5.2	4.5	4.0	3.9	3.9	3.9
Croatia[c]	—	9.7	9.7	13.5	12.8	10.4	10.0	—	—
FYR Macedonia[d]	—	10.3	—	14.4	9.8	10.4	10.7	11.0	10.8
Bosnia-Herzegovina	—	—	—	—	—	—	—	—	—
FR Yugoslavia	—	—	—	—	—	—	—	—	—
Albania	32.4	37.0	42.5	54.2	54.6	55.1	55.9	55.4	62.6
Bulgaria[e f]	10.9	17.7	14.3	11.7	10.3	12.0	13.1	14.6	25.9
Romania	13.9	21.8	18.9	19.0	21.0	19.8	19.9	19.1	18.8
Estonia	—	—	—	12.6	9.8	9.0	7.1	6.8	6.3
Latvia[g]	—	21.1	21.9	17.2	11.7	9.4	10.4	8.7	7.2
Lithuania	—	27.1	16.7	14.3	14.9	11.0	11.9	12.4	12.8
Belarus	—	—	—	23.8	18.3	15.0	17.7	15.9	15.0
Moldova	—	—	—	—	32.0	29.0	33.0	31.0	30.0
Russia	—	—	—	13.4	8.5	6.8	9.6	9.8	9.7
Ukraine	—	24.4	24.4	20.3	21.6	16.0	14.9	6.7	6.0
Armenia[e h]	14.4	17.3	23.6	28.4	49.1	43.5	38.7	33.0	30.1
Azerbaijan	—	26.0	30.4	25.9	26.9	32.2	25.1	24.7	20.0
Georgia	—	—	—	54.5	67.7	28.7	38.0	31.0	28.2
Kazakhstan	—	28.1	29.0	30.4	16.4	14.9	12.3	12.0	10.8
Kyrgyzstan	—	32.0	35.3	37.3	39.0	38.3	40.6	46.6	43.4
Tajikistan[i]	—	—	26.1	27.1	21.0	19.0	15.3	27.7	27.6
Turkmenistan	—	—	46.0	19.0	11.5	9.0	30.3	17.5	19.8
Uzbekistan	—	33.4	37.3	35.4	31.0	38.0	32.0	26.0	29.0

a. 1989: UNECE (1998). 1990-97: EBRD (1998). 1997: estimates.
b. 1989: Czechoslovakia.
c. Includes fishing.
d. According to the concept in former Yugoslavia, whereby the value added by governmental, financial and some personal services is excluded.
e. 1989-90: UNECE (1993).
f. 1995-97: reflects a new industrial classification.
g. In percent of gross value added at current prices.
h. 1991-92: UNICEF (1998).
i. Based on current prices. Variations in shares thus reflect, inter alia, changes in relative prices. 1997: based on January-September 1997 GDP figures.

10.4 Foreign direct investment[a] (net, US$ millions)

	1990	1991	1992	1993	1994	1995	1996	1997	1998
Czech Republic[b]	132.0	513.0	982.9	552.2	748.9	2,525.6	1,387.9	1,275.2	—
Slovakia	24.1	82.0	100.0	106.5	236.3	194.0	199.0	50.7	220.0
Poland[c]	0.0	100.0	300.0	600.0	500.0	1,100.0	2,768.0	3,041.0	4,000.0
Hungary	311.0	1,459.0	1,471.0	2,339.0	1,146.0	4,453.0	1,983.0	2,085.0	1,500.0
Slovenia[d]	0.0	41.3	112.9	111.3	128.1	176.0	185.5	320.8	200.0
Croatia	—	—	13.0	76.6	94.7	82.6	509.0	196.1	450.0
FYR Macedonia	—	—	0.0	0.0	24.0	13.0	12.0	30.0	45.0
Bosnia-Herzegovina	—	—	—	—	—	—	—	—	—
FR Yugoslavia	—	—	—	—	—	—	—	—	—
Albania	—	8.0	32.0	45.0	65.0	89.0	97.0	42.0	95.0
Bulgaria[e]	4.0	56.0	42.0	40.0	105.4	82.0	100.0	497.0	300.0
Romania	18.0	37.0	73.0	97.0	341.0	417.0	263.0	1,224.0	900.0
Estonia[f]	—	—	58.0	157.0	215.0	199.0	110.5	128.0	200.0
Latvia	—	—	43.0	51.0	155.0	244.0	376.0	515.0	344.0
Lithuania[f g]	—	—	43.0	30.2	31.3	71.6	152.3	327.5	800.0
Belarus	—	—	—	18.0	10.5	6.7	69.5	189.7	50.0
Moldova	—	—	17.4	14.0	18.0	73.0	56.0	63.9	100.0
Russia[h]	-400.0	-100.0	700.0	900.0	539.0	1,710.0	1,700.0	3,752.0	1,500.0
Ukraine	—	—	200.0	200.0	100.0	400.0	526.0	600.0	700.0
Armenia	—	—	—	—	2.6	19.1	22.0	51.0	170.0
Azerbaijan[i]	—	—	—	20.0	22.0	282.0	661.0	1,093.0	1,155.0
Georgia	—	—	—	—	8.0	6.0	54.4	189.1	255.0
Kazakhstan	—	—	—	473.0	635.0	964.0	1,137.0	1,320.0	1,200.0
Kyrgyzstan	—	—	—	10.0	44.9	96.1	46.3	83.0	29.0
Tajikistan	—	—	—	9.0	12.0	17.0	20.0	11.0	18.0
Turkmenistan	—	—	—	79.0	103.0	233.0	129.0	108.0	110.0
Uzbekistan	—	—	9.0	48.0	73.0	-24.0	90.0	167.0	60.0

a. EBRD (1998). 1997: estimates. 1998: projections.
b. 1990-91 (which refer only to inflow): UNECE (1998).
c. Balance of payments data based on banking statistics and presented on a settlement basis.
d. Balance of payments data.
e. 1990 (which refers only to inflow): UNECE (1998).
f. 1992 (which refers only to inflow): UNECE (1998).
g. 1993-94: only investment in equity capital. 1995-96: equity capital and reinvested earnings.
h. 1990-93: UNECE (1998).
i. Includes portfolio investment and oil bonus payments to government.

10.5 General government balance[a] (as percent of GDP)

	1990	1991	1992	1993	1994	1995	1996	1997	1998
Czech Republic[b c]	-0.2	-1.9	-3.1	0.5	-1.2	-1.8	-1.2	-2.1	-2.4
Slovakia[b]	—	—	—	-7.0	-1.3	0.2	-1.9	-3.8	-4.0
Poland[b c]	3.1	-6.7	-6.7	-3.1	-3.1	-2.8	-3.3	-3.1	-3.1
Hungary[b]	0.3	-2.9	-6.8	-5.5	-8.4	-6.7	-3.1	-4.9	-4.9
Slovenia[b]	-0.3	2.6	0.2	0.3	-0.2	0.0	0.3	-1.1	-1.0
Croatia[d]	—	—	-3.9	-0.8	1.6	-0.9	-0.4	-1.3	-0.5
FYR Macedonia[b]	—	—	-9.6	-13.8	-2.9	-1.2	-0.5	-0.4	-0.8
Bosnia-Herzegovina[e]	—	—	—	—	-10.6	-0.3	-3.7	-1.2	-1.9
FR Yugoslavia	—	—	—	—	—	—	—	—	—
Albania[b f]	-15.0	-31.0	-20.3	-14.4	-12.4	-10.3	-12.1	-12.7	-13.9
Bulgaria[b]	-	-	-5.2	-10.9	-5.8	-5.6	-10.4	-2.1	-2.0
Romania[b]	1.0	3.3	-4.6	-0.4	-1.9	-2.6	-4.0	-3.6	-5.5
Estonia[b]	—	5.2	-0.3	-0.7	1.3	-1.3	-1.5	2.2	2.5
Latvia[b]	—	—	-0.8	0.6	-4.1	-3.5	-1.4	1.4	1.0
Lithuania[b]	-5.4	2.7	0.5	-3.3	-5.5	-4.5	-4.5	-1.8	-3.6
Belarus[b g]	—	—	0.0	-1.9	-2.5	-1.9	-1.6	-2.1	-3.0
Moldova[b]	—	0.0	-26.2	-7.4	-8.7	-5.7	-6.7	-7.5	-8.0
Russia[h]	—	—	-4.1	-7.4	-9.0	-5.7	-8.3	-7.4	-8.0
Ukraine[b i]	—	—	-25.4	-16.2	-9.1	-7.1	-3.2	-5.6	-3.0
Armenia[j]	—	-1.9	-13.9	-54.7	-10.5	-11.0	-9.3	-6.3	-5.8
Azerbaijan[b]	—	—	—	-15.3	-12.1	-4.9	-2.8	-1.7	-3.6
Georgia[b]	—	-3.0	-25.4	-26.2	-7.4	-4.5	-4.4	-3.8	-2.5
Kazakhstan[b k]	1.4	-7.9	-7.3	-1.4	-7.2	-2.5	-3.1	-3.7	-5.5
Kyrgyzstan[b l]	0.3	—	—	—	—	-17.0	-9.0	-9.4	-8.1
Tajikistan[m]	—	-16.4	-28.4	-23.6	-10.2	-11.2	-5.8	-3.3	-3.3
Turkmenistan[n]	1.2	2.5	13.2	-0.5	-1.4	-1.6	-0.2	0.0	-4.0
Uzbekistan[o]	-1.1	-3.6	-18.4	-10.4	-6.1	-4.1	-7.3	-2.3	-3.0

a. EBRD (1998). 1997: estimates. 1998: projections.
b. Includes state, municipalities, extrabudgetary funds.
c. Excludes privatization revenues.
d. Consolidated central government.
e. Consolidated government balance. For Republika Srpska, excludes municipal governments. 1996-98: excludes external grants for military expenditures; no net financing of budget deficits other than arrears.
f. On a commitment basis.
g. Excludes presidential fund.
h. General consolidated government, including federal, regional and local budgets and extrabudgetary funds and excluding transfers.
i. 1994-98: excluding pension fund.
j. Consolidated accounts of republican government and local authorities.
k. Includes privatization revenues.
l. Includes expenditures through the foreign-financed public investment programme.
m. Central government, excluding state budget transfers to pension and employment funds.
n. Includes state, municipalities, some extrabudgetary funds. Until 1997, some off-budget funds were in operation.
o. Consolidated central government. Includes extrabudgetary funds.

10.6 General government expenditure[a] (as percent of GDP)

	1990	1991	1992	1993	1994	1995	1996	1997
Czech Republic	—	—	—	41.9	43.3	42.8	41.8	41.6
Slovakia	—	—	—	51.2	47.8	46.7	49.3	51.0
Poland[b]	39.8	49.0	49.5	50.5	48.9	47.9	47.5	48.1
Hungary	53.5	55.4	59.4	60.6	60.9	53.9	48.3	52.9
Slovenia	49.6	41.1	45.6	46.7	46.1	45.7	44.9	45.7
Croatia	—	—	36.1	35.0	40.6	44.9	45.6	46.1
FYR Macedonia	—	—	48.2	55.3	50.5	43.1	41.5	39.4
Bosnia-Herzegovina[c]	—	—	—	—	28.1	34.0	43.4	32.6
FR Yugoslavia	—	—	—	—	—	—	—	—
Albania	62.1	61.9	44.0	34.9	31.2	30.8	29.0	27.6
Bulgaria	65.9	45.6	43.6	48.1	45.7	41.3	42.3	33.4
Romania	38.7	38.7	42.0	34.2	33.9	34.5	34.1	34.3
Estonia	—	—	34.9	40.3	39.2	41.4	40.5	37.4
Latvia	—	—	28.2	35.2	38.2	38.2	38.0	38.2
Lithuania[b]	49.1	38.7	31.5	35.1	38.5	36.8	34.1	34.7
Belarus	—	—	46.0	56.2	50.0	44.6	42.6	46.8
Moldova	—	24.7	56.6	29.4	40.6	39.7	38.7	41.8
Russia	—	—	37.2	40.7	45.9	37.0	40.1	40.7
Ukraine	—	—	58.4	54.5	45.8	37.4	31.6	34.8
Armenia	—	28.0	46.7	82.9	42.9	26.6	23.7	24.5
Azerbaijan	—	—	—	55.9	45.9	22.4	20.4	21.4
Georgia	—	33.0	35.7	35.9	23.5	11.6	14.1	14.4
Kazakhstan	31.4	32.9	31.8	25.2	25.9	19.9	18.6	20.3
Kyrgyzstan[b]	38.3	—	—	—	—	33.7	24.9	26.3
Tajikistan[d]	—	49.6	55.0	50.7	54.8	26.5	17.9	17.0
Turkmenistan	43.6	38.2	42.2	19.2	10.4	12.5	16.9	29.2
Uzbekistan[e]	46.1	52.7	43.4	46.4	35.3	38.7	41.6	32.8

a. EBRD (1998). 1997: estimates.
b. Includes net lending.
c. Consolidated government expenditure.
d. Central government expenditure.
e. Consolidated central government expenditure.

10.7 Annual inflation rate[a] (annual average percent change in consumer prices)

	1990	1991	1992	1993	1994	1995	1996	1997	1998
Czech Republic	9.6	56.6	11.1	20.8	10.0	9.1	8.8	8.5	11.0
Slovakia	10.8	61.2	10.1	23.2	13.4	9.9	5.8	6.1	7.5
Poland	585.8	70.3	43.0	35.3	32.2	27.8	19.9	14.9	11.0
Hungary	28.9	35.0	23.0	22.5	18.8	28.2	23.6	18.3	15.0
Slovenia[b]	549.7	117.7	207.3	32.9	21.0	13.5	9.9	8.4	8.5
Croatia[c]	609.5	123.0	665.5	1,517.5	97.6	2.0	3.5	3.6	5.8
FYR Macedonia[c]	608.4	114.9	1,690.7	338.4	126.5	16.4	2.5	1.3	1.3
Bosnia-Herzegovina[c d]	—	114.0	73,109.0	44,069.0	780.0	-4.4	-24.5	13.4	5.0
FR Yugoslavia[e]	580.0	122.0	8,926.0	2.2X10^{14}	7.9X10^{10}	71.8	90.5	23.2	—
Albania[f]	0.0	35.5	226.0	85.0	22.6	7.8	12.7	32.1	21.9
Bulgaria	26.3	333.5	82.0	73.0	96.3	62.0	123.0	1,082.0	25.0
Romania	5.1	161.1	210.4	256.1	136.7	32.3	38.8	154.8	60.0
Estonia	23.1	210.5	1,076.0	89.8	48.0	29.0	23.0	11.0	11.0
Latvia	10.5	172.0	951.2	108.0	36.0	25.0	17.6	8.4	5.3
Lithuania	8.4	224.7	1,020.5	410.4	72.1	39.5	24.7	8.9	5.5
Belarus[g]	5.5	98.6	969.0	1,188.0	2,200.0	709.3	53.0	63.9	50.0
Moldova	4.2	98.0	1,276.4	788.5	329.7	30.2	23.5	11.8	13.0
Russia[h]	5.3	92.7	1,526.0	875.0	311.4	197.7	47.8	14.7	40.0
Ukraine	4.2	91.0	1,210.0	4,735.0	891.0	376.0	80.0	16.0	11.0
Armenia[i]	6.9	174.1	728.7	3,500.0	5,273.4	176.7	18.7	14.0	11.0
Azerbaijan	7.8	107.0	912.0	1,129.0	1,664.0	411.7	19.7	3.5	0.9
Georgia[h]	4.2	79.0	887.4	3,125.4	15,606.5	162.7	39.4	7.3	4.0
Kazakhstan[h]	5.6	78.8	1,381.0	1,662.3	1,892.0	176.3	39.1	17.4	10.0
Kyrgyzstan[h]	5.5	85.0	855.0	772.4	228.7	52.5	30.4	25.5	12.0
Tajikistan	4.0	112.0	1,157.0	2,195.0	350.0	609.0	418.0	87.8	46.3
Turkmenistan	4.6	103.0	493.0	3,102.0	1,748.0	1,005.0	992.0	83.7	19.0
Uzbekistan	3.1	82.2	645.0	534.0	1,568.0	305.0	54.0	72.0	40.0

a. EBRD (1998). 1997: estimates. 1998: projections.
b. 1990-91: retail prices.
c. Retail prices.
d. Federation of B-H. Republika Srpska (based on Yugoslav dinar): 1991: 114, 1992: 7,461, 1993: 2.2X10^{15}, 1994: 1,061, 1995: 117.6, 1996: 65.9, 1997: 2.7, 1998: 10.0.
e. 1990-97: UNECE (1998).
f. 1997: where data collection was possible.
g. 1990-91: UNECE (1998).
h. 1990: UNECE (1998).
i. 1990-92: UNECE (1998).

10.8 Real wages[a] (base year = 100)

	1989	1990	1991	1992	1993	1994	1995	1996	1997
Czech Republic[b]	100.0	93.6	68.9	76.0	78.8	84.9	92.2	100.4	102.3
Slovakia[b]	100.0	94.2	67.3	72.6	69.2	71.4	75.3	81.9	87.4
Poland[c]	100.0	75.6	75.4	73.3	71.2	71.6	73.7	77.9	82.4
Hungary[c]	100.0	94.3	87.7	86.5	83.1	89.1	78.2	74.3	77.1
Slovenia[d]	100.0	73.8	61.8	61.3	70.4	75.4	79.4	83.1	85.4
Croatia	—	—	—	—	—	—	100.0	108.0	117.9
FYR Macedonia	—	—	—	—	—	—	—	—	—
Bosnia-Herzegovina	—	—	—	—	—	—	—	—	—
FR Yugoslavia[e]	100.0	78.1	74.0	38.0	—	—	—	—	—
Albania	—	—	—	—	—	—	—	—	—
Bulgaria[b f]	100.0	111.5	68.0	76.7	77.6	63.7	60.2	49.6	40.1
Romania[d]	100.0	105.2	88.9	77.3	64.4	64.6	72.7	79.8	62.3
Estonia[b]	100.0	102.5	68.2	45.2	46.3	50.9	54.0	55.2	59.5
Latvia[g]	100.0	105.0	71.9	49.0	51.8	57.9	57.7	54.1	60.7
Lithuania[d]	100.0	108.8	75.3	46.6	28.4	32.5	33.5	34.8	39.7
Belarus[b]	—	—	—	—	100.0	60.6	57.6	60.5	69.1
Moldova[b]	100.0	113.7	105.2	64.4	41.8	33.8	34.3	36.3	38.2
Russia[b]	100.0	109.1	102.4	68.9	69.1	63.7	45.9	52.0	54.5
Ukraine	—	—	—	—	—	—	—	—	—
Armenia	—	—	—	—	—	—	—	100.0	96.1
Azerbaijan[f]	100.0	101.1	80.0	95.0	62.4	24.8	19.8	22.5	34.4
Georgia[b]	100.0	111.2	76.5	50.5	24.1	33.5	28.3	42.2	57.0
Kazakhstan[b]	—	—	100.0	64.8	49.1	32.9	33.4	34.4	36.6
Kyrgyzstan[b]	—	100.0	70.7	59.4	49.6	42.0	43.5	44.5	49.1
Tajikistan	—	—	—	—	—	—	—	—	—
Turkmenistan	—	—	—	—	100.0	52.9	24.8	20.2	30.9
Uzbekistan	—	—	—	—	—	—	—	—	—

a. Based on consumer price index. EBRD (1998).
b. Based on gross wages.
c. Real net index calculated by central statistical office.
d. Net wages.
e. FSOY (1996).
f. Public sector only.
g. 1990-93: gross wages. 1994-96: net wages. 1990-96: CSBL (1997).

10.9 Employment growth (1989 = 100)

	1989	1990	1991	1992	1993	1994	1995	1996	1997
Czech Republic[a]	100.0	99.2	90.0	87.7	87.9	88.5	90.9	92.0	—
Slovakia[a]	100.0	97.4	85.9	86.8	84.6	83.7	85.7	84.5	—
Poland[b]	100.0	95.8	90.1	86.3	84.3	85.1	86.7	88.3	93.3
Hungary[c]	100.0	99.3	96.0	86.1	77.7	73.7	72.1	71.1	70.8
Slovenia[b d]	100.0	96.1	88.7	83.8	81.3	79.3	79.1	78.7	78.1
Croatia	100.0	97.1	89.2	79.3	76.6	74.8	73.9	73.9	73.4
FYR Macedonia	100.0	98.5	95.6	91.2	86.2	81.7	73.9	70.6	66.8
Bosnia-Herzegovina	—	—	—	—	—	—	—	—	—
FR Yugoslavia	100.0	97.0	94.1	90.9	88.3	86.5	85.3	84.8	83.6
Albania	100.0	99.3	97.5	76.1	72.7	80.7	79.0	77.5	76.9
Bulgaria	100.0	93.9	81.6	75.0	73.8	74.3	75.2	75.3	73.3
Romania[a d]	100.0	99.0	98.5	95.5	91.9	91.5	86.7	85.7	—
Estonia	100.0	98.6	96.4	91.4	84.5	82.7	78.3	77.0	75.6
Latvia[e]	100.0	100.1	99.3	92.0	85.6	77.0	74.3	72.4	73.7
Lithuania	100.0	97.3	99.7	97.5	93.4	88.0	86.4	87.2	87.7
Belarus	100.0	99.1	96.6	94.1	92.8	90.4	84.8	83.9	84.0
Moldova[f]	100.0	99.0	99.0	98.0	80.7	80.4	80.0	79.4	79.1
Russia[g]	100.0	99.6	97.6	95.4	93.8	90.6	87.9	87.3	86.4
Ukraine[e]	100.0	99.9	98.3	96.3	94.1	90.5	93.3	91.3	88.5
Armenia	100.0	102.4	105.0	99.2	97.0	93.5	92.8	90.2	87.9
Azerbaijan	100.0	100.9	105.8	101.4	101.2	99.0	98.5	100.5	100.7
Georgia	100.0	102.4	93.3	73.5	66.4	64.8	71.6	75.4	82.7
Kazakhstan	100.0	101.3	100.1	98.3	89.9	85.4	85.0	84.6	83.4
Kyrgyzstan	100.0	100.5	100.9	105.6	96.6	94.6	94.4	95.0	97.1
Tajikistan[e]	100.0	103.2	104.9	101.6	98.7	98.7	98.6	92.1	94.8
Turkmenistan[e]	100.0	103.4	105.3	105.4	110.0	111.6	112.1	111.7	114.0
Uzbekistan[e]	100.0	104.2	109.2	108.5	108.3	109.9	110.8	112.3	113.8

a. Year end.
b. 1997: ICDC estimate.
c. Beginning of year.
d. 1989-96: UNECE (1998).
e. 1989-97: UNECE (1998).
f. 1993-97: excludes Transdniestr.
g. 1995-97: UNECE (1998).

10.10 Annual registered unemployment rate (percent)

	1989	1990	1991	1992	1993	1994	1995	1996	1997
Czech Republic[a]	—	0.3	2.6	3.1	3.0	3.3	3.0	3.1	4.3
Slovakia	—	0.6	6.6	11.4	12.7	14.4	13.8	12.6	12.9
Poland	—	3.4	9.2	12.9	14.9	16.5	15.2	14.3	11.5
Hungary[a]	0.4	0.8	8.5	12.3	12.1	10.4	10.4	10.5	10.4
Slovenia	2.9	4.7	8.2	11.5	14.4	14.4	13.9	13.9	14.4
Croatia	8.0	9.3	14.9	15.3	14.8	14.5	14.5	16.4	17.5
FYR Macedonia	22.6	23.0	24.5	26.0	27.7	30.0	35.6	38.8	41.7
Bosnia-Herzegovina	—	—	—	—	—	—	—	—	—
FR Yugoslavia	17.9	19.7	21.4	22.8	23.1	23.1	24.6	25.7	—
Albania	7.0	10.0	9.0	27.0	22.0	18.0	12.9	12.7	13.9
Bulgaria	—	—	—	13.2	15.8	14.0	11.4	11.1	14.0
Romania[a]	—	—	3.0	8.2	10.4	10.9	9.5	6.6	8.8
Estonia	—	—	—	—	3.9	4.4	4.1	4.4	4.0
Latvia	—	—	—	0.9	4.5	6.3	6.4	7.0	7.4
Lithuania	—	—	0.3	1.3	4.4	3.8	6.1	7.1	5.9
Belarus	—	—	0.1	0.5	1.4	2.1	2.7	3.9	2.8
Moldova	—	—	—	0.1	0.7	1.1	1.4	1.5	1.5
Russia[a]	—	—	0.1	0.8	1.1	2.2	3.2	3.4	2.8
Ukraine[a]	—	—	—	0.3	0.4	0.4	0.6	1.6	3.1
Armenia[a]	—	—	—	1.6	5.3	6.1	6.6	9.3	10.6
Azerbaijan	—	—	0.1	0.2	0.7	0.8	1.0	1.1	1.3
Georgia	—	—	0.2	2.3	6.6	3.6	2.6	2.4	5.0
Kazakhstan[a]	—	—	—	0.4	0.6	1.1	2.1	4.2	3.9
Kyrgyzstan[a]	—	—	—	0.1	0.2	0.7	2.9	4.3	3.1
Tajikistan[b]	—	—	—	0.3	1.2	1.7	2.0	2.7	2.9
Turkmenistan	—	—	—	—	—	—	—	—	—
Uzbekistan[b]	—	—	—	0.1	0.3	0.4	0.4	0.4	0.4

a. Year end.
b. EBRD (1998).

10.11 Registered unemployed women (thousands)

	1989	1990	1991	1992	1993	1994	1995	1996	1997
Czech Republic[a]	—	20.2	127.2	77.7	103.6	96.6	88.1	105.1	151.8
Slovakia	—	7.1	85.6	144.4	156.0	176.6	175.0	169.2	173.8
Poland	—	573.7	1,134.1	1,338.8	1,507.3	1,495.0	1,448.6	1,375.6	1,103.2
Hungary[a]	—	—	167.1	273.1	256.0	217.0	210.6	202.1	202.6
Slovenia	13.8	21.4	33.6	45.1	56.6	57.0	56.7	57.6	61.1
Croatia	83.4	91.4	133.1	141.3	138.4	130.5	124.2	129.6	137.3
FYR Macedonia	78.1	79.8	83.1	85.3	86.0	90.1	101.3	109.7	114.9
Bosnia-Herzegovina	—	—	—	—	—	—	—	—	—
FR Yugoslavia	320.1	347.0	374.2	401.6	407.2	405.0	429.9	451.2	456.4
Albania	61.6	78.4	75.0	200.0	141.0	120.9	79.6	70.1	84.6
Bulgaria	—	—	—	264.4	313.3	284.1	237.7	232.5	289.4
Romania[a]	—	—	208.5	563.1	685.5	693.3	551.5	355.4	428.6
Estonia	—	—	—	—	9.3	9.2	9.8	12.4	13.1
Latvia	—	—	—	7.3	32.7	43.4	42.1	46.5	52.4
Lithuania	—	—	3.3	15.2	35.8	34.5	59.6	67.6	55.6
Belarus	—	—	1.8	19.6	44.0	64.5	84.3	116.3	84.0
Moldova	—	—	—	—	21.1	20.9	24.8	25.5	26.5
Russia[a]	—	—	43.1	417.0	567.4	1,051.3	1,454.7	1,575.6	1,277.6
Ukraine[a]	—	—	—	14.7	62.7	59.8	92.2	235.8	416.5
Armenia[a]	—	—	—	35.8	64.5	60.1	91.8	115.8	124.7
Azerbaijan	—	—	2.5	3.6	11.8	14.4	16.9	18.8	22.1
Georgia	—	—	3.5	21.5	55.4	26.0	26.4	19.2	66.4
Kazakhstan[a]	—	—	—	25.1	28.4	45.4	84.0	178.4	171.5
Kyrgyzstan[a]	—	—	—	1.3	2.0	7.7	29.9	44.7	31.9
Tajikistan	—	—	—	—	—	—	—	—	—
Turkmenistan	—	—	—	—	—	—	—	16.7	12.3
Uzbekistan	—	—	—	—	—	—	—	—	—

a. Year end.

10.12 Distribution of earnings: Gini coefficient[a]

	1989	1990	1991	1992	1993	1994	1995	1996	1997
Czech Republic	0.204	—	0.212	0.214	0.258	0.260	0.282	0.254	0.259
Slovakia	0.200	—	—	—	—	—	—	—	—
Poland	0.207	—	0.239	0.247	0.256	0.281	0.290	0.302	0.300
Hungary[b]	0.293	—	—	0.305	0.320	0.324	—	—	0.348
Slovenia	0.219	0.232	0.273	0.260	0.276	0.275	0.358	0.298	0.307
Croatia	—	—	—	—	—	—	—	—	—
FYR Macedonia	—	0.223	0.267	0.235	0.272	0.253	0.270	0.250	0.259
Bosnia-Herzegovina	—	—	—	—	—	—	—	—	—
FR Yugoslavia	0.323	0.268	0.294	0.288	0.334	0.321	0.319	0.338	—
Albania	—	—	—	—	—	—	—	—	—
Bulgaria	—	0.212	0.262	—	0.251	—	—	0.291	—
Romania	0.155	—	0.204	—	0.226	0.276	0.278	0.303	0.422
Estonia	—	—	—	—	—	—	—	—	—
Latvia[c]	0.244	—	0.247	0.333	0.283	0.325	0.346	0.349	0.336
Lithuania[c]	0.260	—	—	0.372	—	0.349	0.341	0.350	0.345
Belarus[c]	0.234	—	—	0.341	0.399	—	—	—	—
Moldova[c]	0.250	—	—	0.411	0.437	0.379	0.390	—	—
Russia	0.271	0.269	0.325	0.371	0.461	0.446	0.471	0.483	—
Ukraine	0.249	—	—	0.251	0.364	—	—	0.413	—
Armenia[c]	0.258	—	0.296	0.355	0.366	0.321	0.381	—	—
Azerbaijan[c]	0.275	—	—	—	—	—	—	0.458	—
Georgia	0.301	—	—	0.369	0.400	—	—	—	0.498
Kazakhstan	—	—	—	—	—	—	—	—	—
Kyrgyzstan[c]	0.260	—	—	0.300	0.445	0.443	0.395	0.428	0.431
Tajikistan	—	—	—	—	—	—	—	—	—
Turkmenistan	—	—	—	—	—	—	—	—	—
Uzbekistan	—	—	—	—	—	—	—	—	—

a. Monthly earnings (w/bonuses) for full-time employees as reported by employers. Small employers often excluded. Some data refer to public sector only.
b. 1989 (which refers to 1988): Atkinson and Micklewright (1992), Table HE1.
c. 1989: Atkinson and Micklewright (1992), Table UE6.

10.13 Income distribution: Gini coefficient[a]

	1989	1990	1991	1992	1993	1994	1995	1996	1997
Czech Republic	0.198	0.190	—	0.215	0.214	0.230	0.216	0.230	0.239
Slovakia	—	—	—	—	—	—	—	0.237	0.249
Poland	0.275	0.268	0.265	0.274	0.317	0.323	0.321	0.328	0.334
Hungary	0.225	—	0.209	—	0.231	0.234	0.242	0.246	0.254
Slovenia	—	—	0.265	0.259	0.320	0.246	0.264	0.252	—
Croatia	—	—	—	—	—	—	—	—	—
FYR Macedonia	—	—	—	—	—	0.273	0.295	0.311	0.295
Bosnia-Herzegovina	—	—	—	—	—	—	—	—	—
FR Yugoslavia	—	—	—	—	—	—	—	—	0.294
Albania	—	—	—	—	—	—	—	—	—
Bulgaria	—	—	—	0.331	0.335	0.374	0.384	0.357	0.366
Romania	0.237	0.227	0.258	0.259	0.267	0.264	0.306	0.302	0.305
Estonia[b]	0.280	—	—	—	—	—	0.398	0.370	0.361
Latvia[b]	0.260	—	—	—	—	—	—	—	—
Lithuania[b]	0.262	—	—	—	—	—	—	0.347	0.309
Belarus[b]	0.229	—	—	—	—	—	0.253	0.244	0.249
Moldova[b]	0.250	—	—	—	—	—	—	—	—
Russia[b c]	0.265	0.236	0.257	0.363	0.381	0.405	0.385	—	—
Ukraine[b]	0.229	—	—	—	—	—	—	—	—
Armenia[b]	0.251	—	—	—	—	—	—	0.420	—
Azerbaijan[b]	0.307	—	—	—	—	—	—	—	—
Georgia[b]	0.280	—	—	—	—	—	—	—	—
Kazakhstan[b]	0.281	—	—	—	—	—	—	—	—
Kyrgyzstan[b]	0.270	—	—	—	—	—	—	—	—
Tajikistan[b]	0.281	—	—	—	—	—	—	—	—
Turkmenistan[b]	0.279	—	—	—	—	—	—	—	—
Uzbekistan[b]	0.280	—	—	—	—	—	—	—	—

a. Interpolated from grouped data from household budget surveys using the procedure described in Atkinson and Micklewright (1992). Survey coverage may have changed over time. Data refer to the distribution of individuals according to household per capita income.
b. 1989: Flemming and Micklewright (1999).
c. 1991: Goskomstat (1992).

Glossary

Abortion: This includes induced early fœtal deaths and excludes spontaneous abortions (miscarriages).

Cause of death: In this publication, causes of death are cited in keeping with the *International Classification of Diseases and Related Health Problems* (ICD) IXth Revision, 1975: "accidents, poisonings and violence" (XVII.800-999); "suicide and self-inflicted injury" (XVII.950-959).

Children in infant homes: The number of children in infant homes is a useful proxy for indicators of child abandonment and institutional care. Infant homes typically care for very young children (0-3 years) who have been left without parental care, although infants may enter the homes on temporary placement, and children may also sometimes be above 3 years old.

Consumer price index: The most widely used measure of inflation, the CPI is a comparison of the price levels of a representative basket of consumer goods and services recorded in retail trade outlets and service units during two periods. The aggregate index is based on actual consumer expenditure patterns gauged through household surveys.

Crime and sentencing rates: Crime data cover reported and registered crime only. Crime and sentencing rates are subject to national legislation, which varies widely within the region. This hinders comparisons among countries and years.

Crude birth rate: The CBR measures the frequency of childbirths in a population. In the Statistical Annex it represents the number of live births per 1,000 mid-year population.

Crude death rate: The CDR measures the frequency of deaths in a population. In the Statistical Annex it represents the number of deaths per 1,000 mid-year population.

Enrolment rates: The net enrolment rate is based on the number of children in a specified age group (corresponding to legislated standards) enrolled at a given level of education divided by the total number of children in the same age group in the general population. The gross enrolment rate is based on the number of children, regardless of age, enrolled at a given level of education divided by the total number of children in the general population that corresponds to the age group specified for that level of education.

Enrolment rates by education level: Selected definitions in the International Standard Classification System of Education Levels (ISCED) are given below as a general guideline, though the situation may differ among countries.

● Kindergarten (ISCED 0): This generally covers children in the 3-5 or 3-6 age group and excludes nursery provision for the 0-2 age group.

● Basic education (ISCED 1 and 2): Basic education, often called "compulsory schooling" or "elementary schooling", normally lasts from age 6 or 7 to age 14 or 15. This is often divided into primary (to age 10) and lower secondary levels.

● General secondary (ISCED 3): General secondary schools (gymnasia/lycees) offer two- to four-year programmes of academic study, often leading to higher education, with entry on a selective basis. In CIS countries, general secondary typically comprises the two or three upper classes of the comprehensive school, while in countries in Central and Eastern Europe

it involves longer programmes at separate institutions. In a number of countries, gymnasium streams begin in lower secondary grades.

● Degree tertiary level (ISCED 6 and 7): This covers programmes for students who have successfully completed prerequisite studies at the secondary level and who wish to earn a first university degree or a recognized equivalent qualification. In this publication, non-degree tertiary level (ISCED 5) or post-secondary programmes which do not lead to a university degree or equivalent are excluded, although in certain countries they account for a substantial number of students.

Foreign direct investment: FDI is a capital flow from one country to another that usually takes the form of the establishment of local production facilities or the purchase of existing businesses.

Gender development index: The GDI follows the framework of the Human Development Index (HDI), but the components are adjusted for gender inequality. The method of calculation renders the index sensitive both to the overall achievements of a nation and to gender disparities. The greater the inequality in basic human capabilities between women and men in a country, the lower the GDI relative to the general HDI. For life expectancy, different age ranges are used for men and women based on the assumption that, on average, women live five years longer than do men. For income distribution, proportional income shares are calculated. These latter take into account the differences in wages by gender and the differing shares of women and men in the labour force, as well as in the population. For educational attainment, scores for women and men are calculated as for the HDI. Equally distributed indices are then calculated for all components. Each index is based on an "harmonic averaging" of the scores by gender, which are weighted according to the shares of the male and the female populations. Finally, the GDI is calculated as a simple "arithmetic average" of the three adjusted indices. (See also *human development index*.)

General government balance: The difference between government revenues and government expenditures, this usually includes local, state and central governments, but the practice may vary among countries. The balance may be positive or negative.

Gini coefficient: The "Gini" is a measure of the degree of inequality in the distribution of earnings and income. It is equal to "0" in the case of total earnings/income equality (everyone receives the same earnings/income) and to "1" in the case of total inequality (one person receives all the earnings/income).

Gross adoption rate: This is used as a proxy for the de-institutionalization of children. The gross adoption rate in the Statistical Annex represents the total number of adoptions per 100,000 children aged 0-3, though there may be adoptions of older children as well.

Gross domestic product: GDP is the most widely used concept of national income defined in the System of National Accounts. It represents the total final output of goods and services produced by an economy during a given period regardless of the allocation to domestic and foreign claims and is calculated without making deductions for depreciation. (See also *net material product*.)

Human development index: The HDI was introduced by the UN Development Programme in 1990 to provide a measure of human well-being that is more inclusive than measures based only on income. It has three components reflecting three important factors in the quality of life: longevity, knowledge and living conditions. The method of calculation has evolved gradually. Currently, the index is established as follows. Life expectancy at birth is used to measure health; literacy figures and combined primary, secondary and tertiary enrolment rates are used as a proxy to measure knowledge, and per capita income adjusted for relative purchasing-power is used as a measure of a decent life. The scores of a country for each variable are standardized on a scale from "0" to "1". The composite index, which reflects a country's overall level of development, is a simple arithmetic average of the three scores. (See also *gender development index*.)

Infant mortality rate: The IMR is a measure of the probability of dying between birth and 1 year of age. It represents the annual number of deaths of infants under 1 year of age per 1,000 live births during the same period. (See also *live births*.)

Life expectancy at birth: A widely used measure of the general level of mortality, this is the theoretical number of years a newborn will live if the age-specific mortality rates in the year of birth are taken as constant. It represents for a given year the sum of the mortality rates for all ages combined.

Live births: According to the standard definition of the World Health Organization, this includes all births, with the exception of stillbirths, regardless of the size, gestation age, or "viability" of the newborn infant, or his or her death soon after birth or before the required birth-registration date. Only a few countries covered in this publication employed this concept before the transition; many used the so-called "Soviet concept", while others relied on national concepts. However, most countries have now adopted the WHO definition, and only a few still use the Soviet concept. The Soviet concept excludes infants born with no breath, but with other signs of life ("stillbirths" in the Soviet concept), and infants born before the end of the 28th week of pregnancy at a weight under 1,000 grams or a length under 35 centimetres and who die during the first seven days of life ("miscarriages").

Maternal mortality rate: This is the annual number of deaths of women due to pregnancy or childbirth-related causes per 100,000 live births.

Net material product: A concept of national income used widely in Central and Eastern Europe and the former Soviet Union before the transition, this includes the total final output of goods and productive services for a given period, but disregards activities (such as health care, education, or public administration) that do not result in material output. (See also *gross domestic product*.)

Population data: These refer to de facto population (all people physically present in an area at the time of a population census or population estimate) as opposed to de jure population (all people who are resident in an area, including those who may be temporarily absent). Typically, refugees not permanently settled in the country of asylum are excluded. For countries for which population data are not available by age cohort, estimates have been made on the basis of data on five-year age groups by gender in the International Database of the US Census Bureau. In cases in which the Census Bureau five-year age-cohort estimates need to be disaggregated to calculate indicators among cohorts, each single-year age group is taken to constitute one-fifth of the five-year cohort estimate.

Public expenditure on education: This represents current and capital expenditures on education by local, regional and national governments, including municipalities. Household contributions are normally excluded.

Rate of natural population increase: This is the difference between the number of births and the number of deaths during a given year divided by the mid-year population. It excludes changes due to migration and may be either positive or negative.

Real wage: A proxy for the quantity of goods and services a money wage can buy, the real wage represents the money wage adjusted for inflation.

Registered and "ILO" unemployment: The registered unemployment rate refers to the segment of the labour force registered at labour offices as unemployed. This administrative approach reflects national rules and conditions and usually generates figures which are different from those resulting from surveys relying on the so-called "ILO concept" of unemployment. The ILO concept is based on three criteria and defines as unemployed those people who (1) have worked less than one hour in the last week, (2) are actively searching for work and (3) are currently available for work.

Teenage birth rate: This measures the frequency of childbirths among very young women. In the Statistical Annex it represents the number of live births among women 15-19 years of age per 1,000 mid-year female population in the same age group.

Total fertility rate: An overall measure of fertility, this represents the theoretical number of births to a woman during her childbearing years taking the given year's age-specific birth rates as a constant. It is calculated as the sum of the age-specific birth rates for all women of childbearing age.

Under-5 mortality rate: The U5MR measures the probability of dying between birth and age 5. It represents the annual number of deaths of children under age 5 per 1,000 live births. In the Statistical Annex the U5MR has been calculated by comparing the number of under-5 deaths to the number of live births in the current year rather than in the year the deceased children were born.

Working-age population: The working-age population refers to individuals above the age of compulsory education and below the official retirement age. Most often this includes men aged 15-59 and women aged 15-54 in the countries of the region. However, this standardized definition may differ from the current definitions of "working age" in some countries due to a gradual increase in the retirement age for both genders.

■

Bibliographic Notes

These Bibliographic Notes are designed mainly as a guide to aid the interested reader in finding additional information. The Bibliography contains a more thorough listing of the information sources used for this Report.

Without offering more explicit descriptions, the text frequently mentions analyses, surveys and other research which have been carried out for this Report. This sort of reference often indicates material which has been produced for the UNICEF International Child Development Centre by the counterparts of the MONEE project network in the transition countries. This material is hereinafter referred to as "MONEE country reports".

More specifically, the majority of these country reports consists of analyses prepared by statistical offices and experts in the region. They are listed in the Bibliography as follows: ASRK (1998), CSBL (1998), FSOY (1998), Gardashkhanova (1998), Gasyuk (1998), Goskomstat (1998a), Kask et al. (1998), Lakatos (1998), LDS (1998), Magloutchiants (1998), NCS (1998), Novák (1998), NSCKR (1998), Papp (1998), Placintar (1998), SDSG (1998), Shircel (1998), SOFYRM (1998), Tafi (1998), and Tzvetkova-Anguelova (1998).

In addition, 10 papers on issues such as government policies concerning gender equity, the labour market participation of women, family support, women's health, and protection against abuse and violence have been expressly prepared as background material. They are listed in the Bibliography as follows: ABW Khujand (1998), Daszynska et al. (1998), Hendrichova and Kucharova (1998), Kupriyanova (1998), Libanova, Makarova and Poznyak (1998), Marnie (1998), MEG (1998), Noncheva (1998), Posarac (1998), and Zamfir and Zamfir (1998).

The text also refers to numerous statistical surveys and databases. Hereafter is a brief description of a selection of those which are not explained in the Bibliographic Notes for individual chapters.

The Azerbaijan Survey of Living Conditions was developed by the State Statistical Committee of the Azerbaijan Republic and the World Bank in November and December 1995. The EUI/Essex Survey in Uzbekistan was carried out by a team from the European University Institute (Florence) and the University of Essex (UK) in summer 1995; see Coudouel (1998). The FR Yugoslavia Labour Force Survey has been conducted since 1994 by the Federal Statistical Office. The Kazakhstan Labour Force Survey was run in November-December 1994 by the Kazakhstan National Centre for Public Opinion and was financed by the government of Japan in conjunction with a World Bank project. The Kazakhstan Living Standards Survey was implemented by the National Statistical Agency in July 1996 through a technical assistance project financed by the World Bank. The Kyrgyzstan Multipurpose Poverty Survey was carried out in autumn 1993 by the World Bank and the government of Kyrgyzstan on a sample of 2,000 households and 9,000 individuals; it covered household income, consumption, living conditions, employment, and education. The Latvian Household Budget Survey was initi-

ated in September 1995 and is updated on a monthly basis by the Central Statistical Bureau; it covers household income, consumption and living conditions, and yearly samples typically comprise around 8,000 households. The Latvian Labour Force Survey was introduced in November 1995 and is run in May and November each year; in November 1996, the sample included 6,000 households and about 12,000 individuals over age 14. The OECD-CCET Labour Market Database is the product of a cooperative effort between the OECD Centre for Cooperation with Economies in Transition and the national statistical offices of Bulgaria, the Czech Republic, Hungary, Latvia, Poland, Romania, Russia, Slovakia, and Slovenia; it includes labour market data based on labour force surveys and contains information on employment, unemployment and wages. The Polish Labour Force Survey is conducted quarterly on a sample of around 32,000 households; it covers employment, unemployment and wages. The Russia Longitudinal Monitoring Survey involved two phases, the first in 1992-93, and the second in 1994-96; more information and datasets are available at http://www.cpc.unc.edu/rlms. The Ukraine Household Income and Expenditures Study was financed by the World Bank and was carried out in June-July 1995 by the International Institute of Sociology in Kiev; a nationally-representative study, it sampled 2,025 households and 4,560 individuals.

The Platform for Action and other material produced for or by the Fourth World Conference on Women (for example UN, 1995a, 1996b) are referred to frequently in the text. Country reports submitted under Article 18 of the Convention on the Elimination of All Forms of Discrimination against Women (CEDAW) and their consideration by the CEDAW Committee can be found on the website at //gopher.un.org:70/00/ga/cedaw/18/country/.

Extensive use has been made of the resources of the Internet. The Bibliographic Notes and the Bibliography reflect this debt. However, references to websites are provided with the hope that readers will understand that the websites are constantly evolving and that the material referred to may sometimes no longer be available in this way.

Chapter 1

The Human Development Index and Gender Development Index scores and the international rankings of countries are included in the annual *Human Development Report* of the UNDP, which also publishes other composite indices on development. The focus of the 1995 *Human Development Report* mentioned in Boxes 1.1 and 1.2 is gender and development. Mehrotra and Jolly (1997) offer case studies of 10 developing countries which have registered particularly good social indicators, and they examine different paths to development and the links among economic growth, poverty reduction and social development. For a critical evaluation of the HDI see, for example, McGillivray (1991) and McGillivray and White (1993).

The discussion on health and education inputs in the early 1990s relies on data from the World Bank (1997a) and

Horton (1996). Information on reassessments of immunization data is provided in IOGU and Macro International (1997), MOHT and UNICEF (1995) and MOHK and UNICEF (1995). For UNICEF's international rankings of countries by achievement, see the annual *The State of the World's Children* (for instance UNICEF, 1997c). In the UNICEF ranking the country with the worst record is placed first; hence the ranking on the basis of the under-5 mortality rate included in the text uses the inverse of the data from the 1997 publication in order to facilitate comparison with the HDI ranking. For the "UNICEF Mission Statement", see http://www.unicef.org/. For a review of UNIFEM's mandate and activities in the region, see UNIFEM (1997).

The data on GDP in Figures 1.7 and 1.8 are drawn from the annual *Transition Report* of the European Bank for Reconstruction and Development (EBRD, 1998). These reports include a detailed survey of privatization and trends related to market reforms in the region. EBRD (1996) gives information on the informal economy in the region; the data used in Box 1.3 are from Johnson, Kaufman and Schleifer (1997). The UN Economic Commission for Europe publishes a biannual macro-economic review of the region; part of the analysis provided in the text is based on this source (for example UNECE, 1998). The data on small-sector development in Hungary are from UNDP (1998b).

Analysis of earnings and income inequality under communism is given in Atkinson and Micklewright (1992). Inequality during the transition is described in Milanovíc (1996, 1998) and Flemming and Micklewright (1999). For a comparison of Gini coefficients for the transition countries and for OECD countries, see Chapter 1 of the fifth Regional Monitoring Report (UNICEF, 1998). The source for the estimate using data from Goskomstat is Frolova (1998); the study referred to that uses data from the Russia Longitudinal Monitoring Survey is Commander and Lee (1998). The 1996 survey in Armenia on child poverty is discussed in Magloutchiants (1998).

Sen's (1995) *Innocenti Lecture*, "Mortality as an Indicator of Economic Success and Failure", is a good stimulus for interest in mortality as a general welfare measure; see also Sen (1998). Mortality during the transition is a focus of the second Regional Monitoring Report (UNICEF, 1994a). The debate on the causes of shifts in mortality in Russia is summarized in Chen, Wittgenstein and McKeon (1996); see also Nell and Stewart (1994) and Cornia (1998).

The analysis provided in Box 1.7 is based mostly on a collection of studies in Harrison and Ziglio (1998). On linkages between the degree of income disparity in a society and the health status of people, see Wilkinson (1996, 1998). For the social capital theory stressing the importance for health of trust and social networks, see Putnam (1993).

The discussion of childhood injuries is based on Ecohost (1998). The 1995 study by the National Institute of Nutrition of Kazakhstan is examined in NINK and Macro International (1996). The fourth Regional Monitoring Report (UNICEF, 1997a) supplies a detailed analysis of children in institutions and of other high-risk groups of children. For data on Russia, see also MLSD (1997). UNICEF (1998) examines reforms and the trends in education. The 1995 international survey of learning achievement among 13-year-olds in 41 countries is presented in Beaton et al. (1996a, 1996b).

Chapter 2

The ILO (1992, 1998) collects data on labour force participation and employment in several transition countries. However, caution is needed when interpreting the numbers

as definitions may vary, and country statistical offices are not always able to verify the data in earlier series. On the divestiture of employee benefits, including childcare, see Rein, Friedman and Wörgötter (1997) and Fajth (1994). For details on gender differences in Poland in success in finding work and in achieving job security (Box 2.2), see Newell and Pastore (1998).

Gimpleson and Lippoldt (1998) studied gender differences in the probability of private-sector employment in five regions of Russia during March 1996. See Newell and Socha (1998) for evidence on the higher wage incentives of private-sector employment in Poland. Using ILO data, Paukert (1997) finds evidence of gender bias in the recruitment practices of employers in Hungary, Poland, the Czech Republic, and Slovakia. The data on part-time work in the European Union is from Eurostat (1998). A sociological survey carried out in 1990-91 in five countries included a question on part-time employment; see Björnberg and Sass (1997). The source of the estimate on informal women workers in Poland is Kowalska (1996). The fact that women dominate in the "shuttle" trade in consumer goods in Central Asia is brought out in Tadjbakhsh (1999). For an econometric analysis using data on women in the informal sector in FR Yugoslavia, see Krstic and Reilly (1998).

Bagratian and Gurgen (1997) observe that payment arrears present a serious problem in the Baltic States, the Russian Federation and other countries of the former Soviet Union, including the Ukraine (Box 2.5). For details about the Ukraine-96 Project, a 1996 initiative of the World Bank and the Kiev International Institute of Sociology to collect information on 850 Ukrainian workers, see Pajaniandy (1998).

The data on the wage gap in Great Britain are taken from Atkinson and Micklewright (1992). Where surveys are referred to as sources for Table 2.2, the gender pay ratios have been calculated based on micro-data from these surveys.

Newell and Reilly (1999) suggest that young male workers receive a wage premium relative to older workers in Russia, but that in most transition economies the age effects are not well understood. For a discussion of the "selection effect" in the gender wage gap, see Hunt (1998) for East Germany, Orazem and Vodopivec (1995) for Slovenia and Reilly (1999) for Russia. For the standard correction procedures adopted to deal with this type of problem, see Heckman (1979). These procedures have been criticized of late; see Manski (1989).

Juhn, Murphy and Pierce (1993) and Blau and Khan (1996) propose a methodology to facilitate the examination of factors influencing the gender pay gap over time. This methodology was developed for application to established capitalist economies. Reilly (1999) highlights potential problems with the application to transition economies. For arguments for a role of labour market institutions in reducing the pay gap in the West, see Rubery (1992).

There is some empirical evidence from advanced capitalist economies that occupations in which there is a high participation of women are also ones which pay less (for instance, see Sorensen, 1990; Lucifora and Reilly, 1990). It is not easy to distinguish the part of the gender differential in occupational distribution that is attributable to female choice and the part that is attributable to employer discrimination. Brown, Moon and Zoloth (1980) and Reilly (1991) have attempted to establish empirically the level of occupational distribution that is "justified" on the basis of different characteristics for two established market economies. They conclude that discrimination cannot be excluded as a significant factor. Gunderson (1989) presents evidence that gender differences in preference play a role, too. Newell and Reilly (1996) undertake a broadly similar analysis for Russia using data from 1992. Blau (1998) draws attention to the possible deleterious effects of occupational segregation on perceptions of the capabilities of women and thereby on the economic status of women.

The dissimilarity index proposed by Duncan and Duncan (1955) has been used extensively in this field, but has also been criticized; see Tzannatos (1990). Silber (1989) proposes the application of the Gini concentration index for the measurement of employment segregation by gender. For the data included for Western Europe, see Blau and Khan (1996). For the data on the US, see Boisso et al. (1994). The latter investigation relied on 51 two-digit occupations for 1985 and 1990, and the sample sizes for both years were around 50,000, in contrast to the more modest sample sizes available in the Russia Longitudinal Monitoring Survey (just over 5,000 in 1992 and about 2,000 in 1996) used in Chapter 2. This type of international comparison is clearly fraught with methodological problems.

On household financial management patterns, see Pahl (1989). Waldfogel (1998a, 1998b) finds that in the US young women with children experience higher gender pay gaps than do women without children and that in the US and the UK maternity leave which involves job guarantees offsets some of the negative wage effects of having children.

Research in various countries has revealed that the receipt of income by women increases their economic power within the household, and this has important effects on household consumption patterns; for example see Alderman et al. (1995).

Chapter 3

Particularly for comparisons to European Union countries, important sources of demographic data include CE (1998), Eurostat (1993, 1997a) and UN (1997a). The survey of countries pursuing pro-natalist objectives in social policies is described in UN (1989a).

The term the "second demographic transition" was introduced by Lesthaeghe and van de Kaa (1986) and van de Kaa (1987). The concept describes changes in values and in demographic behaviour in Europe since the late 1960s (for instance, non-marital childbearing and more diverse family forms, especially single-parent families) and posits that an underlying principle of the changes in demographic behaviour is the right to self-actualization of individuals, especially women.

Chapter 3 draws heavily on the MONEE country reports, previous Regional Monitoring Reports (especially UNICEF, 1997a) and an *Innocenti Occasional Paper* on developments in family policies (Fajth, 1994). The discussion of childcare issues also relies on Cusan and Motivans (1998) and UNICEF (1998). In this regard, a study (Connelly, 1992) in the US calculated that a 10 percent rise in childcare costs reduced the labour force participation of women by 2 percent.

The data on public expenditures on family programmes in 1989 are found in the provisional version of the Social Expenditures Database (SOCX) prepared by the Directorate for Education, Employment, Labour, and Social Policy of the OECD; see OECD (1996). Data for socialist countries are based on the MONEE project database and Fajth (1996).

The chapter cites a cross-national study of attitudes towards family policy and family development in Eastern and Western Europe that is described in Björnberg and Sass (1997). The related surveys were conducted in Germany, Poland, Russia, Hungary, and Sweden in 1991-92. The sample included between 1,000 and 1,400 individuals in each country.

The Population Activities Unit of the Commission for Europe has initiated a series veys focusing on partnership and reproductiv terns in about 20 countries. These include th European countries listed hereafter, followed by the year in which fieldwork was conducted tion of the sample: Bulgaria (1997, 2,500 women the Czech Republic (1997, 5,000 persons aged 15-44), Estonia (1994, 5,000 women aged 20-69), Hungary (1992-93, 5,500 persons aged 18-41), Latvia (1995, 4,200 persons aged 18-49), Lithuania (1994-95, 5,000 persons aged 18-49), Poland (1991, 8,500 persons aged 18-49), and Slovenia (1994-95, 4,600 persons aged 15-45). Further information is available at http://www.unece.org/deap/pau/f_home1.htm. The data on cohabitation are from Klijzing and Macura (1995), who use preliminary results from these surveys.

The data on living standards and poverty among families with children come from several studies. The research relying on the Luxembourg Income Study is described in Bradbury and Jäntti (1998), who examine cross-national differences in relative poverty rates and poverty measurement. The dataset includes household income data for five transition countries: the Czech Republic, Hungary, Poland, Russia, and Slovakia. Further information on the Luxembourg Income Study and data access are available through the website, http://lissy.ceps.lu/access.htm.

Evidence from World Bank studies (for instance Braithwaite and Hoopengardner, 1997) suggests that women have a slightly higher poverty head-count index than men, but the differentials are relatively small. Grootaert and Braithwaite (1998) supply alternative measures. As of May 1999, the World Bank has provided access to a comparative dataset, including household survey data from Bulgaria, Hungary, Poland, Estonia, Kyrgyzstan, and Russia. Known as HEIDE (Household Expenditure and Income Data for Transitional Economies), it is available from the World Bank website, http://www.worldbank.org/research/transition/house.htm.

Lundberg, Pollak and Wales (1997) have analysed the impact on family consumption patterns of changes in child benefit payments. In the UK in the late 1970s, universal child benefits, which up to then had involved a tax deduction (linked mainly to the income of fathers), began to be paid out directly (mainly to mothers). The study found that, for example, expenditures on women's and children's clothing increased relative to those on men's clothing following this switch in the benefit.

Chapter 4

Reproductive health surveys in the Czech Republic in 1993 (CSO et al., 1995), Moldova in 1997 (Serbanescu and Morris, 1998b), Romania in 1993 and 1996 (IMCC and CDC, 1995; Serbanescu and Morris, 1998a), and Russia in 1996 (VCIOM, CDC and USAID, 1998) are information resources. These surveys involved representative samples (4,500 women in the Czech Republic, 5,400 women in Moldova, 4,900 women in 1993 and 4,100 young women in 1996 in Romania, and 6,000 women in three regions of Russia). They cover fertility, abortion, maternal health and care, contraception, sexually transmitted diseases, and sexual experiences.

A demographic and health survey in Kazakhstan in 1995 (NINK and Macro International, 1996) and another in Uzbekistan in 1996 (IOGU and Macro International, 1997) are important sources of information on women's health in Central Asia. Based on representative samples (4,200 households in Kazakhstan and 3,700 in Uzbekistan), these surveys cover fertility, contraception, abortion, infant and child mortality and health, maternal health, and nutrition.

A fertility and family survey among 7,700 individuals in Poland in 1991 (Holzer and Kowalska, 1997) and another among 4,200 individuals in Latvia in 1995 (Zvidrins, Ezera and Greitans, 1998) provide information on household composition, partnership formation and dissolution, fertility, contraception, and abortion.

The Health for All database (WHO, 1998) presents information on demographics, mortality, morbidity, lifestyles, environment, and health care resources and their application for European countries. The database is especially useful for comparisons between Western Europe and the transition countries. The information provides important insights into most of the issues covered by Chapter 4 and are important complements to the MONEE project database.

Details on maternal mortality in Uzbekistan are reported by UNDP (1997e) and Hinrichsen (1995), and information on the disparities within FR Yugoslavia is found in UNICEF (1997b), Posarac (1998) and IPHS, IPHM and UNICEF (1997). The data for Figure 4.4 from Koupilová et al. (1998) have kindly been made available by the copyright holders (©), the American Public Health Association, and have been rounded out with information on neonatal mortality found in Koupilová, McKee and Holcík (1998). Evidence on maternal health and care draws on UNICEF (1997d) and AFHA (1997) for Armenia and on Bauer, Green and Kuehnast (1997) for Kyrgyzstan.

The main sources of information for the analysis of abortion rates are the MONEE country reports. Box 4.1 draws mainly on UNFPA (1997a) and Nowicka (1996). Additional information on the consequences of abortion is from Vikhlayeva and Nikolaeva (1996) for Russia and MOW and UNDP/UNFPA (1998) for Latvia.

Forrai (1996) and Lunin et al. (1995) offer insights into the use of contraceptives and the lack of knowledge about contraceptive methods in Hungary and Russia. The information on the factors in the non-use of contraceptives in Belarus is reported in UNICEF (1995a). NSCKR (1997) provides details about contraceptive use in Kyrgyzstan. The surveys on the perceptions of women and physicians about modern contraception in the 1980s and early 90s are discussed in Oddens (1997). Hendrichova and Kucharova (1998) and Papp (1998) report on the initiatives taken in the Czech Republic and Estonia to promote a shift from abortion to contraception. VCIOM, CDC and USAID (1998) and Stephenson et al. (1998) furnish the information on the small amount of guidance on contraceptive use offered to women in Russia after childbearing or abortion. The initiatives of NGOs in Albania and Uzbekistan are described in Iliriani and Asliani (1995) and Marnie (1998).

The data on the incidence of breast and cervical cancer can be found in WHO (1998). The information on the prevalence of anæmia draws mainly on the MONEE project database and the demographic and health surveys in Kazakhstan and in Uzbekistan mentioned above. The analysis of diets in Russia is based on information contained in the Russia Longitudinal Monitoring Survey, Zohoori et al. (1997) and Welch, Mock and Netrebenko (1998).

The description of the deteriorating access to health care in Central and Southeastern Europe presented in Box 4.2 owes much to Saltman and Figueras (1997), UNDP (1997f) and Pradhan and Zant (1998). The information on Russia comes from Zohoori et al. (1997) and Shulyakovskaya (1998). The case of Moldova is summarized in UNICEF (1997e), of Azerbaijan in UNICEF (1996a), and of Kazakhstan in Ensor and Savelyeva (1998).

The WHO evaluation of the significance of tobacco use as a major cause of death is from WHO and HSPH (1998). It is based on assessments of the number of years of "healthy" life lost because of premature death or disability attributable to various conditions. The discussion of the prevalence of smoking and drinking among adolescents draws on King and Coles (1992), Kalnins and Ranka (1996) and King et al. (1996). The information on street children in Kiev is taken from UNICEF et al. (1998), while the alcohol-related mortality rates in Russia are provided in Nell and Stewart (1994) and Leon et al. (1997). The paragraphs on the incidence of HIV/AIDS are based mainly on documents prepared within the Joint UN Programme on HIV/AIDS (UNAIDS and WHO, 1996, 1998a, 1998b; Dehne, 1998). UNDCP (1995) offers insight into the vulnerability of the transition countries to drug trafficking and drug abuse. Box 4.3 draws mainly on UNFPA (1997b). The figures for Western Europe and for regional averages in the discussion of syphilis are from the Health for All database. Box 4.4 is based on Serbanescu and Morris (1998a), while Box 4.5 relies on Reid (1992) and the international survey presented in UNAIDS (1997).

On the incidence of stress and depression, see Desjarlais et al. (1995) for a general discussion, World Bank (1993) for estimates of the losses due to premature death and disability (based on evaluations similar to those referred to above on tobacco use), and WHO (1998) for information on subjective assessments of health. Table 4.7 is based on the survey of the health of young people that was carried out in transition countries and Western Europe in 1993-94 by King et al. (1996). The survey used to construct Table 4.8 is reported in UNDP (1997a). The information on the mental health of pregnant women comes from the European Longitudinal Survey of Pregnancy and Childhood carried out in districts of England, Russia and the Czech Republic in 1990-92 and discussed in Koupilová et al. (1996) and Dragonas et al. (1996).

Chapter 5

Chapter 5 relies on the definition of violence against women established by the UN Declaration against Violence against Women (UN, 1993b, Article 1) and the recommendations of the UN Fourth World Conference on Women, held in Beijing in 1995 (UN 1995a). The analysis in Heise, Pitanguy and Germain (1994) represents a major source of information and an analytical framework on the issue.

The estimates of the importance of domestic violence and rape within the total burden of disease are found in World Bank (1993), along with the information on tobacco and mental health; see also WHO and HSPH (1998).

Box 5.1 draws on population data from World Bank (1997a) and the Statistical Annex, Tables 1.1 and 1.2, and on two large health surveys, one in Kazakhstan (NINK and Macro International, 1996) and the other in Uzbekistan (IOGU and Macro International, 1997). The information on other forms of violence in Central Asia is supplied in Bauer, Green and Kuehnast (1997) and The Economist (1996).

The discussion on crime, including homicide and rape, is based on the MONEE project database and CIS Stat (1998a). The analysis employs data reported by public authorities. These data are not likely to reflect the actual number of cases, especially with regard to rape. Readers are referred to Alvazzi del Frate and Goryainov (1993) for a discussion of the under-reporting problem and the concealing of crime in Russia.

The information on the extent of domestic violence in transition countries comes mostly from relatively small surveys which are usually not representative, and the results should therefore be interpreted with caution. Figure 5.5 is based on a survey of reproductive health and behaviour involving 3,000 women in Latvia in 1997 (MOW and

UNDP/UNFPA, 1998). The analysis of spousal abuse in Moscow in 1996 is reported in Vannoy et al. (1999), which provides insights into the health of the institution of marriage in Russia. The survey of adolescents in Ukraine reported by Vornik (1997) also examines the attitudes of young people towards sexual abuse. The small survey carried out in Almaty and Jambyl by the Feminist League and UNDP (1997) also investigated issues of violence in the street and in the workplace and women's attitudes towards violence.

In addition to the sources listed above and those used to create Table 5.5, the information on the links between divorce and domestic violence is based on UN (1996a) and NCS (1998) for Romania and on Daszynska et al. (1998) for Poland. The information on the number of family conflicts in Russia is found in Kupriyanova (1998), and the figures advanced by the Russian President's Advisor are reported in HRW (1997). The analysis of spousal homicide in Russia and the US is presented by Gondolf and Shestakov (1997). The survey of women in the Leninabad and Khujand regions of Tajikistan in 1997 is reported in ABW Khujand (1998), and the information on suicides in Uzbekistan is from Marnie (1998).

The information on the prevalence of violence in the workplace is based on the UN Interregional Crime and Justice Research Institute survey used in Figure 5.8 (Chappell and Di Martino, 1998). This is complemented by information on sexual harassment in former Czechoslovakia and the Czech Republic (Cermakova, 1991, 1994; Hendrichova and Kucharova, 1998) and in Russia (Sillaste, 1995, cited in Morvant, 1995). The data on violence in the education system are based on Feminist League and UNDP (1997) for Kazakhstan, Vornik (1997) for Ukraine, UNICEF (1997a) for Romania, and HRW (1998) for Russia.

The estimates of the number of women raped during the conflict in Bosnia-Herzegovina are provided in EC (1993) and UN (1993c, 1994a). An analysis of the trauma experienced by children in Croatia is found in Jagodic and Bunjevac (1995). Most of the information on the number and the demographic profile of refugees and internally displaced persons is supplied in UNHCR (1998), and the estimates regarding the conflict in Kosovo are reported on the UNHCR website, http://www.unhcr.ch/. The analysis of the long-term consequences of conflicts draws on Posarac (1998), MES (1998) and MES and UNICEF (1997).

The definition of trafficking is borrowed from IOM (1996a). Most of the information employed in the examination of trafficking in women for the purpose of sexual exploitation comes from publications and reports by the International Organization for Migration (IOM, 1995, 1996a, 1996b, 1998; IOM and BMFA, 1996) and from Specter (1998) and Caldwell, Galster and Steinzor (1997). The estimates from the Latvian Labour Force Survey and the Latvian police are reported in CSBL (1998).

The information in the section on the recognition of the criminal nature of violence against women is drawn mainly from various MONEE country reports. UNDP (1996a, 1996b, 1997b, 1997c, 1997d, 1997g) and the US Department of State (1998a, 1998b, 1998c, 1998d, 1998e) provide insight into the situation in Albania, Azerbaijan, Belarus, Croatia, Estonia, FYR Macedonia, Kyrgyzstan, Lithuania, Poland, Tajikistan, and Ukraine. The article from the *St Petersburg Times* is Vandendberg (1997).

Signs of the lack of support from the authorities for women victims of violence are reported in HRW (1997) and Alvazzi del Frate and Goryainov (1993) for Russia, Minnesota Advocates for Human Rights (1995, 1996) for Romania and Albania, ABW Khujand (1998) for Tajikistan, and Mrsevic and Hughes (1997) and Posarac (1998) for FR Yugoslavia.

Chapter 6

Women's political participation in Central and Eastern Europe is reviewed in Rueschemeyer (1994) and European Network for Women's Studies (1994). Buckley (1997a) contains essays on women's groups in Russia and the perceptions of women in the media, among other topics. Women's issues in Russia and Ukraine, including the political representation of women, are also discussed in Marsh (1996a). For broader approaches to gender issues, see also Moghadam (1992, 1993, 1996) and Pascall (1997).

The Directorate General for Research of the European Parliament produces a series of working papers on women's rights. The website of the Inter-Parliamentary Union, http://www.ipu.org/wmn-e/world.htm, is a regularly updated source of data on the number of parliamentarians by gender; http://gopher.un.org/ includes various reports on the advancement of women and equality in decision making. For further information, see http://www.un.org/womenwatch and http://www.unifem.undp.org.

The Gender Empowerment Measure is described and analysed in UNDP's annual *Human Development Report*. The measure ranks countries according to gender equity in decision making through the number of women parliamentarians, women administrators and managers, and women professional and technical workers, as well as through women's shares in earned income (a proxy for the weight of women in household decision making). The text on women's status in the Nordic countries (Box 6.1) is based mainly on Allen (1996) and Crompton (1998). Buckley (1997a) quotes politicians who say that women's issues should not be addressed during the crisis of the transition. Wolchik (1994) and Havelkova (1996) comment that the political transformation promised by transition has added to rather than levelled gender inequality. Morvant (1995) and Fischer and Harsányi (1994) describe the gender prejudices of male politicians in Eastern Europe. The source of the quote from Albania in Section 6.1 is Tarifa (1994).

The data on senior government positions occupied by women that appear in Table 6.1 and Figure 6.4 are from UN (1997b). The ILO (1998) furnishes the data in Figure 6.5 on women who are legislators, senior officials and managers. The ILO (1997a) supplies an international review of women in management. The upward occupational mobility of women in established market economies is discussed in Blau, Ferber and Winkler (1998). McCue (1996) has found that promotion in employment in the US tends to be associated with lower wage growth among women than among men. Based on data from Taganrog in the former Soviet Union, Linz (1996) suggests that this phenomenon is not confined to market economies.

The "allergy to feminism" mentioned in Section 6.2 is described in Einhorn (1993). Pavlychko (1997) discusses women's organizations in Ukraine. Lang-Pickvance, Manning and Pickvance (1997), Manning (1998) and Lévai and Kiss (1997) analyse the situation at the grassroots.

Nesporova (1998) finds that the firms owned by women tend to be relatively small in the region. The Kazakh example of the lack of access to bank loans is from Bauer, Boschmann and Green (1997). Arnau (1997) provides data on women entrepreneurs in Western Europe. Blanchflower and Oswald (1998) have investigated a sample of new entrepreneurs in the UK and found that many more have had to rely on savings or family and friends for financing rather than on bank loans. Robson (1991) highlights the importance of liquid assets for self-employment in the UK. The examples in Box 6.5 of women's reliance on family and friendship networks in the procurement of goods, services and employment loans and in kiosk-trading are from Piirainen (1996), Lonkila (1997) and Bruno (1996, 1997). The importance of "social capital" in coping with economic shocks and in improving small-scale agricultural production is described in O'Brien et al. (1996) and Bridger (1997).

The policy recommendations of the UN Commission on the Status of Women are from UN (1994b). Crowley (1997) argues that the role of women entrepreneurs should be publicized as a way to encourage the lowering of barriers. The inadequacy of conventional loan models for small businesses owned by women is examined in, for example, BDBC (1997). Mama Cash is described in Esajas (1997).

■

Bibliography

ABW KHUJAND (Association of Business Women "Khujand") (1998), "Gender Policies in Transition in Tajikistan". Florence: UNICEF International Child Development Centre. Mimeo (7 August).

ADAMIK, MARIA (1994), "Women in Hungary during the Political Transition". Pages 1-7 in European Network for Women's Studies, *Gains and Losses: Women and Transition in Eastern and Central Europe*. Bucharest: European Network for Women's Studies and Centre for Higher Education, UN Educational, Social and Cultural Organization.

ADB and UNESCO (1995), "Technical Assistance for the Education and Training Sector Study: Synthesis Report". *Technical Assistance Report*, No. 2308-KAZ (December). Almaty, Kazakhstan: Asian Development Bank and UN Educational, Social and Cultural Organization.

AFHA (Armenian Family Health Association) (1997), "Assessment of the Reproductive Health Indicators, Infrastructure and Resources in Ararat and Vajots Dzor Marzes". Yerevan, Armenia: UNICEF.

AKINER, SHIRIN (1997), "Between Tradition and Modernity: The Dilemma Facing Contemporary Central Asian Women". Pages 261-304 in Mary Buckley (ed.), *Post-Soviet Women: From the Baltic to Central Asia*. Cambridge, UK: Cambridge University Press.

ALDERMAN, HAROLD, PIERRE-ANDRÉ CHIAPPORI, LAWRENCE HADDAD, JOHN HODDINOTT, and RAVI KANBUR (1995), "Unitary versus Collective Models of the Household: Is it Time to Shift the Burden of Proof?". *World Bank Research Observer*, Vol. 10, No. 1, pages 1-19.

ALLEN, TUOVI (1996), "The Nordic Model of Gender Equality: The Welfare State, Patriarchy and Unfinished Emancipation". Pages 303-26 in Valentine M. Moghadam (ed.), *Patriarchy and Economic Development: Women's Positions at the End of the Twentieth Century*. Oxford: Clarendon Press.

ALVAZZI DEL FRATE, ANNA and KONSTANTIN GORYAINOV (1993), "Latent Crime in Russia". *UNICRI Issues and Reports*, No. 1. http://www.uni-cri.it/unicri/publicat/issues...: UN Interregional Crime and Justice Research Institute and Research Institute, Ministry of the Interior of the Russian Federation.

ARNAU, MIRIAM (1997), "Networks and Tutoring Programmes". Paper presented at the "European Conference on Women: Co-entrepreneurs, Entrepreneurs and Business Owners in Europe", Danish Federation of Small and Medium-sized Enterprises, Copenhagen, 5-6 September.

ASHWIN, SARAH and ELAINE BOWERS (1997), "Do Russian Women Want to Work?". Pages 21-37 in Mary Buckley (ed.), *Post-Soviet Women: From the Baltic to Central Asia*. Cambridge, UK: Cambridge University Press.

ASRK (Agency for Statistics of the Republic of Kazakhstan) (1998), "Demograficheskaya situatsiya v Kazakhstane" ("The Demographic Situation in Kazakhstan"). Florence: UNICEF International Child Development Centre. Mimeo. -In Russian.-

ATKINSON, A. B. and JOHN MICKLEWRIGHT (1992), *Economic Transformation in Eastern Europe and the Distribution of Income*. Cambridge, UK: Cambridge University Press.

ATTWOOD, L. (1997), "'She was Asking for It': Rape and Domestic Violence against Women". Pages 99-118 in Mary Buckley (ed.), *Post-Soviet Women: From the Baltic to Central Asia*. Cambridge, UK: Cambridge University Press.

AVDEEV, ALEXANDRE and ALAIN MONNIER (1996), "Mouvement de la population de la Russie 1959-1994: Tableaux démographiques" ("Movement of the Russian Population, 1959-1994: Demographic Tables"), No. 1. Paris: Institut National d'Etudes Démographiques. -In French.-

BAGRATIAN, H. and E. GURGEN (1997), "Payment Arrears in the Gas and Electric Power Sectors of the Russian Federation and Ukraine". *IMF Working Papers*, No. WP/97/162.

BAUER, ARMIN, NIÑA BOSCHMANN and DAVID GREEN (1997), *Women and Gender Relations in Kazakhstan*. Manila: Asian Development Bank.

BAUER, ARMIN, DAVID GREEN and KATHLEEN KUEHNAST (1997), *Women and Gender Relations: The Kyrgyz Republic in Transition*. Manila: Asian Development Bank.

BDBC (1997), "Canadian Women Entrepreneurs in Growth Sectors: A Survey", November. Toronto: Business Development Bank of Canada.

BEATON, A. E., M. O. MARTIN, I. V. S. MULLIS, E. J. GONZALEZ, T. A. SMITH, and D. L. KELLY (1996a), *Science Achievement in the Middle School Years: IEA's Third International Mathematics and Science Study*. Chestnut Hill, MA: Centre for the Study of Testing, Evaluation and Educational Policy, Boston College.

BEATON, A. E., I. V. S. MULLIS, M. O. MARTIN, E. J. GONZALEZ, D. L. KELLY, and T. A. SMITH (1996b), *Mathematics Achievement in the Middle School Years: IEA's Third International Mathematics and Science Study*. Chestnut Hill, MA: Centre for the Study of Testing, Evaluation and Educational Policy, Boston College.

BECK, BARBARA (1998), "For Better, for Worse: A Survey of Women and Work". *The Economist*, 18 July, Supplement.

BECKER, GARY S. (1991), *A Treatise on the Family*. Cambridge, MA: Harvard University Press.

BELTCHEVA, M. (1996), "Non-marital Births in Bulgaria". Sofia, Bulgaria: National Statistical Institute.

BITTMAN, MICHAEL and ROBERT E. GOODIN (1998), "An Equivalence Scale for Time". *Discussion Papers*, No. 85. http://www.sprc.unsw.edu.au/: Social Policy Research Centre, University of New South Wales.

BJÖRNBERG, ULLA and JÜRGEN SASS (eds) (1997), *Families with Small Children in Eastern and Western Europe*. Aldershot, UK: Ashgate.

BLANCHFLOWER, DAVID G. and ANDREW J. OSWALD (1998), "What Makes an Entrepreneur?". *Journal of Labour Economics*, Vol. 16, No. 1.

BLAU, FRANCINE D. (1998), "Trends in the Well-being of American Women, 1970-1995". *Journal of Economic Literature*, Vol. XXXVI, No. 1 (March), pages 112-65.

BLAU, FRANCINE D. and LAWRENCE M. KHAN (1996), "Wage Structure and Gender Earnings Differentials: An International Comparison". *Economica*, Vol. 63, No. 250 (Supplement, May), pages S29-62.

BLAU, FRANCINE D., MARIANNE A. FERBER and ANNE E. WINKLER (1998), *The Economics of Women, Men and Work*. Englewood Cliffs, NJ: Prentice-Hall.

BOBÁK, MARTIN (1998), "Social Determinants of Health". Pages 17-25 in Dominic Harrison and Erio Ziglio (eds), "Social Determinants of Health: Implications for the Health Professions". *Forum: Trends in Experimental and Clinical Medicine*, No. 8.3, Supplement 4 (July-September). Genoa: Forum Service Editors.

BOBÁK, MARTIN, E. BRUNNER, N. J. MILLER, Z. SKODOVA, and M. MARMOT (1998), "Could Antioxidants Play a Role in the High Rates of Coronary Heart Disease in the Czech Republic?". *European Journal of Clinical Nutrition*, Vol. 52, No. 9 (September), pages 632-36.

BOBÁK, MARTIN, Z. SKODOVA, Z. PISA, R. POLEDNE, and M. MARMOT (1997), "Political Changes and Trends in Cardiovascular Risk Factors in the Czech Republic, 1985-92". *Journal of Epidemiology and Community Health*, Vol. 51, No. 3 (June), pages 272-77.

BODROVA, VALENTINA (1995), "The Russian Family in Flux". *Transition*, Vol. 1, No. 16 (8 September), pages 10-11.

BOISSO, D., K. HAYES, J. HIRSCHBERG, and J. SILBER (1994), "Occupational Segregation in the Multidimensional Case". *Journal of Econometrics*, Vol. 61, pages 161-74.

BORISOV, B. and A. B. SINEL'NIKOV (1996), *Brachnost' i rozhdayemost' v*

Rossii: demograficheskiy analiz (Marriage and Fertility in Russia: A Demographic Analysis). Moscow: Family Research Institute, Ministry of Social Protection. -In Russian.-

BRADBURY, BRUCE and MARKUS JÄNNTI (1998), "Child Poverty across Industrialized Nations". Paper presented at the "25th General Conference of the International Association for Research in Income and Wealth", Cambridge, UK, 23-29 August.

BRAITHWAITE, JEANINE and T. HOOPENGARDNER (1997), "Who are Ukraine's Poor?". In P. K. Cornelius and P. Lenain (eds), *Ukraine: Accelerating the Transition to Market*. Washington, DC: International Monetary Fund.

BRIDGER, S. (1997), "Rural Women and the Impact of Economic Change". Pages 38-55 in Mary Buckley (ed.), *Post-Soviet Women: From the Baltic to Central Asia*. Cambridge, UK: Cambridge University Press.

BROWN, R. S., M. MOON and B. S. ZOLOTH (1980), "Incorporating Occupational Attainment in Studies of Male/Female Earnings Differentials". *Journal of Human Resources*, Vol. 15, pages 3-28.

BRUNO, MARTA (1996), "Employment Strategies and the Formation of New Identities in the Service Sector in Moscow". Pages 39-56 in Hilary Pilkington (ed.), *Gender, Generation and Identity in Contemporary Russia*. London: Routledge.

BRUNO, MARTA (1997), "Women and the Culture of Entrepreneurship". Pages 56-74 in Mary Buckley (ed.), *Post-Soviet Women: From the Baltic to Central Asia*. Cambridge, UK: Cambridge University Press.

BUCKLEY, MARY (ed.) (1997a), *Post-Soviet Women: From the Baltic to Central Asia*. Cambridge, UK: Cambridge University Press.

BUCKLEY, MARY (1997b), "Victims and Agents: Gender in Post-Soviet States". Pages 3-16 in Mary Buckley (ed.), *Post-Soviet Women: From the Baltic to Central Asia*. Cambridge, UK: Cambridge University Press.

BUCKLEY, MARY (1997c), "Adaptation of the Soviet Women's Committee: Deputies Voices from 'Women of Russia'". Pages 157-85 in Mary Buckley (ed.), *Post-Soviet Women: From the Baltic to Central Asia*. Cambridge, UK: Cambridge University Press.

BUMPASS, LARRY (1990), "Redefining Single-parent Families: Cohabitation and Changing Family Reality". *Demography*, Vol. 32, No. 3, pages 425-36.

CALDWELL, GILLIAN, STEVEN GALSTER and NADIA STEINZOR (1997), "Crime and Servitude: An Exposé of the Traffic in Women for Prostitution from the Newly Independent States". Washington, DC: Global Survival Network.

CAMPBELL, M. and M. DALY (1992), "Self-employment into the 1990s". *Employment Gazette*, June, pages 269-92.

CBSC (1996), *Statistical Yearbook, 1996*. Zagreb, Croatia: Central Bureau of Statistics of the Republic of Croatia.

CE (1993), *Recent Demographic Developments in Europe and North America, 1992*. Strasbourg: Council of Europe Press.

CE (1998), *Recent Demographic Developments in Europe and North America, 1997*. Strasbourg: Council of Europe Press.

CEC (1994), "Employment in Europe". COM, No. 314. Luxembourg: Directorate General for Employment, Industrial Relations and Social Affairs, Commission of the European Communities.

CERMAKOVA, MARIA (1991), "Sociálni postaveni zeny v ceskoslovenské spolecnosti" ("The Social Position of Women in Czechoslovak Society"). *Sociologicky ustav*. Prague: CSAW. -In Czech.-

CERMAKOVA, MARIA (1994), "The Social and Economic Status of Women in Czechoslovakia before the Partition". Pages 21-31 in European Network for Women's Studies, *Gains and Losses: Women and Transition in Eastern and Central Europe*. Bucharest: European Network for Women's Studies and Centre for Higher Education, UN Educational, Social and Cultural Organization.

CHAPPELL, DUNCAN and VITTORIO DI MARTINO (1998), *Violence at Work*. Geneva: International Labour Organization.

CHEN, L. C., F. WITTGENSTEIN and E. MCKEON (1996), "The Upsurge of Mortality in Russia: Causes and Policy Implications". *Population and Development Review*, Vol. 22, No. 3 (September), pages 517-30.

CIS STAT (1995a), *Demographic Yearbook, 1994*. Moscow: Interstate Statistical Committee of the Commonwealth of Independent States.

CIS STAT (1995b), *Demographic Yearbook, 1993*. Moscow: Interstate Statistical Committee of the Commonwealth of Independent States.

CIS STAT (Interstate Statistical Committee of the Commonwealth of Independent States) (1996), *1989 USSR Population Census*. Minneapolis, MN: Eastview Publications.

CIS STAT (1997), *Official Statistics of the Countries of the Commonwealth of Independent States, 1997-2*. Moscow: Interstate Statistical Committee of the Commonwealth of Independent States. -CD Rom.-

CIS STAT (1998a), *Official Statistics of the Countries of the Commonwealth of Independent States, 1998*. Moscow: Interstate Statistical Committee of the Commonwealth of Independent States. -CD Rom.-

CIS STAT (1998b), *Sodruzhestvo nezavisimykh gosudarstv v 1997 godu: statisticheskiy yezhigodnik (The Commonwealth of Independent States in 1997: Statistical Yearbook)*. Moscow: Interstate Statistical Committee of the Commonwealth of Independent States. -In Russian.-

CIS STAT (1998c), *Naseleniye i usloviya zhizni v stranakh sodruzhestvo nezavisimykh gosudarstv: statisticheskiy sbornik (Population and Living Conditions in the CIS Countries: Statistical Handbook)*. Moscow: Interstate Statistical Committee of the Commonwealth of Independent States. -In Russian.-

COMMANDER, SIMON and UNE LEE (1998), "How does Public Policy Affect the Income Distribution?: Evidence from Russia, 1992-1996". London: European Bank for Reconstruction and Development and World Bank. Mimeo (12 August).

CONNELLY, R. (1992), "The Effect of Child Care Costs on Married Women's Labour Force Participation". *Review of Economics and Statistics*, Vol. 74, pages 83-90.

CORNIA, GIOVANNI ANDREA (1998), "Labour Market Shocks, Psychosocial Stress and the Transition's Mortality Crisis". Paper presented at the "Arena Meeting I", the Verona Initiative, Verona, 14-17 October, sponsored by Regional Office for Europe, World Health Organization, Copenhagen.

COUDOUEL, ALINE (1998), "Living Standards in Transition: The Case of Uzbekistan", August. Florence: Department of Economics, European University Institute. Ph.D. Thesis.

CROMPTON, ROSEMARY (1997), "Work, Employment and Feminism in the Czech Republic". *Gender, Work and Organization*, Vol. 4, No. 3, pages 137-48.

CROMPTON, ROSEMARY (1998), "Gender Relations, Employment and Occupational Segregation: A Cross-national Study". Mimeo.

CROMPTON, ROSEMARY and FIONA HARRIS (1998), "Gender Relations and Employment: The Impact of Occupation". *Work, Employment and Society*, Vol. 12, No. 2, pages 297-315.

CROWLEY, ROZ (1997), "Networking as an Instrument of Training". Paper presented at the "European Conference on Women: Co-entrepreneurs, Entrepreneurs and Business Owners in Europe", Danish Federation of Small and Medium-sized Enterprises, Copenhagen, 5-6 September.

CSBL (1997), *Statistical Yearbook of Latvia, 1997*. Riga, Latvia: Central Statistical Bureau of Latvia.

CSBL (Central Statistical Bureau of Latvia) (1998), "Women and the Transition in Latvia". Florence: UNICEF International Child Development Centre. Mimeo.

CSO (1998), *Czech Demographic Yearbook*. Prague: Czech Statistical Office.

CSO (Czech Statistical Office), Factum non Fabula, WHO Collaborating Centre for Perinatal Medicine/Institute for the Care of Mother and Child, and Centres for Disease Control and Prevention (1995), *1993 Czech Republic Reproductive Health Survey: Final Report*, March. Washington, DC: US Government Printing Office.

CUSAN, ALESSANDRA and ALBERT MOTIVANS (1998), "Fiscal Adjustment, Education Equity and Access in Transition". Florence: International Child Development Centre. Mimeo.

DANZIGER, SHELDON and MARCIA CARLSON (1999), "Single Parents, Poverty and Social Welfare Policies in the West". Chapter 4 in Jeni Klugman and Albert Motivans (eds), *Single Parents and Child Welfare in the New Russia*. London: Macmillan.

DASZYNSKA, MARIA, MARLENA KUCIARSKA-CIESIELSKA, LONGINA RUTKOWSKA, RENATA SIEMIENSKA, and JOANNA STANCZAK (1998), "Women and the Transition in Poland". Florence: UNICEF International Child Development Centre. Mimeo (July).

DAVANZO, JULIE (ed.) (1996), *Russia's Demographic "Crisis"*. Santa Monica, CA: Rand Centre.

DEHNE, KARL L. (ed.) (1998), "The Determinants of the AIDS Epidemic in Eastern Europe". Geneva: Joint UN Programme on HIV/AIDS. Mimeo.

DESJARLAIS, ROBERT, LEON EISENBERG, BYRON GOOD, and ARTHUR KLEINMAN (1995), World Mental Health: Problems and Priorities in Low-income Countries. New York: Oxford University Press.

DMITRIEVA, ELENA (1996), "Orientations, Re-orientations or Disorient-ation?: Expectations of the Future among Russian School-leavers". Pages 75-93 in Hilary Pilkington (ed.), Gender, Generation and Identity in Contemporary Russia. London: Routledge,

DRAGONAS, THALIA, JEAN GOLDING, ROSEMARY GREENWOOD, and ILONA KOUPILOVÁ (1996), "Maternal Stresses and Strains, Anxiety and Depression, and their Mediators". Pages 38-44 in Thalia Dragonas, Jean Golding, Rimma Ignatyeva, and Remigijus Prohkorskas (eds), Pregnancy in the 90s: The European Longitudinal Study of Pregnancy and Childhood. Bristol, UK: Sansom and Co.

DRAKULIC, SLAVENKA (1998), "What We Learned from Western Feminists". Transitions: Changes in Post-Communist Societies (Prague), Vol. 5, No. 1.

DUNCAN, O. and B. DUNCAN (1955), "A Methodological Analysis of Segregation Indices". American Sociological Review, Vol. 20, pages 210-17.

EBRD (1994), Transition Report 1994: Institutional Reform and Economic Openness. London: European Bank for Reconstruction and Development.

EBRD (1996), Transition Report 1996: Infrastructure and Savings. London: European Bank for Reconstruction and Development.

EBRD (1997), Transition Report 1997: Enterprise Performance and Growth. London: European Bank for Reconstruction and Development.

EBRD (1998), Transition Report 1998: Financial Sector in Transition. London: European Bank for Reconstruction and Development.

EC (European Community) (1993), "Report to European Community Foreign Ministers on the Investigative Mission into the Treatment of Muslim Women in the Former Yugoslavia". Document No. S/25240, January. New York: Permanent Representative of Denmark to the United Nations.

ECOHOST (1998), "Childhood Injuries: A Priority Area for the Transition Countries of Central and Eastern Europe and the Newly Independent States", September. London: European Centre on Health of Societies in Transition, London School of Hygiene and Tropical Medicine.

THE ECONOMIST (1996), "The Stolen Brides of Kyrgyzstan", 23 November.

THE ECONOMIST (1998), "The Sex Industry", 14 February, pages 23-25.

EINHORN, BARBARA (1993), Cinderella Goes to Market: Citizenship, Gender and Women's Movements in East Central Europe. London: Verso.

ELIZAROV, VALERY (1996), "The Socio-economic Potential of Families". Florence: UNICEF International Child Development Centre. Mimeo.

ENSOR, TIM and LARISA SAVELYEVA (1998), "Informal Payments for Health Care in the Former Soviet Union: Some Evidence from Kazakhstan". Health Policy and Planning, Vol. 13, No. 1, pages 41-49.

ENTWHISTLE, B., L. WATTERSON and D. DONOHUE (1997), "Family Planning and Abortion in the Russian Federation: Trends 1992-1996". Chapel Hill, NC: Carolina Population Centre, University of North Carolina.

ERMISCH, JOHN (1990), "Demographic Aspects of the Growing Number of Lone-parent Families". Pages 27-41 in OECD, Lone-parent Families: The Economic Challenge. Paris: Organization for Economic Cooperation and Development.

ESAJAS, JOS (1997), "Helping Women to Set Up or Develop Business". Paper presented at the "European Conference on Women: Co-entrepre-neurs, Entrepreneurs and Business Owners in Europe", Danish Federation of Small and Medium-sized Enterprises, Copenhagen, 5-6 September.

EUROPEAN NETWORK FOR WOMEN'S STUDIES (1994), Gains and Losses: Women and Transition in Eastern and Central Europe. Bucharest: European Network for Women's Studies and Centre for Higher Education, UN Educational, Social and Cultural Organization.

EUROPEAN OBSERVATORY ON NATIONAL FAMILY POLICIES (1990), Families and Policies, Evolutions and Trends in 1988-89: Interim Report. Luxembourg: Commission of the European Communities.

EUROPEAN PARLIAMENT (1996), "Central and Eastern European Women: A Portrait". Women's Rights Working Papers, No. W8 (March). Strasbourg: Directorate General for Research, European Parliament.

EUROSTAT (1993), Demographic Statistics, 1993. Luxembourg: Office for Official Publications of the European Communities.

EUROSTAT (1997a), Demographic Statistics, 1997. Luxembourg: Office for Official Publications of the European Communities.

EUROSTAT (1997b), Eurostat Yearbook '97: A Statistical Eye on Europe, 1986-1996. Luxembourg: Office for Official Publications of the European Communities.

EUROSTAT (1998), Labour Force Survey: Results 1997. Luxembourg: Office for Official Publications of the European Communities.

FAJTH, GÁSPÁR (1994), "Family Support Policies in Transitional Economies: Challenges and Constraints". Innocenti Occasional Papers, No. EPS 43 (August). Florence: UNICEF International Child Development Centre.

FAJTH, GÁSPÁR (1996), "Family Support Policies in Central and Eastern Europe". Paper presented at the workshop "Economic Transformation, Institutional Change and Social Sector Reform", Task Force on Economies in Transition, National Research Council, Washington, DC, September.

FEMINIST LEAGUE and UNDP (1997), "Republic of Kazakhstan: Report on the Status of Women 1997". Almaty, Kazakhstan: Malvina Publishing House.

FESTI, PATRICK and LYDIA PROKOFIEVA (1996), "Alimenty, posobiya i dokhody semey posle razvoda" ("Alimony, Benefits and Family Income after Divorce"). Naseleniye i Obshehestvo (Population and Society), No. 15 (December). Moscow: Centre for Demography and Human Ecology. -In Russian.-

FISCHER, MARY ELLEN and DOINA PASCA HARSÁNYI (1994), "From Tradition and Ideology to Elections and Competition: The Changing Status of Women in Romanian Politics". Pages 201-23 in Marilyn Rueschemeyer (ed.), Women in the Politics of Postcommunist Eastern Europe. Armonk, NY: M. E. Sharpe.

FLEMMING, J. and JOHN MICKLEWRIGHT (1999), "Income Distribution, Economic Systems and Transition". Innocenti Occasional Papers, No. EPS 70. Florence: UNICEF International Child Development Centre.

FODOR, EVA (1994), "The Political Woman?: Women in Politics in Hungary". Pages 171-99 in Marilyn Rueschemeyer (ed.), Women in the Politics of Postcommunist Eastern Europe. Armonk, NY: M. E. Sharpe.

FONG, MONICA S. (1993), "The Role of Women in Rebuilding the Russian Economy". Studies of Economies in Transformation, No. 10. Washington, DC: World Bank.

FORRAI, JUDITH (1996), "Adolescent Sexuality in Hungary Today". Choices, Vol. 25, No. 3, pages 32-36.

FOUNDATION ROSA (1997), I will not Kill You Today: A Report on Home Violence. Prague: Foundation ROSA.

FROLOVA, ELENA B. (1998), "Problems in Poverty Measurement and Income Inequality in the Russian Federation: Methodological Issues and Conclusions". Paper presented at "Statistics for Economic and Social Development", Joint Conference of the International Association of Survey Statisticians and the International Association for Official Statistics, Aguascalientes, Mexico, 1-4 September.

FSOY (1996), Statistical Yearbook of Yugoslavia, 1996. Belgrade: Federal Statistical Office, FR Yugoslavia.

FSOY (Federal Statistical Office, FR Yugoslavia) (1998), "Women and the Transition in the Federal Republic of Yugoslavia". Florence: UNICEF International Child Development Centre. Mimeo.

GANTCHEVA, ROUMIANA (1999) "Does the Transition to a Market Economy Influence Violence against Children". Florence: UNICEF International Child Development Centre. Mimeo.

GARDASHKHANOVA, MERI (1998), "Women and the Transition in the Azerbaijan Republic". Florence: UNICEF International Child Development Centre. Mimeo.

GASYUK, GALINA (1998), "The Situation of Women in Belarus during the Transitional Period of 1991-97". Florence: UNICEF International Child Development Centre. Mimeo.

GIMPLESON, V. and D. LIPPOLDT (1998), "Private-sector Employment in Russia: Scale, Composition and Performance, Evidence from the Russian Labour Force Survey". Moscow: Moscow University. Mimeo.

GOLDSTEIN, ELLEN, ALEXANDER S. PREKER, OLUSOJI ADEYI, and GNANARAJ CHELLARAJ (1996), "Trends in Health Status, Services and Finance: The Transition in Central and Eastern Europe". *World Bank Technical Papers*, No. 341, Vol. 1 (October).

GONDOLF, EDWARD W. and DMITRI SHESTAKOV (1997), "Spousal Homicide in Russia: Gender Inequality in a Multifactor Model". *Violence against Women*, Vol. 3, No. 5 (October), pages 533-46.

GOSKOMSTAT (1988), *Naseleniye SSSR (Population of the USSR)*. Moscow: Finansy i statistika. -In Russian.-

GOSKOMSTAT (1990), *Demograf/cheskiy yezhigodnik SSSR (Demographic Yearbook USSR)*. Moscow: Finansy i statistika. -In Russian.-

GOSKOMSTAT (1991a), *Social'noye razvitiye SSSR (Social Development of the USSR)*. Moscow: Finansy i statistika. -In Russian.-

GOSKOMSTAT (1991b), *Narodnoye khozyaystvo SSSR v 1990 godu (National Economy of the USSR, 1990)*. Moscow: Finansy i statistika. -In Russian.-

GOSKOMSTAT (1992), *Narodnoye khozyaystvo Rossiyskoy federatsii, 1992 (Economy of the Russian Federation, 1992)*. Moscow: Goskomstat RF. -In Russian.-

GOSKOMSTAT (1995a), *Typy i sostav domokhozyastv v Rossii (Household Types and Structure in Russia)*. Moscow: Goskomstat RF. -In Russian.-

GOSKOMSTAT (1995b), *Sostoyaniye v brake i rozhdayemost' v Rossii (Marital Status and Fertility in Russia)*. Moscow: Goskomstat RF. -In Russian.-

GOSKOMSTAT (1996a), *Rossiyskiy statisticheskiy yezhigodnik (Russian Statistical Yearbook)*. Moscow: Goskomstat RF. -In Russian.-

GOSKOMSTAT (1996b), *Demograf/cheskiy yezhigodnik (Demographic Yearbook)*. Moscow: Goskomstat RF. -In Russian.-

GOSKOMSTAT (1998a), "Women and the Transition in Russia". Florence: UNICEF International Child Development Centre. Mimeo.

GOSKOMSTAT (1998b), *Population of Russia, 1897-1997: Statistical Handbook*. Moscow: Goskomstat RF.

GROOTAERT, CHRISTIAAN and JEANINE BRAITHWAITE (1998), "Poverty Correlates and Indicator-based Targeting in Eastern Europe and the Former Soviet Union", May. Washington, DC: World Bank.

GRÜNER, ELISABETH (1998), "Times are Changing and So is Entrepreneurship". Paper presented at "The V International Conference 'Women in a Changing World'", St Petersburg, 25-26 June.

GUNDERSON, M. (1989), "Male-Female Wage Differentials and Policy Responses". *Journal of Economic Literature*, Vol. 27, No. 1, pages 46-72.

GUS (1994), *Rocznik Statystyczny 1994 (Statistical Yearbook 1994)*. Warsaw: Central Statistical Office (GUS). -In Polish.-

GUS (1997), *Rocznik Statystyczny 1997 (Statistical Yearbook 1997)*. Warsaw: Central Statistical Office (GUS). -In Polish.-

HARRISON, DOMINIC (1998), "Integrating Health-sector Action on the Social and Economic Determinants of Health". Pages 51-70 in Dominic Harrison and Erio Ziglio (eds), "Social Determinants of Health: Implications for the Health Professions". *Forum: Trends in Experimental and Clinical Medicine*, No. 8.3, Supplement 4 (July-September). Genoa: Forum Service Editors.

HARRISON, DOMINIC and ERIO ZIGLIO (eds) (1998), "Social Determinants of Health: Implications for the Health Professions". *Forum: Trends in Experimental and Clinical Medicine*, No. 8.3, Supplement 4 (July-September). Genoa: Forum Service Editors.

HAUB, CARL (1996), "Demographic Change and the Status of Women in Belarus". Washington, DC: World Bank. Mimeo.

HAVELKOVA, HANA (1996), "Ignored but Assumed: Family and Gender between Public and Private Realm". *Czech Sociological Review*, Vol. 4, No. 1 (Spring), pages 63-79.

HEALY, JUDITH and MARTIN MCKEE (1997), "Health-sector Reform in Central and Eastern Europe: The Professional Dimension". *Health Policy and Planning*, Vol. 12, No. 4, pages 286-95.

HECKMAN, J. (1979), "Sample Selection Bias as a Specification Error". *Econometrica*, Vol. 47, pages 153-61.

HEISE, LORI L., JACQUELINE PITANGUY and ADRIENNE GERMAIN (1994), "Violence against Women: The Hidden Health Burden". *World Bank Discussion Papers*, No. 255.

HENDRICHOVA, JANA and VERA KUCHAROVA (1998), "Gender Policies in Transition in the Czech Republic". Florence: UNICEF International Child Development Centre. Mimeo (July).

HERNANDEZ, DONALD (1993), *America's Children: Resources from Family, Government and the Economy*. New York: Russell Sage Foundation.

HESLI, VICKI L. and ARTHUR H. MILLER (1993), "The Gender Base of Institutional Support in Lithuania, Ukraine and Russia". *Europe-Asia Studies*, Vol. 45, No. 3, pages 505-32.

HINRICHSEN, DON (1995), "Requiem for a Dying Sea". *People and the Planet*, Vol. 4, No. 2.

HOLZER, JERZY Z. and IRENA KOWALSKA (1997), "Fertility and Family Surveys in Countries of the ECE Region, Standard Country Report: Poland". *Economic Studies*, No. 10d. Geneva: UN Economic Commission for Europe and UN Population Fund.

HORTON, MARK A. (1996), "Health and Education Expenditures in Russia, the Baltic States and the Other Countries of the Former Soviet Union". *IMF Working Papers*, No. WP/96/126 (November).

HRW (1997), "Russia, too Little, too Late: State Response to Violence against Women". *Reports*, Vol. 9, No. 13 (D) (December). http://www.hrw.org/reports97/: Human Rights Watch.

HRW (1998), "Abandoned to the State: Cruelty and Neglect in Russian Orphanages", December. http://www.hrw.org/reports98/: Human Rights Watch.

HUNT, J. (1998), "The Transition in East Germany: When is a Ten Point Fall in the Gender Pay Gap Bad News?". *CEPR Discussion Paper Series*, No. 1,805 (March). London: Centre for Economic Policy Research.

ILIRIANI, EDA and PERSIDA ASLIANI (1995), "Albania's Students Teach their Peers about Sexuality and Safer Sex". *Planned Parenthood Challenges*, No. 1995/1.

ILO (1992), *Yearbook of Labour Statistics*. Geneva: International Labour Organization.

ILO (1997a), *Breaking through the Glass Ceiling: Women in Management*. Geneva: Sectoral Activities Programme, International Labour Organization.

ILO (1997b), *Yearbook of Labour Statistics*. Geneva: International Labour Organization.

ILO (1998), *Yearbook of Labour Statistics*. Geneva: International Labour Organization.

IMCC and CDC (1995), *Reproductive Health Survey, Romania 1993: Final Report*, March. Bucharest: Institute for Mother and Child Care and Centres for Disease Control and Prevention.

INTERFAX (1997), *Interfax Statistical Report*, Vol. VI, No. 51/274 (12-26 December). Denver: Interfax International.

IOGU and MACRO INTERNATIONAL (1997), *Uzbekistan: Demographic and Health Survey, 1996*. Calverton, MD: Institute of Obstetrics and Gynæcology (Uzbekistan) and Macro International.

IOM (1995), "Trafficking and Prostitution: The Growing Exploitation of Migrant Women from Central and Eastern Europe", May. Budapest: Migration Information Programme, International Organization for Migration.

IOM (1996a), "Trafficking of Women to Countries of the European Union: Characteristics, Trends and Policy Issues". Paper presented at the "Conference on Trafficking in Women for Sexual Exploitation", Vienna, June. Geneva: International Organization for Migration.

IOM (1996b), "Trafficking in Women to Italy for Sexual Exploitation", June. Budapest: Migration Information Programme, International Organization for Migration.

IOM (1997), "CIS Migration Report, 1996". Geneva: International Organization for Migration.

IOM (1998), "Information Campaign against Trafficking in Women from Ukraine: Research Report", July. Geneva: International Organization for Migration.

IOM and BMFA (Office of the Austrian Minister for Women's Affairs) (1996), "Trafficking in Women to Austria for Sexual Exploitation", June. Budapest: Migration Information Programme, International Organization for Migration.

IPHS (Institute of Public Health of Serbia), IPHM (Institute of Public Health of Montenegro) and UNICEF (1997), *FR Yugoslavia 1996: Multiple Indicator Cluster Survey*. Belgrade: UNICEF-Belgrade.

IPU (1995), "Women in Parliaments 1945-1995: A World Statistical Survey". *Reports and Documents*, No. 23. Geneva: Inter-Parliamentary Union.

IPU (1999), "Women in National Parliaments". http://www.ipu.org/wmn-e/world.htm: Inter-Parliamentary Union.

IVANOVA, ELENA I. (1997) "Braky i razvody" ("Marriage and Divorce"). Pages 54-74 in Anatoly G. Vishnevskiy (ed.), *Naseleniye Rossii: 1996 (Population of Russia, 1996)*. Moscow: Centre for Human Demography and Ecology. -In Russian.-

IZHEVSKA, TATIANA (1994), "Ukrainian Women during the Transitional Period: Basic Trends". Pages 8-14 in European Network for Women's Studies, *Gains and Losses: Women and Transition in Eastern and Central Europe*. Bucharest: European Network for Women's Studies and Centre for Higher Education, UN Educational, Social and Cultural Organization.

JAGODIC, GORDANA KUTEROVAC and TOMISLAV BUNJEVAC (1995), "Report on the UNICEF Psychosocial Programmes for Children in Croatia, 1992-1994". Zagreb, Croatia: UNICEF-Zagreb.

JAIN, PANKAJ S. (1996), "Managing Credit for the Rural Poor: Lessons from the Grameen Bank". *World Development*, Vol. 24, No. 1, pages 79-89.

JALUSIC, VLASTA (1998), "Freedom versus Equality?". *Working Papers*, No. 1/1998. Vienna: Institute for Human Sciences (IWM).

JANOVA, MIRA and MARIETTE SINEAU (1992), "Women's Participation in Political Power in Europe: An Essay in East-West Comparison". *Women's Studies International Forum*, Vol. 15, No. 1, pages 115-28.

JOHNSON, S., D. KAUFMAN and A. SCHLEIFER (1997), "Politics and Entrepreneurship in Transition Economies". *Working Paper Series*, No. 57. Ann Arbor, MI: William Davidson Institute, University of Michigan.

JONES, ELLEN and FRED GRUPP (1987), *Modernization, Value Change and Fertility in the Soviet Union*. Cambridge, UK: Cambridge University Press.

JUHN, C., K. MURPHY and B. PIERCE (1993), "Wage Inequality and the Rise in Returns to Skill". *Journal of Political Economy*, Vol. 101, pages 410-42.

KALNINS, ILZE and IEVA RANKA (1996), "Attitudes et comportements des jeunes Lettoniens à l'égard de la santé dans un contexte de changements rapides" ("The Attitudes and Behaviour of Young Latvians towards Health in a Rapidly Changing Environment"). In Renée B. Dandurand, Roch Hurtubise and Céline Le Bourdais (eds), *Enfances: Perspectives sociales et pluriculturelles (Childhoods: Social and Pluricultural Perspectives)*. Sainte-Foy, Canada: Institut Québécois de Recherche sur la Culture. -In French.-

KALOYANOV, T. (1995), "Desired Number of Children by Ethnic Group". Sofia, Bulgaria: National Statistical Institute.

KARL, MARILEE (ed.) (1995), *Women and Empowerment: Participation and Decision Making*. London: Zed Books.

KARRO, HELLE (1997), "Abortion in the Framework of Family Planning in Estonia". *Acta Obstetricia et Gynecologica Scandinavica*, Vol. 76, No. 164 (Supplement), pages 46-50.

KASK, URVE, ÜLLE PETTAI, MARE RUUGE, ENE PALO, ARVO VALTIN, and MARE KUSMA (1998), "Women in the Transition Period in Estonia". Florence: UNICEF International Child Development Centre. Mimeo.

KATUS, K. (1998), "Rahvastikuareng" ("Population Development"). *Sotsiaaltrendid (Social Trends)* (Tallinn, Estonia), pages 7-23. -In Estonian.-

KAY, REBECCA (1997), "Images of an Ideal Woman: Perceptions of Russian Womanhood through the Media, Education and Women's Own Eyes". Pages 77-98 in Mary Buckley (ed.), *Post-Soviet Women: From the Baltic to Central Asia*. Cambridge, UK: Cambridge University Press.

KING, ALAN J. C. and BEVERLY COLES (1992), "The Health of Canada's Youth: Views and Behaviours of 11-, 13- and 15-year-olds from 11 Countries". Ottawa: Minister of National Health and Welfare.

KING, ALAN J. C., BENTE WOLD, CHRIS TUDOR-SMITH, and YOSSI HAREL (1996), "The Health of Youth: A Cross-national Survey". *WHO Regional Publications, European Series*, No. 69. Copenhagen: Regional Office for Europe, World Health Organization.

KLIJZING, ERIC and MIROSLAV MACURA (1995), "Cohabitation and Extra-marital Childbearing: Early FFS Evidence". Paper presented at "The United Nations Fourth World Conference on Women", Beijing, September. Geneva: Population Activities Unit, UN Economic Commission for Europe.

KLUGMAN, JENI (ed.) (1996), *Poverty in Russia: Public Policy and Private Responses*. Washington, DC: Economic Development Institute, World Bank.

KLUGMAN, JENI and ALEXANDRE KOLEV (1999), "Single Parenthood and Poverty in Russia". Chapter 6 in Jeni Klugman and Albert Motivans (eds), *Single Parents and Child Welfare in the New Russia*. London: Macmillan.

KLUGMAN, JENI and ALBERT MOTIVANS (eds) (1999), *Single Parents and Child Welfare in the New Russia*. London: Macmillan.

KLUGMAN, JENI, SHEILA MARNIE, JOHN MICKLEWRIGHT, and PHILIP O'KEEFE (1997), "The Impact of Kindergarten Divestiture on Household Welfare in Central Asia". Pages 183-201 in Jane Falkingham, Jeni Klugman, Sheila Marnie, and John Micklewright (eds), *Household Welfare in Central Asia*. London: Macmillan.

KOSTOVA, DOBRINKA (1994), "Similar or Different?: Women in Post-communist Bulgaria". Pages 117-32 in Marilyn Rueschemeyer (ed.), *Women in the Politics of Postcommunist Eastern Europe*. Armonk, NY: M. E. Sharpe.

KOUPILOVÁ, ILONA, MARTIN MCKEE and JAN HOLCÍK (1998), "Neonatal Mortality in the Czech Republic during the Transition". *Health Policy*, Vol. 46, No. 1, pages 43-52.

KOUPILOVÁ, ILONA, MARTIN BOBÁK, JAN HOLCÍK, HYNEK PIKHART, and DAVID A. LEON (1998), "Increasing Social Variation in Birth Outcomes in the Czech Republic after 1989". *American Journal of Public Health*, Vol. 88, No. 9, pages 1,343-47. -© American Public Health Association.-

KOUPILOVÁ, ILONA, THALIA DRAGONAS, ROSEMARY GREENWOOD, RIMMA IGNATYEVA, LUBOMIR KUKLA, and JAROSLAV STEJSKAL (1996), "International Differences in Social Support Systems of Pregnant Women". Paper presented at the EUPHA Annual Meeting, London, 12-14 December.

KOWALSKA, A. (1996), "Economic Activity of Women and their Position in the Labour Market". Warsaw: Department of Labour Statistics, Central Statistical Office (GUS). Mimeo.

KRENGEL, M. (1997), "Studie über die Lebensentwürfe von Jugendlichen, ihre Kenntnisse und Vorstellungen von Sexualität, Geschlechtlichkeit und Verhütung" ("Study of the Ideas of Young People on their Future Lives, their Knowledge and Ideas on Sexuality, Sex and Contraception"). Bad Homburg, Germany: EPOS Health Consultants and the German Society for Technical Cooperation. -In German.-

KRSTIC, G. and BARRY REILLY (1998), "Modelling Secondary Job Holding in Yugoslavia". Brighton, UK: University of Sussex. Mimeo.

KSH (1995), *Statistical Yearbook of Hungary*. Budapest: Central Statistical Office (KSH).

KUPRIYANOVA, ELENA IVANOVNA (1998), "Gender Policies in Transition in the Russian Federation". Florence: UNICEF International Child Development Centre. Mimeo (27 July).

LACZKO, ZSUZSA and ANIKÓ SOLTÉSZ (eds) (1997), "The Status of Women in the Labour Market in Hungary: Entrepreneurship as an Alternative". Budapest: Small Enterprise Economic Development Foundation.

LAKATOS, JUDIT (1998), "Women and the Transition in Hungary". Florence: UNICEF International Child Development Centre. Mimeo (June).

LAND, HILARY and JANE LEWIS (1997), "The Emergence of Lone Motherhood as a Problem in Late Twentieth Century Britain". *Welfare State Programme Discussion Papers*, No. WSP/134. London: STICERD, London School of Economics.

LANG-PICKVANCE, K., N. MANNING and C. PICKVANCE (eds) (1997), *Environmental and Housing Movements: Grassroots Experience in Hungary, Russia and Estonia*. Aldershot, UK: Avebury.

LAPORTE, B. and D. RINGOLD (1997), "Trends in Education Access and Financing during the Transition in Central and Eastern Europe". *World Bank Technical Papers*, No. 361.

LDS (Lithuanian Department of Statistics) (1998), "Women and the Transition in Lithuania". Florence: UNICEF International Child Development Centre. Mimeo.

LEON, D. A. *et al.* (1997), "Huge Variation in Russian Mortality Rates, 1984-94: Artifact, Alcohol, or What?". *The Lancet*, Vol. 350, No. 9,075 (9 August), pages 383-88.

LESTHAEGHE, RON and DIRK J. VAN DE KAA (1986), "Twee Demografische Transities?" ("Two Demographic Transitions?"). Pages 9-24 in Dirk J. van de Kaa and Ron Lesthaeghe (eds), *Bevolking: Groei en Krimp (Population: Growing and Shrinking)*. Deventer, the Netherlands: van

Loghum Slaterus. -In Dutch.-

LÉVAI, KATALIN and RÓBERT KISS (1997), "Nök a közéletben" ("Women in Public Life"). Pages 52-70 in Katalin Lévai and István György Tóth (eds), *Szerepváltozások: Jelentés a nök helyzetéröl 1997 (Changing Roles: Report on the Situation of Women, 1997).* Budapest: Tárki. -In Hungarian.-

LÉVAI, KATALIN and ISTVÁN GYÖRGY TÓTH (eds) (1997), *Szerepváltozások: Jelentés a nök helyzetéröl 1997 (Changing Roles: Report on the Situation of Women, 1997).* Budapest: Tárki. -In Hungarian.-

LIBANOVA, ELLA, HELEN MAKAROVA and OLEXLY POZNYAK (1998), "Gender Policies in Transition in Ukraine". Florence: UNICEF International Child Development Centre. Mimeo.

LIBORAKINA, MARINA (1998), "The Unappreciated Mothers of Civil Society". *Transitions: Changes in Post-Communist Societies* (Prague), Vol. 5, No. 1.

LINZ, S. J. (1996), "Gender Differences in the Russian Labour Market". *Journal of Economic Issues*, Vol. 30, pages 161-85.

LIPOVSKAYA, OLGA (1997), "Women's Groups in Russia". Pages 186-99 in Mary Buckley (ed.), *Post-Soviet Women: From the Baltic to Central Asia.* Cambridge, UK: Cambridge University Press.

LONKILA, M. (1997), "Informal Exchange Relations in Post-Soviet Russia: A Comparative Perspective". http://www.socresonline.org.uk/socresonline/2/2/9.html: *Sociological Research Online*.

LUCIFORA, C. and BARRY REILLY (1990), "Wage Discrimination and Female Occupational Intensity". *Labour*, Vol. 4, No. 2, pages 147-68.

LUNDBERG, SHELLY J., ROBERT A. POLLAK and TERENCE J. WALES (1997), "Do Husbands and Wives Pool their Resources?: Evidence from the UK Child Benefit". *Journal of Human Resources*, Vol. 32, No. 3 (Summer), pages 463-80.

LUNIN, IGOR, THOMAS L. HALL, JEFFREY S. MANDEL, JULIA KAY, and NORMAN HEARST (1995), "Adolescent Sexuality in St Petersburg, Russia". *AIDS*, Vol. 9, Supplement 1, pages S53-S60.

MAGLOUTCHIANTS, JULIETTE (1998), "Women and the Transition in Armenia". Florence: UNICEF International Child Development Centre. Mimeo.

MANNING, N. (1998), "Patterns of Environmental Movements in Eastern Europe". *Environmental Politics*, Vol. 7, No. 2, pages 100-34.

MANSKI, C. (1989), "Anatomy of the Selection Problem". *Journal of Human Resources*, Vol. 24, pages 343-60.

MARMOT, MICHAEL G., H. BOSMA, H. HEMINGWAY, E. BRUNNER, and S. STANSFELD (1997), "Contribution of Job Control and Other Risk Factors to Social Variations in Coronary Heart Disease Incidence". *The Lancet*, No. 350, pages 235-39.

MARNIE, SHEILA (1998), "Uzbekistan: Summary Report". Florence: UNICEF International Child Development Centre. Mimeo (August).

MARNIE, SHEILA and ALBERT MOTIVANS (1994), "Women in the Labour Market in the Former Soviet Union". Washington, DC: World Bank. Mimeo.

MARSH, R. (ed.) (1996a), *Women in Russia and Ukraine.* Cambridge, UK: Cambridge University Press.

MARSH, R. (1996b), "Anastasiia Posadskaia, the Dubna Forum and the Independent Women's Movement in Russia". Pages 286-97 in R. Marsh (ed.), *Women in Russia and Ukraine.* Cambridge, UK: Cambridge University Press.

MCAULEY, ALASTAIR (1981), *Women's Work and Wages in the Soviet Union.* Oxford: Katerprint.

MCCUE, K. (1996), "Promotions and Wage Growth". *Journal of Labour Economics*, Vol. 14, No. 3, pages 175-209.

MCGILLIVRAY, M. (1991), "The Human Development Index: Yet Another Redundant Composite Development Indicator?". *World Development*, Vol. 19, No. 10.

MCGILLIVRAY, M. and H. WHITE (1993), "Measuring Development?: The UNDP's Human Development Index". *Journal of International Development, Policy, Economics, and International Relations*, Vol. 5, No. 2.

MCKEOWN, T. (1976), *The Modern Rise of Population.* New York: Academic Press.

MCLANAHAN, SARA and LYNNE CASPAR (1995), "Growing Diversity and Inequality in the American Family". Pages 1-45 in R. Fanley (ed.), *State of the Union: America in the 1990s.* New York: Russell Sage Foundation.

MEG (Ministry of the Economy of Georgia) (1998), "Gender Policies in Transition in Georgia". Florence: UNICEF International Child Development Centre. Mimeo.

MEHROTRA, SANTOSH and RICHARD JOLLY (1997), *Development with a Human Face: Experiences in Social Achievement and Economic Growth.* Oxford: Clarendon Press.

MES (1998), "Available Data about Suicide Incidence in the Republic of Croatia". Zagreb, Croatia: Ministry of Education and Sports. Mimeo.

MES and UNICEF (1997), "Modules 1, 3 and 5: Evaluation of Psychosocial Projects in Croatia between 1992 and 1996". Zagreb, Croatia: Ministry of Education and Sports and UNICEF-Zagreb.

MICKLEWRIGHT, JOHN and KITTY STEWART (1999), "Is Child Welfare Converging in the European Union?". *Innocenti Occasional Papers*, No. EPS 69 (May). Florence: UNICEF International Child Development Centre.

MILANOVÍC, BRANKO (1996), "Income, Inequality and Poverty during the Transition". *Research Papers*, No. 11. Washington, DC: World Bank.

MILANOVÍC, BRANKO (1998), "Income, Inequality and Poverty during the Transition from Planned to Market Economy". *World Bank Regional and Sectoral Studies.* Washington, DC: World Bank.

MINNESOTA ADVOCATES FOR HUMAN RIGHTS (1995), "Lifting the Last Curtain: A Report on Domestic Violence in Romania". Minneapolis, MN: Minnesota Advocates for Human Rights.

MINNESOTA ADVOCATES FOR HUMAN RIGHTS (1996), *Domestic Violence in Albania.* Minneapolis, MN: Minnesota Advocates for Human Rights.

MLSD (Ministry of Labour and Social Development) (1995), "O polozhenii detey v Rossiyskoy Federatsii" ("The Situation of Children in the Russian Federation"). Moscow: International Publishing House "Energy". -In Russian.-

MLSD (Ministry of Labour and Social Development) (1997), "O polozhenii detey v Rossiyskoy Federatsii" ("The Situation of Children in the Russian Federation"). Moscow: International Publishing House "Energy". -In Russian.-

MOCKIENE, B., R. KLEPACIENE and Z. JACKUNAS (1997), "Lithuania: Education in Transition". Florence: UNICEF International Child Development Centre. Mimeo (September).

MOGHADAM, VALENTINE M. (ed.) (1992), "Privatization and Democratization in Central and Eastern Europe and the Soviet Union: The Gender Dimension". *Research for Action.* Helsinki: UNU-WIDER.

MOGHADAM, VALENTINE M. (ed.) (1993), "Gender, Development and Policy: Towards Equity and Empowerment". *Research for Action.* Helsinki: UNU-WIDER.

MOGHADAM, VALENTINE M. (1996), "Patriarchy and Post-communism: Eastern Europe and the Former Soviet Union". Pages 327-53 in Valentine M. Moghadam (ed.), *Patriarchy and Economic Development: Women's Positions at the End of the Twentieth Century.* Oxford: Clarendon Press.

MOHG and UNICEF (1996), "EPI Coverage Survey in Georgia". Tbilisi: Ministry of Health (Georgia) and UNICEF-Tbilisi.

MOHK and UNICEF (1995), "MICS, Multiple Indicator Cluster Survey: Kyrgyz Republic, 1995". Bishkek, Kyrgyz Republic: Ministry of Health (Kyrgyz Republic) and UNICEF-Bishkek.

MOHT and UNICEF (1995), "MICS, Multiple Indicator Cluster Survey: Turkmenistan, 1995". Ashgabat, Turkmenistan: Ministry of Health (Turkmenistan) and UNICEF-Ashgabat.

MORVANT, PENNY (1995), "Bearing the 'Double Burden' in Russia". *Transition*, Vol. 1, No. 16 (8 September).

MOTIVANS, ALBERT (1999), "Family Stability and Structure in Russia". Chapter 2 in Jeni Klugman and Albert Motivans (eds), *Single Parents and Child Welfare in the New Russia.* London: Macmillan.

MOW (Ministry of Welfare) and UNDP/UNFPA (UN Development Programme/UN Population Fund) (1998), "Reproductive Health in Latvia: Evaluation and Recommendations". Riga, Latvia: Jana Seta.

MOZHINA, M. and ELENA PROKOFIEVA (1997), "Living Standards of Families in Russia". Paper presented at the "Seminar on Family Structure, Welfare and Policies", UNICEF International Child Development Centre, Florence, November.

MRSEVIC, ZORICA and DONNA M. HUGHES (1997), "Violence against Women in Belgrade, Serbia: SOS Hotline 1990-1993". *Violence against Women*, Vol. 3, No. 2, pages 101-28.

MSP (Ministry of Social Protection) (1996), *O polozheniye detey v Rossiyskoy Federatsii, 1995 (The Situation of Children in the Russian Federation, 1995)*. Moscow: Government publication. -In Russian.-

NCES (National Centre for Education Statistics) (1993), *Youth Indicators 1993: Trends in the Well-being of American Youth*, No. NCES 93-242. Washington, DC: US Department of Education.

NCS (National Commission for Statistics, Romania) (1998), "Women and the Transition in Romania". Florence: UNICEF International Child Development Centre. Mimeo.

NELL, JACOB and KITTY STEWART (1994), "Death in Transition: The Rise in the Death Rate in Russia since 1992". *Innocenti Occasional Papers*, No. EPS 45 (December). Florence: UNICEF International Child Development Centre.

NESPOROVA, A. (1998), "Women in the Labour Markets of Central and Eastern Europe". Budapest: International Labour Organization. Mimeo.

NEWELL, ANDREW and F. PASTORE (1998), "Labour Market Flows in Poland: Some Empirical Evidence Using the Polish Labour Force Surveys". Brighton, UK: University of Sussex. Mimeo.

NEWELL, ANDREW and BARRY REILLY (1996), "The Gender Wage Gap in Russia: Some Empirical Evidence". *Labour Economics*, Vol. 3, No. 3 (October), pages 337-56.

NEWELL, ANDREW and BARRY REILLY (1999), "Returns to Educational Qualifications in the Transitional Economies". *Education Economics*.

NEWELL, ANDREW and M. SOCHA (1998), "Wage Distribution in Poland: The Roles of Privatization and International Trade, 1992-96". *Economics of Transition*, Vol. 6, No. 1, pages 47-65.

NHS (1994), "NHS Executive North West Strategic Statement". Warrington, UK: National Health Service Executive, North West.

NINK and MACRO INTERNATIONAL (1996), *Kazakhstan: Demographic and Health Survey, 1995*. Calverton, MD: National Institute of Nutrition (Kazakhstan) and Macro International.

NONCHEVA, THEODORA IVANOVA (1998), "Gender Policies in Transition in Bulgaria". Florence: UNICEF International Child Development Centre. Mimeo (10 June).

NOVÁK, JAROSLAV (1998), "Women and the Transition in the Czech Republic". Florence: UNICEF International Child Development Centre. Mimeo.

NOWICKA, WANDA (1996), "The Effects of the 1993 Anti-Abortion Law in Poland". *Entre Nous*, Nos 34-35, pages 13-15.

NSCKR (1997), "Women of the Kyrgyz Republic: Statistical Book". Bishkek, Kyrgyz Republic: National Statistical Committee of the Kyrgyz Republic.

NSCKR (National Statistical Committee of the Kyrgyz Republic) (1998), "O polozhenii zhenshchin v Kyrgyzstane" ("The Situation of Women in Kyrgyzstan"). Florence: UNICEF International Child Development Centre. Mimeo. -In Russian.-

NSI (National Statistical Institute) (various years), "Household Budgets in the Republic of Bulgaria". Sofia, Bulgaria: Statistical Publishing and Printing House.

NSI (1997), *Naselenie '97 (Population '97)*, December. Sofia, Bulgaria: National Statistical Institute. -In Bulgarian.-

NSI (National Statistical Institute) (1998), *Employment and Unemployment*, Vol. 1998, No. 1. Sofia, Bulgaria: Statistical Publishing and Printing House.

O'BRIEN, D., V. V. PATSIORKOVSKI, L. DERSHEM, and O. LYLOVA (1996), *Social Capital and Adaptation to Social Change in Russian Villages*. Glasgow: University of Strathclyde.

ODDENS, B. J. (1997), "Acceptance and Acceptability of Modern Family Planning in Eastern Europe". Pages 103-17 in E. Johannisson, L. Kovács, B. A. Resch, and N. P. Bruyniks (eds), *Assessment of Research and Service Needs in Reproductive Health in Eastern Europe: Concerns and Commitments*. London: Parthenon.

OECD (1995), *Literacy, Economy and Society: Results of the First International Adult Literacy Survey*. Paris: Organization for Economic Cooperation and Development and Statistics Canada.

OECD (1996), "Social Expenditure Statistics of OECD Member Countries". *Labour Market and Social Policy Occasional Papers*, No. 17. Paris: Organization for Economic Cooperation and Development.

OECD (1997), *Literacy Skills for the Knowledge Society: Further Results from the International Adult Literacy Survey*. Paris: Organization for Economic Cooperation and Development, Human Resources Development Canada and Statistics Canada.

ONITA, M. (1998), "Micro Credits in Central Asian Republics: An Overview of Micro Credits in Central Asian Countries". Paper presented at the conference "Central Asia 2010", Almaty, Kazakhstan, 20-22 July.

ORAZEM, P. and M. VODOPIVEC (1995), "Winners and Losers in Transition: Returns to Education, Experience and Gender in Slovenia". *World Bank Economic Review*, Vol. 9, No. 2, pages 201-30.

PAHL, J. (1989), *Money and Marriage*. London: Macmillan.

PAI (1997), "Contraceptive Choice: Developed Country Contraceptive Choice Index". http://www.populationaction.org/programs/developed.htm: Population Action International.

PAJANIANDY, C. (1998), "An Empirical Analysis of Wage Arrears among Employees in the Ukraine in 1996". Brighton, UK: University of Sussex. MA dissertation.

PAPP, ÜLLE-MARIKE (1998), "Gender Policies in Transition in Estonia". Florence: UNICEF International Child Development Centre. Mimeo (July).

PASCALL, GILLIAN (1997), *Social Policy: A New Feminist Analysis*. London: Routledge.

PAUKERT, L. (1997), "Economic Transition and Women's Employment in Four Central European Countries, 1989-1994". *Labour Market Papers*, No. 7. Geneva: Employment Department, International Labour Organization.

PAVLYCHKO, SOLOMEA (1997), "Progress on Hold: The Conservative Faces of Women in Ukraine". Pages 219-34 in Mary Buckley (ed.), *Post-Soviet Women: From the Baltic to Central Asia*. Cambridge, UK: Cambridge University Press.

PIIRAINEN, TIMO (1996), *Towards a New Social Order in Russia: Transforming Structures and Everyday Life*. Aldershot, UK: Dartmouth.

PIO, ALESSANDRO (ed.) (1996), *From Adjustment to Long-run Growth: The Role of Human Capital and the Informal Sector*. Milan: Università Commerciale "Luigi Bocconi".

PLACINTAR, EUGEN (1998), "Report on Women and the Transition in the Slovak Republic". Florence: UNICEF International Child Development Centre. Mimeo (May).

PONGRÁCZ, TIBORNÉ and EDIT S. MOLNÁR (1997), "A gyermekvállalási magatartás alakulása" ("Changes in Childbearing Behaviour"). Pages 86-103 in Katalin Lévai and István György Tóth (eds), *Szerepváltozások: Jelentés a nök helyzetéröl 1997 (Changing Roles: Report on the Situation of Women, 1997)*. Budapest: Tárki. -In Hungarian.-

POSADSKAYA, ANASTASIYA and NATALIYA ZAKHAROVA (1990), "To be a Manager: Changes for Women in the USSR". *Training Discussion Papers*, No. 65. Geneva: International Labour Organization.

POSARAC, ALEKSANDRA (1998), "Gender Policies in Transition in the Federal Republic of Yugoslavia". Florence: UNICEF International Child Development Centre. Mimeo (August).

PRADHAN, MENNO and WOUTER ZANT (1998), "Incidence of Publicly Provided Education and Health Care Expenditures in Bulgaria", draft (July). Washington, DC: World Bank. Mimeo.

PUTNAM, R. D. (1993), "The Prosperous Community: Social Capital and Public Life". *American Prospect*, No. 13, pages 35-42.

RAO, V. V. B. (1991), "Human Development Report 1990: Review and Assessment". *World Development*, Vol. 19, No. 10.

REGULSKA, JOANNA (1994), "Transition to Local Democracy: Do Polish Women have a Chance?". Pages 35-62 in Marilyn Rueschemeyer (ed.), *Women in the Politics of Postcommunist Eastern Europe*. Armonk, NY: M. E. Sharpe.

REID, ELIZABETH (1992), "Gender, Knowledge and Responsibility". *Issues Papers*, No. 10. New York: HIV and Development Programme, UN Development Programme.

REILLY, BARRY (1991), "Occupational Segregation and Selectivity Bias in Occupational Wage Equations: An Empirical Analysis Using Irish Data". *Applied Economics*, Vol. 23, January, pages 1-7.

REILLY, BARRY (1999), "The Gender Pay Gap in Russia during the Transition, 1992-96". *Economics of Transition*, Vol. 7, No. 1, pages 245-64.

REIN, MARTIN, BARRY L. FRIEDMAN and ANDREAS WÖRGÖTTER (eds)

(1997), *Enterprise and Social Benefits after Communism*. Cambridge, UK: Cambridge University Press.

RILEY, NANCY (1997), "Gender, Power and Population Change". *Population Bulletin*, Vol. 52, No. 1 (May).

ROBSON, M. (1991), "Self-employment and New Firm Formation". *Scottish Journal of Political Economy*, Vol. 38, No. 4, pages 352-68.

ROBSON, M. (1994), "Self-employment in the UK Regions". Newcastle, UK: Department of Economics, University of Newcastle. Mimeo (July).

RUBERY, J. (1992), "Pay, Gender and the Social Dimension to Europe". *British Journal of Industrial Relations*, Vol. 30, No. 4, pages 605-21.

RUESCHEMEYER, MARILYN (ed.) (1994), *Women in the Politics of Postcommunist Eastern Europe*. Armonk, NY: M. E. Sharpe.

RULE, WILMA and STEVEN HILL (1998), "Ain't I a Victor?: Voting Rights for Women". http://open.igc.org/cvd/on_line_library/Women/voting-rights.htm: Centre for Voting and Democracy.

SALTMAN, RICHARD B. and JOSEP FIGUERAS (1997), "European Health Care Reform: Analysis of Current Strategies". *WHO Regional Publications, European Series*, No. 72. Copenhagen: Regional Office for Europe, World Health Organization.

SAMPSON, R. J. *et al.* (1997), "Neighbourhoods and Violent Crime: A Multilevel Study of Collective Efficacy". *Science*, No. 277, pages 918-24.

SARGEANT, E. (1996), "The 'Woman Question' and Problems of Maternity in Post-Communist Russia". Pages 269-85 in R. Marsh (ed.), *Women in Russia and Ukraine*. Cambridge, UK: Cambridge University Press.

SASS, JÜRGEN and MONIKA JAECKEL (1997), "The Compatibility of Family and Work". Pages 61-92 in Ulla Björnberg and Jürgen Sass (eds), *Families with Small Children in Eastern and Western Europe*. Aldershot, UK: Ashgate.

SDSG (State Department for Statistics of Georgia) (1998), "Georgia: Women and Transition". Florence: UNICEF International Child Development Centre. Mimeo.

SEN, AMARTYA (1995), "Mortality as an Indicator of Economic Success and Failure". *Innocenti Lectures*, No. 1. Florence: UNICEF International Child Development Centre.

SEN, AMARTYA (1998), "Mortality as an Indicator of Economic Success and Failure". *Economic Journal*, Vol. 108, January, pages 1-25.

SERBANESCU, FLORINA and LEO MORRIS (1998a), "Young Adult Reproductive Health Survey: Romania 1996", February. Bucharest: National Institute of Mother and Child Care.

SERBANESCU, FLORINA and LEO MORRIS (1998b), "Reproductive Health Survey, Moldova 1997: Preliminary Report", May. Chisinau, Moldova: Institute for Scientific Research of Mother and Child Care, Moldovan Ministry of Health.

SHIRCEL, MILIVOIJA (1998), "The Analytical Report on Women in Slovenia". Florence: UNICEF International Child Development Centre. Mimeo.

SHOMINA, Y. (1997), "Housing Movements in Russia". Pages 143-97 in K. Lang-Pickvance, N. Manning and C. Pickvance (eds), *Environmental and Housing Movements: Grassroots Experience in Hungary, Russia and Estonia*. Aldershot, UK: Avebury.

SHULYAKOVSKAYA, NATALYA (1998), "Pharmacies Run Short of Drugs for Elderly". *Moscow Times*, 16 December.

SIEMIENSKA, RENATA (1994), "The Postcommunist Gender Gap in Political Representation in Poland". Pages 52-67 in European Network for Women's Studies, *Gains and Losses: Women and Transition in Eastern and Central Europe*. Bucharest: European Network for Women's Studies and Centre for Higher Education, UN Educational, Social and Cultural Organization.

SILBER, J. (1989), "On the Measurement of Employment Segregation". *Economics Letters*, Vol. 30, pages 237-43.

SILLASTE, G. G. (1995), "Evolyutsiya sotsialnykh pozitsii zhenshchin v menyayushchemsya rossiiskom obshchestve" ("Evolution of the Situation of Women in Russia's Changing Society"). *Sotsiologicheskiye issledovaniye (Sociological Research)*, No. 4, pages 58-64. -In Russian.-

SILLASTE, J. and Ü. PURGA (1995), "Elutingimused Eestis 1994" ("Living Conditions in Estonia, 1994"). *Aasa Lopul*, No. 4. Tallinn, Estonia: Tervis Ja Turvatunne (Health and Security). -In Estonian.-

SINEL'NIKOV, A. B. (1997), "Perspektivy izmeneniya norm brachnosti i razvodimosti v Rossiyskoy Federatsii" ("Perspectives on Changes in Marriage and Divorce Norms in the Russian Federation"). *Sem'ya v Rossii (Family in Russia)*, No. 2. -In Russian.-

SOFYRM (Statistical Office, FYR Macedonia) (1998), "Analytical Report: Women in Transition". Florence: UNICEF International Child Development Centre. Mimeo.

SORENSEN, E. (1990), "The Crowding Hypothesis and Comparable Worth Issues". *Journal of Human Resources*, Vol. 25, No. 1 (Winter), pages 55-89.

SOSR (1996), *Social Statistics, 1996*. Bratislava: Statistical Office of the Slovak Republic.

SPECTER, MICHAEL (1998), "Traffickers' New Cargo: Naïve Slavic Women". *The New York Times*, 11 January.

STEPHENSON, PATRICIA, FRANCE DONNAY, OLGA FROLOVA, TATIANA MELNICK, and CHANTAL WORZALA (1998), "Improving Women's Health Services in the Russian Federation: Results of a Pilot Project". *World Bank Technical Papers*, No. 404 (April).

TADJBAKHSH, SHARHBANOU (1999), "Impact of Restructuring on Women in Central Asia and Policy Recommendations: A Regional Overview on Central Asia". Pages 192-99 in UNDP, *Central Asia, 2010: Prospects for Human Development*. New York: Regional Bureau for Europe and the CIS, UN Development Programme.

TAFI, JANA (1998), "Women and the Transition in the Republic of Moldova". Florence: UNICEF International Child Development Centre. Mimeo.

TAFI, JANA and DOSRM (Department of Statistics, Republic of Moldova) (1997), "Moldova: Education in Transition". Florence: UNICEF International Child Development Centre. Mimeo (June).

TARIFA, FATOS (1994), "Disappearing from Politics: Social Change and Women in Albania". Pages 133-51 in Marilyn Rueschemeyer (ed.), *Women in the Politics of Postcommunist Eastern Europe*. Armonk, NY: M. E. Sharpe.

TARTAKOVSKAIA, IRINA (1996), "Women's Career Patterns in Industry: A Generational Comparison". Pages 57-74 in Hilary Pilkington (ed.), *Gender, Generation and Identity in Contemporary Russia*. London: Routledge.

TITKOW, ANNA (1994), "Polish Women in Politics: An Introduction to the Status of Women in Poland". Pages 29-34 in Marilyn Rueschemeyer (ed.), *Women in the Politics of Postcommunist Eastern Europe*. Armonk, NY: M. E. Sharpe.

TOKHTAKHODZHAEVA, M. (1998), "Traditsionnyy steriotipi" ("Traditional Stereotypes"). *Zhenshchina Srednogo Asii (Women of Central Asia)*, No. 2. -In Russian.-

TZANNATOS, Z. (1990), "Employment Segregation: Can We Measure It, and What does the Measure Mean?". *British Journal of Industrial Relations*, Vol. 28, pages 105-11.

TZVETKOVA-ANGUELOVA, JAKLINA (1998), "Some Aspects of Women's Situation and the Transition in Bulgaria". Florence: UNICEF International Child Development Centre. Mimeo.

UN (1986), *Demographic Yearbook, 1984*. New York: United Nations.

UN (1989a), "Trends in Population Policy". *Population Studies*, No. 114. New York: United Nations.

UN (1989b), "Convention on the Rights of the Child". General Assembly Resolution, No. 44/25 (20 November). New York: United Nations.

UN (1992), *Demographic Yearbook, 1990*. New York: United Nations.

UN (1993a), *Demographic Yearbook: Population Ageing and the Situation of Elderly Persons*. New York: United Nations.

UN (1993b), "Declaration on the Elimination of Violence against Women". General Assembly Resolution, No. 48/104 (20 December). New York: United Nations.

UN (1993c), "Situation of Human Rights in the Territory of the Former Yugoslavia". Document No. E/CN.4/1993/50 (10 February). New York: United Nations.

UN (1994a), "Rape and Abuse of Women in the Areas of Armed Conflict in the Former Yugoslavia". General Assembly Resolution, No. 49/205 (23 December). New York: United Nations.

UN (1994b), "Priority Themes, Equality: Equality in Economic Decision Making". Document No. E/CN.6/1995/10 (23 December). http://gopher.un.org/...1995-10.en: United Nations.

UN (1994c), "Report of the Committee on the Elimination of Discrimination against Women: Supplement No. 38". Document No.

A/49/38 (12 April). New York: United Nations.

UN (1994d), "Consideration of Reports Submitted by States Parties under Article 18 of the Convention on the Elimination of All Forms of Discrimination against Women: Bulgaria". Document No. CEDAW/C/BGR/2-3 (3 November). gopher://gopher.un.org:70/00/ga/cedaw/18/country/bulgaria/c-bgr2-3.en: United Nations.

UN (1995a), "Report of the Fourth World Conference on Women". Document No. A/CONF.177/20 (17 October). New York: United Nations.

UN (1995b), "Consideration of Reports Submitted by States Parties under Article 18 of the Convention: Armenia". Document No. CEDAW/C/ARM/1 (26 September). New York: United Nations.

UN (1995c), "Report of the Committee on the Elimination of Discrimination against Women: Note". Document No. A/50/38 (31 May). New York: United Nations.

UN (1995d), "The World's Women 1995: Trends and Statistics". *Social Statistics and Indicators*, Series K, No. 12. New York: United Nations.

UN (1996a), "Report of the Special Rapporteur on Violence against Women, its Causes and Consequences". Document No. E/CN.4/1996/53 (5 February). New York: United Nations.

UN (1996b), *The United Nations and the Advancement of Women, 1945-1996*. New York: Department of Public Information, United Nations.

UN (1996c), "Consideration of Reports Submitted by States Parties under Article 18 of the Convention on the Elimination of All Forms of Discrimination against Women: Azerbaijan". Document No. CEDAW/C/AZE/1 (16 September). gopher://gopher.un.org:70/00/ga/cedaw/18/country/azerbaijan/c-aze1.en: United Nations.

UN (1996d), "Report of the Committee on the Elimination of Discrimination against Women: Supplement No. 38". Document No. A/51/38 (9 May). New York: United Nations.

UN (1996e), "Consideration of Reports Submitted by States Parties under Article 18 of the Convention on the Elimination of All Forms of Discrimination against Women: Slovakia". Document No. CEDAW/C/SVK/1 (20 July). New York: United Nations.

UN (1997a), *Demographic Yearbook, 1995*. New York: United Nations.

UN (1997b), "Statistics and Indicators on the World's Women", 1 December. http://www.un.org/Depts/unsd/gender/6-2dev.htm: Statistics Division, Department of Economic and Social Affairs, United Nations.

UN (1997c), "Consideration of Reports Submitted by States Parties under Article 18 of the Convention on the Elimination of All Forms of Discrimination against Women: Armenia, Corrigendum". Document No. CEDAW/C/ARM/1/Corr.1 (11 February). New York: United Nations.

UN (1998), "Role of Microcredit in the Eradication of Poverty". Document No. A/53/223 (1 September). New York: United Nations.

UNAIDS (1997), "Impact of HIV and Sexual Health Education on the Sexual Behaviour of Young People: A Review Update". Geneva: Joint UN Programme on HIV/AIDS.

UNAIDS and WHO (1996), "HIV/AIDS: The Global Epidemic, December", 28 November. http://www.unaids.org/unaids/document/epi-demio/situat96.html: Joint UN Programme on HIV/AIDS.

UNAIDS and WHO (1998a), "Report on the Global HIV/AIDS Epidemic", June. Geneva: Joint UN Programme on HIV/AIDS and World Health Organization.

UNAIDS and WHO (1998b), "AIDS Epidemic Update", December. http://www.unaids.org: Joint UN Programme on HIV/AIDS.

UNDAW (1997a), "Women 2000: Women and Decision Making". http://gopher.un.org: UN Division for the Advancement of Women.

UNDAW (1997b), "Status of Women Commission Focus on Women in Power and Decision Making", 12 March. http://gopher.un.org/...w961.txt: UN Division for the Advancement of Women.

UNDCP (1995), "The Vulnerability of Transition Countries to Drug Trafficking, Drug Abuse and Organized Crime", October. Vienna: UN International Drug Control Programme.

UNDP (1990), *Human Development Report 1990*. New York: Oxford University Press.

UNDP (1993), *Human Development Report 1993*. New York: Oxford University Press.

UNDP (1995), *Human Development Report 1995*. New York: Oxford University Press.

UNDP (1996a), "Albanian Human Development Report 1996". Tirana, Albania: UN Development Programme.

UNDP (1996b), "Estonian Human Development Report, 1996". Tallinn, Estonia: UN Development Programme.

UNDP (1997a), "Estonian Human Development Report, 1997". Tallinn, Estonia: UN Development Programme.

UNDP (1997b), *Belarusian Women as Seen through an Era*. http://www.un.minsk.by/wid/97/content.html: UN Development Programme.

UNDP (1997c), "Azerbaijan: Human Development Report 1997". Baku, Azerbaijan: UN Development Programme.

UNDP (1997d), "Tajikistan: Human Development Report, 1997". Dushanbe, Tajikistan: UN Development Programme.

UNDP (1997e), "Human Development Report: Uzbekistan 1997". Tashkent, Uzbekistan: UN Development Programme.

UNDP (1997f), "Human Development Report: Czech Republic 1997". Prague: UN Development Programme.

UNDP (1997g), "Human Development Report: Croatia 1997". Zagreb, Croatia: UN Development Programme.

UNDP (1997h), *Human Development Report 1997*. New York: Oxford University Press.

UNDP (1998a), *Human Development Report 1998*. New York: Oxford University Press.

UNDP (1998b), *Poverty in Transition?*, July. New York: Regional Bureau for Europe and the CIS, UN Development Programme.

UNECE (1993), *Economic Survey of Europe in 1992-1993*. Geneva: UN Economic Commission for Europe.

UNECE (1998), *Economic Survey of Europe*, No. 1 (May). Geneva: UN Economic Commission for Europe.

UNESCO (1997), *Statistical Yearbook, 1996*. Lanham, MD: UN Educational, Social and Cultural Organization and Bernan Press.

UNFPA (1997a), "Maternal Mortality and Abortion in Romania, 1989-1996", July. Bucharest: UN Population Fund, Romania.

UNFPA (1997b), *The State of the World Population 1997: The Right to Choose, Reproductive Rights and Reproductive Health*. http://www.unfpa.org...: UN Population Fund.

UNHCR (1998), "Refugees and Others of Concern to UNHCR: 1997 Statistical Overview", 11 December. http://www.unhcr.ch/refworld/ref-bib/refstat/1998/: Statistical Unit, UN High Commissioner for Refugees.

UNICEF (1990a), "First Call for Children", December. New York: UNICEF.

UNICEF (1990b), "The World Summit for Children". New York: UNICEF.

UNICEF (1993), "Public Policy and Social Conditions". *Regional Monitoring Reports*, No. 1. Florence: UNICEF International Child Development Centre.

UNICEF (1994a), "Crisis in Mortality, Health and Nutrition". *Regional Monitoring Reports*, No. 2. Florence: UNICEF International Child Development Centre.

UNICEF (1994b), "Women and Gender in Countries in Transition: A UNICEF Perspective", October. New York: Regional Office for Central and Eastern Europe, Commonwealth of Independent States and Baltic States, UNICEF.

UNICEF (1995a), "Children and Women of Belarus Today and Tomorrow: A Situation Analysis". Minsk, Belarus: UNICEF-Minsk.

UNICEF (1995b), "Poverty, Children and Policy: Responses for a Brighter Future". *Regional Monitoring Reports*, No. 3. Florence: UNICEF International Child Development Centre.

UNICEF (1996a), "Study of Health Care Demand and Health Care Expenditures in Kuba District, Azerbaijan". *Bamako Initiative Technical Reports*, No. 35 (April). New York: UNICEF.

UNICEF (1996b), "UNICEF Mission Statement". http://www.unicef.org/...: UNICEF.

UNICEF (1997a), "Children at Risk in Central and Eastern Europe: Perils and Promises". *Regional Monitoring Reports*, No. 4. Florence: UNICEF International Child Development Centre.

UNICEF (1997b), "Annual Report: Federal Republic of Yugoslavia", Part 3. http://www.intranet.unicef.org/...: UNICEF.

UNICEF (1997c), *The State of the World's Children 1997*. New York: Oxford University Press.

UNICEF (1997d), "Annual Report: Armenia", Part 3.

http://www.intranet.unicef.org/...: UNICEF.

UNICEF (1997e), "Summary Report: The Investigation of the Accessibility of Health Services to the Population of the Republic of Moldova and the Evaluation of Expenditures for Health". Chisinau, Moldova: UNICEF-Chisinau.

UNICEF (1998), "Education for All?". *Regional Monitoring Reports*, No. 5. Florence: UNICEF International Child Development Centre.

UNICEF, Ukrainian State Centre of Social Services for Youth, Social Service for Juveniles Kiev City State Administration, Public Movement "Vira, Nadiya, Lyubov", and Ukrainian Institute of Social Studies (1998), "Analytical Report on the Project 'The Street Children'". Kiev: Ukraine: UNICEF-Kiev.

UNIFEM (1997), "Annual Report 1997". New York: UN Development Fund for Women.

US CENSUS BUREAU (1997), *International Data Base (IDB)*. http://www.census.gov/ftp/pub/ipc/: International Programmes Centre, US Bureau of the Census.

US CENSUS BUREAU (1998), *International Data Base (IDB)*, June. http://www.census.gov/ipc/idbnew.htm: International Programmes Centre, US Bureau of the Census.

US DEPARTMENT OF STATE (1998a), "Poland Country Report on Human Rights Practices for 1997", 30 January. http://www.state.gov/www/global/human_rights/1997_hrp_report/poland.html: Bureau of Democracy, Human Rights and Labour, US Department of State.

US DEPARTMENT OF STATE (1998b), "Lithuania Country Report on Human Rights Practices for 1997", 30 January. http://www.state.gov/www/global/human_rights/1997_hrp_report/lithuani.html: Bureau of Democracy, Human Rights and Labour, US Department of State.

US DEPARTMENT OF STATE (1998c), "Ukraine Country Report on Human Rights Practices for 1997", 30 January. http://www.state.gov/www/global/human_rights/1997_hrp_report/ukraine.html: Bureau of Democracy, Human Rights and Labour, US Department of State.

US DEPARTMENT OF STATE (1998d), "Kyrgyz Republic Report on Human Rights Practices for 1997", 30 January. http://www.state.gov/www/global/human_rights/1997_hrp_report/kyrgyzre.html: Bureau of Democracy, Human Rights and Labour, US Department of State.

US DEPARTMENT OF STATE (1998e), "Macedonia Country Report on Human Rights Practices for 1997", 30 January. http://www.state.gov/www/global/human_rights/1997_hrp_report/macedoni.html: Bureau of Democracy, Human Rights and Labour, US Department of State.

VAN DE KAA, DIRK J. (1987), "Europe's Second Demographic Transition". *Population Bulletin*, Vol. 4, No. 1.

VANDENDBERG, MARTINA (1997), "'Invisible' Women Shown in Russia's Demographics". *St Petersburg Times*, 6-12 October.

VANNOY, DANA, NATALIA RIMASHEVSKAYA, LISA CUBBINS, MARINA MALYSHEVA, ELENA MESHTERKINA, and MARINA PISLAKOVA (1999), *Russian Marriages: Couples during the Transition*. Westport, CT: Greenwood Publishing Group.

VCIOM, CDC and USAID (1998), *1996 Russia Women's Reproductive Health Survey: A Study of Three Sites, Final Report*, May. Moscow: All-Russian Centre for Public Opinion and Market Research, Centres for Disease Control and Prevention and US Agency for International Development.

VIKHLAYEVA, EKATERINA M. and E. NIKOLAEVA (1996), "Epidemiology of Abortions in Russia". *Entre Nous*, Nos 34-35, page 18.

VISCUSI, K. (1992), *Fatal Tradeoffs: Public and Private Responsibilities for Risk*. New York: Oxford University Press.

VISHNEVSKIY, ANATOLY G. (1996), "Family, Fertility and Demographic Dynamics in Russia: Analysis and Forecast". In Julie DaVanzo (ed.), *Russia's Demographic "Crisis"*. Santa Monica, CA: Rand Centre.

VISHNEVSKIY, ANATOLY G. (1997), "Chislennost' naseleniye" ("Population Trends"). Pages 5-14 in Anatoly G. Vishnevskiy (ed.), *Naseleniye Rossii: 1996 (Population of Russia, 1996)*. Moscow: Centre for Human Demography and Ecology. -In Russian.-

VORNIK, BORIS (1997), "Sexual Victimization of Adolescents in Ukraine". *Choices*, Vol. 26, No. 2.

WALDFOGEL, JANE (1998a), "Understanding the 'Family Gap' in Pay for Women with Children". *Journal of Economic Perspectives*, Vol. 12, No. 1 (Winter), pages 137-56.

WALDFOGEL, JANE (1998b), "The Family Gap for Young Women in the United States and Britain: Can Maternity Leave Make a Difference?". *Journal of Labour Economics*, Vol. 16, No. 3, pages 505-45.

WELCH, K. J., N. MOCK and O. NETREBENKO (1998), "Measuring Hunger in the Russian Federation Using the Radimer/Cornell Hunger Scale". *Bulletin of the World Health Organization*, Vol. 76, No. 2, pages 143-48.

WHITE, NICOLE (1997), "Women in Changing Societies: Latvia and Lithuania". Pages 203-18 in Mary Buckley (ed.), *Post-Soviet Women: From the Baltic to Central Asia*. Cambridge, UK: Cambridge University Press.

WHO (1998), "Health for All Database, European Region", June. Copenhagen: Regional Office for Europe, World Health Organization.

WHO and HSPH (1998), *The Executive Summary of the Global Burden of Disease Series*. http://www.hsph.harvard.edu/organizations/bdu/summary.html: Harvard School of Public Health.

WILKINSON, RICHARD (1996), *Unhealthy Societies: The Afflictions of Inequality*. London: Routledge.

WILKINSON, RICHARD (1998), "What Health Tells Us about Society". *IDS Bulletin*, Vol. 29, No. 1 (January), pages 77-84.

WINKEL, R. and E. KERKHOFF (1995), "Zur Lage junger erwerbstätiger Mütter in den neuen Bundesländern, insbesondere zur Wirksamkeit von Erziehungsurlaub und Erziehungsgeld" ("The Situation of Young Employed Mothers in the New Federal Länder: The Effectiveness of the Parental Leave and the Child Allowance"). *Schriftenreihe des Bundesministeriums für Familie, Senioren, Frauen und Jugend (Reports of the Federal Ministry of Family Affairs, Senior Citizens, Women, and Youth)*, Vol. 100. Stuttgart: Kohlhammer. -In German.-

WIRTH, LINDA (1998) "Women in Management: Closer to Breaking through the Glass Ceiling?". *International Labour Review*, Vol. 137, No. 1, pages 93-102.

WOLCHIK, SHARON L. (1994), "Women and the Politics of Transition in the Czech and Slovak Republics". Pages 3-27 in Marilyn Rueschemeyer (ed.), *Women in the Politics of Postcommunist Eastern Europe*. Armonk, NY: M. E. Sharpe.

WONG, YIN-LING, IRWIN GARFINKEL and SARA MCLANAHAN (1993), "Single-mother Families in Eight Countries: Economic Status and Social Policy". *Social Service Review*, June, pages 177-97.

WORLD BANK (1993), *World Development Report 1993: Investing in Health*. New York: Oxford University Press.

WORLD BANK (1996) "Estonia: Living Standards during the Transition". Report No. 15637-EE. Washington, DC: World Bank.

WORLD BANK (1997a), *World Development Indicators*. Washington, DC: World Bank.

WORLD BANK (1997b), "Kazakhstan: Living Standards during the Transition". Report No. KZ-SR-19398 (22 September). Washington, DC: Human Development Sector Unit, Europe and Central Asia Region, World Bank.

ZAKHAROV, SERGEI V. and ELENA I. IVANOVA (1996), "Fertility Decline and Recent Changes in Russia: On the Threshold of the Second Demographic Transition". In Julie DaVanzo (ed.) (1996), *Russia's Demographic "Crisis"*. Santa Monica, CA: Rand Centre.

ZAMFIR, ELENA and CATALIN ZAMFIR (1998), "Gender Policies in Transition in Romania". Florence: UNICEF International Child Development Centre. Mimeo (17 June).

ZATONSKI, W. A., A. J. MCMICHAEL and J. W. POWLES (1998), "Ecological Study of the Reasons for the Sharp Decline in Mortality from Ischaemic Heart Disease in Poland since 1991". *British Medical Journal*, Vol. 316, No. 7,137 (4 April), pages 1,047-51.

ZIGLIO, ERIO, LOWELL S. LEVIN and LUIGI BERTINATO (1998), "Social and Economic Determinants of Health: Implications for Promoting the Health of the Public". Pages 6-16 in Dominic Harrison and Erio Ziglio (eds), "Social Determinants of Health: Implications for the Health Professions". *Forum: Trends in Experimental and Clinical Medicine*, No. 8.3, Supplement 4 (July-September). Genoa: Forum Service Editors.

ZOHOORI, NAMVAR, LAURA KLINE, BARRY M. POPKIN, and LENORE KOHLMEIER (1997), "Monitoring Health Conditions in the Russian Federation: The Russia Longitudinal Monitoring Survey, 1992-96". Chapel Hill, NC: Carolina Population Centre, University of North Carolina.

ZVIDRINS, PETERIS, LIGITA EZERA and AIGARS GREITANS (1998), "Fertility and Family Surveys in Countries of the ECE Region, Standard Country Report: Latvia". *Economic Studies*, No. 10f. Geneva: UN Economic Commission for Europe and UN Population Fund. ∎

"Public Policy and Social Conditions", 1993

In the early 1990s considerable attention was given to the issues of stabilization, privatization, taxation, and labour market adjustment in the Eastern Europe transition, but demographic and welfare issues received less attention. While the economic and social reforms undertaken were desirable, they faced severe problems of implementation and involved economic, social and political costs far greater than anticipated. This first Report highlights the fact that initial hopes for rapid transformation and economic prosperity were quickly tempered by a considerable decline in output, employment and incomes, a worsening of some social indicators and the appearance of new welfare problems. The Report warns against neglecting the social costs of transition that affect children and adults, but also threaten the entire reform process.

■ Regional Monitoring Report No. 2

"Crisis in Mortality, Health and Nutrition", 1994

After the collapse of the communist system in 1989, most Eastern European countries experienced a mortality and health crisis. However, this did not hit the traditionally most vulnerable groups – children, adolescents, women, and the elderly – but male adults in the 20-59 age group. The Report indicates that the surge is largely dependent on three transition-related factors: widespread impoverishment, erosion of preventive health services and sanitary and medical services, and social stress. Although infants, children and young adolescents have not been greatly or directly affected by the mortality crisis, the Report points out that their situation has been severely threatened by more frequent sickness and greater nutritional imbalances, while the upturn in adult deaths is leading to a considerably heightened risk of poverty, abandonment, or orphanhood.

■ Regional Monitoring Report No. 3

"Poverty, Children and Policy: Responses for a Brighter Future", 1995

Despite improved economic performance in the region in 1994 and 1995, there was still no clear and comprehensive evidence that the welfare crisis was ending. This third Report confirms the social trends observed since 1989; in particular that children have suffered disproportionately in the field of childcare, education, adolescent protection, and poverty. The Report maintains that untimely, partial, or clearly erroneous policies have contributed to this deterioration in child welfare and proposes a series of policy guidelines for a "transition with a human face". These guidelines include the promotion of an employment- and self-employment-based anti-poverty strategy and some important measures in the fields of health, education and childcare.

■ Regional Monitoring Report No. 4

"Children at Risk in Central and Eastern Europe: Perils and Promises", 1997

This Report looks at the changes in risks facing the 100 million children in the 18 countries of Central and Eastern Europe and the Caucasus. Eight types of risk are considered in turn: poverty; war and dislocation; environmental degradation; health and health service deterioration; changes in family formation, including rising family-breakdown rates; falling access to education and rising truancy; youth lifestyle, including an increase in drug abuse and the occurrence of sexually transmitted diseases; and juvenile crime. The Report also indicates that institutional care, foster care and adoption remain in need of sweeping reform; it examines the failure of substitute care and emphasizes the preventive role of family support policies.

■ Regional Monitoring Report No. 5

"Education for All?", 1998

Education is vitally important for the welfare of children and for the development of society. The Report covers a broad range of issues, including enrolment and other measures of educational access, learning achievement, the schooling costs faced by families, education for children with special needs, early childhood development, and the decentralization of educational systems. The Report emphasizes the need for public policy to promote good education for all children and warns of growing inequalities in educational systems.